STOCK TRADER'S ALMANAC 2026

Jeffrey A. Hirsch & Christopher Mistal

WILEY

www.stocktradersalmanac.com

Copyright © 2026 by John Wiley & Sons, Inc. All rights reserved, including rights for text and data mining and training of artificial intelligence technologies or similar technologies.

Published by John Wiley & Sons, Inc., Hoboken, New Jersey.

Published simultaneously in Canada.

Editor-in-Chief	Jeffrey A. Hirsch
Director of Research	Christopher Mistal
Graphic Design	Darlene Dion Design
Publisher 1966–2000 & Editor 1966–2003	Yale Hirsch (1923–2021)

No part of this publication may be reproduced, stored in a retrieval system, or transmitted in any form or by any means, electronic, mechanical, photocopying, recording, scanning, or otherwise, except as permitted under Section 107 or 108 of the 1976 United States Copyright Act, without either the prior written permission of the Publisher, or authorization through payment of the appropriate per-copy fee to the Copyright Clearance Center, Inc., 222 Rosewood Drive, Danvers, MA 01923, (978) 750-8400, fax (978) 750-4470, or on the web at www.copyright.com. Requests to the Publisher for permission should be addressed to the Permissions Department, John Wiley & Sons, Inc., 111 River Street, Hoboken, NJ 07030, (201) 748-6011, fax (201) 748-6008, or online at http://www.wiley.com/go/permission.

The manufacturer's authorized representative according to the EU General Product Safety Regulation is Wiley-VCH GmbH, Boschstr. 12, 69469 Weinheim, Germany, e-mail: Product_Safety@wiley.com.

Trademarks: Wiley and the Wiley logo are trademarks or registered trademarks of John Wiley & Sons, Inc. and/or its affiliates in the United States and other countries and may not be used without written permission. All other trademarks are the property of their respective owners. John Wiley & Sons, Inc. is not associated with any product or vendor mentioned in this book.

Limit of Liability/Disclaimer of Warranty: While the publisher and author have used their best efforts in preparing this book, they make no representations or warranties with respect to the accuracy or completeness of the contents of this book and specifically disclaim any implied warranties of merchantability or fitness for a particular purpose. No warranty may be created or extended by sales representatives or written sales materials. The advice and strategies contained herein may not be suitable for your situation. You should consult with a professional where appropriate. Further, readers should be aware that websites listed in this work may have changed or disappeared between when this work was written and when it is read. Neither the publisher nor authors shall be liable for any loss of profit or any other commercial damages, including but not limited to special, incidental, consequential, or other damages.

For general information on our other products and services or for technical support, please contact our Customer Care Department within the United States at (800) 762-2974, outside the United States at (317) 572-3993 or fax (317) 572-4002.

Wiley also publishes its books in a variety of electronic formats. Some content that appears in print may not be available in electronic formats. For more information about Wiley products, visit our web site at www.wiley.com.

ISBN: 9781394362684 (paper)
ISBN: 9781394362714 (ePDF)
ISBN: 9781394362707 (ePub)

SKY10119688_072225

THE 2026 STOCK TRADER'S ALMANAC

CONTENTS

- 7 Introduction to the Fifty-Ninth Edition
- 10 2026 Outlook
- 12 2026 Strategy Calendar
- **14 January Almanac**
- 16 January's First Five Days: An Early Warning System
- 18 The Incredible January Barometer (Devised 1972): Only 12 Significant Errors in 75 Years
- 20 Bulls Win When Market Hits the January Trifecta
- **22 February Almanac**
- 24 Down Januarys: A Remarkable Record
- 26 Market Charts of Midterm Election Years
- 28 Midterm Election Years: Where Bottom Picker's Find Paradise
- **30 March Almanac**
- 32 Prosperity More Than Peace Determines the Outcome of Midterm Congressional Races
- 34 Why a 50% Gain in the Dow is Possible from Its 2026 Low to Its 2027 High
- 36 The December Low Indicator: A Useful Prognosticating Tool
- 38 How to Trade Best Months Switching Strategies
- **40 April Almanac**
- 42 Dow Jones Industrials & S&P 500 One-Year Seasonal Pattern Charts Since 1901 & 1950
- 44 NASDAQ, Russell 1000 & 2000 One-Year Seasonal Pattern Charts Since 1971 & 1979
- 46 Welcome to the Sweet Spot of the 4-Year Cycle: Q4 Midterm Year to Q2 Pre-Election Year
- **48 May Almanac**
- 50 Summer Market Volume Doldrums Drive Worst Six Months
- 52 Top-Performing Months: Standard & Poor's 500 and Dow Jones Industrials
- 54 Best Six Months: Still an Eye-Popping Strategy
- 56 MACD-Timing Triples Best-Six-Months Results
- **58 June Almanac**
- 60 Top-Performing NASDAQ Months
- 62 Get More out of NASDAQ's Best Eight Months with MACD Timing
- 64 Triple Returns, Fewer Trades: Best 6 + 4–Year Cycle

66	**July Almanac**
68	First Month of Quarters Is the Most Bullish
70	2024 Daily Dow Point Changes (Dow Jones Industrial Average)
72	Market Gains More on Super-8 Days Each Month Than on All 13 Remaining Days Combined
74	**August Almanac**
76	A Rally for All Seasons
78	Take Advantage of Down Friday/Down Monday Warning
80	Market Behavior Three Days Before and Three Days After Holidays
82	Fourth-Quarter Market Magic
84	**September Almanac**
86	Best Investment Books of the Year
88	A Correction for All Seasons
90	First-Trading-Day-of-the-Month Phenomenon
92	**October Almanac**
94	Sector Seasonality: Selected Percentage Plays
96	Sector Index Seasonality Strategy Calendar
100	**November Almanac**
102	Midterm Election Time Unusually Bullish
104	Traders Feast on Small Stocks Thanksgiving Through Santa Claus Rally
106	Trading the Thanksgiving Market
108	Aura of the Triple Witch—4th Quarter Most Bullish: Down Weeks Trigger More Weakness Week After
110	**December Almanac**
112	Most of the So-Called January Effect Takes Place in the Last Half of December
114	January Effect Now Starts in Mid-December
116	Wall Street's Only "Free Lunch" Served Before Christmas
118	If Santa Claus Should Fail to Call, Bears May Come to Broad and Wall
120	2027 Strategy Calendar

DIRECTORY OF TRADING PATTERNS AND DATABANK

123	Dow Jones Industrials Market Probability Calendar 2026
124	<u>Recent</u> Dow Jones Industrials Market Probability Calendar 2026
125	S&P 500 Market Probability Calendar 2026
126	<u>Recent</u> S&P 500 Market Probability Calendar 2026
127	NASDAQ Composite Market Probability Calendar 2026
128	<u>Recent</u> NASDAQ Composite Market Probability Calendar 2026
129	Russell 1000 Index Market Probability Calendar 2026
130	Russell 2000 Index Market Probability Calendar 2026
131	Decennial Cycle: A Market Phenomenon
132	Presidential Election/Stock Market Cycle: The 192-Year Saga Continues

133	Dow Jones Industrials Bull and Bear Markets Since 1900
134	Standard & Poor's 500 Bull and Bear Markets Since 1929/ NASDAQ Composite Since 1971
135	Dow Jones Industrials 10-Year Daily Point Changes: January and February
136	Dow Jones Industrials 10-Year Daily Point Changes: March and April
137	Dow Jones Industrials 10-Year Daily Point Changes: May and June
138	Dow Jones Industrials 10-Year Daily Point Changes: July and August
139	Dow Jones Industrials 10-Year Daily Point Changes: September and October
140	Dow Jones Industrials 10-Year Daily Point Changes: November and December
141	A Typical Day in the Market
142	Through the Week on a Half-Hourly Basis
143	Tuesday & Wednesday, Best Days of Week
144	NASDAQ Strongest Last 3 Days of Week
145	S&P Daily Performance Each Year Since 1952
146	NASDAQ Daily Performance Each Year Since 1971
147	Monthly Cash Inflows into S&P Stocks
148	Monthly Cash Inflows into NASDAQ Stocks
149	November, December, and January: Year's Best Three-Month Span
150	November through June: NASDAQ's Eight-Month Run
151	Dow Jones Industrials Annual Highs, Lows, & Closes Since 1901
153	S&P 500 Annual Highs, Lows, & Closes Since 1930
154	NASDAQ Annual Highs, Lows, & Closes Since 1971
155	Russell 1000 and 2000 Annual Highs, Lows, & Closes Since 1979
156	Dow Jones Industrials Monthly Percent Changes Since 1950
158	Dow Jones Industrials Monthly Point Changes Since 1950
160	Dow Jones Industrials Monthly Closing Prices Since 1950
162	Standard & Poor's 500 Monthly Percent Changes Since 1950
164	Standard & Poor's 500 Monthly Closing Prices Since 1950
166	NASDAQ Composite Monthly Percent Changes Since 1971
168	NASDAQ Composite Monthly Closing Prices Since 1971
170	Russell 1000 Index Monthly Percent Changes Since 1979
171	Russell 1000 Index Monthly Closing Prices Since 1979
172	Russell 2000 Index Monthly Percent Changes Since 1979
173	Russell 2000 Index Monthly Closing Prices Since 1979
174	10 Best Days by Percent and Point
175	10 Worst Days by Percent and Point
176	10 Best Weeks by Percent and Point
177	10 Worst Weeks by Percent and Point
178	10 Best Months by Percent and Point
179	10 Worst Months by Percent and Point
180	10 Best Quarters by Percent and Point

181	10 <u>Worst</u> Quarters by Percent and Point
182	10 <u>Best</u> Years by Percent and Point
183	10 <u>Worst</u> Years by Percent and Point

STRATEGY PLANNING AND RECORD SECTION

185	Portfolio at Start of 2026
186	Additional Purchases
188	Short-Term Transactions
190	Long-Term Transactions
192	Interest/Dividends Received During 2026/Brokerage Account Data 2026
193	Weekly Portfolio Price Record 2026
195	Weekly Indicator Data 2026
197	Monthly Indicator Data 2026
198	Portfolio at End of 2026
199	If You Don't Profit from Your Investment Mistakes, Someone Else Will/ Performance Record of Recommendations
200	Individual Retirement Accounts: Most Awesome Investment Incentive Ever Devised
201	G.M. Loeb's "Battle Plan" for Investment Survival
202	G.M. Loeb's Investment Survival Checklist

INTRODUCTION TO THE FIFTY-NINTH EDITION

We are honored to present the 59th annual edition of the *Stock Trader's Almanac*. The *Almanac* provides you with the necessary tools and data to invest and trade successfully in the twenty-first century.

J.P. Morgan's classic retort "Stocks will fluctuate" is often quoted with a wink-of-the-eye implication that the only prediction one can make about the stock market is that it will go up, down, or sideways. Many investors and traders agree that no one ever really knows which way the market will move. Nothing could be further from the truth.

We discovered many years ago that while stocks do indeed fluctuate, they do so in well-defined, often predictable patterns. These patterns recur too frequently to be the result of chance or coincidence. How else do we explain that since 1950 the Dow has gained 29918.50 points during November through April compared to 10536.53 May through October? (See page 54.)

The *Almanac* is a practical investment tool. It alerts you to those little-known market patterns and tendencies on which shrewd professionals enhance profit potential. You will be able to forecast market trends with accuracy and confidence when you use the *Almanac* to help you understand:

- How our presidential elections affect the economy and the stock market—just as the moon affects the tides. Many investors have made fortunes following the political-cycle. You can be sure that money managers who control billions of dollars are also political-cycle watchers. Astute people do not ignore a pattern that has been working effectively throughout most of our economic history.

- How the passage of the Twentieth Amendment to the Constitution fathered the January Barometer. This barometer has an outstanding record for predicting the general course of the stock market each year with only 12 major errors since 1950 for an 84.0% accuracy ratio. (See page 18.)

- Why there is a significant market bias at certain times of the day, week, month and year.

Even if you are an investor who pays scant attention to cycles, indicators, and patterns, your investment survival could hinge on your interpretation of one of the recurring patterns found within these pages. One of the most intriguing and important patterns is the symbiotic relationship between Washington and Wall Street. Aside from the potential profitability in seasonal patterns, there's the pure joy of seeing the market very often do just what you expected.

The *Stock Trader's Almanac* is also an organizer. Its wealth of information is presented on a calendar basis. The *Almanac* puts investing in a business framework and makes it easier because it:

- Updates investment knowledge and informs you of new techniques and tools.
- Is a monthly reminder and refresher course.
- Alerts you to both seasonal opportunities and dangers.

- Furnishes a historical viewpoint by providing pertinent statistics on past market performance.
- Supplies forms necessary for portfolio planning, record keeping, and tax preparation.

The WITCH icon signifies THIRD FRIDAY OF THE MONTH on calendar pages and alerts you to extraordinary volatility due to expiration of monthly equity options, index options, and index futures contracts. "Triple-Witching" days appear during March, June, September, and December (see page 108).

The BULL icon on calendar pages signifies favorable trading days based on the S&P 500 rising 60% or more of the time on a particular trading day during the 21-year period January 2004 to December 2024.

A BEAR icon on calendar pages signifies unfavorable trading days based on the S&P falling 60% or more of the time for the same 21-year period.

Clusters of two or more BULLs or BEARs can be especially helpful in identifying periods of strength or weakness throughout the year. Clusters can also be three out of four days or three out of five days. An example of four BEARs in five days can be observed on page 91 during the last full week of September. One of the most bullish weeks of the year is illustrated by a streak of five BULLs in a row during the first week of November on page 103.

On pages 123–130 you will find complete Market Probability Calendars both long term and the recent 21-year period for the Dow, S&P and NASDAQ, as well as for the Russell 1000 and Russell 2000 indices. To give you even greater perspective we have listed on the weekly planner pages next to the date every day that the market is open the market probability numbers for the same 21-year period for the Dow (D), S&P 500 (S) and NASDAQ (N). You will see a "D," "S" and "N" followed by a number signifying the actual market probability number for that trading day based on the recent 21-year period.

Other seasonalities near the ends, beginnings, and middles of months; options expirations, around holidays and other times are noted for *Almanac* investors' convenience on the weekly planner pages. All other important economic releases are provided in the Strategy Calendar every month in our digital newsletter, *Almanac Investor*, available at our website *www.stocktradersalmanac.com*. Please see the insert for a special offer for new subscribers.

One-year seasonal pattern charts for Dow, S&P 500, NASDAQ, Russell 1000, and Russell 2000 appear on pages 42 and 44. There is one chart of the Dow that spans our entire database starting in 1901, one each for the Dow and S&P 500 back to 1950 and one each for the younger indices. As 2026 is a midterm election year, each chart contains typical midterm election year performance compared to all years.

The Russell 2000 is an excellent proxy for small- and mid-caps and the Russell 1000 provides a broader view of large caps. Annual highs and lows for all five indices covered in the *Almanac* appear on pages 151–155. Top "10 Best & Worst" days, weeks, months, quarters and years for all five indices are listed on pages 174–183.

We have converted many of the paper forms in our Record Keeping section into spreadsheets for our own internal use. As a service to our faithful readers, we are making these forms available at our website *www.stocktradersalmanac.com*. Look for a link titled "Forms" at the bottom of the home page.

You can find all the market charts of midterm election years from 1942 to 2022 on page 26. "Midterm Election Years: Where Bottom Picker's Find Paradise" on page 28 highlights the uncanny record of major market bottoms occurring in the midterm election year particularly in October. "Prosperity More Than Peace Determines the Outcome of Midterm Congressional Races" on page 32 shows how market performance and inflation impact the notorious loss of House seats by the president's party in the midterms. "Why A 50% Move in the Dow Is Possible From Its 2026 Low to Its 2027 High" is detailed on page 34. Bullish market behavior around the midterm elections in November appears on page 102, "Midterm Election Time Unusually Bullish."

"Welcome to the Sweet Spot of the 4-Year Cycle" on page 46 explains the usual weakness that occurs during Q2 and Q3 of the midterm setting up the "Sweet Spot" of the 4-Year Cycle from Q4 in the midterm year through Q2 pre-election year and beyond. On page 86, by popular demand, we have brought back the "Best Investment Books of the Year" with half a dozen hand-picked recently published investment and trading books from the brightest minds on Wall Street that run the gamut from technical analysis to quantitative research to dividend investing to the dos and don'ts of wealth management to Bitcoin.

"Bulls Win When Market Hits the January Trifecta" on page 20 shows a new indicator we built in 2013 that combines our Santa Claus Rally (page 118) and January Barometer (page 18) with the First Five Days (page 16), creating a more powerful indicator. On page 104 is a new trading strategy, "Traders Feast on Small Stocks Thanksgiving through Santa Claus Rally."

"How to Trade Best Months Switching Strategies" appears on page 38. How "Summer Market Volume Doldrums Drives Worst Six Months" is updated on page 50. Revised sector seasonalities including several consistent shorting opportunities, appear on pages 94–98.

Our 2026 Outlook on pages 10–11 calls for tougher trading through the first three quarters of 2026 in line with the historic performance of midterm years. After modest gains during the first quarter look for the market to consolidate gains and retreat through Q2 and Q3, the 4-Year Cycle "Weak Spot," with increased risk of recession and a bear market, before the bull returns and the market rallies in Q4 of 2026 at the outset of the "Sweet Spot" of the 4-Year Cycle.

We are constantly searching for new insights and nuances about the stock market and welcome any suggestions from our readers.

May 2026 bring you health, happiness, and success!

2026 OUTLOOK

Welcome to the "Sweet Spot" of the 4-Year Cycle. This uncanny market cycle revolves around the forces generated by the regular election of the President of the United States of America every four years. It has provided us with a reliable framework and guided our analysis and market forecasting from our beginnings in the 1960s to the present day. Presidents and their parties engage in a quadrennial dance to hold power that impacts geopolitics, economics, and the stock market profoundly.

During the first two years of their term their efforts are focused on implementing the agendas they campaigned on. They attempt to push through their most sweeping changes and least savory policy initiatives early on, fueling uncertainty and market volatility. Then they prime the pump in the third and fourth year with rhetoric and policy that is intended to juice the economy and buoy the stock market so the country is rich and happy when they go to the polls four years later. This political rhythm is what drives the 4-Year Presidential Stock Market Cycle.

The first two years have been more prone to wars, recessions, and bear markets whereas the latter two years have experienced greater peace, prosperity, and bull markets. The cycle has evolved slightly over the years with the most significant change being the improvement in the market performance in the first year of the president's term, the post-election year. What remains the same is clear weakness in the second year, the midterm election year and the outperformance of the third year, the pre-election year. And this creates the "Sweet Spot" of the 4-Year Cycle.

Midterm election year 2026 promises to be fraught with crisis, bear market action and economic weakness. Ten of the last 16 bear markets bottomed in the midterm year – 2022 case in point. Effects of the current administration's fiscal, trade, tax, and immigration policies will likely cause inflation to tick up next year threatening to slow economic activity and impact the market most dramatically in Q2 and Q3 of 2026. During this "Weak Spot" of the 4-year Cycle the market averages losses of -2.0% for the Dow, -2.5% for S&P 500 and -6.6% for NASDAQ over the two-quarter span.

As the congressional midterm election battles take centerstage the president and congress will be focused on retaining power and less on their agenda, increasing the potential for a decline that could culminate in bear market. But where there is great danger, there is also great opportunity. This sets up the "Sweet Spot" and the next great buying opportunity. After the invariable loss of seats by the president's party and potentially control of congress, the president will likely

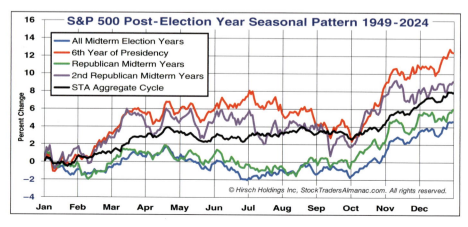

tack to the center and adjust fiscal policy to get spending and income up and interest rates and inflation down over the next two years to keep his party in the White House.

The "S&P 500 Midterm Election Seasonal Pattern" chart on page 10 illustrates a rather bleak outlook for the first three quarters of 2026. After reaching negative territory in Q2 and Q3 stocks should rally in Q4 at the outset of the "Sweet Spot" pushing the market into the black with a net gain for the year of 4-8%.

The Super Boom we forecasted in May 2010 for Dow 38820 by 2025 is still in play and has room to run. We hit Dow 38820 in early 2024 a year ahead of schedule but the current tech boom continues to gather momentum that will likely push this secular bull to new heights. Based on the Super Boom pattern depicted in the chart below and with the benefit of hindsight, the secular bear and launching pad for the current Super Boom was not completed until 2013 when Dow broke out to new all-time highs and never looked back. The final mini bear bottomed on October 3, 2011, at Dow 10655.30. A 500% move from the intraday low on October 4, 2011, of 10405 takes Dow to our new target of 62430. Based upon the Dow's average 8.5% annual return since 1949 we could hit that level within 5 years.

The tech stack that drives these booms is always evolving. We refer to these innovative and disruptive technologies that change the world as "culturally-enabling-paradigm-shifting technologies." AI clearly fits the bill, and its moat is constantly expanding to new industries and uses. Quantum computing is another promising technology that could change the world and has been gaining traction lately.

Bitcoin may also play a role in this boom. In his new *Little Book of Bitcoin* (one of our Best Investment Books of the Year, page 86) Anthony Scaramucci compares BTC to Apple or Amazon circa 2000: "The investment equivalent of the fire or the wheel." "Bitcoin is the Internet of money." He relates how Bitcoin fulfills Peter Diamandis' Six Ds of exponential technology that changes every industry it touches: Digitize, Dematerialize, Demonetize, Democratize, Deception, and Disruption. Everything is now just data, and Bitcoin is money data.

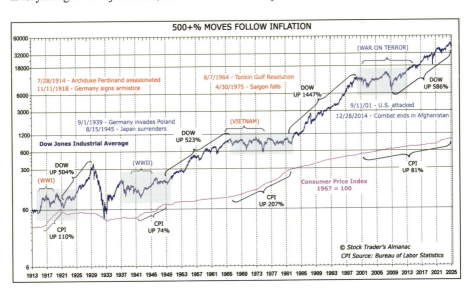

Jeffrey A. Hirsch, May 30, 2025

2026 STRATEGY CALENDAR
(Option expiration dates circled)

	MONDAY	TUESDAY	WEDNESDAY	THURSDAY	FRIDAY	SATURDAY	SUNDAY
JANUARY	29	30	31	1 JANUARY — New Year's Day	2	3	4
	5	6	7	8	9	10	11
	12	13	14	15	(16)	17	18
	19 — Martin Luther King Jr. Day	20	21	22	23	24	25
	26	27	28	29	30	31	1 FEBRUARY
FEBRUARY	2	3	4	5	6	7	8
	9	10	11	12	13	14 ♥	15
	16 — Presidents' Day	17	18 — Ash Wednesday	19	(20)	21	22
	23	24	25	26	27	28	1 MARCH
MARCH	2	3	4	5	6	7	8 — Daylight Saving Time Begins
	9	10	11	12	13	14	15
	16	17 ♣ — St. Patrick's Day	18	19	(20)	21	22
	23	24	25	26	27	28	29
	30	31	1 APRIL	2 Passover	3 Good Friday	4	5 Easter
APRIL	6	7	8	9	10	11	12
	13	14	15 — Tax Deadline	16	(17)	18	19
	20	21	22	23	24	25	26
	27	28	29	30	1 MAY	2	3
MAY	4	5	6	7	8	9	10 — Mother's Day
	11	12	13	14	(15)	16	17
	18	19	20	21	22	23	24
	25 — Memorial Day	26	27	28	29	30	31
JUNE	1 JUNE	2	3	4	5	6	7
	8	9	10	11	12	13	14
	15	16	17	(18)	19 — Juneteenth	20	21 — Father's Day
	22	23	24	25	26	27	28
	29	30	1 JULY	2	3	4 — Independence Day	5

Market closed on shaded weekdays; closes early when half-shaded.

2026 STRATEGY CALENDAR
(Option expiration dates circled)

MONDAY	TUESDAY	WEDNESDAY	THURSDAY	FRIDAY	SATURDAY	SUNDAY	
6	7	8	9	10	11	12	JULY
13	14	15	16	(17)	18	19	
20	21	22	23	24	25	26	
27	28	29	30	31	1 AUGUST	2	
3	4	5	6	7	8	9	AUGUST
10	11	12	13	14	15	16	
17	18	19	20	(21)	22	23	
24	25	26	27	28	29	30	
31	1 SEPTEMBER	2	3	4	5	6	SEPTEMBER
7 Labor Day	8	9	10	11	12 Rosh Hashanah	13	
14	15	16	17	(18)	19	20	
21 Yom Kippur	22	23	24	25	26	27	
28	29	30	1 OCTOBER	2	3	4	OCTOBER
5	6	7	8	9	10	11	
12 Columbus Day	13	14	15	(16)	17	18	
19	20	21	22	23	24	25	
26	27	28	29	30	31	1 NOVEMBER Daylight Saving Time Ends	
2	3 Election Day	4	5	6	7	8	NOVEMBER
9	10	11 Veterans' Day	12	13	14	15	
16	17	18	19	(20)	21	22	
23	24	25	26 Thanksgiving Day	27	28	29	
30	1 DECEMBER	2	3	4	5 Chanukah	6	DECEMBER
7	8	9	10	11	12	13	
14	15	16	17	(18)	19	20	
21	22	23	24	25 Christmas	26	27	
28	29	30	31	1 JANUARY New Year's Day	2	3	

JANUARY ALMANAC

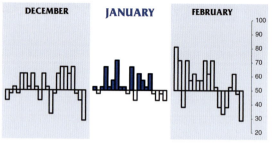

Market Probability Chart above is a graphic representation of the S&P 500 Recent Market Probability Calendar on page 126.

◆ January Barometer predicts year's course with .733 batting average (page 18) ◆ 11 of last 19 midterm election years followed January's direction ◆ Every down January on the S&P since 1950, *without exception*, preceded a new or extended bear market, a flat market, or a 10% correction (page 24) ◆ S&P gains January's first five days preceded full-year gains 83.3% of the time, 9 of last 19 midterm election years followed first five day's direction (page 16) ◆ November, December, and January constitute the year's best three-month span, a 4.4% S&P gain (pages 52 & 149) ◆ January NASDAQ powerful 2.6% since 1971 (pages 60 & 150) ◆ January Effect now starts in mid-December and favors small-cap stocks (pages 112 & 114) ◆ 2009 has the dubious honor of the worst S&P 500 January on record ◆ Dow gained more than 1000 points in 2018 & 2019 ◆ See January Indicator Trifecta (page 20)

January Vital Statistics

	DJIA		S&P 500		NASDAQ		Russell 1K		Russell 2K	
Rank	5		5		1		5		3	
Up	48		46		37		29		26	
Down	28		30		18		18		21	
Average % Change	1.0		1.1		2.6		1.1		1.5	
Midterm Yr Avg % Chg	−0.7		−0.9		−0.7		−1.1		−1.4	
Best & Worst January										
	% Change		% Change		% Change		% Change		% Change	
Best	1976	14.4	1987	13.2	1975	16.6	1987	12.7	1985	13.1
Worst	2009	−8.8	2009	−8.6	2008	−9.9	2009	−8.3	2009	−11.2
Best & Worst January Weeks										
Best	1/9/76	6.1	1/2/09	6.8	1/12/01	9.1	1/2/09	6.8	1/9/87	7.0
Worst	1/8/16	−6.2	1/8/16	−6.0	1/28/00	−8.2	1/8/16	−6.0	1/21/22	−8.1
Best & Worst January Days										
Best	1/17/91	4.6	1/3/01	5.0	1/3/01	14.2	1/3/01	5.3	1/21/09	5.3
Worst	1/8/88	−6.9	1/8/88	−6.8	1/2/01	−7.2	1/8/88	−6.1	1/20/09	−7.0
First Trading Day of Monthly Options Expiration Week: 1980–2025										
Record (#Up–#Down)	28–18		25–21		23–23		23–23		23–23	
Current streak	U1		U1		D2		U1		U1	
Avg % Change	0.03		0.02		0.02		−0.00		−0.06	
Monthly Options Expiration Day: 1980–2025										
Record (#Up–#Down)	27–19		27–19		28–18		27–19		28–18	
Current streak	U3		U3		U3		U3		U3	
Avg % Change	0.05		0.10		0.08		0.08		0.11	
Monthly Options Expiration Week: 1980–2025										
Record (#Up–#Down)	26–20		22–24		28–18		22–24		25–11	
Current streak	U2		U2		U3		U2		U1	
Avg % Change	−0.06		0.06		0.38		0.06		0.21	
Week After Monthly Options Expiration: 1980–2025										
Record (#Up–#Down)	27–19		29–17		28–18		29–17		31–15	
Current streak	U4		U4		U4		U4		U3	
Avg % Change	0.13		0.28		0.26		0.26		0.17	
First Trading Day Performance										
% of Time Up	59.2		48.7		54.5		44.7		46.8	
Avg % Change	0.23		0.14		0.16		0.11		0.03	
Last Trading Day Performance										
% of Time Up	53.9		59.2		61.8		55.3		68.1	
Avg % Change	0.15		0.21		0.26		0.24		0.21	

Dow & S&P 1950–May 2, 2025; NASDAQ 1971–May 2, 2025; Russell 1K & 2K 1979–May 2, 2025.

*20th Amendment made "lame ducks" disappear.
Now, "as January goes, so goes the year."*

DECEMBER 2025/JANUARY 2026

MONDAY
D 42.9
S 47.6
N 38.1
29

Get inside information from the president and you will probably lose half your money. If you get it from the chairman of the board, you will lose all your money.
— Jim Rogers (Financier, b. 1942)

TUESDAY
D 42.9
S 42.9
N 38.1
30

First-rate people hire first-rate people; second-rate people hire third-rate people.
— Leo Rosten (American author, 1908–1997)

Last Trading Day of the Year, NASDAQ Down 19 of last 25
NASDAQ Was Up 29 Years in a Row 1971-1999

WEDNESDAY
D 33.3
S 28.6
N 28.6
31

Exercising the right of occasional suppression and slight modification, it is truly absurd to see how plastic a limited number of observations become, in the hands of men with preconceived ideas.
— Sir Francis Galton, FRS (English polymath, statistical pioneer, *Meteorographica* 1863, 1822–1911)

New Years Day *(Market Closed)*

THURSDAY
1

If more of us valued food and cheer and song above hoarded gold, it would be a merrier world.
— J. R. R. Tolkien (English writer, poet, philologist, and academic, *The Hobbit*, 1892–1973)

First Trading Day of Year NASDAQ Up 18 of Last 28

FRIDAY
D 66.7
S 52.4
N 61.9
2

I'm not nearly so concerned about the return on my capital as I am the return of my capital.
— Will Rogers (American humorist and showman, 1879–1935)

SATURDAY
3

January Almanac Investor Sector Seasonalities: See Pages 94, 96, and 98

SUNDAY
4

JANUARY'S FIRST FIVE DAYS: AN EARLY WARNING SYSTEM

The last 48 up First Five Days were followed by full-year gains 40 times for an 83.3% accuracy ratio and a 14.2% average gain in all 48 years. The eight exceptions include flat years 1994, 2011, 2015, four related to war, and 2018. Vietnam military spending delayed start of 1966 bear market. Ceasefire imminence early in 1973 raised stocks temporarily. Saddam Hussein turned 1990 into a bear. The war on terrorism, instability in the Mideast and corporate malfeasance shaped 2002 into one of the worst years on record. In 2018 a partially inverted yield curve and trade tensions triggered a fourth quarter selloff. The 27 down First Five Days were followed by 15 up years and 12 down (44.4% accurate) and an average gain of 1.1%.

In midterm election years this indicator has a poor record. In the last 19 midterm election years only 9 full years followed the direction of the First Five Days. See January Indicator Trifecta (page 20).

THE FIRST-FIVE-DAYS-IN-JANUARY INDICATOR

Chronological Data | Ranked by Performance

Year	Previous Year's Close	January 5th Day	5-Day Change	Year Change	Rank	Year	5-Day Change	Year Change
1950	16.76	17.09	2.0%	21.8%	1	1987	6.2%	2.0%
1951	20.41	20.88	2.3	16.5	2	1976	4.9	19.1
1952	23.77	23.91	0.6	11.8	3	1999	3.7	19.5
1953	26.57	26.33	–0.9	–6.6	4	2003	3.4	26.4
1954	24.81	24.93	0.5	45.0	5	2006	3.4	13.6
1955	35.98	35.33	–1.8	26.4	6	1983	3.3	17.3
1956	45.48	44.51	–2.1	2.6	7	1967	3.1	20.1
1957	46.67	46.25	–0.9	–14.3	8	1979	2.8	12.3
1958	39.99	40.99	2.5	38.1	9	2018	2.8	–6.2
1959	55.21	55.40	0.3	8.5	10	2019	2.7	28.9
1960	59.89	59.50	–0.7	–3.0	11	2010	2.7	12.8
1961	58.11	58.81	1.2	23.1	12	1963	2.6	18.9
1962	71.55	69.12	–3.4	–11.8	13	1958	2.5	38.1
1963	63.10	64.74	2.6	18.9	14	1984	2.4	1.4
1964	75.02	76.00	1.3	13.0	15	1951	2.3	16.5
1965	84.75	85.37	0.7	9.1	16	2013	2.2	29.6
1966	92.43	93.14	0.8	–13.1	17	1975	2.2	31.5
1967	80.33	82.81	3.1	20.1	18	1950	2.0	21.8
1968	96.47	96.62	0.2	7.7	19	2012	1.8	13.4
1969	103.86	100.80	–2.9	–11.4	20	2021	1.8	26.9
1970	92.06	92.68	0.7	0.1	21	2004	1.8	9.0
1971	92.15	92.19	0.04	10.8	22	1973	1.5	–17.4
1972	102.09	103.47	1.4	15.6	23	2023	1.4	24.2
1973	118.05	119.85	1.5	–17.4	24	1972	1.4	15.6
1974	97.55	96.12	–1.5	–29.7	25	1964	1.3	13.0
1975	68.56	70.04	2.2	31.5	26	2017	1.3	19.4
1976	90.19	94.58	4.9	19.1	27	1961	1.2	23.1
1977	107.46	105.01	–2.3	–11.5	28	1989	1.2	27.3
1978	95.10	90.64	–4.7	1.1	29	2011	1.1	–0.003
1979	96.11	98.80	2.8	12.3	30	2002	1.1	–23.4
1980	107.94	108.95	0.9	25.8	31	1997	1.0	31.0
1981	135.76	133.06	–2.0	–9.7	32	1980	0.9	25.8
1982	122.55	119.55	–2.4	14.8	33	1966	0.8	–13.1
1983	140.64	145.23	3.3	17.3	34	1994	0.7	–1.5
1984	164.93	168.90	2.4	1.4	35	1965	0.7	9.1
1985	167.24	163.99	–1.9	26.3	36	2009	0.7	23.5
1986	211.28	207.97	–1.6	14.6	37	2020	0.7	16.3
1987	242.17	257.28	6.2	2.0	38	1970	0.7	0.1
1988	247.08	243.40	–1.5	12.4	39	2025	0.6	??
1989	277.72	280.98	1.2	27.3	40	1952	0.6	11.8
1990	353.40	353.79	0.1	–6.6	41	1954	0.5	45.0
1991	330.22	314.90	–4.6	26.3	42	1996	0.4	20.3
1992	417.09	418.10	0.2	4.5	43	1959	0.3	8.5
1993	435.71	429.05	–1.5	7.1	44	1995	0.3	34.1
1994	466.45	469.90	0.7	–1.5	45	1992	0.2	4.5
1995	459.27	460.83	0.3	34.1	46	1968	0.2	7.7
1996	615.93	618.46	0.4	20.3	47	2015	0.2	–0.7
1997	740.74	748.41	1.0	31.0	48	1990	0.1	–6.6
1998	970.43	956.04	–1.5	26.7	49	1971	0.04	10.8
1999	1229.23	1275.09	3.7	19.5	50	2024	–0.1	23.3
2000	1469.25	1441.46	–1.9	–10.1	51	2007	–0.4	3.5
2001	1320.28	1295.86	–1.8	–13.0	52	2014	–0.6	11.4
2002	1148.08	1160.71	1.1	–23.4	53	1960	–0.7	–3.0
2003	879.82	909.93	3.4	26.4	54	1957	–0.9	–14.3
2004	1111.92	1131.91	1.8	9.0	55	1953	–0.9	–6.6
2005	1211.92	1186.19	–2.1	3.0	56	1974	–1.5	–29.7
2006	1248.29	1290.15	3.4	13.6	57	1998	–1.5	26.7
2007	1418.30	1412.11	–0.4	3.5	58	1988	–1.5	12.4
2008	1468.36	1390.19	–5.3	–38.5	59	1993	–1.5	7.1
2009	903.25	909.73	0.7	23.5	60	1986	–1.6	14.6
2010	1115.10	1144.98	2.7	12.8	61	2001	–1.8	–13.0
2011	1257.64	1271.50	1.1	–0.003	62	1955	–1.8	26.4
2012	1257.60	1280.70	1.8	13.4	63	2022	–1.9	–19.4
2013	1426.19	1457.15	2.2	29.6	64	2000	–1.9	–10.1
2014	1848.36	1837.49	–0.6	11.4	65	1985	–1.9	26.3
2015	2058.90	2062.14	0.2	–0.7	66	1981	–2.0	–9.7
2016	2043.94	1922.03	–6.0	9.5	67	1956	–2.1	2.6
2017	2238.83	2268.90	1.3	19.4	68	2005	–2.1	3.0
2018	2673.61	2747.71	2.8	–6.2	69	1977	–2.3	–11.5
2019	2506.85	2574.41	2.7	28.9	70	1982	–2.4	14.8
2020	3230.78	3253.05	0.7	16.3	71	1969	–2.9	–11.4
2021	3756.07	3824.68	1.8	26.9	72	1962	–3.4	–11.8
2022	4766.18	4677.03	–1.9	–19.4	73	1991	–4.6	26.3
2023	3839.50	3892.09	1.4	24.2	74	1978	–4.7	1.1
2024	4769.83	4763.54	–0.1	23.3	75	2008	–5.3	–38.5
2025	5881.63	5918.35	0.6	??	76	2016	–6.0	9.5

Based on S&P 500

JANUARY 2026

MONDAY
Second Trading Day of the Year, Dow Up 21 of Last 32
Santa Claus Rally Ends *(Page 118)*
Almanac Investor Subscribers Emailed Official Results (See Insert)
D 61.9
S 47.6
N 38.1

5

I'd be a bum on the street with a tin cup, if the markets were always efficient.
— Warren Buffett (CEO Berkshire Hathaway, investor & philanthropist, b. 1930)

TUESDAY
D 47.6
S 52.4
N 47.6

6

Oil has fostered massive corruption in almost every country that has been "blessed" with it, and the expectation that oil wealth will transform economies has lead to disastrous policy choices.
— Ted Tyson (Chief Investment Officer, Mastholm Asset Management)

WEDNESDAY
D 61.9
S 66.7
N 61.9

7

I'm always turned off by an overly optimistic letter from the president in the annual report. If his letter is mildly pessimistic to me, that's a good sign.
— Philip Carret (Centenarian, Founded Pioneer Fund in 1928, 1896–1998)

January's First Five Days Act as an "Early Warning" *(Page 16)*
Almanac Investor Subscribers Emailed Official Results (See Insert)

THURSDAY
D 42.9
S 52.4
N 71.4

8

I've always preached to my clients that how you do in bad markets is more important than how you do in good markets. Managing your risk is more important than finding avenues to make money.
— Thomas Buck (*Barron's* Top 100 Advisor)

January Ends "Best Three-Month Span" *(Pages 52, 60, 149, and 150)*

FRIDAY
D 52.4
S 57.1
N 66.7

9

Imagination is more important than knowledge.
— Albert Einstein (German-American physicist, 1921 Nobel Prize, 1879–1955)

SATURDAY

10

SUNDAY

11

THE INCREDIBLE JANUARY BAROMETER (DEVISED 1972): ONLY 12 SIGNIFICANT ERRORS IN 75 YEARS

Devised by Yale Hirsch in 1972, our January Barometer states that as the S&P 500 goes in January, so goes the year. The indicator has registered **12 major errors since 1950 for an 84.0% accuracy ratio**. Vietnam affected 1966 and 1968; major bull market started in August 1982; two January rate cuts and 9/11 affected 2001; anticipation of military action in Iraq held stocks down in January 2003; new bull market began in 2009; the Fed saved 2010 with QE2; QE3 likely staved off declines in 2014; global growth fears sparked selling in January 2016; a partially inverted yield curve and trade tensions fueled Q4 selling in 2018; and Covid-19 disrupted 2020 and 2021. (*Almanac Investor* subscribers receive full analysis of each reading.)

Including the eight flat-year errors (less than +/- 5%) yields a 73.3% accuracy ratio. A full comparison of all monthly barometers for the Dow, S&P and NASDAQ can be seen at *www.stocktradersalmanac.com* in the January 11, 2024 issue. Full years followed January's direction in 11 of the last 19 midterm election years. See pages 20 and 24 for more.

AS JANUARY GOES, SO GOES THE YEAR

Market Performance in January

	Previous Year's Close	January Close	January Change	Year Change	
1950	16.76	17.05	1.7%	21.8%	
1951	20.41	21.66	6.1	16.5	
1952	23.77	24.14	1.6	11.8	
1953	26.57	26.38	−0.7	−6.6	
1954	24.81	26.08	5.1	45.0	
1955	35.98	36.63	1.8	26.4	
1956	45.48	43.82	−3.6	2.6	flat
1957	46.67	44.72	−4.2	−14.3	
1958	39.99	41.70	4.3	38.1	
1959	55.21	55.42	0.4	8.5	
1960	59.89	55.61	−7.1	−3.0	flat
1961	58.11	61.78	6.3	23.1	
1962	71.55	68.84	−3.8	−11.8	
1963	63.10	66.20	4.9	18.9	
1964	75.02	77.04	2.7	13.0	
1965	84.75	87.56	3.3	9.1	
1966	92.43	92.88	0.5	−13.1	X
1967	80.33	86.61	7.8	20.1	
1968	96.47	92.24	−4.4	7.7	X
1969	103.86	103.01	−0.8	−11.4	
1970	92.06	85.02	−7.6	0.1	flat
1971	92.15	95.88	4.0	10.8	
1972	102.09	103.94	1.8	15.6	
1973	118.05	116.03	−1.7	−17.4	
1974	97.55	96.57	−1.0	−29.7	
1975	68.56	76.98	12.3	31.5	
1976	90.19	100.86	11.8	19.1	
1977	107.46	102.03	−5.1	−11.5	
1978	95.10	89.25	−6.2	1.1	flat
1979	96.11	99.93	4.0	12.3	
1980	107.94	114.16	5.8	25.8	
1981	135.76	129.55	−4.6	−9.7	
1982	122.55	120.40	−1.8	14.8	X
1983	140.64	145.30	3.3	17.3	
1984	164.93	163.41	−0.9	1.4	flat
1985	167.24	179.63	7.4	26.3	
1986	211.28	211.78	0.2	14.6	
1987	242.17	274.08	13.2	2.0	flat
1988	247.08	257.07	4.0	12.4	
1989	277.72	297.47	7.1	27.3	
1990	353.40	329.08	−6.9	−6.6	
1991	330.22	343.93	4.2	26.3	
1992	417.09	408.79	−2.0	4.5	flat
1993	435.71	438.78	0.7	7.1	
1994	466.45	481.61	3.3	−1.5	flat
1995	459.27	470.42	2.4	34.1	
1996	615.93	636.02	3.3	20.3	
1997	740.74	786.16	6.1	31.0	
1998	970.43	980.28	1.0	26.7	
1999	1229.23	1279.64	4.1	19.5	
2000	1469.25	1394.46	−5.1	−10.1	
2001	1320.28	1366.01	3.5	−13.0	X
2002	1148.08	1130.20	−1.6	−23.4	
2003	879.82	855.70	−2.7	26.4	X
2004	1111.92	1131.13	1.7	9.0	
2005	1211.92	1181.27	−2.5	3.0	flat
2006	1248.29	1280.08	2.5	13.6	
2007	1418.30	1438.24	1.4	3.5	flat
2008	1468.36	1378.55	−6.1	−38.5	
2009	903.25	825.88	−8.6	23.5	X
2010	1115.10	1073.87	−3.7	12.8	X
2011	1257.64	1286.12	2.3	−0.003	flat
2012	1257.60	1312.41	4.4	13.4	
2013	1426.19	1498.11	5.0	29.6	
2014	1848.36	1782.59	−3.6	11.4	X
2015	2058.90	1994.99	−3.1	−0.7	flat
2016	2043.94	1940.24	−5.1	9.5	X
2017	2238.83	2278.87	1.8	19.4	
2018	2673.61	2823.81	5.6	−6.2	X
2019	2506.85	2704.10	7.9	28.9	
2020	3230.78	3225.52	−0.2	16.3	X
2021	3756.07	3714.24	−1.1	26.9	X
2022	4766.18	4515.55	−5.3	−19.4	
2023	3839.50	4076.60	6.2	24.2	
2024	4769.83	4845.65	1.6	23.3	
2025	5881.63	6040.53	2.7	??	

January Performance by Rank

Rank		January Change	Year Change	
1	1987	13.2%	2.0%	flat
2	1975	12.3	31.5	
3	1976	11.8	19.1	
4	2019	7.9	28.9	
5	1967	7.8	20.1	
6	1985	7.4	26.3	
7	1989	7.1	27.3	
8	1961	6.3	23.1	
9	2023	6.2	24.2	
10	1997	6.1	31.0	
11	1951	6.1	16.5	
12	1980	5.8	25.8	
13	2018	5.6	−6.2	X
14	1954	5.1	45.0	
15	2013	5.0	29.6	
16	1963	4.9	18.9	
17	2012	4.4	13.4	
18	1958	4.3	38.1	
19	1991	4.2	26.3	
20	1999	4.1	19.5	
21	1971	4.0	10.8	
22	1988	4.0	12.4	
23	1979	4.0	12.3	
24	2001	3.5	−13.0	X
25	1965	3.3	9.1	
26	1983	3.3	17.3	
27	1996	3.3	20.3	
28	1994	3.3	−1.5	flat
29	2025	2.7	??	
30	1964	2.7	13.0	
31	2006	2.5	13.6	
32	1995	2.4	34.1	
33	2011	2.3	−0.003	flat
34	1972	1.8	15.6	
35	1955	1.8	26.4	
36	2017	1.8	19.4	
37	1950	1.7	21.8	
38	2004	1.7	9.0	
39	2024	1.6	23.3	
40	1952	1.6	11.8	
41	2007	1.4	3.5	flat
42	1998	1.0	26.7	
43	1993	0.7	7.1	
44	1966	0.5	−13.1	X
45	1959	0.4	8.5	
46	1986	0.2	14.6	
47	2020	−0.2	16.3	X
48	1953	−0.7	−6.6	
49	1969	−0.8	−11.4	
50	1984	−0.9	1.4	flat
51	1974	−1.0	−29.7	
52	2021	−1.1	26.9	X
53	2002	−1.6	−23.4	
54	1973	−1.7	−17.4	
55	1982	−1.8	14.8	X
56	1992	−2.0	4.5	flat
57	2005	−2.5	3.0	flat
58	2003	−2.7	26.4	X
59	2015	−3.1	−0.7	flat
60	2014	−3.6	11.4	X
61	1956	−3.6	2.6	flat
62	2010	−3.7	12.8	X
63	1962	−3.8	−11.8	
64	1957	−4.2	−14.3	
65	1968	−4.4	7.7	X
66	1981	−4.6	−9.7	
67	1977	−5.1	−11.5	
68	2000	−5.1	−10.1	
69	2016	−5.1	9.5	X
70	2022	−5.3	−19.4	
71	2008	−6.1	−38.5	
72	1978	−6.2	1.1	flat
73	1990	−6.9	−6.6	
74	1960	−7.1	−3.0	flat
75	1970	−7.6	0.1	flat
76	2009	−8.6	23.5	X

X = major error Based on S&P 500

JANUARY 2026

First Trading Day of January Monthly Expiration Week, Dow Up 20 of Last 33, But Down 8 of Last 12

MONDAY
D 61.9
S 71.4
N 71.4
12

When I stand before God at the end of my life, I would hope that I would not have a single bit of talent left, and could say, "I used everything you gave me."
— Erma Bombeck (American humorist, columnist, & writer, 1927–1996)

TUESDAY
D 52.4
S 52.4
N 61.9
13

If I owe a million dollars I am lost. But if I owe $50 billion the bankers are lost.
— Celso Ming (Brazilian journalist)

January Monthly Expiration Week, Dow Up 11 of Last 15

WEDNESDAY
D 47.6
S 52.4
N 47.6
14

A senior European diplomat said he was convinced that the choice of starting a war this spring was made for political as well as military reasons. [The President] clearly does not want to have a war raging on the eve of his presumed reelection campaign.
— Reported by Steven R. Weisman (*NY Times*, 3/14/03)

THURSDAY
D 42.9
S 47.6
N 42.9
15

The single best predictor of overall excellence is a company's ability to attract, motivate, and retain talented people.
— Bruce Pfau (Vice chair human resources KPMG, *Fortune* 1998)

January Monthly Expiration Day Improving Since 2011, Dow Up 13 of Last 15
Day Before Martin Luther King Jr. Day, NASDAQ Up 8 of Last 10

FRIDAY
D 57.1
S 66.7
N 66.7
16

He who knows nothing is confident of everything.
— Anonymous

SATURDAY
17

SUNDAY
18

BULLS WIN WHEN MARKET HITS THE JANUARY TRIFECTA

We invented our January Indicator Trifecta in 2013 by combining our Santa Claus Rally (page 118) and January Barometer (page 18), both invented by our late founder Yale Hirsch in 1972 published in the *1973 Almanac*, with the age-old First Five Days Early Warning System (page 16).

The predicative power of the three is considerably greater than any of them alone; we have been rather impressed by its forecasting prowess. When the market hits this trifecta, the bulls win. Since 1950 when our January Barometer, Santa Claus Rally and First Five Days indicators are all positive for the S&P 500 the odds of the rest of the year—and the year as a whole—being up increase dramatically.

When all three are up, the S&P 500 has been up 90.6% of the time, 29 of 32 years, with an average gain of 17.7%, and the next 11 months are up 87.5 % of the time, 28 of 32 years, with an average gain of 12.6%. When any of them are down the year's results are reduced with S&P up 60.5% of the time, 26 of 43 years, with an average gain of 3.4%. When all three are down the S&P was down 3 of 8 years with an average loss of –3.6% with bear markets in 1969 (–11.4%), 2000 (–10.1%) and 2008 (–38.5%), flat years in 1956 (2.6%), 1978 (1.1%), and 2005 (3.0%). Down Trifecta's were followed by gains in 1982 (14.8%) and 2016 (9.5%).

When the January Indicator Trifecta was preceded by a bear market in the year prior the results were even more striking. Next 11-months and full-year performance were always positive, up 14-0, with average gains of 16.8% and 22.2%, respectively. We did not hit this trifecta in 2025, the Santa Claus Rally was negative. *Almanac Investor* newsletter subscribers received our full analysis.

S&P 500 JANUARY INDICATOR TRIFECTA — THREE POSITIVE

Year	SC Rally	FFD	JB	Feb	Feb-Dec	Full Year
1950	1.3%	2.0%	1.7%	1.0%	19.7%	21.8
1951	3.1	2.3	6.1	0.6	9.7	16.5
1952	1.4	0.6	1.6	–3.6	10.1	11.8
1954	1.7	0.5	5.1	0.3	38.0	45.0
1958	3.5	2.5	4.3	–2.1	32.4	38.1
1959	3.6	0.3	0.4	–0.02	8.1	8.5
1961	1.7	1.2	6.3	2.7	15.8	23.1
1963	1.7	2.6	4.9	–2.9	13.3	18.9
1964	2.3	1.3	2.7	1.0	10.0	13.0
1965	0.6	0.7	3.3	–0.1	5.6	9.1
1966	0.1	0.8	0.5	–1.8	–13.5	–13.1
1971	1.9	0.04	4.0	0.9	6.5	10.8
1972	1.3	1.4	1.8	2.5	13.6	15.6
1975	7.2	2.2	12.3	6.0	17.2	31.5
1976	4.3	4.9	11.8	–1.1	6.5	19.1
1979	3.3	2.8	4.0	–3.7	8.0	12.3
1983	1.2	3.2	3.3	1.9	13.5	17.3
1987	2.4	6.2	13.2	3.7	–9.9	2.0
1989	0.9	1.2	7.1	–2.9	18.8	27.3
1995	0.2	0.3	2.4	3.6	30.9	34.1
1996	1.8	0.4	3.3	0.7	16.5	20.3
1997	0.1	1.0	6.1	0.6	23.4	31.0
1999	1.3	3.7	4.1	–3.2	14.8	19.5
2004	2.4	1.8	1.7	1.2	7.1	9.0
2006	0.4	3.4	2.5	0.05	10.8	13.6
2011	1.1	1.1	2.3	3.2	–2.2	–0.003
2012	1.9	1.8	4.2	4.1	8.7	13.4
2013	2.0	2.2	4.8	1.1	23.4	29.6
2017	0.4	1.3	1.8	3.7	17.3	19.4
2018	1.1	2.8	5.6	–3.9	–11.2	–6.2
2019	1.3	2.7	7.9	3.0	19.5	28.9
2023	0.8	1.4	6.2	–2.6	20.1	24.2
Average				0.4%	12.6%	17.7%
# Up				20	28	29
#Down				12	4	3

JANUARY 2026

Martin Luther King Jr. Day *(Market Closed)*

MONDAY
19

I never won a fight in the ring; I always won in preparation.
— Muhammad Ali (American boxer, activist, "The Greatest," 1942–2016)

Day After Martin Luther King Jr. Day, NASDAQ Down 7 of Last 10

D 42.9
S 42.9
N 47.6

TUESDAY
20

The death of contrarians has been greatly exaggerated. The reason is that the crowd is the market for most of any cycle. You cannot be contrarian all the time, otherwise you end up simply fighting the tape the whole way up (or down), therefore being wildly wrong.
— Barry L. Ritholtz (Founder/CIO Ritholtz Wealth Management, *Bailout Nation*, The Big Picture blog, Bloomberg View 12/20/2013, b. 1961)

D 52.4
S 61.9
N 47.6

WEDNESDAY
21

Look for an impending crash in the economy when the best seller lists are filled with books on business strategies and quick-fix management ideas.
— Peter Drucker (Austrian-born pioneer management theorist, 1909–2005)

D 42.9
S 57.1
N 52.4

THURSDAY
22

The bigger a man's head gets, the easier it is to fill his shoes.
— Anonymous

D 47.6
S 52.4
N 66.7

FRIDAY
23

Low volatility is where trends are born, high volatility is where they go to die.
— John Bollinger, CMT, CFA (American author, technical/financial analyst, developer of Bollinger Bands, Bollinger Capital Management, *Capital Growth Letter, Bollinger on Bollinger Bands*, b. 1950)

SATURDAY
24

SUNDAY
25

FEBRUARY ALMANAC

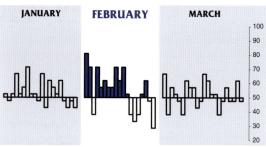

Market Probability Chart above is a graphic representation of the S&P 500 Recent Market Probability Calendar on page 126.

◆ February is the weak link in "Best Six Months" (pages 52, 54, & 149)
◆ RECENT RECORD: S&P up 9, down 6, average change +0.9% last 15 years
◆ #4 NASDAQ month in midterm election years average gain 0.4%, up 6 down 7 (page 166), #6 Dow, up 12 down 7 and #6 S&P, up 10, down 9 (pages 156 & 162) ◆ Day before Presidents' Day weekend S&P down 21 of 34, 11 straight 1992–2002, day after mixed up 18 down 16 (see page 102 & 135) ◆ Many technicians modify market predictions based on January's market in February

February Vital Statistics

	DJIA		S&P 500		NASDAQ		Russell 1K		Russell 2K	
Rank	8		11		10		11		6	
Up	44		41		29		27		27	
Down	32		35		26		20		20	
Average % Change	0.1		−0.02		0.5		0.2		1.0	
Midterm Yr Avg % Chg	0.5		0.3		0.4		0.5		1.3	
Best & Worst February										
	% Change		% Change		% Change		% Change		% Change	
Best	1976	14.4	1987	13.2	1975	16.6	1987	12.7	1985	13.1
Worst	2009	−8.8	2009	−8.6	2008	−9.9	2009	−8.3	2009	−11.2
Best & Worst February Weeks										
Best	2/1/08	4.4	2/6/09	5.2	2/4/00	9.2	2/6/09	5.3	2/5/21	7.7
Worst	2/28/20	−12.4	2/28/20	−11.5	2/28/20	−10.5	2/28/20	−11.6	2/28/20	−12.0
Best & Worst February Days										
Best	2/24/09	3.3	2/24/09	4.0	2/11/99	4.2	2/24/09	4.1	2/24/09	4.5
Worst	2/10/09	−4.6	2/10/09	−4.9	2/16/01	−5.0	2/10/09	−4.8	2/10/09	−4.7
First Trading Day of Monthly Options Expiration Week: 1980–2025										
Record (#Up–#Down)	28–18		31–15		27–19		31–15		28–18	
Current streak	U3		U1		U1		U1		U3	
Avg % Change	0.30		0.27		0.14		0.25		0.20	
Monthly Options Expiration Day: 1980–2025										
Record (#Up–#Down)	23–23		18–28		18–28		19–27		22–24	
Current streak	D2		D6		D4		D6		D2	
Avg % Change	−0.07		−0.17		−0.33		−0.17		−0.10	
Monthly Options Expiration Week: 1980–2025										
Record (#Up–#Down)	26–20		23–23		24–22		23–23		29–17	
Current streak	D4		D6		D2		D6		D1	
Avg % Change	0.38		0.21		0.12		0.21		0.37	
Week After Monthly Options Expiration: 1980–2025										
Record (#Up–#Down)	22–24		22–24		26–20		22–24		23–23	
Current streak	U2		D1		D1		D1		D3	
Avg % Change	−0.49		−0.44		−0.50		−0.42		−0.41	
First Trading Day Performance										
% of Time Up	64.5		63.2		70.9		68.1		68.1	
Avg % Change	0.17		0.20		0.40		0.26		0.41	
Last Trading Day Performance										
% of Time Up	46.1		51.3		50.9		48.9		55.3	
Avg % Change	−0.06		−0.03		−0.03		−0.08		0.01	

Dow & S&P 1950–May 2, 2025; NASDAQ 1971–May 2, 2025; Russell 1K & 2K 1979–May 2, 2025.

Either go short or stay away the day before Presidents' Day.

JANUARY/FEBRUARY 2026

MONDAY
D 57.1
S 61.9
N 57.1
26

One thing John Chambers (Cisco CEO) does well is stretch people's responsibilities and change the boxes they are in. It makes our jobs new all the time.
— Mike Volpi (Senior VP of business development and alliances at Cisco, *Fortune*)

TUESDAY
D 57.1
S 47.6
N 61.9
27

An autobiography must be such that one can sue oneself for libel.
— Thomas Hoving (Museum Director)

FOMC Meeting

WEDNESDAY
D 52.4
S 42.9
N 57.1
28

Small volume is usually accompanied by a fall in price; large volume by a rise in price.
— Charles C. Ying ("Stock Market Prices and Volumes of Sales," *Econometrica*, July 1966)

THURSDAY
D 47.6
S 47.6
N 42.9
29

If investing is entertaining, if you're having fun, you're probably not making any money. Good investing is boring.
— George Soros (Financier, philanthropist, political activist, author and philosopher, b. 1930)

"January Barometer" 84.0% Accurate (Page 18)
Almanac Investor Subscribers Emailed Official Results (See Insert)

FRIDAY
D 38.1
S 42.9
N 52.4
30

The reason that "guru" is such a popular word is because "charlatan" is so hard to spell.
— Barry L. Ritholtz (Founder/CIO Ritholtz Wealth Management, *How Not to Invest*, b. 1961)

SATURDAY
31

February Almanac Investor Sector Seasonalities: See Pages 94, 96, and 98

SUNDAY
1

DOWN JANUARYS: A REMARKABLE RECORD

In the first third of the 20th century there was no correlation between January markets and the year as a whole. Then in 1972 Yale Hirsch discovered that the 1933 "Lame Duck" Amendment to the Constitution changed the political calendar and the January Barometer was born—its record has been quite accurate (page 18).

Down Januarys are harbingers of trouble ahead, in the economic, political, or military arenas. Eisenhower's heart attack in 1955 cast doubt on whether he could run in 1956—a flat year. Two other election years with down Januarys were also flat (1984 & 1992). Sixteen bear markets began and 10 continued into second years with poor Januarys. 1968 started down as we were mired in Vietnam, but Johnson's "bombing halt" changed the climate. Imminent military action in Iraq held January 2003 down before the market triple-bottomed in March. After Baghdad fell, pre-election and recovery forces fueled 2003 into a banner year. 2005 was flat, registering the narrowest Dow trading range on record. 2008 was the worst January on record and preceded the worst bear market since the Great Depression. A negative reading in 2015 and 2016 preceded an official Dow bear market declaration in February 2016. In 2020 the shortest bear market in history began after the close on February 19. ZIRP and QE fueled a banner 2021 however, NASDAQ did correct 10.5% during February and March. Aggressive interest rate hikes triggered a bear in 2022.

Unfortunately, bull and bear markets do not start conveniently at the beginnings and ends of months or years. Though some years ended higher, **every down January since 1950 was followed by a new or continuing bear market, a 10% correction or a flat year. Down Januarys were followed by substantial declines averaging** *minus* **13.3%**, providing excellent buying opportunities later in most years.

FROM DOWN JANUARY S&P CLOSES TO LOW NEXT 11 MONTHS

Year	January Close	% Change	11-Month Low	Date of Low	Jan Close to Low %	% Feb to Dec	Year % Change	
1953	26.38	−0.7%	22.71	14-Sep	−13.9%	−6.0%	−6.6%	bear
1956	43.82	−3.6	43.42	14-Feb	−0.9	6.5	2.6	bear/FLAT
1957	44.72	−4.2	38.98	22-Oct	−12.8	−10.6	−14.3	Cont. bear
1960	55.61	−7.1	52.30	25-Oct	−6.0	4.5	−3.0	bear
1962	68.84	−3.8	52.32	26-Jun	−24.0	−8.3	−11.8	bear
1968	92.24	−4.4	87.72	5-Mar	−4.9	12.6	7.7	−10%/bear
1969	103.01	−0.8	89.20	17-Dec	−13.4	−10.6	−11.4	Cont. bear
1970	85.02	−7.6	69.20	26-May	−18.6	8.4	0.1	Cont. bear
1973	116.03	−1.7	92.16	5-Dec	−20.6	−15.9	−17.4	bear
1974	96.57	−1.0	62.28	3-Oct	−35.5	−29.0	−29.7	Cont. bear
1977	102.03	−5.1	90.71	2-Nov	−11.1	−6.8	−11.5	bear
1978	89.25	−6.2	86.90	6-Mar	−2.6	7.7	1.1	Cont. bear/bear
1981	129.55	−4.6	112.77	25-Sep	−13.0	−5.4	−9.7	bear
1982	120.40	−1.8	102.42	12-Aug	−14.9	16.8	14.8	Cont. bear
1984	163.42	−0.9	147.82	24-Jul	−9.5	2.3	1.4	Cont. bear/FLAT
1990	329.07	−6.9	295.46	11-Oct	−10.2	0.4	−6.6	bear
1992	408.79	−2.0	394.50	8-Apr	−3.5	6.6	4.5	FLAT
2000	1394.46	−5.1	1264.74	20-Dec	−9.3	−5.3	−10.1	bear
2002	1130.20	−1.6	776.76	9-Oct	−31.3	−22.2	−23.4	bear
2003	855.70	−2.7	800.73	11-Mar	−6.4	29.9	26.4	Cont. bear
2005	1181.27	−2.5	1137.50	20-Apr	−3.7	5.7	3.0	FLAT
2008	1378.55	−6.1	752.44	20-Nov	−45.4	−34.5	−38.5	bear
2009	825.88	−8.6	676.53	9-Mar	−18.1	35.0	23.5	Cont. bear
2010	1073.87	−3.7	1022.58	2-Jul	−4.8	17.1	12.8	−10%/no bear
2014	1782.59	−3.6	1741.89	3-Feb	−2.3	15.5	11.4	−10% intraday
2015	1994.99	−3.1	1867.61	25-Aug	−6.4	2.5	−0.7	bear
2016	1940.24	−5.1	1829.08	11-Feb	−5.7	15.4	9.5	Cont. bear
2020	3225.52	−0.2	2237.40	23-Mar	−30.6	16.4	16.3	bear
2021	3714.24	−1.1	3768.47	4-Mar	1.5	28.3	26.9	−10% NAS
2022	4515.55	−5.3	3577.03	12-Oct	−20.8	15.0	−19.4	bear
				Totals	−398.7%	92.0%	−52.2%	
				Average	−13.3%	3.1%	−1.7%	

FEBRUARY 2026

First Trading Day in February, Dow Up 19 of Last 23

MONDAY
D 85.7
S 81.0
N 81.0
2

There have been three great inventions since the beginning of time: Fire, the wheel, and central banking.
— Will Rogers (American humorist and showman, 1879–1935)

TUESDAY
D 57.1
S 71.4
N 66.7
3

There is a perfect inverse correlation between inflation rates and price/earnings ratios...
When inflation has been very high…P/E has been [low].
— Liz Ann Sonders (Chief Investment Strategist Charles Schwab, June 2006)

WEDNESDAY
D 47.6
S 38.1
N 33.3
4

If you can buy all you want of a new issue, you do not want any; if you cannot obtain any, you want all you can buy.
— Rod Fadem (Stifel Nicolaus & Co., Barron's, 1989)

THURSDAY
D 66.7
S 71.4
N 61.9
5

Letting your emotions override your plan or system is the biggest cause of failure.
— J. Welles Wilder Jr. (Creator of several technical indicators including Relative Strength Index (RSI), 1935–2021)

FRIDAY
D 61.9
S 57.1
N 57.1
6

Under capitalism man exploits man: under socialism the reverse is true.
— Polish proverb

SATURDAY
7

SUNDAY
8

MARKET CHARTS OF MIDTERM ELECTION YEARS

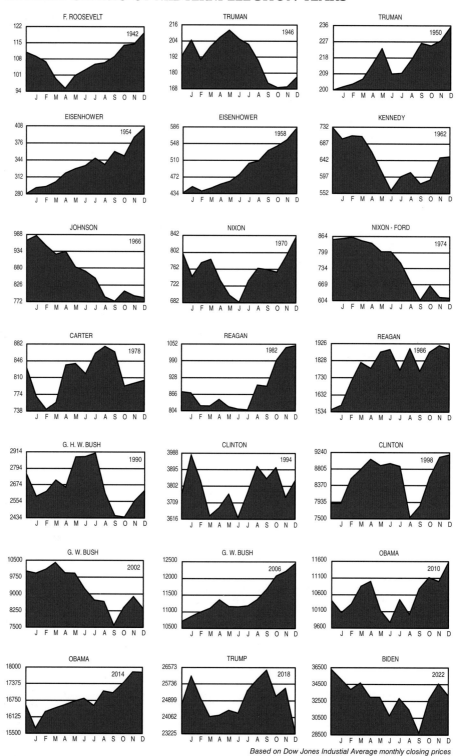

Based on Dow Jones Industial Average monthly closing prices

FEBRUARY 2026

MONDAY
D 47.6
S 61.9
N 61.9
9

As for it being different this time, it is different every time. The question is in what way, and to what extent.
— Tom McClellan (Market analyst and technician, *The McClellan Market Report*)

Week Before February Monthly Expiration Week, NASDAQ Up 11 of Last 16

TUESDAY
D 52.4
S 57.1
N 61.9
10

Whenever you see a successful business, someone once made a courageous decision.
— Peter Drucker (Austrian-born pioneer management theorist, 1909–2005)

WEDNESDAY
D 61.9
S 57.1
N 57.1
11

Politicians use statistics in the same way that a drunk uses lamp-posts—for support rather than illumination.
— Andrew Lang (Scottish writer, literary critic, anthropologist, 1844–1912)

THURSDAY
D 57.1
S 71.4
N 71.4
12

The worst crime against working people is a company that fails to make a profit.
— Samuel Gompers

Day Before Presidents' Day Weekend, S&P Up 10 of Last 15

FRIDAY
D 47.6
S 61.9
N 81.0
13

Pretending to know everything closes the door to finding out what's really there.
— Neil deGrasse Tyson (American astrophysicist, cosmologist, Director Hayden Planetarium, *Cosmos: A Spacetime Odyssey*, b. 1958)

Valentine's Day ♥

SATURDAY
14

SUNDAY
15

MIDTERM ELECTION YEARS: WHERE BOTTOM PICKER'S FIND PARADISE

American presidents have danced the Quadrennial Quadrille over the past two centuries. After the midterm congressional election and the invariable seat loss by his party, the president during the next two years jiggles fiscal policies to get federal spending, disposable income and social security benefits up and interest rates and inflation down. By Election Day, he will have danced his way into the wallets and hearts of the electorate and, hopefully, will have choreographed four more years in the White House for his party.

After the Inaugural Ball is over, however, we pay the piper. Practically all bear markets began and ended in the two years after presidential elections. Bottoms often occurred in an air of crisis: the Cuban Missile Crisis in 1962, tight money in 1966, Cambodia in 1970, Watergate and Nixon's resignation in 1974, threat of international monetary collapse in 1982, and Asian currency crisis in 1998. In the last 16 quadrennial cycles since 1961, 10 of the 19 bear markets bottomed in the midterm year. *See pages 133–134 for further detail.*

THE RECORD SINCE 1914

Year	President	Notes
1914	Wilson (D)	Bottom in July. War closed markets.
1918	Wilson (D)	**Bottom 12 days prior to start of year.**
1922	Harding (R)	**Bottom 4½ months prior to start of year.**
1926	Coolidge (R)	Only drop (7 wks, –17%) ends Mar. 30.
1930	Hoover (R)	**'29 Crash continues through 1930. No bottom.**
1934	Roosevelt (D)	1st Roosevelt bear, Feb to July 26 bottom (–23%).
1938	Roosevelt (D)	Big 1937 break ends in March, DJI off 49%.
1942	Roosevelt (D)	World War II bottom in April.
1946	Truman (D)	Market tops in May, bottoms in October.
1950	Truman (D)	June 1949 bottom, June 1950 Korean War outbreak causes 14% drop.
1954	Eisenhower (R)	**September 1953 bottom, then straight up.**
1958	Eisenhower (R)	**October 1957 bottom, then straight up.**
1962	Kennedy (D)	Bottoms in June and October.
1966	Johnson (D)	Bottom in October.
1970	Nixon (R)	Bottom in May.
1974	Nixon, Ford (R)	December Dow bottom, S&P bottom in October.
1978	Carter (D)	March bottom, despite October massacre later.
1982	Reagan (R)	Bottom in August.
1986	Reagan (R)	**No bottom in 1985 or 1986.**
1990	Bush (R)	Bottom October 11 (Kuwaiti Invasion).
1994	Clinton (D)	Bottom April 4 after 10% drop.
1998	Clinton (D)	October 8 bottom (Asian currency crisis, hedge fund debacle).
2002	Bush, GW (R)	October 9 bottom (Corp malfeasance, terrorism, Iraq).
2006	Bush, GW (R)	**No Bottom in 2006** (Iraq success, credit bubble).
2010	Obama (D)	**No Bear,** July low, –13.6% from April high.
2014	Obama (D)	**No Bear, No Bottom** (Fed QE).
2018	Trump (R)	**No Bear, December bottom** (Fed, rates)
2022	Biden (D)	Dow bottom Sept. 30, S&P Oct. 12, NAS Dec. 28

Bold = No bottom in midterm election year

Graph shows Midterm years screened
Based on Dow Jones industial average monthly ranges

FEBRUARY 2026

Presidents' Day *(Market Closed)*

MONDAY
16

Bear markets don't act like a medicine ball rolling down a smooth hill. Instead, they behave like a basketball bouncing down a rock-strewn mountainside; there's lots of movement up and sideways before the bottom is reached.
— Daniel Turov (*Turov on Timing, Barron's,* May 21, 2001, b. 1947)

Day After Presidents Day, NASDAQ Down 19 of Last 31, But Up 8 of Last 13
First Trading Day of February Monthly Expiration Week Dow Up 22 of Last 32

D 71.4
S 71.4
N 71.4

TUESDAY
17

Losses loom larger than gains. The aggravation that one experiences in losing a sum of money appears to be greater than the pleasure associated with gaining the same amount.
— Daniel Kahneman (Israeli-American psychologist and economist, "Prospect Theory: An Analysis of Decision under Risk," *Econometrica,* March 1979, 2002 Nobel Prize, 1934–2024)

Ash Wednesday

D 61.9
S 52.4
N 42.9

WEDNESDAY
18

Savor the joy of others. It is abundant and free and it will lift your spirits and boost your wellbeing even as you add positive energy to the world.
— Phil Pearlman (Founder, Pearl Institute, b. 1967)

D 42.9
S 38.1
N 38.1

THURSDAY
19

While markets often make double bottoms, three pushes to a high is the most common topping pattern.
— John Bollinger (Bollinger Capital Management, *Capital Growth Letter, Bollinger on Bollinger Bands*)

February Monthly Expiration Day, NASDAQ Down 15 of Last 22

D 38.1
S 33.3
N 33.3

FRIDAY
20

The years teach much which the days never know.
— Ralph Waldo Emerson (American author, poet and philosopher, *Self-Reliance,* 1803–1882)

SATURDAY
21

SUNDAY
22

MARCH ALMANAC

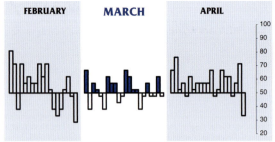

Market Probability Chart above is a graphic representation of the S&P 500 Recent Market Probability Calendar on page 126.

◆ Mid-month strength and late-month choppiness are most evident above ◆ RECENT RECORD: S&P 13 up, 8 down, average gain 1.0%, fourth best ◆ Rather turbulent in recent years with wild fluctuations and large gains and losses ◆ March 2020 Dow declined 13.7%, worst March loss since 1938 ◆ March has been taking some mean end-of-quarter hits (page 136), down 1469 Dow points March 9-22, 2001 ◆ Last three or four days Dow a net loser 22 out of last 36 years ◆ NASDAQ hard hit in 2001, down 14.5% after 22.4% drop in February ◆ #3 NASDAQ month during midterm election years average gain 1.4%, up 8, down 5 ◆ Third Dow month to gain more than 1000 points in 2016

March Vital Statistics

	DJIA	S&P 500	NASDAQ	Russell 1K	Russell 2K
Rank	6	6	9	8	8
Up	49	49	35	31	32
Down	27	27	20	16	15
Average % Change	0.9	1.0	0.7	0.8	0.6
Midterm Yr Avg % Chg	1.1	1.2	1.4	1.7	2.5
Best & Worst March					
	% Change	% Change	% Change	% Change	% Change
Best	2000 7.8	2000 9.7	2009 10.9	2000 8.9	1979 9.7
Worst	2020 −13.7	2020 −12.5	1980 −17.1	2020 −13.4	2020 −21.9
Best & Worst March Weeks					
Best	3/27/20 12.8	3/13/09 10.7	3/13/09 10.6	3/13/09 10.7	3/13/09 12.0
Worst	3/20/20 −17.3	3/20/20 −15.0	3/20/20 −12.6	3/20/20 −15.3	3/13/20 −16.5
Best & Worst March Days					
Best	3/24/20 11.4	3/24/20 9.4	3/13/20 9.4	3/24/20 9.5	3/24/20 9.4
Worst	3/16/20 −12.9	3/16/20 −12.0	3/16/20 −12.3	3/16/20 −12.2	3/16/20 −14.3
First Trading Day of Monthly Options Expiration Week: 1980–2025					
Record (#Up–#Down)	30–16	28–18	24–22	26–20	24–22
Current streak	U2	U1	U1	U1	U1
Avg % Change	−0.09	−0.17	−0.44	−0.22	−0.58
Monthly Options Expiration Day: 1980–2025					
Record (#Up–#Down)	24–22	26–20	24–22	25–21	23–22
Current streak	U1	U1	U1	U1	D1
Avg % Change	−0.04	−0.07	−0.05	−0.06	−0.09
Monthly Options Expiration Week: 1980–2025					
Record (#Up–#Down)	30–15	30–16	28–18	29–17	25–21
Current streak	U1	U1	U1	U1	U1
Avg % Change	0.52	0.51	0.12	0.45	−0.11
Week After Monthly Options Expiration: 1980–2025					
Record (#Up–#Down)	21–25	17–29	22–24	17–29	20–26
Current streak	D1	D1	D1	D1	D1
Avg % Change	−0.03	0.03	0.08	0.02	−0.11
First Trading Day Performance					
% of Time Up	67.1	63.2	61.8	59.6	66.0
Avg % Change	0.21	0.22	0.31	0.23	0.29
Last Trading Day Performance					
% of Time Up	43.4	43.4	61.8	51.1	78.7
Avg % Change	−0.09	0.01	0.19	0.10	0.38

Dow & S&P 1950–May 2, 2025; NASDAQ 1971–May 2, 2025; Russell 1K & 2K 1979–May 2, 2025

March has Ides and St. Patrick's Day;
Begins bullishly, then fades away.

FEBRUARY/MARCH 2026

End of February Miserable in Recent Years (Page 22 and 135)

MONDAY
D 47.6
S 38.1
N 42.9
23

Governments last as long as the under-taxed can defend themselves against the over-taxed.
— Bernard Berenson (American art critic, 1865–1959)

Week After February Monthly Expiration Week, Dow Down 15 of Last 27, But Up 9 of Last 14, 2020 Down 12.4% 5th Worst Week Since 1950

TUESDAY
D 47.6
S 52.4
N 42.9
24

Regret for the things we did can be tempered by time; it is regret for the things we did not do that is inconsolable.
— Sydney J. Harris (American journalist and author, 1917–1986)

WEDNESDAY
D 57.1
S 61.9
N 76.2
25

In bull markets promises trade at a premium, but in bear markets reality trades at a discount.
— Jim Chanos (Short seller, Founder Kynikos Associates, b. 1957)

THURSDAY
D 42.9
S 47.6
N 61.9
26

If there's anything duller than being on a board in Corporate America, I haven't found it.
— H. Ross Perot (American businessman, NY Times, 10/28/92, 2-time 3rd-party presidential candidate 1992 & 1996, 1930–2019)

FRIDAY
D 28.6
S 28.6
N 33.3
27

When everybody thinks alike, everyone is likely to be wrong.
— Humphrey B. Neill (Investor, analyst, author, *Art of Contrary Thinking* 1954, 1895–1977)

SATURDAY
28

March Almanac Investor Sector Seasonalities: See Pages 94, 96, and 98

SUNDAY
1

PROSPERITY MORE THAN PEACE DETERMINES THE OUTCOME OF MIDTERM CONGRESSIONAL RACES

Though the stock market in presidential election years very often is able to predict if the party in power will retain or lose the White House, the outcome of congressional races in midterm years is another matter entirely. Typically, the president's party will lose a number of House seats in these elections (1934, 1998, and 2002 were exceptions). It is considered a victory for the president when his party loses a small number of seats, and a repudiation of sorts when a large percentage of seats is lost.

The table below would seem to indicate that there is no relationship between the stock market's behavior in the 10 months prior to the midterm election and the magnitude of seats lost in the House. Roaring bull markets preceded the elections of 1954 and 1958, yet Republicans lost few seats during one, and a huge number in the other.

If the market does not offer a clue to the outcome of House races, does anything besides the popularity and performance of the administration? Yes! In the two years prior to the elections in the first 12 midterm years listed, no war or major recession began. As a result, the percentage of House seats lost was minimal. A further observation is that the market gained ground in the last seven weeks of the year, except 2002.

Our five major wars began under four Democrats and one Republican in the shaded area. The percentage of seats lost was greater during these midterm elections. But the eight worst repudiations of the president are at the bottom of the list. These were preceded by: a Fed interest rate tightening cycle in 2018, the sick economy in 1930, the botched health proposals in 1994, the severe recession in 1937, the post-war contraction in 1946, the recession in 1957, financial crisis and the second worst bear market in history from 2007 to 2009, Watergate in 1974, and rumors of corruption (Teapot Dome) in 1922. **Obviously, prosperity is of greater importance to the electorate than peace!**

LAST 27 MIDTERM ELECTIONS RANKED BY % LOSS OF SEATS BY PRESIDENT'S PARTY

	% Seats Gained or Lost	Year	President	Dow Jones Industrials Jan 1 to Elec Day	Dow Jones Industrials Elec Day to Dec 31	Year's CPI% Change
1	3.6 %	2002	R: G.W. Bush	−14.5 %	−2.7 %	1.6 %
2	2.9	1934	D: Roosevelt	−3.8	8.3	1.5
3	2.4	1998	D: Clinton	10.1	5.5	1.6
4	−1.5	1962	D: Kennedy	−16.5	6.8	1.3
5	−2.7	1986	R: Reagan	22.5	0.1	1.1
6	−3.2	2022	D: Biden	−9.7	1.0	6.5
7	−4.0	1926	R: Coolidge	−3.9	4.4	−1.1
8	−4.6	1990	R: G.H.W. Bush	−9.1	5.3	6.1
9	−5.1	1978	D: Carter	−3.7	0.6	9.0
10	−6.3	1970	R: Nixon	−5.3	10.7	5.6
11	−6.5	2014	D: Obama	7.3	3.5	0.8
12	−8.1	1954	R: Eisenhower	26.0	14.2	−0.7
13	−9.0	1918	D: Wilson (WW1)	15.2	−4.1	20.4
14	−11.0	1950	D: Truman (Korea)	11.2	−5.8	5.9
15	−12.9	2006	R: G.W. Bush (Iraq)	13.4	2.5	2.6
16	−13.5	1982	R: Reagan	14.9	4.1	3.8
17	−15.9	1966	D: Johnson (Vietnam)	−17.2	−2.1	3.5
18	−16.9	1942	D: Roosevelt (WW2)	3.4	4.1	9.0
19	−17.4	2018	R: Trump	3.0	−8.3	1.9
20	−18.4	1930	R: Hoover	−25.4	−11.2	−6.4
21	−20.9	1994	D: Clinton	1.5	0.7	2.7
22	−21.3	1938	D: Roosevelt	28.2	−0.1	−2.8
23	−22.6	1946	D: Truman	−9.6	1.6	18.1
24	−23.9	1958	R: Eisenhower	25.1	7.1	1.8
25	−24.6	2010	D: Obama	7.3	3.5	1.5
26	−25.0	1974	R: Ford	−22.8	−6.2	12.3
27	−25.0	1922	R: Harding	21.4	0.3	−2.3

MARCH 2026

First Trading Day in March, S&P Up 17 of Last 26

MONDAY
D 66.7
S 66.7
N 61.9

2

An economist is a man who, when he finds something works in practice, wonders if it works in theory.
— Walter Heller (American economist, Chairman Council Economic Advisors 1961–1964, 1915–1987)

TUESDAY
D 33.3
S 38.1
N 42.9

3

If we did all the things we are capable of doing, we would literally astound ourselves.
— Thomas Alva Edison (American inventor, 1093 patents, 1847–1931)

WEDNESDAY
D 52.4
S 57.1
N 47.6

4

Marx's great achievement was to place the system of capitalism on the defensive.
— Charles A. Madison (1977)

March Historically Strong Early in the Month (Pages 30 and 136)

THURSDAY
D 47.6
S 52.4
N 38.1

5

People somehow think you must buy at the bottom and sell at the top. That's nonsense. The idea is to buy when the probability is greatest that the market is going to advance.
— Martin Zweig (Fund manager, Winning on Wall Street, 1943–2013)

FRIDAY
D 47.6
S 47.6
N 33.3

6

Regulatory agencies within five years become controlled by industries they were set up to regulate.
— Gabriel Kolko (American historian and author, 1932–2014)

SATURDAY

7

Daylight Saving Time Begins

SUNDAY

8

WHY A 50% GAIN IN THE DOW IS POSSIBLE FROM ITS 2026 LOW TO ITS 2027 HIGH

Normally, major corrections occur sometime in the first or second years following presidential elections. In the last 16 midterm election years, bear markets began or were in progress 10 times—we experienced bull years in 1986, 2006, 2010, and 2014, while 1994 was flat. A correction in 2018 ended on Christmas Eve day.

The puniest midterm advance, 14.5% from the 1946 low, was during the industrial contraction after World War II. The next five smallest advances were: 2014 (tepid global growth) 19.1%, 1978 (OPEC–Iran) 21.0%, 1930 (economic collapse) 23.4%, 1966 (Vietnam) 26.7%, and 2022 (Fed interest rate tightening) 31.3%.

Since 1914 the Dow has gained 46.3% on average from its midterm election year low to its subsequent high in the following pre-election year. A swing of such magnitude is equivalent to a move from 40000 to 60000.

POST-ELECTION HIGH TO MIDTERM LOW: –20.2%

Conversely, since 1913 the Dow has dropped –20.2% on average from its post-election-year high to its subsequent low in the following midterm year. At press-time the Dow's 2025 post-election-year high is 44882.13. A 20.2% decline would put the Dow back at 35815 at the 2026 midterm bottom. At press time, lingering tariff uncertainty could make a decline to this level possible. Whatever the level, the rally off the 2026 midterm low could be another great buying opportunity.

Pretty impressive seasonality! There is no reason to think the quadrennial Presidential Election/Stock Market Cycle will not continue. Page 132 shows how effectively most presidents "managed" to have much stronger economies in the third and fourth years of their terms than in their first two.

% CHANGE IN DOW JONES INDUSTRIALS BETWEEN THE MIDTERM YEAR LOW AND THE HIGH IN THE FOLLOWING YEAR

	Midterm Year Low				Pre-Election Year High			
	Date of Low			Dow	Date of High		Dow	% Gain
1	Jul	30	1914*	52.32	Dec	27	1915	99.21	89.6%
2	Jan	15	1918**	73.38	Nov	3	1919	119.62	63.0
3	Jan	10	1922**	78.59	Mar	20	1923	105.38	34.1
4	Mar	30	1926*	135.20	Dec	31	1927	202.40	49.7
5	Dec	16	1930*	157.51	Feb	24	1931	194.36	23.4
6	Jul	26	1934*	85.51	Nov	19	1935	148.44	73.6
7	Mar	31	1938*	98.95	Sep	12	1939	155.92	57.6
8	Apr	28	1942*	92.92	Jul	14	1943	145.82	56.9
9	Oct	9	1946	163.12	Jul	24	1947	186.85	14.5
10	Jan	13	1950**	196.81	Sep	13	1951	276.37	40.4
11	Jan	11	1954**	279.87	Dec	30	1955	488.40	74.5
12	Feb	25	1958**	436.89	Dec	31	1959	679.36	55.5
13	Jun	26	1962*	535.74	Dec	18	1963	767.21	43.2
14	Oct	7	1966*	744.32	Sep	25	1967	943.08	26.7
15	May	26	1970*	631.16	Apr	28	1971	950.82	50.6
16	Dec	6	1974*	577.60	Jul	16	1975	881.81	52.7
17	Feb	28	1978*	742.12	Oct	5	1979	897.61	21.0
18	Aug	12	1982*	776.92	Nov	29	1983	1287.20	65.7
19	Jan	22	1986	1502.29	Aug	25	1987	2722.42	81.2
20	Oct	11	1990*	2365.10	Dec	31	1991	3168.84	34.0
21	Apr	4	1994	3593.35	Dec	13	1995	5216.47	45.2
22	Aug	31	1998*	7539.07	Dec	31	1999	11497.12	52.5
23	Oct	9	2002*	7286.27	Dec	31	2003	10453.92	43.5
24	Jan	20	2006	10667.39	Oct	9	2007	14164.53	32.8
25	Jul	2	2010**	9686.48	Apr	29	2011	12810.54	32.3
26	Feb	3	2014	15372.80	May	19	2015	18312.39	19.1
27	Dec	24	2018	21792.20	Dec	27	2019	28645.26	31.4
28	Sep	30	2022*	28725.51	Dec	28	2023	37710.10	31.3
							Average		**46.3%**

*Bear Market ended ** Bear previous year

The perfect companion to *Stock Trader's Almanac*

FOR TRADERS OF STOCKS, ETFS, COMMODITIES, & FOREX

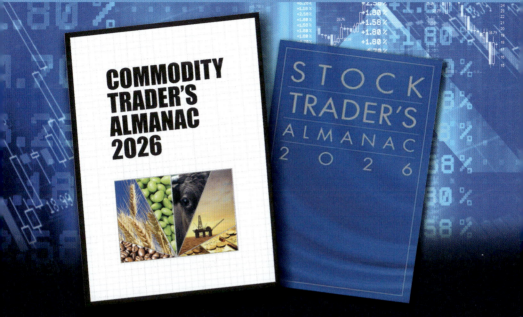

Commodity Trader's Almanac is the ultimate guide to actively trading commodities and commodity-related assets. Whether you're a seasoned investor or just getting started, this vital calendar reference is packed with easy-to-follow strategy guides, seasonality trends, trading how-tos, and invaluable data.

Plus you'll get actionable information on specific stocks, ETFs, and more!

2026 Features Include:

- ◆ Essential commodity trading specs and guide to related securities
- ◆ Key trades and vital data including the S&P 500, 30-year bond futures, with case studies to walk you through how these trades really work
- ◆ Commodity seasonality strategy calendar
- ◆ Tips on using the COT report – commodity trader's "inside scoop"

And so much more!

As a loyal *Stock Trader's Almanac* reader…
Get 20% off your *2026 Commodity Trader's Almanac*!

ORDER YOURS TODAY!

Visit www.stocktradersalmanac.com and use promo code CTA2026

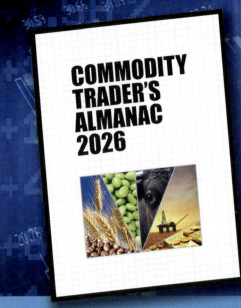

Returning after an 13-year hiatus, *Commodity Trader's Almanac* for 2026 will provide you the information needed to effectively trade commodities and forex using futures, ETFs, or highly correlated stocks. Futures traders will benefit from the years of historical data available along with contract specific trade ideas. Stock and ETF traders will be able to take advantage of seasonal moves in commodities and forex by using highly-correlated individual stocks and exchange-traded funds.

Commodities & Forex Covered in the *Commodity Trader's Almanac* include:

- S&P 500
- Heating Oil
- Corn
- Coffee
- NASDAQ 100
- 30-year Treasury Bond
- Copper
- Soybeans
- Sugar
- Euro
- Crude Oil
- Gold
- Wheat
- Platinum
- Russell 2000
- Natural Gas
- Silver
- Cocoa
- Gasoline
- Japanese Yen

As an existing *Stock Trader's Almanac* user, you can expect a similar calendar-style layout in the *Commodity Trader's Almanac*. Each month will alert you to upcoming trade setups with a full break down of their historical track record and chart of the commodity or currency overlaid with a correlating stock or ETF and seasonal trend. Armed with the data, you will be better informed of potential risks and rewards before placing any trade.

Weekly diary pages are a place to put notes, quickly view when trade ideas begin and end plus key reminders for important dates. Carefully curated daily quotes lend support and spur creative thought.

It is impossible to predict the future. That is why we rely on seasonal and historical analysis to help understand, or better yet, to remind us of what price trends have occurred in the past and how often these trends perform. These patterns typically occur as a direct result of perennial supply and demand changes year after year. Every year has differences, from changes in monetary and fiscal policies to global macroeconomic situations to presidential election year cycles to extreme weather events and other exogenous events. With the *Commodity Trader's Almanac* as a reference guide you can compare current events against history and potentially improve your trades.

Get 20% off your *2026 Commodity Trader's Almanac*!

ORDER YOURS TODAY!

Visit www.stocktradersalmanac.com and use promo code CTA2026

MARCH 2026

MONDAY
D 38.1
S 38.1
N 42.9
9

The difference between the almost right word [or trade] and the right word [trade] is really a large matter
—'tis the difference between the lightning-bug and the lightning.
— Mark Twain (American novelist and satirist, pen name of Samuel Longhorne Clemens, 1835–1910)

TUESDAY
D 66.7
S 61.9
N 57.1
10

In Wall Street, the man who does not change his mind will soon have no change to mind.
— William D. Gann (Trader, technical analyst, author, publisher, 1878–1955)

Dow Down 1469 Points March 9–22 in 2001

WEDNESDAY
D 47.6
S 57.1
N 42.9
11

Whoso neglects learning in his youth, loses the past and is dead for the future.
— Euripides (Greek tragedian, *Medea*, 485–406 BC)

THURSDAY
D 52.4
S 57.1
N 61.9
12

There are two kinds of people who lose money: those who know nothing and those who know everything.
— Henry Kaufman (German-American economist, b. 1927, to Robert Lenzner in Forbes 10/19/98 who added, "With two Nobel Prize winners in the house, Long-Term Capital clearly fits the second case.")

FRIDAY
D 66.7
S 42.9
N 47.6
13

The number one thing that has made us successful, by far, is obsessive, compulsive focus on the customer, as opposed to obsession over the competitor.
— Jeff Bezos (Founder & CEO Amazon, technology entrepreneur, investor, & philanthropist, b. 1964)

SATURDAY
14

SUNDAY
15

THE DECEMBER LOW INDICATOR: A USEFUL PROGNOSTICATING TOOL

When the Dow closes below its December closing low in the first quarter, it is frequently an excellent warning sign. Jeffrey Saut brought this to our attention years ago. The December Low Indicator was originated by Lucien Hooper, a *Forbes* columnist and Wall Street analyst back in the 1970s. Hooper dismissed the importance of January and January's first week as reliable indicators. He noted that the trend could be random or even manipulated during a holiday-shortened week. Instead, said Hooper, "Pay much more attention to the December low. If that low is violated during the first quarter of the New Year, watch out!"

Twenty-two of the 38 occurrences were followed by gains for the rest of the year—and 20 full-year gains—after the low for the year was reached. For perspective we've included the January Barometer readings for the selected years. Hooper's "Watch Out" warning was absolutely correct, though. All but two of the instances since 1952 experienced further declines, as the Dow fell an additional 10.9% on average when December's low was breached in Q1. At press time, Dow was rebounding after closing below its December closing low and suffering a 10.2% additional decline triggered by broad, steep tariff rate increases.

Only three significant drops occurred (not shown) when December's low was not breached in Q1 (1974, 1981, and 1987). If the December low is not crossed, turn to our January Barometer (page 18) and January Indicator Trifecta (page 20) for guidance.

YEARS DOW FELL BELOW DECEMBER LOW IN FIRST QUARTER

Year	Previous Dec Low	Date Crossed	Crossing Price	Subseq. Low	% Change Cross-Low	Rest of Year % Change	Full Year % Change	Jan Bar
1952	262.29	2/19/52	261.37	256.35	–1.9%	11.7%	8.4%	1.6%[2]
1953	281.63	2/11/53	281.57	255.49	–9.3	–0.2	–3.8	–0.7[3]
1956	480.72	1/9/56	479.74	462.35	–3.6	4.1	2.3	–3.6[1,2,3]
1957	480.61	1/18/57	477.46	419.79	–12.1	–8.7	–12.8	–4.2
1960	661.29	1/12/60	660.43	566.05	–14.3	–6.7	–9.3	–7.1
1962	720.10	1/5/62	714.84	535.76	–25.1	–8.8	–10.8	–3.8
1966	939.53	3/1/66	938.19	744.32	–20.7	–16.3	–18.9	0.5[1]
1968	879.16	1/22/68	871.71	825.13	–5.3	8.3	4.3	–4.4[1,2,3]
1969	943.75	1/6/69	936.66	769.93	–17.8	–14.6	–15.2	–0.8
1970	769.93	1/26/70	768.88	631.16	–17.9	9.1	4.8	–7.6[2,3]
1973	1000.00	1/29/73	996.46	788.31	–20.9	–14.6	–16.6	–1.7
1977	946.64	2/7/77	946.31	800.85	–15.4	–12.2	–17.3	–5.1
1978	806.22	1/5/78	804.92	742.12	–7.8	0.01	–3.1	–6.2[3]
1980	819.62	3/10/80	818.94	759.13	–7.3	17.7	14.9	5.8[2]
1982	868.25	1/5/82	865.30	776.92	–10.2	20.9	19.6	–1.8[1,2]
1984	1236.79	1/25/84	1231.89	1086.57	–11.8	–1.6	–3.7	–0.9[3]
1990	2687.93	1/15/90	2669.37	2365.10	–11.4	–1.3	–4.3	–6.9[3]
1991	2565.59	1/7/91	2522.77	2470.30	–2.1	25.6	20.3	4.2[2]
1993	3255.18	1/8/93	3251.67	3241.95	–0.3	15.5	13.7	0.7[2]
1994	3697.08	3/30/94	3626.75	3593.35	–0.9	5.7	2.1	3.3[2,3]
1996	5059.32	1/10/96	5032.94	5032.94	NC	28.1	26.0	3.3[2]
1998	7660.13	1/9/98	7580.42	7539.07	–0.5	21.1	16.1	1.0[2]
2000	10998.39	1/4/00	10997.93	9796.03	–10.9	–1.9	–6.2	–5.1
2001	10318.93	3/12/01	10208.25	8235.81	–19.3	–1.8	–7.1	3.5[1]
2002	9763.96	1/16/02	9712.27	7286.27	–25.0	–14.1	–16.8	–1.6
2003	8303.78	1/24/03	8131.01	7524.06	–7.5	28.6	25.3	–2.7[1,2]
2005	10440.58	1/21/05	10392.99	10012.36	–3.7	3.1	–0.6	–2.5[3]
2006	10717.50	1/20/06	10667.39	10667.39	NC	16.8	16.3	2.5[2]
2007	12194.13	3/2/07	12114.10	12050.41	–0.5	9.5	6.4	1.4[2]
2008	13167.20	1/2/08	13043.96	7552.29	–42.1	–32.7	–33.8	–6.1
2009	8149.09	1/20/09	7949.09	6547.05	–17.6	31.2	18.8	–8.6[1,2]
2010	10285.97	1/22/10	10172.98	9686.48	–4.8	13.8	11.0	–3.7[1,2]
2014	15739.43	1/29/14	15738.79	15372.80	–2.3	13.2	7.5	–3.6[1,2]
2016	17128.55	1/6/16	16906.51	15660.18	–7.4	16.9	13.4	–5.1[1,2]
2018	24140.91	2/8/18	23860.46	21792.20	–8.7	–2.2	–5.6	5.6[1]
2020	27502.81	2/25/20	27081.36	18591.93	–31.3	13.0	7.2	–0.2[1,2]
2022	34022.04	2/22/22	33596.61	28725.51	–14.5	–1.3	–8.8	–5.3
2023	32757.54	2/28/23	32656.70	31819.14	–2.6	15.4	13.7	6.2[2]
2025	42326.87	1/10/2025	41938.45	37645.59	–10.2	*As of May 13, 2025		
				Average Drop	**–10.9%**			

[1] January Barometer wrong. [2] December Low Indicator wrong. [3] Year Flat.

MARCH 2026

Monday Before March Triple Witching, Dow Up 27 of Last 38

MONDAY
D 61.9
S 47.6
N 47.6
16

Enlightenment isn't something you get or find, it's something you rediscover – a state of being that has always been in you but that has been covered with made-up stories and false concepts....our true nature. It's not something we can become, because it's something we already are. We just have to realize it.
— Noah Rasheta (Founder Secular Buddhism, *No-Nonsense Buddhism for Beginners*)

St. Patrick's Day ♣

TUESDAY
D 61.9
S 66.7
N 71.4
17

I learned that courage was not the absence of fear, but the triumph over it. The brave man is not he who does not feel afraid, but he who conquers that fear.
— Nelson Mandela (1st President of South Africa, 1918–2013)

FOMC Meeting

WEDNESDAY
D 61.9
S 61.9
N 71.4
18

English stocks…are springing up like mushrooms this year…forced up to a quite unreasonable level and then, for most part, collapse. In this way, I have made over 400 pounds…[Speculating] makes small demands on one's time, and it's worth while running some risk in order to relieve the enemy of his money.
— Karl Marx (German social philosopher and revolutionary, in an 1864 letter to his uncle, 1818–1883)

Dow Lost 4012 Points (17.3%) on the Week Ending 3/20/2020
Worst Dow Weekly Point Loss and 2nd-Worst Percent Loss Overall

THURSDAY
D 61.9
S 52.4
N 76.2
19

Self-discipline is a form of freedom. Freedom from laziness and lethargy, freedom from expectations and demands of others, freedom from weakness and fear—and doubt.
— Harvey A. Dorfman (Sports psychologist, *The Mental ABC's of Pitching*, b. 1935)

March Triple-Witching Day Mixed Last 30 Years, but NASDAQ Up 8 of Last 11

FRIDAY
D 52.4
S 52.4
N 61.9
20

On Wall Street, to know what everyone else knows is to know nothing.
— Newton Zinder (Investment advisor and analyst, E.F. Hutton, b. 1927)

SATURDAY
21

SUNDAY
22

HOW TO TRADE BEST MONTHS SWITCHING STRATEGIES

Our Best Months Switching Strategies found on pages 54, 56, 62, and 64 are simple and reliable, with a proven 75-year track record. Thus far we have failed to find a similar trading strategy that even comes close over the past six decades. And to top it off, the strategy has only been improving since we first discovered it in 1986.

Exogenous factors and cultural shifts must be considered. "Backward" tests that go back to 1925 or even 1896 and conclude that the pattern does not work are best ignored. They do not take into account these factors. Farming made August the best month from 1900–1951. Since 1988 it is the second worst month of the year for Dow and S&P. Panic caused by financial crisis in 2007–08 caused every asset class aside from U.S. Treasuries to decline substantially. But the bulk of the major decline in equities in the worst months of 2008 was sidestepped using these strategies. Much of the 2022 bear market and 2023's August through October correction were also avoided.

Our Best Months Switching Strategy will not make you an instant millionaire as other strategies claim they can do. What it will do is steadily build wealth over time with possibly less risk of a "buy and hold" approach and the strategy can be applied to any portion of your portfolio.

A sampling of tradable funds for the Best and Worst Months appears in the table below. These are just a starting point and only skim the surface of possible trading vehicles currently available to take advantage of these strategies. Your specific situation and risk tolerance will dictate a suitable choice. If you are trading in a tax-advantaged account such as a company sponsored 401(k) or Individual Retirement Account (IRA), your investment options may be limited to what has been selected by your employer or IRA administrator. But if you are a self-directed trader with a brokerage account, then you likely have unlimited choices (perhaps too many).

TRADABLE BEST AND WORST MONTHS SWITCHING STRATEGY FUNDS

Best Months Exchange Traded Funds (ETF)		Worst Months Exchange Traded Funds (ETF)	
Symbol	Name	Symbol	Name
DIA	SPDR Dow Jones Industrial Average	SGOV	iShares 0-3 Month Treasury Bond
SPY	SPDR S&P 500	SHV	iShares Short Treasury Bond
QQQ	Invesco QQQ	IEF	iShares 7–10 Year Treasury Bond
IWM	iShares Russell 2000	TLT	iShares 20+ Year Treasury Bond
Mutual Funds		Mutual Funds	
Symbol	Name	Symbol	Name
VWNDX	Vanguard Windsor Fund	VFSTX	Vanguard Short-Term Investment-Grade Bond Fund
FMAGX	Fidelity Magellan Fund	FBNDX	Fidelity Investment Grade Bond Fund
AMCPX	American Funds AMCAP Fund	ABNDX	American Funds Bond Fund of America
FCGAX	Franklin Growth Fund	FKFSX	Franklin U.S. Government Securities Fund

Generally speaking, during the Best Months you want to be invested in equities that offer similar exposure to the companies that constitute Dow, S&P 500, and NASDAQ indices. These would typically be large-cap growth and value stocks as well as technology concerns. Reviewing the holdings of a particular ETF or mutual fund and comparing them to the index members is an excellent way to correlate.

During the Worst Months switch into Treasury bonds, money market funds or a bear/short fund. **Leuthold Grizzly Short** (GRZZX) and **AdvisorShares Ranger Equity Bear** (HDGE) are two possible choices. Money market funds will be the safest, but are likely to offer the smallest return, while bear/short funds offer potentially greater returns, but more risk. If the market moves sideways or higher during the Worst Months, a bear/short fund is likely to lose money. Treasuries can offer a combination of reasonable returns with limited risk.

Additional Worst Month possibilities include precious metals and the companies that mine them. **SPDR Gold Shares** (GLD), **VanEck Gold Miners** (GDX) and **Abrdn Physical Gold** (SGOL) are a few well recognized names available from the ETF universe.

BECOME AN ALMANAC INVESTOR

Almanac Investor subscribers receive specific buy and sell trade ideas based upon the Best Months Switching Strategies online and via email. Sector Index Seasonalities, found on page 94, are also put into action throughout the year with corresponding ETF trades. Buy limits, stop losses, and auto-sell price points for the majority of seasonal trades are delivered directly to your inbox. Visit *www.stocktradersalmanac.com* or see the insert for details and a special offer for new subscribers.

MARCH 2026

Week after Triple Witching, Dow Down 23 of Last 38, 2000 Up 4.9%, 2009 Up 6.8%, 2020 Up 12.8% Best Week Since 1931

MONDAY
D 42.9
S 38.1
N 42.9
23

To an imagination of any scope the most far-reaching form of power is not money, it is the command of ideas.
— Oliver Wendell Holmes Jr. (U.S. Supreme Court Justice 1902-1932, *The Mind and Faith of Justice Holmes*, edited by Max Lerner, 1841–1935)

March Historically Weak Later in the Month (Pages 30 and 136)

TUESDAY
D 42.9
S 47.6
N 52.4
24

People do not change when you tell them they should; they change when they tell themselves they must.
— Michael Mandelbaum (Johns Hopkins foreign policy specialist, *NY Times*, 6/24/2009, b. 1946)

WEDNESDAY
D 61.9
S 57.1
N 66.7
25

News on stocks is not important. How the stock reacts to it is important.
— Michael L. Burke (*Investors Intelligence*, 1935–2014)

THURSDAY
D 47.6
S 47.6
N 38.1
26

It's no coincidence that three of the top five stock option traders in a recent trading contest were all former Marines.
— Robert Prechter, Jr. (American financial author & stock market analyst, *The Elliott Wave Theorist*, b. 1949)

Start Looking for Dow and S&P MACD SELL Signal on April 1 (Pages 56 & 64)
Almanac Investor Subscribers Emailed when It Triggers (See Insert)

FRIDAY
D 47.6
S 47.6
N 47.6
27

If you can buy more of your best idea, why put [the money] into your 10th-best idea or your 20th-best idea? The more positions you have, the more average you are.
— Bruce Berkowitz (Fairholme Fund, *Barron's* 3/17/08)

SATURDAY
28

April Almanac Investor Sector Seasonalities: See Pages 94, 96, and 98

SUNDAY
29

APRIL ALMANAC

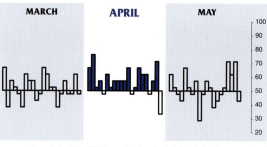

	APRIL							MAY					
S	M	T	W	T	F	S	S	M	T	W	T	F	S
		1	2	3	4						1	2	
5	6	7	8	9	10	11	3	4	5	6	7	8	9
12	13	14	15	16	17	18	10	11	12	13	14	15	16
19	20	21	22	23	24	25	17	18	19	20	21	22	23
26	27	28	29	30			24	25	26	27	28	29	30
							31						

Market Probability Chart above is a graphic representation of the S&P 500 Recent Market Probability Calendar on page 126.

◆ April is the #2 Dow month (average 1.8%) since 1950 (page 52) ◆ April 1999 first month ever to gain 1000 Dow points, 856 in 2001, knocked off its high horse in 2002 down 458, 2003 up 488 ◆ Up 16 straight, 2006 to 2021 ◆ April 2020 Dow +11.1%, best April since 1938 ◆ Exhibits strength after tax deadline recent years ◆ Stocks anticipate great first quarter earnings by rising sharply before earnings are reported, rather than after ◆ Rarely a dangerous month, recent exceptions are 2002, 2004, 2005, 2022, 2024, and 2025 ◆ "Best Six Months" of the year end with April (page 54) ◆ Midterm election year Aprils since 1950, Dow 0.4%, S&P 0.3%, NASDAQ 1.1% ◆ End of April NASDAQ strength fading (pages 127 & 128)

April Vital Statistics

	DJIA	S&P 500	NASDAQ	Russell 1K	Russell 2K
Rank	2	2	4	2	5
Up	51	53	36	32	28
Down	25	23	19	15	19
Average % Change	1.8	1.4	1.3	1.5	1.2
Midterm Yr Avg % Chg	0.4	−0.3	−1.1	−0.9	−0.2
Best & Worst April					
	% Change	% Change	% Change	% Change	% Change
Best	2020 11.1	2020 12.7	2020 15.4	2020 13.1	2009 15.3
Worst	1970 −6.3	1970 −9.0	2000 −15.6	2022 −9.0	2022 −10.0
Best & Worst April Weeks					
Best	4/9/20 12.7	4/9/20 12.1	4/12/01 14.0	4/9/20 12.6	4/9/20 18.5
Worst	4/4/25 −7.9	4/14/00 −10.5	4/14/00 −25.3	4/14/00 −11.2	4/14/00 −16.4
Best & Worst April Days					
Best	4/9/25 7.9	4/9/25 9.5	4/9/25 12.2	4/9/25 9.6	4/9/25 8.7
Worst	4/14/00 −5.7	4/4/25 −6.0	4/14/00 −9.7	4/4/25 −6.0	4/14/00 −7.3
First Trading Day of Monthly Options Expiration Week: 1980–2025					
Record (#Up–#Down)	26–20	24–22	24–22	24–22	20–26
Current streak	U1	U1	U1	U1	U1
Avg % Change	0.13	0.05	0.04	0.05	−0.06
Monthly Options Expiration Day: 1980–2025					
Record (#Up–#Down)	29–17	29–17	25–21	29–17	29–17
Current streak	D1	U1	D2	U1	U3
Avg % Change	0.18	0.14	−0.12	0.14	0.24
Monthly Options Expiration Week: 1980–2025					
Record (#Up–#Down)	35–11	30–16	29–17	28–18	33–13
Current streak	D1	D4	D4	D4	U1
Avg % Change	0.89	0.68	0.69	0.67	0.67
Week After Monthly Options Expiration: 1980–2025					
Record (#Up–#Down)	29–17	30–16	31–15	30–16	31–15
Current streak	U3	U3	U3	U3	U2
Avg % Change	0.37	0.49	0.81	0.49	0.81
First Trading Day Performance					
% of Time Up	57.9	61.8	49.1	59.6	48.9
Avg % Change	0.10	0.09	−0.13	0.07	−0.21
Last Trading Day Performance					
% of Time Up	48.7	52.6	56.4	51.1	55.3
Avg % Change	−0.004	−0.03	−0.04	−0.11	−0.20

Dow & S&P 1950–May 2, 2025; NASDAQ 1971–May 2, 2025; Russell 1K & 2K 1979–May 2, 2025.

April "Second Best Month" for Dow since 1950; Day-before-Good-Friday gains are nifty.

MARCH/APRIL 2026

MONDAY
D 66.7
S 61.9
N 71.4
30

Cannot people realize how large an income is thrift?
— Marcus Tullius Cicero (Great Roman Orator, Politician, 106–43 B.C.)

Last Day of March, Dow Down 21 of Last 36, Russell 2000 Up 26 of Last 36

TUESDAY
D 47.6
S 47.6
N 52.4
31

In the business world, everyone is paid in two coins: cash and experience.
Take the experience first; the cash will come later.
— Harold S. Geneen (British-American businessman, CEO ITT Corp, 1910–1977)

First Trading Day in April, S&P Up 22 of Last 31

WEDNESDAY
D 66.7
S 66.7
N 61.9
1

If you could kick the person in the pants responsible for most of your trouble, you wouldn't sit for a month.
— Theodore Roosevelt (26th U.S. President, 1858–1919)

Passover
NASDAQ Up 21 of Last 25 Days Before Good Friday

THURSDAY
D 71.4
S 76.2
N 71.4
2

Securities pricing is, in every sense a psychological phenomenon that arises from the interaction of human beings with fear. Why not greed and fear as the equation is usually stated? Because greed is simply fear of not having enough.
— John Bollinger, CMT, CFA (American author, technical/financial analyst, developer of Bollinger Bands, Bollinger Capital Management, *Capital Growth Letter, Bollinger on Bollinger Bands*, b. 1950)

Good Friday *(Market Closed)*

FRIDAY
3

Of all manifestations of power, restraint impresses men most.
— Thucydides (Greek historian and general, 460–400 BC)

SATURDAY
4

Easter

SUNDAY
5

DOW JONES INDUSTRIALS & S&P 500 ONE-YEAR SEASONAL PATTERN CHARTS SINCE 1901 & 1950

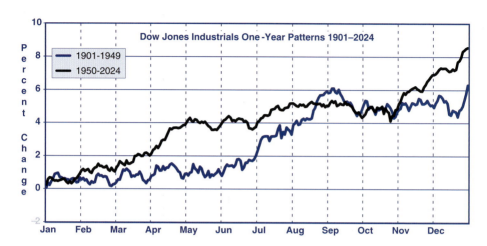

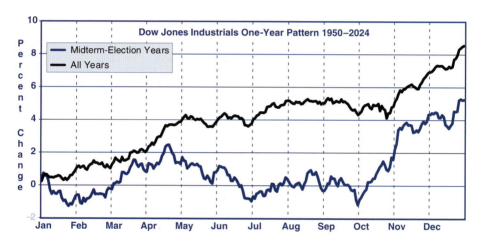

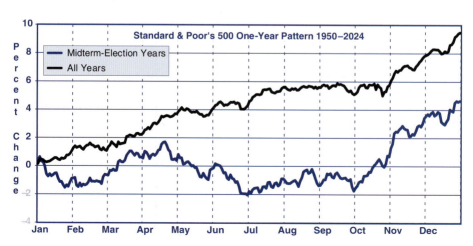

APRIL 2026

Day After Easter, Second Worst Post-Holiday (Page 80)

MONDAY
D 47.6
S 52.4
N 57.1
6

Nothing is more uncertain than the favor of the crowd.
— Marcus Tullius Cicero (Great Roman Orator, Politician, 106–43 B.C.)

April is the Second Best Month for the Dow, Average 1.8% Gain Since 1950

TUESDAY
D 57.1
S 57.1
N 52.4
7

Never tell people how to do things. Tell them what to do and they will surprise you with their ingenuity.
— General George S. Patton, Jr. (U.S. Army field commander WWII, 1885–1945)

April 1999 First Month Ever to Gain 1000 Dow Points

WEDNESDAY
D 47.6
S 47.6
N 33.3
8

We are nowhere near a capitulation point because it's at that point where it's despair, not hope, that reigns supreme, and there was scant evidence of any despair at any of the meetings I gave.
— David Rosenberg (Economist, Merrill Lynch, Barron's 4/21/2008)

THURSDAY
D 66.7
S 61.9
N 66.7
9

There is only one corner of the universe you can be certain of improving, and that's yourself.
— Aldous Huxley (English author, Brave New World, 1894–1963)

April Is 2nd Best Month for S&P, 4th Best for NASDAQ (Since 1971)

FRIDAY
D 47.6
S 52.4
N 47.6
10

I will never knowingly buy any company that has a real time quote of their stock price in the building lobby.
— Robert Mahan (A trader commenting on Enron)

SATURDAY
11

SUNDAY
12

NASDAQ, RUSSELL 1000 & 2000 ONE-YEAR SEASONAL PATTERN CHARTS SINCE 1971 & 1979

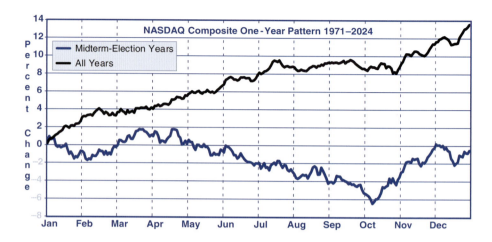

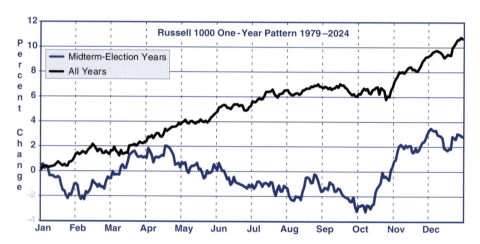

APRIL 2026

Monday Before April Monthly Expiration, Dow Up 22 of Last 37, Down 12 of Last 21

MONDAY
D 47.6
S 57.1
N 61.9
13

Don't delay! A good plan, violently executed now, is better than a perfect plan next week. War is a very simple thing, [like stock trading] and the determining characteristics are self-confidence, speed, and audacity.
— General George S. Patton, Jr. (U.S. Army field commander WWII, 1885–1945)

TUESDAY
D 52.4
S 57.1
N 47.6
14

Learn from the mistakes of others; you can't live long enough to make them all yourself.
— Eleanor Roosevelt (First Lady, 1884–1962)

Income Tax Deadline
April Exhibits Strength After Tax Deadline Recent Years (Pages 40 and 136)

WEDNESDAY
D 61.9
S 57.1
N 42.9
15

Fight until death over taxes? Oh, no. Women, country, God, things like that. Taxes? No.
— Daniel Patrick Moynihan (U.S. Senator New York 1977-2001, "Meet The Press" 5/23/1993, 1927–2003)

THURSDAY
D 52.4
S 57.1
N 42.9
16

Stocks are super-attractive when the Fed is loosening and interest rates are falling. In sum: Don't fight the Fed!
— Martin Zweig (Fund manager, Winning on Wall Street, 1943–2013)

April Monthly Expiration Day Dow Up 19 of Last 29

FRIDAY
D 61.9
S 66.7
N 66.7
17

A person's greatest virtue is his ability to correct his mistakes and continually make a new person of himself.
— Yang-Ming Wang (Chinese philosopher, 1472–1529)

SATURDAY
18

SUNDAY
19

WELCOME TO THE SWEET SPOT OF THE 4-YEAR CYCLE: Q4 MIDTERM YEAR TO Q2 PRE-ELECTION YEAR

"Fourth-Quarter Market Magic" is detailed on page 82 and the "50% Gain in the Dow" from the midterm year low to the pre-election year high is highlighted on page 34. The intersection of the annual seasonal pattern and the 4-Year Cycle produces the quadrennial Sweet Spot. We created the charts here to highlight this critical juncture of 4-Year Cycle.

The second and third quarters of the midterm year have been the weakest period of the entire 4-year pattern averaging losses over the 2-quarter period of -2.0% for the Dow, -2.5% for the S&P 500 and -6.6% for the NASDAQ Composite Index. But thankfully, this sets up the even more important Sweet Spot of the cycle where the Dow gains 19.3%, S&P 500 increases 20.2% and NASDAQ jumps 29.4% over the three-quarter span from midterm year Q4 to pre-election year Q2.

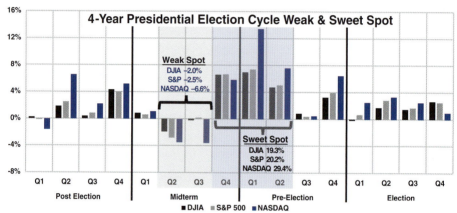

It is for this reason that we call midterm election years a "Bottom Picker's Paradise." From the midterm low to the pre-election year high DJIA gains 46.3% since 1914 and NASDAQ gains a whopping 66.6% since 1974! Should the market begin to falter in Q2 or Q3 of 2026 be on the lookout for a late Q3 or early Q4 low in the August to October period. Then be prepared for the rally off that low into the Sweet Spot and beyond to new highs.

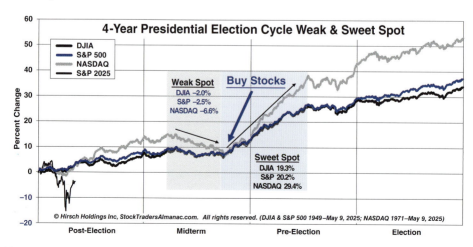

APRIL 2026

MONDAY
D 47.6
S 47.6
N 33.3
20

Wall Street has a uniquely hysterical way of thinking the world will end tomorrow but be fully recovered in the long run, then a few years later believing the immediate future is rosy but that the long term stinks.
— Kenneth L. Fisher (*Wall Street Waltz*)

TUESDAY
D 66.7
S 52.4
N 57.1
21

A weak currency is the sign of a weak economy, and a weak economy leads to a weak nation.
— H. Ross Perot (American businessman, *The Dollar Crisis*, 2-time 3rd-party presidential candidate 1992 & 1996, 1930–2019)

End of "Best Six Months" of the Year (Pages 54, 56, 64, and 149)

WEDNESDAY
D 61.9
S 66.7
N 61.9
22

It's a lot of fun finding a country nobody knows about. The only thing better is finding a country everybody's bullish on and shorting it.
— Jim Rogers (Financier, *Investment Biker*, b. 1942)

THURSDAY
D 66.7
S 61.9
N 52.4
23

The possession of gold has ruined fewer men than the lack of it.
— Thomas Bailey Aldrich (American author, poet and editor, 1903, 1836–1907)

FRIDAY
D 52.4
S 61.9
N 61.9
24

The longer you can look back, the farther you can look forward.
— Winston Churchill (British statesman, 1874–1965)

SATURDAY
25

May Almanac Investor Sector Seasonalities: See Pages 94, 96, and 98

SUNDAY
26

MAY ALMANAC

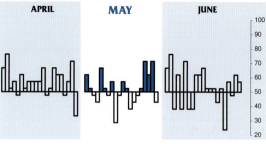

Market Probability Chart above is a graphic representation of the S&P 500 Recent Market Probability Calendar on page 126.

◆ "May/June disaster area" between 1965 and 1984 with S&P down 15 out of 20 Mays ◆ Between 1985 and 1997 May was the best month with 13 straight gains, gaining 3.3% per year on average, up 19, down 9 since ◆ Worst six months of the year begin with May (page 54) ◆ A $10,000 investment compounded to $1,316,635 gain for November-April in 75 years compared to a $4,253 gain for May-October ◆ Dow Memorial Day week record: up 12 years in a row (1984-1995), down 17 of the last 30 years ◆ Since 1950 midterm election year Mays rank, #8 Dow, #9 S&P and #6 NASDAQ

May Vital Statistics

	DJIA		S&P 500		NASDAQ		Russell 1K		Russell 2K	
Rank	9		8		5		6		4	
Up	41		46		33		32		29	
Down	34		29		21		14		17	
Average % Change	–0.02		0.3		1.1		0.9		1.3	
Midterm Yr Avg % Chg	–0.6		–0.7		–0.8		0.1		–1.0	
Best & Worst May										
	% Change		% Change		% Change		% Change		% Change	
Best	1990	8.3	1990	9.2	1997	11.1	1990	8.9	1997	11.0
Worst	2010	–7.9	1962	–8.6	2000	–11.9	2010	–8.1	2019	–7.9
Best & Worst May Weeks										
Best	5/27/22	6.2	5/27/22	6.6	5/17/02	8.8	5/27/22	6.6	5/22/20	7.8
Worst	5/25/62	–6.0	5/25/62	–6.8	5/7/10	–8.0	5/7/10	–6.6	5/7/10	–8.9
Best & Worst May Days										
Best	5/27/70	5.1	5/27/70	5.0	5/30/00	7.9	5/10/10	4.4	5/18/20	6.1
Worst	5/28/62	–5.7	5/28/62	–6.7	5/23/00	–5.9	5/18/22	–4.0	5/20/10	–5.1
First Trading Day of Monthly Expiration Week: 1980–2025										
Record (#Up–#Down)	27–18		28–17		25–20		26–19		23–22	
Current streak	D1		D1		U2		D1		U2	
Avg % Change	0.10		0.10		0.08		0.07		–0.04	
Monthly Options Expiration Day: 1980–2025										
Record (#Up–#Down)	24–21		25–20		20–25		25–20		22–23	
Current streak	U1		U1		D4		U1		D3	
Avg % Change	–0.05		–0.07		–0.10		–0.06		0.03	
Monthly Options Expiration Week: 1980–2025										
Record (#Up–#Down)	21–24		21–24		23–22		20–25		23–22	
Current streak	U2		U2		U2		U2		U2	
Avg % Change	–0.08		–0.06		0.12		–0.06		–0.22	
Week After Monthly Options Expiration: 1980–2025										
Record (#Up–#Down)	25–20		30–15		32–13		29–16		32–13	
Current streak	D2		U5		U5		D1		D2	
Avg % Change	0.19		0.40		0.59		0.42		0.65	
First Trading Day Performance										
% of Time Up	56.6		57.9		60.0		57.4		63.8	
Avg % Change	0.16		0.19		0.28		0.18		0.19	
Last Trading Day Performance										
% of Time Up	56.0		58.7		61.1		52.2		56.5	
Avg % Change	0.13		0.20		0.14		0.13		0.17	

Dow & S&P 1950–May 2, 2025; NASDAQ 1971–May 2, 2025; Russell 1K & 2K 1979–May 2, 2025.

Better to reposition in May
Than to sell in May and go away.

APRIL/MAY 2026

MONDAY 27
D 52.4
S 47.6
N 33.3

Whenever a well-known bearish analyst is interviewed [Cover story] in the financial press, it usually coincides with an important near-term market bottom.
— Clif Droke (Clifdroke.com, 11/15/04)

TUESDAY 28
D 66.7
S 57.1
N 52.4

I've never been poor, only broke. Being poor is a frame of mind. Being broke is only a temporary situation.
— Mike Todd (Movie Producer, 1903–1958)

FOMC Meeting

WEDNESDAY 29
D 71.4
S 71.4
N 81.0

No horse gets anywhere until he is harnessed. No steam or gas ever drives anything until it is confined. No Niagara is ever turned into light and power until it is tunneled. No life ever grows great until it is focused, dedicated, disciplined.
— Harry Emerson Fosdick (Protestant minister, author, 1878–1969)

THURSDAY 30
D 28.6
S 33.3
N 28.6

There is no tool to change human nature…people are prone to recurring bouts of optimism and pessimism that manifest themselves from time to time in the buildup or cessation of speculative excesses.
— Alan Greenspan (Fed Chairman 1987–2006, July 18, 2001 monetary policy report to the Congress)

First Trading Day in May, S&P Up 19 of Last 28

FRIDAY 1
D 57.1
S 61.9
N 61.9

Government is like fire—useful when used legitimately, but dangerous when not.
— David Brooks (*NY Times* columnist, 10/5/07)

SATURDAY 2

SUNDAY 3

SUMMER MARKET VOLUME DOLDRUMS DRIVE WORST SIX MONTHS

In recent years, Memorial Day weekend has become the unofficial start of summer. Not long afterwards, trading activity typically begins to slowly decline (barring any external event triggers) towards a later summer low. We refer to this summertime slowdown in trading as the doldrums due to the anemic volume and uninspired trading on Wall Street. The individual trader, if they are looking to sell a stock, is generally met with disinterest from The Street. It becomes difficult to sell a stock at a good price. That is also why many summer rallies tend to be short lived and are quickly followed by a pullback or correction.

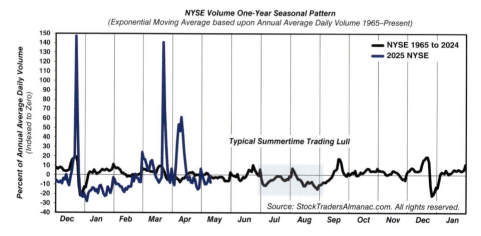

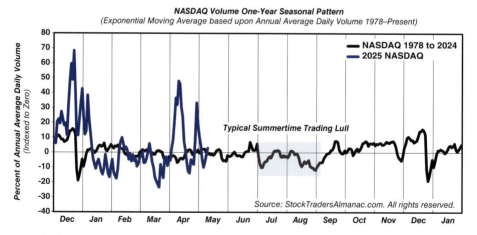

Above are plotted the one-year seasonal volume patterns since 1965 for the NYSE and since 1978 for NASDAQ against the annual average daily volume moving average for 2025 as of the close on May 9, 2025. The typical summer lull is highlighted in blue. A prolonged surge in volume during the typically quiet summer months, especially when accompanied by gains, can be an encouraging sign that the bull market will continue. However, should traders lose their conviction and participate in the annual summer exodus from The Street, a market pullback or correction could quickly unfold.

MAY 2026

MONDAY
D 66.7
S 52.4
N 57.1
4

What is conservatism? Is it not adherence to the old and tried, against the new and untried?
— Abraham Lincoln (16th U.S. President, 1809–1865)

TUESDAY
D 52.4
S 47.6
N 42.9
5

If you're wrong, you can just change your mind. It's not that big of a deal. You don't have to live this depressing life of trend fighting. That's no good.
— J. C. Parets, CMT (Founder All Star Charts, Stock Market Media and TrendLabs, b. 1982)

WEDNESDAY
D 38.1
S 42.9
N 47.6
6

A market is the combined behavior of thousands of people responding to information, misinformation and whim.
— Kenneth Chang (*NY Times* journalist)

THURSDAY
D 66.7
S 66.7
N 57.1
7

Only those who will risk going too far can possibly find out how far one can go.
— T.S. Eliot (English poet, essayist and critic, *The Wasteland*, 1888–1965)

Friday Before Mother's Day, Dow Up 20 of Last 31

FRIDAY
D 66.7
S 52.4
N 66.7
8

Under capitalism, the seller chases after the buyer, and that makes both of them work better; under socialism, the buyer chases the seller, and neither has time to work.
— Andrei Sakharov's Uncle Ivan

SATURDAY
9

Mother's Day

SUNDAY
10

TOP-PERFORMING MONTHS:
STANDARD & POOR'S 500 AND DOW JONES INDUSTRIALS

Monthly performance of the S&P and the Dow are ranked over the past 75 1/3 years. NASDAQ monthly performance is shown on page 60.

April, November, and December still hold the top three positions in both the Dow and S&P. Disastrous Januarys in 2008, 2009, 2016, and 2022 knocked January into fifth. This, in part, led to our discovery in 1986 of the market's most consistent seasonal pattern. You can divide the year into two sections and have practically all the gains in one six-month section and very little in the other. September is the worst month on both lists. (See "Best Six Months" on page 54.)

MONTHLY % CHANGES (JANUARY 1950–APRIL 2025)

	Standard & Poor's 500					Dow Jones Industrials			
Month	Total % Change	Avg. % Change	# Up	# Down	Month	Total % Change	Avg. % Change	# Up	# Down
Jan	82.0%	1.1%	46	30	Jan	73.6%	1.0%	48	28
Feb	–1.8	–0.02	41	35	Feb	4.3	0.1	44	32
Mar	78.6	1.0	49	27	Mar	68.3	0.9	49	27
Apr	109.5	1.4	53	23	Apr	134.9	1.8	51	25
May	21.3	0.3	46	29	May	–1.8	–0.02	41	34
Jun	11.4	0.2	42	33	Jun	–12.3	–0.2	36	39
Jul	96.0	1.3	45	30	Jul	105.0	1.4	50	25
Aug	1.4	0.02	41	34	Aug	–7.3	–0.1	42	33
Sep*	–51.2	–0.7	33	41	Sep	–61.8	–0.8	30	45
Oct	66.6	0.9	44	31	Oct	54.6	0.7	44	31
Nov	140.4	1.9	52	23	Nov	143.8	1.9	52	23
Dec	107.3	1.4	55	20	Dec	109.9	1.5	52	23
% Rank					**% Rank**				
Nov	140.4%	1.9%	52	23	Nov	143.8%	1.9%	52	23
Apr	109.5	1.4	53	23	Apr	134.9	1.8	51	25
Dec	107.3	1.4	55	20	Dec	109.9	1.5	52	23
Jul	96.0	1.3	45	30	Jul	105.0	1.4	50	25
Jan	82.0	1.1	46	30	Jan	73.6	1.0	48	28
Mar	78.6	1.0	49	27	Mar	68.3	0.9	49	27
Oct	66.6	0.9	44	31	Oct	54.6	0.7	44	31
May	21.3	0.3	46	29	Feb	4.3	0.1	44	32
Jun	11.4	0.2	42	33	May	–1.8	–0.02	41	34
Aug	1.4	0.02	41	34	Aug	–7.3	–0.1	42	33
Feb	–1.8	–0.02	41	35	Jun	–12.3	–0.2	36	39
Sep*	–51.2	–0.7	33	41	Sep	–61.8	–0.8	30	45
Totals	661.5%	8.8%			Totals	611.2%	8.2%		
Average		0.73%			Average		0.68%		

*No change 1979

Anticipators, shifts in cultural behavior and faster information flow have altered seasonality in recent years. Here is how the months ranked over the past 15 1/3 years (185 months) using total percentage gains on the S&P 500: November 46.4, July 43.0, October 31.9, April 17.9, February 15.8, Janaury 15.4, March 13.3, December 8.9, June 8.7, May –2.4, August –6.6, and September –14.2.

January has declined in 13 of the last 26 years. Sizeable turnarounds in "bear killing" October were a common occurrence from 1999 to 2007 and 2022. Recent big Dow losses in the period were: September 2001 (9/11 attack), off 11.1%; September 2002 (Iraq war drums), off 12.4%; June 2008, off 10.2%; October 2008, off 14.1%; February 2009, off 11.7% (financial crisis); and March 2020 (Covid-19 shutdown), off 13.7%.

MAY 2026

Monday After Mother's Day, Dow Up 19 of Last 31
Monday Before May Monthly Expiration, Dow Up 26 of Last 38,
But Down 9 of Last 15

MONDAY
D 38.1
S 47.6
N 52.4
11

There is no one who can replace America. Without American leadership, there is no leadership.
That puts a tremendous burden on the American people to do something positive. You can't be tempted
by the usual nationalism.
— Lee Hong-koo (South Korean prime minister 1994–1995 and ambassador to U.S. 1998–2000, *NY Times* 2/25/2009)

TUESDAY
D 57.1
S 57.1
N 42.9
12

He who hesitates is poor.
— Mel Brooks (Writer, director, comedian, b. 1926)

WEDNESDAY
D 28.6
S 28.6
N 52.4
13

Every time everyone's talking about something, that's the time to sell.
— George Lindemann (Billionaire, *Forbes*)

THURSDAY
D 57.1
S 47.6
N 57.1
14

Three ways a smart person can go broke: liquor, ladies and leverage
— Charlie Munger (Vice-Chairman Berkshire Hathaway, 1924–2023)

May Monthly Expiration Day, Dow Up 16 of Last 24

FRIDAY
D 66.7
S 57.1
N 47.6
15

A fundamental analyst goes into each store and studies the products to decide whether to buy or not. A technical
analyst sits on a bench watching people go into stores. Disregarding the intrinsic value, the technical analyst's
decision is based on the patterns or activity of people.
— Investopedia.com on Technical Analysis (Hat tip JC Parets of All Star Charts via Ari Wald of Oppenheimer)

SATURDAY
16

SUNDAY
17

BEST SIX MONTHS: STILL AN EYE-POPPING STRATEGY

Our Best Six Months Switching Strategy consistently delivers. Investing in the Dow Jones Industrial Average between November 1st and April 30th each year and then switching into fixed income for the other six months has produced reliable returns with reduced risk since 1950.

The chart on page 149 shows November, December, January, March, and April to be the top months since 1950. Add February, and an excellent strategy is born! These six consecutive months gained 29918.50 Dow points in 75 years, while the remaining May through October months gained 10536.53 points. The S&P gained 3724.33 points in the same best six months versus 1826.66 points in the worst six.

Percentage changes are shown along with a compounding $10,000 investment. The November-April $1,316,635 gain overshadows May-October's $4,253 gain. (S&P results were $1,147,286 to $16,592.) Just four November-April losses were double-digit: April 1970 (Cambodian invasion), 1973 (OPEC oil embargo), 2008 (financial crisis) and 2019 (Covid-19 shutdown). Similarly, Iraq muted the Best Six and inflated the Worst Six in 2003. When we discovered this strategy in 1986, November-April outperformed May-October by $88,163 to minus $1,522. Results improved substantially these past 39 years, $1,218,472 to $5,775. A simple timing indicator nearly triples results (page 56).

SIX-MONTH SWITCHING STRATEGY

	DJIA % Change May 1–Oct 31	Investing $10,000	DJIA % Change Nov 1–Apr 30	Investing $10,000
1950	5.0%	$10,500	15.2%	$11,520
1951	1.2	10,626	–1.8	11,313
1952	4.5	11,104	2.1	11,551
1953	0.4	11,148	15.8	13,376
1954	10.3	12,296	20.9	16,172
1955	6.9	13,144	13.5	18,355
1956	–7.0	12,224	3.0	18,906
1957	–10.8	10,904	3.4	19,549
1958	19.2	12,998	14.8	22,442
1959	3.7	13,479	–6.9	20,894
1960	–3.5	13,007	16.9	24,425
1961	3.7	13,488	–5.5	23,082
1962	–11.4	11,950	21.7	28,091
1963	5.2	12,571	7.4	30,170
1964	7.7	13,539	5.6	31,860
1965	4.2	14,108	–2.8	30,968
1966	–13.6	12,189	11.1	34,405
1967	–1.9	11,957	3.7	35,678
1968	4.4	12,483	–0.2	35,607
1969	–9.9	11,247	–14.0	30,622
1970	2.7	11,551	24.6	38,155
1971	–10.9	10,292	13.7	43,382
1972	0.1	10,302	–3.6	41,820
1973	3.8	10,693	–12.5	36,593
1974	–20.5	8,501	23.4	45,156
1975	1.8	8,654	19.2	53,826
1976	–3.2	8,377	–3.9	51,727
1977	–11.7	7,397	2.3	52,917
1978	–5.4	6,998	7.9	57,097
1979	–4.6	6,676	0.2	57,211
1980	13.1	7,551	7.9	61,731
1981	–14.6	6,449	–0.5	61,422
1982	16.9	7,539	23.6	75,918
1983	–0.1	7,531	–4.4	72,578
1984	3.1	7,764	4.2	75,626
1985	9.2	8,478	29.8	98,163
1986	5.3	8,927	21.8	119,563
1987	–12.8	7,784	1.9	121,835
1988	5.7	8,228	12.6	137,186
1989	9.4	9,001	0.4	137,735
1990	–8.1	8,272	18.2	162,803
1991	6.3	8,793	9.4	178,106
1992	–4.0	8,441	6.2	189,149
1993	7.4	9,066	0.03	189,206
1994	6.2	9,628	10.6	209,262
1995	10.0	10,591	17.1	245,046
1996	8.3	11,470	16.2	284,743
1997	6.2	12,181	21.8	346,817
1998	–5.2	11,548	25.6	435,602
1999	–0.5	11,490	0.04	435,776
2000	2.2	11,743	–2.2	426,189
2001	–15.5	9,923	9.6	467,103
2002	–15.6	8,375	1.0	471,774
2003	15.6	9,682	4.3	492,060
2004	–1.9	9,498	1.6	499,933
2005	2.4	9,726	8.9	544,427
2006	6.3	10,339	8.1	588,526
2007	6.6	11,021	–8.0	541,444
2008	–27.3	8,012	–12.4	474,305
2009	18.9	9,526	13.3	537,388
2010	1.0	9,621	15.2	619,071
2011	–6.7	8,976	10.5	684,073
2012	–0.9	8,895	13.3	775,055
2013	4.8	9,322	6.7	826,984
2014	4.9	9,779	2.6	848,436
2015	–1.0	9,681	0.6	853,577
2016	2.1	9,884	15.4	985,223
2017	11.6	11,031	3.4	1,018,721
2018	3.9	11,461	5.9	1,078,826
2019	1.7	11,656	–10.0	970,943
2020	8.9	12,693	27.8	1,240,865
2021	5.7	13,417	–7.9	1,142,837
2022	–0.7	13,323	4.2	1,190,836
2023	–3.1	12,910	14.4	1,362,316
2024	10.4	14,253	–2.6	1,326,635
Average/Gain	**0.9%**	**$4,253**	**7.2%**	**$1,316,635**
# Up/Down	**46/29**		**58/17**	

MAY 2026

MONDAY 18
D 47.6
S 52.4
N 57.1

But how do we know when irrational exuberance has unduly escalated asset values, which then become subject to unexpected and prolonged contractions as they have in Japan over the past decade?
— Alan Greenspan (Fed Chairman 1987–2006, 12/5/96 speech to American Enterprise Institute, b. 1926)

TUESDAY 19
D 38.1
S 38.1
N 38.1

Trading is not a science. It's an art. But it helps to know a lot of science.
— Senior Member of Central Bank of Spain (*The Energy World is Flat: Opportunities from the End of Peak Oil* by Daniel Lacalle)

WEDNESDAY 20
D 38.1
S 42.9
N 42.9

It wasn't raining when Noah built the ark.
— Howard Ruff (Financial advisor and author, *The Ruff Times*, 1930–2016)

THURSDAY 21
D 47.6
S 47.6
N 47.6

The usual bull market successfully weathers a number of tests until it is considered invulnerable, whereupon it is ripe for a bust.
— George Soros (Financier, philanthropist, political activist, author and philosopher, b. 1930)

Friday Before Memorial Day Tends to Be Lackluster with Light Trading, Dow Mixed, Up 13 Down 13, Average –0.05%

FRIDAY 22
D 47.6
S 52.4
N 47.6

Intense concentration hour after hour can bring out resources in people they didn't know they had.
— Edwin Land (Polaroid inventor and founder, 1909–1991)

SATURDAY 23

SUNDAY 24

MACD-TIMING TRIPLES BEST-SIX-MONTHS RESULTS

Using the simple MACD (Moving Average Convergence Divergence) indicator developed by our friend Gerald Appel to better time entries and exits into and out of the Best Six Months (page 54) period nearly triples the results. Sy Harding enhanced our Best-Six-Months Switching Strategy with MACD triggers, dubbing it the "best mechanical system ever." In 2006 we improved results with just four trades every four years (page 64).

Our *Almanac Investor* (see insert) implements this system with quite a degree of success. Starting on the first trading day of October we look to catch the market's first hint of an uptrend after the summer doldrums, and beginning on the first trading day of April we prepare to exit these seasonal positions as soon as the market falters.

In up-trending markets MACD signals get you in earlier and keep you in longer. But if the market is trending down, entries are delayed until the market turns up and exit points can come a month earlier.

The results are astounding applying the simple MACD signals. Instead of $10,000 gaining $1,316,635 over the 75 recent years when invested only during the Best Six Months (page 54), the gain nearly tripled to $3,743,209. The $4,253 gain during the worst six months became a loss of $4,931.

Impressive results for being invested during only 6.3 months of the year on average! For the rest of the year consider money markets, bonds, puts, bear funds, covered calls or credit call spreads.

Updated signals are emailed to our *Almanac Investor* subscribers as soon as they are triggered. Visit www.stocktradersalmanac.com or see the insert for details and a special offer for new subscribers.

BEST SIX-MONTH SWITCHING STRATEGY+TIMING

	DJIA % Change May 1–Oct 31*	Investing $10,000	DJIA % Change Nov 1–Apr 30*	Investing $10,000
1950	7.3%	$10,730	13.3%	$11,330
1951	0.1	10,741	1.9	11,545
1952	1.4	10,891	2.1	11,787
1953	0.2	10,913	17.1	13,803
1954	13.5	12,386	16.3	16,053
1955	7.7	13,340	13.1	18,156
1956	−6.8	12,433	2.8	18,664
1957	−12.3	10,904	4.9	19,579
1958	17.3	12,790	16.7	22,849
1959	1.6	12,995	−3.1	22,141
1960	−4.9	12,358	16.9	25,883
1961	2.9	12,716	−1.5	25,495
1962	−15.3	10,770	22.4	31,206
1963	4.3	11,233	9.6	34,202
1964	6.7	11,986	6.2	36,323
1965	2.6	12,298	−2.5	35,415
1966	−16.4	10,281	14.3	40,479
1967	−2.1	10,065	5.5	42,705
1968	3.4	10,407	0.2	42,790
1969	−11.9	9,169	−6.7	39,923
1970	−1.4	9,041	20.8	48,227
1971	−11.0	8,046	15.4	55,654
1972	−0.6	7,998	−1.4	54,875
1973	−11.0	7,118	0.1	54,930
1974	−22.4	5,524	28.2	70,420
1975	0.1	5,530	18.5	83,448
1976	−3.4	5,342	−3.0	80,945
1977	−11.4	4,733	0.5	81,350
1978	−4.5	4,520	9.3	88,916
1979	−5.3	4,280	7.0	95,140
1980	9.3	4,678	4.7	99,612
1981	−14.6	3,995	0.4	100,010
1982	15.5	4,614	23.5	123,512
1983	2.5	4,729	−7.3	114,496
1984	3.3	4,885	3.9	118,961
1985	7.0	5,227	38.1	164,285
1986	−2.8	5,081	28.2	210,613
1987	−14.9	4,324	3.0	216,931
1988	6.1	4,588	11.8	242,529
1989	9.8	5,038	3.3	250,532
1990	−6.7	4,700	15.8	290,116
1991	4.8	4,926	11.3	322,899
1992	−6.2	4,621	6.6	344,210
1993	5.5	4,875	5.6	363,486
1994	3.7	5,055	13.1	411,103
1995	7.2	5,419	16.7	479,757
1996	9.2	5,918	21.9	584,824
1997	3.6	6,131	18.5	693,016
1998	−12.4	5,371	39.9	969,529
1999	−6.4	5,027	5.1	1,018,975
2000	−6.0	4,725	5.4	1,074,000
2001	−17.3	3,908	15.8	1,243,692
2002	−25.2	2,923	6.0	1,318,314
2003	16.4	3,402	7.8	1,421,142
2004	−0.9	3,371	1.8	1,446,723
2005	−0.5	3,354	7.7	1,558,121
2006	4.7	3,512	14.4	1,782,490
2007	5.6	3,709	−12.7	1,556,114
2008	−24.7	2,793	−14.0	1,338,258
2009	23.8	3,458	10.8	1,482,790
2010	4.6	3,617	7.3	1,591,034
2011	−9.4	3,277	18.7	1,888,557
2012	0.3	3,287	10.0	2,077,413
2013	4.1	3,422	7.1	2,224,909
2014	2.3	3,501	7.4	2,389,552
2015	−6.0	3,291	4.9	2,506,640
2016	3.5	3,406	13.1	2,835,010
2017	15.7	3,941	0.4	2,846,350
2018	5.0	4,138	5.2	2,994,360
2019	1.5	4,200	−13.3	2,596,110
2020	22.1	5,128	19.1	3,091,967
2021	2.8	5,272	−0.5	3,076,507
2022	−12.3	4,624	10.6	3,402,617
2023	0.2	4,633	16.6	3,967,451
2024	9.4	5,069	−5.4	3,753,209
Average	−0.4%		8.7%	
# Up	43		63	
# Down	32		12	
75-Year Gain (Loss)		($4,931)		$3,743,209

*MACD generated entry and exit points (earlier or later) can lengthen or shorten six-month periods.

MAY 2026

Memorial Day *(Market Closed)*

MONDAY
25

The soul is dyed the color of its thoughts. Think only on those things that are in line with your principles and can bear the light of day. The content of your character is your choice. Day by day, what you do is who you become.
— Heraclitus (Greek philosopher, 535–475 BC)

Day After Memorial Day, Dow Up 23 of Last 39, But Down 8 of Last 10

D 57.1
S 71.4
N 71.4

TUESDAY
26

…the most successful positions I've taken have been those about which I've been most nervous (and ignored that emotion anyway). Courage is not about being fearless; courage is about acting appropriately even when you are fearful.
— Daniel Turov (*Turov on Timing*, b. 1947)

Memorial Day Week Dow Down 17 of Last 29, Up 12 Straight 1984-1995

D 52.4
S 61.9
N 66.7

WEDNESDAY
27

If you create an act, you create a habit. If you create a habit, you create a character. If you create a character, you create a destiny.
— André Maurois (Novelist, biographer, essayist, 1885–1967)

D 66.7
S 71.4
N 66.7

THURSDAY
28

A small debt produces a debtor; a large one, an enemy.
— Publilius Syrus (Syrian-born Roman mime and former slave, 83–43 B.C.)

Start Looking for NASDAQ MACD Sell Signal on June 1 (Page 62)
Almanac Investor Subscribers Emailed when It Triggers (See Insert)

D 28.6
S 42.9
N 42.9

FRIDAY
29

If you want to raise a crop for one year, plant corn. If you want to raise a crop for decades, plant trees. If you want to raise a crop for centuries, raise men. If you want to plant a crop for eternities, raise democracies.
— Carl A. Schenck (German forester, 1868–1955)

SATURDAY
30

June Almanac Investor Sector Seasonalities: See Pages 94, 96, and 98

SUNDAY
31

JUNE ALMANAC

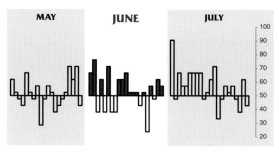

Market Probability Chart above is a graphic representation of the S&P 500 Recent Market Probability Calendar on page 126.

◆ The "summer rally" in most years is the weakest rally of all four seasons (page 76) ◆ Week after June Triple-Witching Day Dow down 28 of last 34 (page 108) ◆ RECENT RECORD: S&P up 13, down 8, average gain 0.005%, ranks eleventh ◆ Summer doldrums can begin in late June (page 50) ◆ Watch out for end-of-quarter "portfolio pumping" on last day of June, Dow down 19 of last 34, NASDAQ up 10 of last 14 ◆ Midterm election year Junes: #12 S&P, #12 Dow, #12 NASDAQ ◆ June ends NASDAQ's Best Eight Months (page 62)

June Vital Statistics

	DJIA	S&P 500	NASDAQ	Russell 1K	Russell 2K
Rank	11	9	6	9	7
Up	36	42	31	29	29
Down	39	33	23	17	17
Average % Change	–0.2	0.2	1.0	0.4	0.8
Midterm Yr Avg % Chg	–1.9	–2.1	–1.9	–1.8	–2.1
Best & Worst June					
	% Change	% Change	% Change	% Change	% Change
Best	2019 7.2	1955 8.2	2000 16.6	2019 6.9	2000 8.6
Worst	2008 –10.2	2008 –8.6	2002 –9.4	2022 –8.5	2022 –8.4
Best & Worst June Weeks					
Best	6/5/20 6.8	6/2/00 7.2	6/2/00 19.0	6/2/00 8.0	6/2/00 12.2
Worst	6/30/50 –6.8	6/30/50 –7.6	6/15/01 –8.4	6/17/22 –5.9	6/12/20 –7.9
Best & Worst June Days					
Best	6/28/62 3.8	6/28/62 3.4	6/2/00 6.4	6/24/22 3.1	6/2/00 4.2
Worst	6/11/20 –6.9	6/11/20 –5.9	6/11/20 –5.3	6/11/20 –5.9	6/11/20 –7.6
First Trading Day of Monthly Options Expiration Week: 1980–2025					
Record (#Up–#Down)	24–18	27–18	22–23	25–20	19–25
Current streak	U2	U2	U2	U2	U2
Avg % Change	–0.06	–0.12	–0.21	–0.13	–0.31
Monthly Options Expiration Day: 1980–2025					
Record (#Up–#Down)	24–21	25–20	22–23	25–20	23–22
Current streak	U1	D2	D3	D2	U1
Avg % Change	–0.11	–0.03	–0.05	–0.05	–0.07
Monthly Options Expiration Week: 1980–2025					
Record (#Up–#Down)	26–19	25–20	21–24	23–22	22–23
Current streak	U2	U2	U2	U2	U2
Avg % Change	–0.12	–0.10	–0.14	–0.14	–0.36
Week After Monthly Options Expiration: 1980–2025					
Record (#Up–#Down)	14–31	20–25	25–20	20–25	24–21
Current streak	D2	D2	U1	D2	U1
Avg % Change	–0.36	–0.07	0.25	–0.04	0.08
First Trading Day Performance					
% of Time Up	57.3	54.7	59.3	60.9	65.2
Avg % Change	0.14	0.12	0.14	0.10	0.21
Last Trading Day Performance					
% of Time Up	56.0	53.3	66.7	56.5	67.4
Avg % Change	0.08	0.13	0.32	0.09	0.41

Dow & S&P 1950–May 2, 2025; NASDAQ 1971–May 2, 2025; Russell 1K & 2K 1979–May 2, 2025

Week after June Triple Witch very poor; Dow Down 28 of 34!

JUNE 2026

First Trading Day in June, Dow Up 28 of Last 37, Down 4 of 5 2008–2012

MONDAY
D 71.4
S 66.7
N 61.9

1

There's nothing wrong with cash. It gives you time to think.
— Robert Prechter, Jr. (American financial author & stock market analyst, *The Elliott Wave Theorist*, b. 1949)

June Ends NASDAQ's "Best Eight Months" (Pages 60, 62, and 150)

TUESDAY
D 66.7
S 76.2
N 71.4

2

The game [or market] can be reduced to a social science; that it is simply a matter of figuring out the odds, and exploiting the laws of probability; that baseball players [or investors] follow strikingly predictable patterns.
— Michael Lewis (American author & journalist, what Oakland A's GM Billy Beane claims to believe, *Moneyball: The Art of Winning an Unfair Game*, b. 1960)

WEDNESDAY
D 33.3
S 38.1
N 42.9

3

History must repeat itself because we pay such little attention to it the first time.
— Blackie Sherrod (Sportswriter, 1919–2016)

THURSDAY
D 71.4
S 61.9
N 61.9

4

Buy a stock the way you would buy a house. Understand and like it such that you'd be content to own it in the absence of any market.
— Warren Buffett (CEO Berkshire Hathaway, investor and philanthropist, b. 1930)

FRIDAY
D 61.9
S 38.1
N 42.9

5

The reason the market did so well in the last several years is because the Federal Reserve drove interest rates down to extraordinary low levels—like 1%.
— George Roche (Chairman, T. Rowe Price, *Barron's* 12/18/06)

SATURDAY

6

SUNDAY

7

TOP-PERFORMING NASDAQ MONTHS

NASDAQ stocks continue to run away during three consecutive months, November, December and January, with an average gain of 6.2% despite the slaughter of November 2000, down 22.9%; December 2000, –4.9%; December 2002, –9.7%; November 2007, –6.9%; January 2008, –9.9%; November 2008, –10.8%; January 2009, –6.4%; January 2010, –5.4%; January 2016, –7.9%; December 2018, –9.5%; January 2022, –9.0%; and December 2022 –8.7%. Solid gains in November and December 2004 offset January 2005's 5.2% Iraq-turmoil-fueled drop.

You can see the months graphically on page 150. January by itself is impressive, up 2.6% on average. April, May, and June also shine, creating our NASDAQ Best Eight Months strategy. What appears as a Death Valley abyss occurs during NASDAQ's leanest months, August and September. NASDAQ's Best Eight Months seasonal strategy using MACD timing is displayed on page 62.

MONTHLY % CHANGES (JANUARY 1971–APRIL 2025)

	NASDAQ Composite*					Dow Jones Industrials			
Month	Total % Change	Avg. % Change	# Up	# Down	Month	Total % Change	Avg. % Change	# Up	# Down
Jan	144.7%	2.6%	37	18	Jan	63.9%	1.2%	34	21
Feb	28.0	0.5	29	26	Feb	9.9	0.2	32	23
Mar	36.4	0.7	35	20	Mar	47.1	0.9	36	19
Apr	73.0	1.3	36	19	Apr	103.9	1.9	36	19
May	59.2	1.1	33	21	May	11.6	0.2	31	23
Jun	53.9	1.0	31	23	Jun	4.9	0.09	28	26
Jul	47.3	0.9	31	23	Jul	61.5	1.1	34	20
Aug	17.2	0.3	30	24	Aug	–10.0	–0.2	30	24
Sep	–47.7	–0.9	28	26	Sep	–57.9	–1.1	20	34
Oct	38.1	0.7	29	25	Oct	43.2	0.8	32	22
Nov	114.9	2.1	39	15	Nov	99.8	1.8	38	16
Dec	82.9	1.5	33	21	Dec	73.6	1.4	37	17
% Rank					% Rank				
Jan	144.7%	2.6%	37	18	Apr	103.9%	1.9%	36	19
Nov	114.9	2.1	39	15	Nov	99.8	1.8	38	16
Dec	82.9	1.5	33	21	Dec	73.6	1.4	37	17
Apr	73.0	1.3	36	19	Jan	63.9	1.2	34	21
May	59.2	1.1	33	21	Jul	61.5	1.1	34	20
Jun	53.9	1.0	31	23	Mar	47.1	0.9	36	19
Jul	47.3	0.9	31	23	Oct	43.2	0.8	32	22
Oct	38.1	0.7	29	25	May	11.6	0.2	31	23
Mar	36.4	0.7	35	20	Feb	9.9	0.2	32	23
Feb	28.0	0.5	29	26	Jun	4.9	0.09	28	26
Aug	17.2	0.3	30	24	Aug	–10.0	–0.2	30	24
Sep	–47.7	–0.9	28	26	Sep	–57.9	–1.1	20	34
Totals	647.9%	11.8%			Totals	451.5%	8.3%		
Average		0.98%			Average		0.69%		

*Based on NASDAQ composite, prior to Feb. 5, 1971, based on National Quotation Bureau indices.

For comparison, Dow figures are shown. During this period NASDAQ averaged a 0.98% gain per month, 42.0% more than the Dow's 0.69% per month. Between January 1971 and January 1982 NASDAQ's composite index doubled in 12 years, while the Dow stayed flat. But while NASDAQ plummeted 77.9% from its 2000 highs to the 2002 bottom, the Dow only lost 37.8%. The Great Recession and bear market of 2007-2009 spread its carnage equally across Dow and NASDAQ. Recent market moves are increasingly more correlated, but NASDAQ still retains a sizable advantage.

JUNE 2026

2008 Second Worst June Ever, Dow –10.2%, S&P –8.6%,
Only 1930 Was Worse, NASDAQ June 2008 –9.1%, June 2002 –9.4%

MONDAY
D 71.4
S 71.4
N 61.9

8

If you can ever buy with a P/E equivalent to growth, that's a good starting point.
— Alan Lowenstein (co-portfolio manager, John Hancock Technology Fund, *TheStreet.com* 3/12/2001)

TUESDAY
D 38.1
S 38.1
N 38.1

9

The most important lesson in investing is humility.
— Sir John Templeton (Founder Templeton Funds, philanthropist, 1912–2008)

WEDNESDAY
D 33.3
S 38.1
N 42.9

10

Let me end my talk by abusing slightly my status as an official representative of the Federal Reserve.
I would like to say to Milton [Friedman]: regarding the Great Depression, you're right; we did it.
We're very sorry. But thanks to you, we won't do it again.
— Ben Bernanke (Fed Chairman 2006-2014, 11/8/02 speech as Fed Govenor, b. 1953)

THURSDAY
D 57.1
S 61.9
N 57.1

11

Develop interest in life as you see it; in people, things, literature, music—the world is so rich, simply throbbing
with rich treasures, beautiful souls and interesting people. Forget yourself.
— Henry Miller (American writer, *Tropic of Cancer, Tropic of Capricorn*, 1891–1980)

FRIDAY
D 52.4
S 61.9
N 71.4

12

Civility is not a sign of weakness, and sincerity is always subject to proof. Let us never negotiate out of fear.
But let us never fear to negotiate.
— John F. Kennedy (35th U.S. President, Inaugural Address 1/20/1961, 1917–1963)

SATURDAY

13

SUNDAY

14

GET MORE OUT OF NASDAQ'S BEST EIGHT MONTHS WITH MACD TIMING

NASDAQ's amazing eight-month run from November through June is hard to miss on pages 60 and 150. A $10,000 investment in these eight months since 1971 gained $1,569,428 versus $996 during the void that is the four-month period July-October (as of May 12, 2025).

Using the same MACD timing indicators on the NASDAQ as is done for the Dow (page 56) has enabled us to capture much of October's improved performance, pumping up NASDAQ's results considerably. Over the 54 years since NASDAQ began, the gain on the same $10,000 nearly triples to $3,487,640 and the gain during the four-month void becomes a loss of $5,128. Only five double-digit losses occurred during the favorable period and the bulk of many NASDAQ's bear markets were avoided.

Updated signals are emailed to *Almanac Investor* subscribers as soon as they are triggered. Visit *www.stocktradersalmanac.com*, or see insert for details and a special offer for new subscribers.

BEST EIGHT MONTHS STRATEGY + TIMING

MACD Signal Date	Worst 4 Months July 1–Oct 31* NASDAQ	% Change	Investing $10,000	MACD Signal Date	Best 8 Months Nov 1–June 30* NASDAQ	% Change	Investing $10,000
22-Jul-71	109.54	–3.6	$9,640	4-Nov-71	105.56	24.1	$12,410
7-Jun-72	131.00	–1.8	9,466	23-Oct-72	128.66	–22.7	9,593
25-Jun-73	99.43	–7.2	8,784	7-Dec-73	92.32	–20.2	7,655
3-Jul-74	73.66	–23.2	6,746	7-Oct-74	56.57	47.8	11,314
11-Jun-75	83.60	–9.2	6,125	7-Oct-75	75.88	20.8	13,667
22-Jul-76	91.66	–2.4	5,978	19-Oct-76	89.45	13.2	15,471
27-Jul-77	101.25	–4.0	5,739	4-Nov-77	97.21	26.6	19,586
7-Jun-78	123.10	–6.5	5,366	6-Nov-78	115.08	19.1	23,327
3-Jul-79	137.03	–1.1	5,307	30-Oct-79	135.48	15.5	26,943
20-Jun-80	156.51	26.2	6,697	9-Oct-80	197.53	11.2	29,961
4-Jun-81	219.68	–17.6	5,518	1-Oct-81	181.09	–4.0	28,763
7-Jun-82	173.84	12.5	6,208	7-Oct-82	195.59	57.4	45,273
1-Jun-83	307.95	–10.7	5,544	3-Nov-83	274.86	–14.2	38,844
1-Jun-84	235.90	5.0	5,821	15-Oct-84	247.67	17.3	45,564
3-Jun-85	290.59	–3.0	5,646	1-Oct-85	281.77	39.4	63,516
10-Jun-86	392.83	–10.3	5,064	1-Oct-86	352.34	20.5	76,537
30-Jun-87	424.67	–22.7	3,914	2-Nov-87	328.33	20.1	91,921
8-Jul-88	394.33	–6.6	3,656	29-Nov-88	368.15	22.4	112,511
13-Jun-89	450.73	0.7	3,682	9-Nov-89	454.07	1.9	114,649
11-Jun-90	462.79	–23.0	2,835	2-Oct-90	356.39	39.3	159,706
11-Jun-91	496.62	6.4	3,016	1-Oct-91	528.51	7.4	171,524
11-Jun-92	567.68	1.5	3,061	14-Oct-92	576.22	20.5	206,686
7-Jun-93	694.61	9.9	3,364	1-Oct-93	763.23	–4.4	197,592
17-Jun-94	729.35	5.0	3,532	11-Oct-94	765.57	13.5	224,267
1-Jun-95	868.82	17.2	4,140	13-Oct-95	1018.38	21.6	272,709
3-Jun-96	1238.73	1.0	4,181	7-Oct-96	1250.87	10.3	300,798
4-Jun-97	1379.67	24.4	5,201	3-Oct-97	1715.87	1.8	306,212
1-Jun-98	1746.82	–7.8	4,795	15-Oct-98	1611.01	49.7	458,399
1-Jun-99	2412.03	18.5	5,682	6-Oct-99	2857.21	35.7	622,047
29-Jun-00	3877.23	–18.2	4,648	18-Oct-00	3171.56	–32.2	421,748
1-Jun-01	2149.44	–31.1	3,202	1-Oct-01	1480.46	5.5	444,944
3-Jun-02	1562.56	–24.0	2,434	2-Oct-02	1187.30	38.5	616,247
20-Jun-03	1644.72	15.1	2,802	6-Oct-03	1893.46	4.3	642,746
21-Jun-04	1974.38	–1.6	2,757	1-Oct-04	1942.20	6.1	681,954
8-Jun-05	2060.18	1.5	2,798	19-Oct-05	2091.76	2.9	701,731
7-Jun-06	2151.80	7.2	2,999	5-Oct-06	2306.34	10.2	773,308
7-Jun-07	2541.38	7.9	3,236	1-Oct-07	2740.99	–9.1	702,937
2-Jun-08	2491.53	–31.3	2,223	17-Oct-08	1711.29	6.1	745,816
15-Jun-09	1816.38	17.8	2,619	9-Oct-09	2139.28	1.6	757,749
7-Jun-10	2173.90	18.6	3,106	4-Nov-10	2577.34	7.4	813,822
1-Jun-11	2769.19	–10.5	2,780	7-Oct-11	2479.35	10.8	901,715
1-Jun-12	2747.48	9.6	3,047	6-Nov-12	3011.93	14.4	1,031,562
4-Jun-13	3445.26	10.1	3,355	15-Oct-13	3794.01	15.4	1,190,423
26-Jun-14	4379.05	0.9	3,385	21-Oct-14	4419.48	14.5	1,363,034
4-Jun-15	5059.12	–5.5	3,199	5-Oct-15	4781.26	1.4	1,382,116
13-Jun-16	4848.44	9.5	3,503	24-Oct-16	5309.83	16.9	1,615,694
9-Jun-17	6207.92	11.3	3,899	28-Nov-17	6912.36	11.6	1,803,115
21-Jun-18	7712.95	–5.3	3,692	31-Oct-18	7305.90	11.5	2,010,473
19-Jul-19	8146.49	–1.1	3,651	11-Oct-19	8057.04	17.8	2,368,337
11-Jun-20	9492.73	25.3	4,575	5-Nov-20	11890.93	23.2	2,917,791
14-Jul-21	14644.95	–0.4	4,557	8-Oct-21	14579.54	–25.9	2,162,083
13-Jun-22	10809.23	3.4	4,712	4-Oct-22	11176.41	20.7	2,609,634
23-Jun-23	13492.52	–0.1	4,707	9-Oct-23	13484.24	31.4	3,429,059
25-Jun-24	17717.65	3.5	4,872	11-Oct-24	18342.94	2.0**	3,497,640**
25-May-12**	18708.34						
	Average	–0.4%				12.9%	
	54-Year Loss	($5,128)				54-Year Gain	$3,487,640

** As of 5/12/2025 – NASDAQ Seasonal Sell NOT triggered yet
* MACD-generated entry and exit points (earlier or later) can lengthen or shorten eight-month periods.

JUNE 2026

Monday of Triple-Witching Week, Dow Down 15 of Last 28

MONDAY
D 57.1
S 66.7
N 66.7
15

Today we deal with 65,000 more pieces of information each day than did our ancestors 100 years ago.
— Dr. Jean Houston (A founder of the Human Potential Movement, b. 1937)

Triple-Witching Week Often Up in Bull Markets and Down in Bears (Page 108)

TUESDAY
D 52.4
S 52.4
N 52.4
16

The generally accepted view is that markets are always right—that is, market prices tend to discount future developments accurately even when it is unclear what those developments are. I start with the opposite point of view. I believe that market prices are always wrong in the sense that they present a biased view of the future.
— George Soros (1987, Financier, philanthropist, political activist, author and philosopher, b. 1930)

FOMC Meeting

WEDNESDAY
D 52.4
S 52.4
N 61.9
17

An inventor fails 999 times, and if he succeeds once, he's in. He treats his failures simply as practice shots.
— Charles Kettering (Inventor of electric ignition, founded Delco in 1909, 1876–1958)

June Triple-Witching Day Mixed, But Down 8 of Last 10

THURSDAY
D 52.4
S 52.4
N 47.6
18

What people in the Middle East tell you in private is irrelevant. All that matters is what they will defend in public in their language.
— Thomas L. Friedman (*NY Times* Foreign Affairs columnist, "Meet the Press" 12/17/06)

Juneteenth National Independence Day *(Market Closed)*

FRIDAY
19

Behold, my son, with what little wisdom the world is ruled.
— Count Axel Gustafsson Oxenstierna (1648 letter to his son at conclusion of Thirty Years War, 1583–1654)

SATURDAY
20

Father's Day

SUNDAY
21

TRIPLE RETURNS, FEWER TRADES: BEST 6 + 4-YEAR CYCLE

We first introduced this strategy to *Almanac Investor* subscribers in October 2006. Recurring seasonal stock market patterns and the Four-Year Presidential Election/Stock Market Cycle (page 132) have been integral to our research since the first *Almanac* over 50 years ago. Yale Hirsch discovered the Best Six Months in 1986 (page 54) and it has been a cornerstone of our seasonal investment analysis and strategies ever since.

Most of the market's gains have occurred during the Best Six Months and the market generally hits a low point every four years in the first (post-election) or second (midterm) year and exhibits the greatest gains in the third (pre-election) year. This strategy combines the best of these two market phenomena, the Best Six Months and the 4-Year Cycle, timing entries and exits with MACD (pages 56 and 62).

We've gone back to 1949 to include the full four-year cycle that began with post-election year 1949. Only four trades every four years are needed to more than triple the results of the Best Six Months. Buy and sell during the post-election and midterm years and then hold from the midterm MACD seasonal buy signal sometime on/after October 1 until the post-election MACD seasonal sell signal sometime on/after April 1, approximately 2.5 years. Solid returns, less effort, lower transaction fees and fewer taxable events.

BEST SIX MONTHS+TIMING+4-YEAR CYCLE STRATEGY

	DJIA		DJIA	
	% Change	Investing	% Change	Investing
	May 1–Oct 31*	$10,000	Nov 1–Apr 30*	$10,000
1949	3.0%	$10,300	17.5%	$11,750
1950	7.3	11,052	19.7	14,065
1951		11,052		14,065
1952		11,052		14,065
1953	0.2	11,074	17.1	16,470
1954	13.5	12,569	35.7	22,350
1955		12,569		22,350
1956		12,569		22,350
1957	–12.3	11,023	4.9	23,445
1958	17.3	12,930	27.8	29,963
1959		12,930		29,963
1960		12,930		29,963
1961	2.9	13,305	–1.5	29,514
1962	–15.3	11,269	58.5	46,780
1963		11,269		46,780
1964		11,269		46,780
1965	2.6	11,562	–2.5	45,611
1966	–16.4	9,666	22.2	55,737
1967		9,666		55,737
1968		9,666		55,737
1969	–11.9	8,516	–6.7	52,003
1970	–1.4	8,397	21.5	63,184
1971		8,397		63,184
1972		8,397		63,184
1973	–11.0	7,473	0.1	63,247
1974	–22.4	5,799	42.5	90,127
1975		5,799		90,127
1976		5,799		90,127
1977	–11.4	5,138	0.5	90,578
1978	–4.5	4,907	26.8	114,853
1979		4,907		114,853
1980		4,907		114,853
1981	–14.6	4,191	0.4	115,312
1982	15.5	4,841	25.9	145,178
1983		4,841		145,178
1984		4,841		145,178
1985	7.0	5,180	38.1	200,491
1986	–2.8	5,035	33.2	267,054
1987		5,035		267,054
1988		5,035		267,054
1989	9.8	5,528	3.3	275,867
1990	–6.7	5,158	35.1	372,696
1991		5,158		372,696
1992		5,158		372,696
1993	5.5	5,442	5.6	393,455
1994	3.7	5,643	88.2	740,482
1995		5,643		740,482
1996		5,643		740,482
1997	3.6	5,846	18.5	877,471
1998	–12.4	5,121	36.3	1,195,993
1999		5,121		1,195,993
2000		5,121		1,195,993
2001	–17.3	4,235	15.8	1,384,960
2002	–25.2	3,168	34.2	1,858,616
2003		3,168		1,858,616
2004		3,168		1,858,616
2005	–0.5	3,152	7.7	2,001,729
2006	4.7	3,300	–31.7	1,367,181
2007		3,300		1,367,181
2008		3,300		1,367,181
2009	23.8	4,085	10.8	1,514,738
2010	4.6	4,273	27.4	1,929,777
2011		4,273		1,929,777
2012		4,273		1,929,777
2013	4.1	4,448	7.1	2,066,791
2014	2.3	4,550	24.0	2,562,820
2015		4,550		2,562,820
2016		4,550		2,562,820
2017	15.7	5,265	0.4	2,573,072
2018	5.0	5,528	34.6	3,463,354
2019		5,528		3,463,354
2020		5,528		3,463,354
2021	2.8	5,683	–0.5	3,446,038
2022	–12.3	4,984	33.7	4,607,352
2023		4,984		4,607,352
2024		4,984		4,607,352
2025	4.6**	5,213**		
Average	–0.6%		9.6%	
# Up	21		33	
# Down	17		5	
76-Year Gain (Loss)		($4,787)		$4,597,352

* MACD and 2.5-year hold lengthen and shorten six-month periods.
** As of May 12, 2025 Close – Switching – Not in totals.

FOUR TRADES EVERY FOUR YEARS

Year	Worst Six Months May–Oct	Best Six Months Nov–April
Post-election	Sell	Buy
Midterm	Sell	Buy
Pre-election	Hold	Hold
Election	Hold	Hold

JUNE 2026

Week After June Triple-Witching, Dow Down 29 of Last 35
Average Loss Since 1990, 0.8%

MONDAY
D 38.1
S 42.9
N 47.6
22

The worse a situation becomes, the less it takes to turn it around, the bigger the upside.
— George Soros (Financier, philanthropist, political activist, author and philosopher, b. 1930)

TUESDAY
D 47.6
S 52.4
N 47.6
23

The difference between life and the movies is that a script has to make sense, and life doesn't.
— Joseph L. Mankiewicz (Film director, writer, producer, 1909–1993)

WEDNESDAY
D 28.6
S 23.8
N 19.0
24

It was never my thinking that made the big money for me. It was always my sitting. Got that? My sitting tight!
— Jesse Livermore (Early 20th century stock trader & speculator, How to Trade in Stocks, 1877–1940)

THURSDAY
D 47.6
S 57.1
N 57.1
25

The market can stay irrational longer than you can stay solvent.
— John Maynard Keynes (British economist, 1883–1946)

FRIDAY
D 47.6
S 47.6
N 61.9
26

Throughout the centuries there were men who took first steps down new roads armed with nothing but their own vision.
— Ayn Rand (Russian-born American novelist and philosopher, The Fountainhead, 1943, 1905–1982)

SATURDAY
27

July Almanac Investor Sector Seasonalities: See Pages 94, 96, and 98

SUNDAY
28

JULY ALMANAC

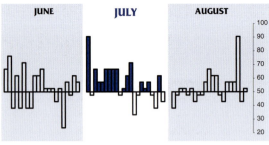

Market Probability Chart above is a graphic representation of the S&P 500 Recent Market Probability Calendar on page 126.

◆ July is the best month of the third quarter (page 68) ◆ Start of 2nd half brings an inflow of retirement funds ◆ First trading day S&P up 32 of last 36 ◆ Graph above shows strength in the first half of July ◆ Huge gain in July usually provides better buying opportunity over next four months ◆ Start of NASDAQ's worst four months of the year (page 60 & 150) ◆ Midterm election Julys are ranked #3 Dow (up 12, down 7), #3 S&P (up 11, down 8), and #7 NASDAQ (up 5, down 8)

July Vital Statistics

	DJIA		S&P 500		NASDAQ		Russell 1K		Russell 2K	
Rank	4		4		7		4		9	
Up	50		45		31		26		25	
Down	25		30		23		20		21	
Average % Change	1.4		1.3		0.9		1.2		0.4	
Midterm Yr Avg % Chg	1.6		1.3		−0.8		0.2		−2.5	
	Best & Worst July									
	% Change		% Change		% Change		% Change		% Change	
Best	1989	9.0	2022	9.1	2022	12.3	2022	9.2	1980	11.0
Worst	1969	−6.6	2002	−7.9	2002	−9.2	2002	−7.5	2002	−15.2
	Best & Worst July Weeks									
Best	7/17/09	7.3	7/17/09	7.0	7/17/09	7.4	7/17/09	7.0	7/17/09	8.0
Worst	7/19/02	−7.7	7/19/02	−8.0	7/28/02	−10.5	7/19/02	−7.4	7/2/10	−7.2
	Best & Worst July Days									
Best	7/24/02	6.4	7/24/02	5.7	7/29/02	5.8	7/24/02	5.6	7/29/02	4.9
Worst	7/19/02	−4.6	7/19/02	−3.8	7/28/00	−4.7	7/19/02	−3.6	7/23/02	−4.1
	First Trading Day of Monthly Options Expiration Week: 1980–2025									
Record (#Up–#Down)	29–16		28–17		30–15		28–17		25–20	
Current streak	U2		U2		U2		U2		U2	
Avg % Change	0.13		0.02		−0.01		−0.01		−0.05	
	Monthly Options Expiration Day: 1980–2025									
Record (#Up–#Down)	19–24		22–23		18–27		22–23		17–28	
Current streak	D1		D1		D2		D1		D2	
Avg % Change	−0.20		−0.23		−0.35		−0.23		−0.38	
	Monthly Options Expiration Week: 1980–2025									
Record (#Up–#Down)	28–17		25–20		21–24		25–20		25–20	
Current streak	U2		D1		D7		D1		U2	
Avg % Change	0.49		0.10		−0.09		0.05		−0.05	
	Week After Monthly Options Expiration: 1980–2025									
Record (#Up–#Down)	26–19		23–22		21–24		24–21		19–26	
Current streak	U4		D1		D1		D1		U4	
Avg % Change	0.10		0.01		−0.21		0.004		−0.10	
	First Trading Day Performance									
% of Time Up	68.0		74.7		66.7		78.3		67.4	
Avg % Change	0.27		0.28		0.20		0.34		0.14	
	Last Trading Day Performance									
% of Time Up	52.0		61.3		51.9		58.7		63.0	
Avg % Change	0.03		0.09		0.05		0.03		0.002	

Dow & S&P 1950–May 2, 2025; NASDAQ 1971–May 2, 2025; Russell 1K & 2K 1979–May 2, 2025.

When Dow and S&P in July are inferior, NASDAQ days tend to be even drearier.

Studying Market History Can Produce Gains

LIKE THESE
- SPDR Financial (XLF) **up 25.5%** in 6 months
- Invescos QQQ (QQQ) **up 30.0%** in 9 months
- SPDR Utilities (XLU) **up 20.2%** in 5.5 months
- iShares US Technology (IYW) **up 34.3%** in 8 months

AND THESE
- InterDigital (IDCC) **up 125.2%** in 18.5 months
- Emcor Group (EME) **up 110.5%** in 18.5 months
- OSI Systems (OSISI) **up 53.6%** in 7 months
- Avid Tech Inc (AVID) **up 132.4%** in 9 months

What do all these big winners have in common? All were undervalued and off Wall Street's radar screen when we selected them. All were chosen by my team of highly trained veteran market analysts with decades of experience trading and investing in the market with real money. All passed through our multi-disciplined approach that combines our renowned *Stock Trader's Almanac* behavioral finance analysis of the 4-Year Election Cycle, market and sector seasonality in conjunction with our proprietary fundamental stock screening criteria with the entries and exits pinpointed using old-school technical analysis. We refer to our blend of historical rules-based strategy with technical and fundamental tactical signals as DYNAMIC Investing.

Jeffrey A. Hirsch
Editor *Stock Trader's Almanac*

My name is Jeffrey A. Hirsch, I am the editor-in chief of the *Stock Trader's Almanac* and I want to introduce you to the **ALMANAC INVESTOR**. ALMANAC INVESTOR is a unique service that brings you top stocks and top sectors at the right time every week. Subscribe to my highly acclaimed weekly digital subscription service, *Almanac Investor*, which culminates over 50 years of independent market research and publishing. Every Thursday you will receive a detailed report updating our market outlook and portfolio positions plus timely Alerts as warranted on our seasonal signals and indicators, bringing you actionable trades and investment ideas with clear and specific buy and sell points.

771.4% Gain Since 2001 Vs. 384.3% for S&P 500

Almanac Investor, is the culmination of all we've done with the *Almanac* and newsletters over the years. Our *Almanac Investor* stock portfolio currently has a total return of 771.4% since inception in 2001 versus a 384.3% return for the S&P 500 over the same timeframe. This includes all of our sold positions.

- Excludes dividends, fees and any foreign currency gains or losses
- No margin or leverage used
- Long and Short stock trades across Small-, Mid-, and Large-Cap companies
- Rarely fully invested, cash balance maintained

Get The 2027 Stock Trader's Almanac FREE

Save over 55% Off the Regular Pricing and get a **FREE** *Stock Trader's Almanac* (Retail value $55). Your subscription includes, weekly issues via email, interim buy and sell signal alerts, full access to the website and a **FREE** annual copy of the *Stock Trader's Almanac*. Subscribe today at www.StockTradersAlmanac.com click "Subscribe Now". TWO WAYS TO SAVE:

- **1-Year @ $179** – 46% Off vs. Quarterly – Use promo code **1YRSTA26**
- **2-Years @ $299 – BEST DEAL**, over 55% Off – Use promo code **2YRSTA26**

Go to www.STOCKTRADERSALMANAC.com
and click "Subscribe Now" or CALL 914-750-5860

Those who understand market history are bound to profit from it!

"I'm a mechanical engineer, and an investment advisor, and been in this business for over 30 years. Throughout the years I subscribed to the most expensive newsletters in the country, and never made a profit because of the momentum stocks they all recommend, and most of their recommendations made a round trip no exception. In 8 weeks I followed your recommendations regarding the seasonality trends and I made over $135,000.00."
– Sam C. from Mississippi

ACT NOW! Visit www.STOCKTRADERSALMANAC.com
CALL 914-750-5860. TWO WAYS TO SAVE:

♦ **1-Year @ $179** – 46% Off vs. Quarterly – Use promo code **1YRSTA26**

♦ **2-Years @ $299** – BEST DEAL, over 55% Off – Use promo code **2YRSTA26**

Now you can find out which seasonal trends are on schedule and which are not, and how to take advantage of them. You will be kept abreast of upcoming market-moving events and what our indicators are saying about the next major market move. Every week you will receive timely dispatches about bullish and bearish seasonal patterns.

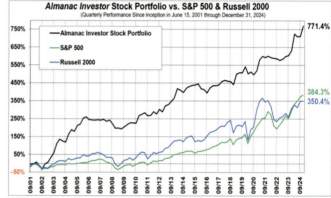

Our digital subscription service, *Almanac Investor*, provides all this plus unusual investing opportunities – exciting small-, mid- and large-cap stocks; seasoned, undervalued equities; timely sector ETF trades and more. Our **Data-Rich and Data-Driven Market Cycle Analysis** is the only investment tool of its kind that helps traders and investors forecast market trends with accuracy and confidence.

YOU RECEIVE WEEKLY EMAILS CONTAINING:
- ♦ Opportune ETF and Stock Trading Ideas with Specific Buy and Sell Price Limits
- ♦ Timely Data-Rich and Data-Driven Market Analysis
- ♦ Access to Webinars, Videos, Tools, and Resources
- ♦ Market-Tested and Time-Proven Short- and Long-Term Trading Strategies
- ♦ Best Six-Months Switching Strategy MACD Timing Signals

Copyright © 2000-2025 by Jeffrey A. Hirsch and Hirsch Holdings Inc. All rights reserved. www.stocktradersalmanac.com

JUNE/JULY 2026

MONDAY 29
D 61.9
S 61.9
N 61.9

The symbol of all relationships among such men, the moral symbol of respect for human beings, is the trader.
— Ayn Rand (Russian-born American novelist and philosopher, from Galt's Speech, *Atlas Shrugged*, 1957, 1905–1982)

Last Day of Q2 Bearish for Dow, Down 19 of Last 34, But Up 10 of Last 14, Bullish for NASDAQ, Up 22 of 33

TUESDAY 30
D 57.1
S 57.1
N 52.4

It is wise to remember that too much success [in the stock market] is in itself an excellent warning.
— Gerald M. Loeb (E.F. Hutton, *The Battle for Investment Survival*, predicted 1929 Crash, 1900–1974)

First Trading Day in July, S&P Up 32 of Last 36, Average Gain 0.5%

WEDNESDAY 1
D 81.0
S 90.5
N 85.7

The world hates change, but it is the only thing that has brought progress.
— Charles Kettering (Inventor of electric ignition, founded Delco in 1909, 1876–1958)

July is the Best Performing Dow and S&P Month of Third Quarter (Page 68)

THURSDAY 2
D 38.1
S 47.6
N 47.6

Great things are not accomplished by those who yield to trends and fads and popular opinion.
— Jack Kerouac (Beat Generation novelist and poet, *On the Road*, 1922–1969)

(Market Closed – Independence Day Observed)

FRIDAY 3

Press on. Nothing in the world can take the place of persistence. Talent will not: nothing is more common than unrewarded talent. Education alone will not: the world is full of educated failures. Persistence alone is omnipotent.
— Calvin Coolidge (30th U.S. President, 1872–1933)

Independence Day

SATURDAY 4

SUNDAY 5

FIRST MONTH OF QUARTERS IS THE MOST BULLISH

We have observed over the years that the investment calendar reflects the annual, semi-annual, and quarterly operations of institutions during January, April, and July. The opening month of the first three quarters produces the greatest gains in the Dow Jones Industrials, S&P 500, and NASDAQ. Recent January weakness has given March the advantage in Q1 for Dow Jones Industrials and S&P 500 from 1991 through April 2025.

The fourth quarter had behaved quite differently since it is affected by year-end portfolio adjustments and Presidential and Congressional elections in even-numbered years. Since 1991 major turnarounds have helped October join the ranks of bullish first months of quarters. October transformed into a bear-killing-turnaround month, posting Dow gains in 18 of the last 27 years, 2008 was a significant exception (See pages 156–173.)

After experiencing the most powerful bull market of all time during the 1990s, followed by two ferocious bear markets early in the millennium, we divided the monthly average percent changes into two groups: before 1991 and after. Comparing the month-by-month quarterly behavior of the three major U.S. averages in the table, you'll see that first months of the first three quarters perform best overall. Nasty selloffs in April 2000, 2002, 2004, 2005, and 2022 and July 2000–2002 and 2004, hit the NASDAQ hardest. The bear market of October 2007-March 2009, which more than cut the markets in half, took a toll on every first month except April. October 2008 was the worst month in a decade. January was also a difficult month in 13 of the last 26 years pulling its performance lower. (See pages 156–173.)

Between 1950 and 1990, the S&P 500 gained 1.3% (Dow, 1.4%) on average in first months of the first three quarters. Second months barely eked out any gain, while third months, thanks to March, moved up 0.23% (Dow, 0.07%) on average. NASDAQ's first month of the first three quarters averages 1.67% from 1971–1990 with July being a negative drag.

DOW JONES INDUSTRIALS, S&P 500 AND NASDAQ
AVERAGE MONTHLY % CHANGES BY QUARTER

	DJIA 1950–1990			S&P 500 1950–1990			NASDAQ 1971–1990		
	1st Mo	2nd Mo	3rd Mo	1st Mo	2nd Mo	3rd Mo	1st Mo	2nd Mo	3rd Mo
1Q	1.5%	−0.01%	1.0%	1.5%	−0.1%	1.1%	3.8%	1.2%	0.9%
2Q	1.6	−0.4	0.1	1.3	−0.1	0.3	1.7	0.8	1.1
3Q	1.1	0.3	−0.9	1.1	0.3	−0.7	−0.5	0.1	−1.6
Tot	4.2%	−0.1%	0.2%	3.9%	0.1%	0.7%	5.0%	2.1%	0.4%
Avg	1.40%	−0.04%	0.07%	1.30%	0.03%	0.23%	1.67%	0.70%	0.13%
4Q	−0.1%	1.4%	1.7%	0.4%	1.7%	1.6%	−1.4%	1.6%	1.4%

	DJIA 1991-April 2025			S&P 500 1991-April 2025			NASDAQ 1991-April 2025		
1Q	0.4%	0.1%	0.7%	0.6%	0.1%	0.9%	2.0%	0.1%	0.5%
2Q	1.9	0.4	−0.4	1.6	0.8	0.02	1.1	1.2	1.0
3Q	1.8	−0.6	−0.8	1.5	−0.3	−0.7	1.7	0.4	−0.5
Tot	4.1%	−0.1%	−0.5%	3.7%	0.6%	0.2%	4.8%	1.7%	1.0%
Avg	1.37%	−0.02%	−0.17%	1.23%	0.18%	0.07%	1.60%	0.56%	0.33%
4Q	1.7%	2.5%	1.2%	1.5%	2.1%	1.2%	1.9%	2.5%	1.6%

	DJIA 1950–April 2025			S&P 500 1950–April 2025			NASDAQ 1971–April 2025		
1Q	1.0%	0.1%	0.9%	1.1%	−0.02%	1.0%	2.6%	0.5%	0.7%
2Q	1.8	−0.02	−0.2	1.4	0.3	0.2	1.3	1.1	1.0
3Q	1.4	−0.1	−0.8	1.3	0.02	−0.7	0.9	0.3	−0.9
Tot	4.2%	−0.02%	−0.1%	3.8%	0.3%	0.5%	4.8%	1.9%	0.8%
Avg	1.40%	−0.01%	−0.03%	1.27%	0.10%	0.15%	1.59%	0.64%	0.27%
4Q	0.7%	1.9%	1.5%	0.9%	1.9%	1.4%	0.7%	2.1%	1.5%

JULY 2026

Market Subject to Elevated Volatility After July 4th

MONDAY
D 57.1
S 66.7
N 66.7
6

Margin clerks are the most ruthless sellers Wall Street has ever known.
— John Mendelson (Morgan Stanely)

TUESDAY
D 57.1
S 57.1
N 61.9
7

Bitcoin is digital photography. Before you know it, it will digitize and dematerialize the entire financial system, and the same thing that happened to Kodak will happen to many traditional financial institutions.
— Peter Diamandis (American engineer, physician, entrepreneur, futurist, b. 1961)

Beware the "Summer Rally" Hype
Historically the Weakest Rally of All Seasons (Page 76)

WEDNESDAY
D 52.4
S 57.1
N 61.9
8

If you bet on a horse, that's gambling. If you bet you can make three spades, that's entertainment. If you bet cotton will go up three points, that's business. See the difference?
— Blackie Sherrod (Sportswriter, 1919–2016)

THURSDAY
D 61.9
S 66.7
N 76.2
9

If we hire people bigger than ourselves, we will become a company of giants—smaller than ourselves, a company of midgets.
— David Oglivy (Forbes ASAP)

FRIDAY
D 57.1
S 66.7
N 66.7
10

There is nothing more powerful than a market that has changed its mind.
— Arthur D. Cashin, Jr. (Legendary NYSE floor trader, director of floor operations UBS Financial Services, 1941–2024)

SATURDAY
11

SUNDAY
12

2024 DAILY DOW POINT CHANGES
(DOW JONES INDUSTRIAL AVERAGE)

Week #	Month	Monday**	Tuesday	Wednsday	Thursday	Friday**	Weekly Dow Close	Net Point Change
						2023 Close	37689.54	
1		Holiday	25.50	−284.85	10.15	25.77	37466.11	−223.43
2	JAN	216.90	−157.85	170.57	15.29	−118.04	37592.98	126.87
3		Holiday	−231.86	−94.45	201.94	395.19	37863.80	270.82
4		138.01	−96.36	−99.06	242.74	60.30	38109.43	245.63
5		224.02	133.86	−317.01	369.54	134.58	38654.42	544.99
6		−274.30	141.24	156.00	48.97	−54.64	38671.69	17.27
7	FEB	125.69	−524.63	151.52	348.85	−145.13	38627.99	−43.70
8		Holiday	−64.19	48.44	456.87	62.42	39131.53	503.54
9		−62.30	−96.82	−23.39	47.37	90.99	39087.38	−44.15
10		−97.55	−404.64	75.86	130.30	−68.66	38722.69	−364.69
11	MAR	46.97	235.83	37.83	−137.66	−190.89	38714.77	−7.92
12		75.66	320.33	401.37	269.24	−305.47	39475.90	761.13
13		−162.26	−31.31	477.75	47.29	Holiday	39807.37	331.47
14		−240.52	−396.61	−43.10	−530.16	307.06	38904.04	−903.33
15		−11.24	−9.13	−422.16	−2.43	−475.84	37983.24	−920.80
16	APR	−248.13	63.86	−45.66	22.07	211.02	37986.40	3.16
17		253.58	263.71	−42.77	−375.12	153.86	38239.66	253.26
18		146.43	−570.17	87.37	322.37	450.02	38675.68	436.02
19		176.59	31.99	172.13	331.37	125.08	39512.84	837.16
20	MAY	−81.33	126.60	349.89	−38.62	134.21	40003.59	490.75
21		−196.82	66.22	−201.95	−605.78	4.33	39069.59	−934.00
22		Holiday	−216.73	−411.32	−330.06	574.84	38686.32	−383.27
23		−115.29	140.26	96.04	78.84	−87.18	38798.99	112.67
24	JUN	69.05	−120.62	−35.21	−65.11	−57.94	38589.16	−209.83
25		188.94	56.76	Holiday	299.90	15.57	39150.33	561.17
26		260.88	−299.05	15.64	36.26	−45.20	39118.86	−31.47
27		50.66	162.33	−23.85*	Holiday	67.87	39375.87	257.01
28		−31.08	−52.82	429.39	32.39	247.15	40000.90	625.03
29	JUL	210.82	742.76	243.60	−533.06	−377.49	40287.53	286.63
30		127.91	−57.35	−504.22	81.20	654.27	40589.34	301.81
31		−49.41	203.40	99.46	−494.82	−610.71	39737.26	−852.08
32		−1033.99	294.39	−234.21	683.04	51.05	39497.54	−239.72
33	AUG	−140.53	408.63	242.75	554.67	96.70	40659.76	1162.22
34		236.77	−61.56	55.52	−177.71	462.30	41175.08	515.32
35		65.44	9.98	−159.08	243.63	228.03	41563.08	388.00
36		Holiday	−626.15	38.04	−219.22	−410.34	40345.41	−1217.67
37	SEP	484.18	−92.63	124.75	235.06	297.01	41393.78	1048.37
38		228.30	−15.90	−103.08	522.09	38.17	42063.36	669.58
39		61.29	83.57	−293.47	260.36	137.89	42313.00	249.64
40		17.15	−173.18	39.55	−184.93	341.16	42352.75	39.75
41		−398.51	126.13	431.63	−57.88	409.74	42863.86	511.11
42	OCT	201.36	−324.80	337.28	161.35	36.86	43275.91	412.05
43		−344.31	−6.71	−409.94	−140.59	−259.96	42114.40	−1161.51
44		273.17	−154.52	−91.51	−378.08	288.73	42052.19	−62.21
45		−257.59	427.28	1508.05	−0.59	259.65	43988.99	1936.80
46	NOV	304.14	−382.15	47.21	−207.33	−305.87	43444.99	−544.00
47		−55.39	−120.66	139.53	461.88	426.16	44296.51	851.52
48		440.06	123.74	−138.28	Holiday	188.62*	44910.65	614.14
49		−128.65	−76.47	308.51	−248.33	−123.19	44642.52	−268.13
50	DEC	−240.59	−154.10	−99.27	−234.44	−86.06	43828.06	−814.46
51		−110.58	−267.58	−1123.03	15.37	498.02	42840.26	−987.80
52		66.69	390.08*	Holiday	28.77	−333.59	42992.21	151.95
53		−418.48	−29.51			Year Close:	42544.22	−447.99
TOTALS		−1121.62	−124.18	1084.81	1549.96	3465.71		4854.68

Outline Bold Color: Down Friday, Down Monday *Shortened trading day: Jul 3, Nov 29, & Dec 24
** Monday denotes first trading day of week, Friday denotes last trading day of week

JULY 2026

Monday Before July Monthly Expiration, Dow Up 17 of Last 22

MONDAY
D 76.2
S 66.7
N 52.4
13

Over time, you weed out luck.
— Billy Beane (American baseball player and general manager, b. 1962)

TUESDAY
D 76.2
S 66.7
N 71.4
14

The reasonable man adapts himself to the world; the unreasonable one persists in trying to adapt the world to himself. Therefore, all progress depends on the unreasonable man.
— George Bernard Shaw (Irish dramatist, 1856–1950)

WEDNESDAY
D 71.4
S 47.6
N 57.1
15

Patriotism is when love of your own people comes first. Nationalism is when hate for people other than your own comes first.
— Charles De Gaulle (French president and WWII General, 1890–1970, May 1969)

THURSDAY
D 52.4
S 52.4
N 57.1
16

The more feted by the media, the worse a pundit's accuracy.
— Sharon Begley (Senior editor Newsweek, 2/23/2009, referencing Philip E. Tetlock's 2005 Expert Political Judgment)

July Monthly Expiration Day, Dow Down 16 of Last 25, –4.6% 2002, –2.5% 2010

FRIDAY
D 66.7
S 61.9
N 66.7
17

The best time to be wrong is with money in one's pocket.
— George Brooks (60-year market veteran, hired by Yale Hirsch in 1974, mentor, confidant, Investors First Read, b. 1937)

SATURDAY
18

SUNDAY
19

MARKET GAINS MORE ON SUPER-8 DAYS EACH MONTH THAN ON ALL 13 REMAINING DAYS COMBINED

For many years the last day plus the first four days were the best days of the month. The market currently exhibits greater bullish bias from the last three trading days of the previous month through the first two days of the current month, and shows significant bullishness during the middle three trading days, nine to eleven, due to 401(k) cash inflows (see pages 147 and 148). This pattern was not as pronounced during the boom years of the 1990s, with market strength all month long. Since the 2009 market bottom, the Super-8 advantage has been sporadic. So far in 2025, the Super 8 have performed well. The Super 8 lagged badly in 2024 after soaring in 2023. When compared to the last 26 and third-year record (at the bottom of the page), the Super-8 edge has dulled recently.

SUPER-8 DAYS* S&P 500 % CHANGES VS. REST OF MONTH

	Super 8 Days	Rest of Month	Super 8 Days	Rest of Month	Super 8 Days	Rest of Month
	2017		**2018**		**2019**	
Jan	0.15%	1.08%	2.49%	4.57%	−0.04%	7.19%
Feb	0.73	2.17	−1.13	−3.28	4.22	1.47
Mar	1.30	−1.51	−3.30	0.07	0.99	−0.19
Apr	−0.05	1.32	−0.33	−0.39	2.34	1.45
May	0.22	0.89	−0.57	3.69	−1.35	−2.92
Jun	1.12	−0.93	0.68	−0.61	0.37	3.72
Jul	1.07	1.33	0.04	4.16	2.05	1.64
Aug	1.07	−2.40	−0.88	3.03	−4.31	−0.90
Sep	0.78	1.36	−0.30	0.93	2.26	1.73
Oct	1.61	0.92	−0.99	−7.90	−1.36	3.24
Nov	0.07	1.53	2.57	−1.65	2.22	0.87
Dec	1.91	1.11	−3.30	−4.86	0.27	3.11
Totals	9.98%	6.88%	−5.02%	−2.24%	7.65%	20.39%
Average	0.83%	0.57%	−0.42%	−0.19%	0.64%	1.70%
	2020		**2021**		**2022**	
Jan	0.71%	0.40%	−0.51%	3.59%	−3.01%	−6.30%
Feb	0.38	−4.88	−0.03	0.85	4.73	−7.25
Mar	−16.43	0.61	1.51	0.88	3.88	4.24
Apr	−2.60	12.37	3.69	1.59	0.02	−8.77
May	−1.46	5.48	1.93	−1.86	1.86	−6.44
Jun	−1.01	4.13	0.65	1.55	2.00	−3.89
Jul	3.44	0.90	0.70	2.11	−1.01	1.56
Aug	2.79	5.16	1.22	0.34	6.49	−2.83
Sep	4.31	−9.10	1.61	−2.18	−4.75	−5.63
Oct	0.05	2.74	−0.52	3.51	6.87	−1.73
Nov	0.87	6.29	2.01	0.75	−0.97	6.14
Dec	1.65	1.08	−2.69	4.62	−1.27	−3.67
Totals	−7.30%	25.17%	9.55%	15.75%	14.84%	−34.57%
Average	−0.61%	2.10%	0.80%	1.31%	1.24%	−2.88%
	2023		**2024**		**2025**	
Jan	−0.75%	6.84%	−2.31%	4.86%	1.01%	−0.51%
Feb	4.38	−5.33	1.54	2.08	0.78	−2.62
Mar	0.01	−1.03	0.07	2.86	−1.66	−2.46
Apr	3.47	−0.91	−2.15	−1.13	1.70	−4.89
May	1.14	0.80	1.95	3.09		
Jun	5.22	0.23	0.68	2.38		
Jul	2.57	1.68	2.22	−2.35		
Aug	−1.85	−1.09	1.58	1.45		
Sep	1.12	−4.67	−1.20	2.95		
Oct	−1.11	−2.11	0.39	1.38		
Nov	6.44	3.34	−3.76	6.83		
Dec	2.06	2.81	0.88	−0.04		
Totals	22.70%	0.58%	−0.10%	24.35%	1.84%	−10.48%
Average	1.89%	0.05%	−0.01%	2.03%	0.46%	−2.62%

		Super Eight Days		Rest of Month (13 days)	
316		Net % Changes	177.60%	Net % Changes	10.77%
Month		Average Period	0.56%	Average Period	0.03%
Totals		Average Day	0.07%	Average Day	0.003%

Super 8 Days = Last 3 + First 2 + Middle 3

JULY 2026

MONDAY
D 76.2
S 71.4
N 71.4
20

Your organization will never get better unless you are willing to admit that there is something wrong with it.
— General Norman Schwartzkof (Ret. Commander of Allied Forces in 1990–1991 Gulf War)

TUESDAY
D 28.6
S 33.3
N 19.0
21

If everyone's waiting for a pullback to buy, either the market doesn't have a pullback or, if it does, you shouldn't buy into it.
— Robert J. Farrell (Farrell Advisory, Chief Market Analyst Merrill Lynch 1957–1992, b. 1932)

Week After July Monthly Expiration Prone to Swings, Dow Up 17 of Last 23
2002 +3.1%, 2006 +3.2%, 2007 –4.2%, 2009 +4.0%, 2010 +3.2, 2015 –2.9%

WEDNESDAY
D 52.4
S 47.6
N 57.1
22

Make sure you have a jester because people in high places are seldom told the truth.
— Radio caller to President Ronald Reagan

THURSDAY
D 52.4
S 57.1
N 52.4
23

The greatest discovery of my generation is that human beings can alter their lives by altering their attitudes.
— William James (Philosopher, psychologist, 1842–1910)

FRIDAY
D 38.1
S 52.4
N 47.6
24

The greatest good you can do for another is not just to share your riches, but to reveal to him his own.
— Benjamin Disraeli (British prime minister, 1804–1881)

SATURDAY
25

SUNDAY
26

AUGUST ALMANAC

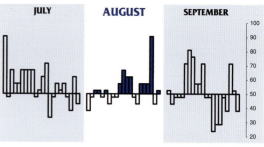

Market Probability Chart above is a graphic representation of the S&P 500 Recent Market Probability Calendar on page 126.

◆ Harvesting made August the best stock market month 1901–1951 ◆ Now about 2% farm, August is the worst Dow and second worst S&P and NASDAQ (2000 up 11.7%, 2001 down 10.9%) month since 1988 ◆ Second-shortest bear in history (45 days) caused by turmoil in Russia, currency crisis, and hedge fund debacle ended here in 1998, 1344.22-point drop in the Dow, 15th worst monthly point loss, off 15.1% second worst percent loss since 1941 ◆ Saddam Hussein triggered a 10.0% slide in 1990 ◆ Best Dow gains: 1982 (11.5%) and 1984 (9.8%) as bear markets ended ◆ Next to last day S&P down 19 times last 29 years ◆ Midterm election year Augusts' rankings #8 S&P, #10 Dow, and #10 NASDAQ

August Vital Statistics

	DJIA	S&P 500	NASDAQ	Russell 1K	Russell 2K
Rank	10	10	11	10	10
Up	42	41	30	28	25
Down	33	34	24	18	21
Average % Change	−0.1	0.02	0.3	0.3	0.1
Midterm Yr Avg % Chg	−0.7	−0.4	−1.4	−0.2	−1.4
Best & Worst August					
	% Change	% Change	% Change	% Change	% Change
Best	1982 11.5	1982 11.6	2000 11.7	1982 11.3	1984 11.5
Worst	1998 −15.1	1998 −14.6	1998 −19.9	1998 −15.1	1998 −19.5
Best & Worst August Weeks					
Best	8/20/82 10.3	8/20/82 8.8	8/3/84 7.4	8/20/82 8.5	8/3/84 7.0
Worst	8/23/74 −6.1	8/5/11 −7.2	8/28/98 −8.8	8/5/11 −7.7	8/5/11 −10.3
Best & Worst August Days					
Best	8/17/82 4.9	8/17/82 4.8	8/9/11 5.3	8/9/11 5.0	8/9/11 6.9
Worst	8/31/98 −6.4	8/31/98 −6.8	8/31/98 −8.6	8/8/11 −6.9	8/8/11 −8.9
First Trading Day of Monthly Options Expiration Week: 1980–2025					
Record (#Up–#Down)	28–17	33–12	33–12	32–13	27–18
Current streak	D1	U5	U3	D1	D2
Avg % Change	0.20	0.25	0.33	0.23	0.21
Monthly Options Expiration Day: 1980–2025					
Record (#Up–#Down)	24–21	24–21	25–20	26–19	26–19
Current streak	U2	U1	U1	U2	U2
Avg % Change	−0.07	−0.04	−0.10	−0.04	0.10
Monthly Options Expiration Week: 1980–2025					
Record (#Up–#Down)	20–25	24–21	23–22	24–21	25–20
Current streak	U1	U1	U1	U1	U1
Avg % Change	−0.01	0.17	0.31	0.17	0.17
Week After Monthly Options Expiration: 1980–2025					
Record (#Up–#Down)	27–18	30–15	29–16	30–15	29–16
Current streak	U1	U2	U2	U2	U1
Avg % Change	0.24	0.34	0.57	0.35	0.27
First Trading Day Performance					
% of Time Up	45.3	46.7	51.9	41.3	43.5
Avg % Change	−0.004	0.01	−0.08	0.04	−0.09
Last Trading Day Performance					
% of Time Up	57.3	61.3	64.8	56.5	65.2
Avg % Change	0.09	0.11	0.07	−0.03	0.04

Dow & S&P 1950–May 2, 2025; NASDAQ 1971–May 2, 2025; Russell 1K & 2K 1979–May 2, 2025.

August's a good month to go on vacation;
Trading stocks will likely lead to frustration.

JULY/AUGUST 2026

MONDAY
D 66.7
S 57.1
N 52.4
27

The mind is not a vessel to be filled but a fire to be kindled.
— Plutarch (Greek biographer and philosopher, *Parallel Lives*, 46–120 AD)

TUESDAY
D 52.4
S 47.6
N 47.6
28

The choice of starting a war this [pre-election] spring was made for political as well as military reasons… [The president] cleary does not want to have a war raging on the eve of his presumed reelection campaign.
— Senior European diplomat (*NY Times* 3/14/03)

FOMC Meeting

WEDNESDAY
D 42.9
S 38.1
N 42.9
29

The Stone Age didn't end for lack of stone, and the oil age will end long before the world runs out of oil.
— Sheik Ahmed Zaki Yamani (Saudi oil minister 1962–1986, b. 1930–2021)

THURSDAY
D 52.4
S 61.9
N 71.4
30

To succeed in the markets, it is essential to make your own decisions. Numerous traders cited listening to others as their worst blunder.
— Jack D. Schwager (Investment manager, author, *Stock Market Wizards: Interviews with America's Top Stock Traders*, b. 1948)

Last Trading Day in July, NASDAQ and S&P Down 12 of Last 20, Dow Down 13 of Last 20

FRIDAY
D 38.1
S 42.9
N 42.9
31

We always live in an uncertain world. What is certain is that the United States will go forward over time.
— Warren Buffett (CEO Berkshire Hathaway, investor & philanthropist, CNBC 9/22/2010, b. 1930)

SATURDAY
1

August Almanac Investor Sector Seasonalities: See Pages 94, 96, and 98

SUNDAY
2

A RALLY FOR ALL SEASONS

Most years, especially when the market sells off during the first half, prospects for the perennial summer rally become the buzz on the street. Parameters for this "rally" were defined by the late Ralph Rotnem as the lowest close in the Dow Jones Industrials in May or June to the highest close in July, August, or September. Such a big deal is made of the "summer rally" that one might get the impression the market puts on its best performance in the summertime. Nothing could be further from the truth! Not only does the market "rally" in every season of the year, but it does so with more gusto in the winter, spring, and fall than in the summer.

Winters in 62 years averaged a 12.9% gain as measured from the low in November or December to the first quarter closing high. Spring rose 11.5% followed by fall with 11.3%. Last and least was the average 9.5% "summer rally." Even 2020's impressive 25.2% "summer rally" was outmatched by spring. Nevertheless, no matter how thick the gloom or grim the outlook, don't despair! There's always a rally for all seasons, statistically.

SEASONAL GAINS IN DOW JONES INDUSTRIALS

	WINTER RALLY Nov/Dec Low to Q1 High	SPRING RALLY Feb/Mar Low to Q2 High	SUMMER RALLY May/Jun Low to Q3 High	FALL RALLY Aug/Sep Low to Q4 High
1964	15.3%	6.2%	9.4%	8.3%
1965	5.7	6.6	11.6	10.3
1966	5.9	4.8	3.5	7.0
1967	11.6	8.7	11.2	4.4
1968	7.0	11.5	5.2	13.3
1969	0.9	7.7	1.9	6.7
1970	5.4	6.2	22.5	19.0
1971	21.6	9.4	5.5	7.4
1972	19.1	7.7	5.2	11.4
1973	8.6	4.8	9.7	15.9
1974	13.1	8.2	1.4	11.0
1975	36.2	24.2	8.2	8.7
1976	23.3	6.4	5.9	4.6
1977	8.2	3.1	2.8	2.1
1978	2.1	16.8	11.8	5.2
1979	11.0	8.9	8.9	6.1
1980	13.5	16.8	21.0	8.5
1981	11.8	9.9	0.4	8.3
1982	4.6	9.3	18.5	37.8
1983	15.7	17.8	6.3	10.7
1984	5.9	4.6	14.1	9.7
1985	11.7	7.1	9.5	19.7
1986	31.1	18.8	9.2	11.4
1987	30.6	13.6	22.9	5.9
1988	18.1	13.5	11.2	9.8
1989	15.1	12.9	16.1	5.7
1990	8.8	14.5	12.4	8.6
1991	21.8	11.2	6.6	9.3
1992	14.9	6.4	3.7	3.3
1993	8.9	7.7	6.3	7.3
1994	9.7	5.2	9.1	5.0
1995	13.6	19.3	11.3	13.9
1996	19.2	7.5	8.7	17.3
1997	17.7	18.4	18.4	7.3
1998	20.3	13.6	8.2	24.3
1999	15.1	21.6	8.2	12.6
2000	10.8	15.2	9.8	3.5
2001	6.4	20.8	1.7	23.1
2002	14.8	7.9	2.8	17.6
2003	6.5	23.9	14.3	15.7
2004	11.6	5.2	4.4	10.6
2005	9.0	2.1	5.6	5.3
2006	8.8	8.3	9.5	13.0
2007	6.7	13.5	6.6	10.3
2008	2.5	11.2	3.8	4.5
2009	19.6	34.4	19.7	15.5
2010	11.6	13.1	11.1	16.0
2011	12.6	10.3	7.0	14.7
2012	18.0	4.5	12.4	5.7
2013	16.2	11.8	6.9	12.2
2014	6.0	10.2	5.5	10.3
2015	7.1	5.5	3.0	14.4
2016	3.4	15.6	8.7	10.8
2017	18.0	8.3	8.8	14.6
2018	14.4	7.6	11.8	6.6
2019	19.7	6.8	10.3	12.4
2020	8.1	48.3	25.2	14.8
2021	23.2	15.1	7.0	7.8
2022	8.2	7.7	14.3	20.4
2023	7.2	8.1	8.7	12.5
2024	19.6	4.5	11.7	16.3
2025	7.4	3.5*		
Totals	800.5%	714.3%	577.4%	686.4%
Average	12.9%	11.5%	9.5%	11.3%

* As of 5/9/2025

AUGUST 2026

First Trading Day in August, Dow Down 19 of Last 28
First Nine Trading Days of August Are Historically Weak (Pages 74 and 138)

MONDAY 3
D 38.1
S 38.1
N 52.4

> Benjamin Graham was correct in suggesting that while the stock market in the short run may be a voting mechanism, in the long run it is a weighing mechanism. True value will win out in the end.
> — Burton G. Malkiel (Economist, April 2003 Princeton Paper, *A Random Walk Down Wall Street*, b. 1932)

TUESDAY 4
D 42.9
S 47.6
N 42.9

> Life is what happens, while you're busy making other plans.
> — John Lennon (Beatle, 1940–1980)

WEDNESDAY 5
D 57.1
S 52.4
N 57.1

> The four most expensive words in the English language, "This time it's different."
> — Sir John Templeton (Founder Templeton Funds, philanthropist, 1912–2008)

THURSDAY 6
D 47.6
S 52.4
N 57.1

> A generation from now, Americans may marvel at the complacency that assumed the dollar's dominance would never end.
> — Floyd Norris (Chief financial correspondent, *NY Times*, 2/2/07)

FRIDAY 7
D 52.4
S 47.6
N 38.1

> Thieves of private property pass their lives in chains; thieves of public property in riches and luxury.
> — Marcus Porcius Cato (Roman soldier, senator, historian, Cato the Elder, 234–149 B.C.)

SATURDAY 8

SUNDAY 9

TAKE ADVANTAGE OF DOWN FRIDAY/ DOWN MONDAY WARNING

Fridays* and Mondays* are the most important days of the week. Friday* is the day for squaring positions—trimming longs or covering shorts before taking off for the weekend. Traders want to limit their exposure (particularly to stocks that are not acting well) since there could be unfavorable developments before trading resumes two or more days later.

Monday* is important because the market then has the chance to reflect any weekend news, plus what traders think after digesting the previous week's action and the many Monday* morning research and strategy comments.

For over 30 years, a down Friday* followed by down Monday* has frequently corresponded with important market inflection points that typically exhibit a negative bias, often coinciding with market tops and on a few climactic occasions, such as in October 2002, March 2009, March 2020, and August–October 2022, near major market bottoms.

One simple way to get a quick reading on which way the market may be heading is to keep track of the performance of the Dow Jones Industrial Average on Fridays* and the following Mondays*. Since 1995 there have been 302 occurrences of Down Friday/Down Monday* (DF/DM) with 92 falling in the bear market years of 2001, 2002, 2008, 2011, 2015, 2020, and 2022, producing an average decline of 12.5% (shaded).

To illustrate how DF/DM* can telegraph market infection points we created the chart below of the Dow Jones Industrials from November 2023 to May 9, 2025, with arrows pointing to occurrences of DF/DM*. Use DF/DM* as a warning to examine market conditions carefully.

DOWN FRIDAY/DOWN MONDAY

Year	Total Number Down Friday/ Down Monday	Subsequent Average % Dow Loss*	Average Number of Days it took
1995	8	−1.2%	18
1996	9	−3.0%	28
1997	6	−5.1%	45
1998	9	−6.4%	47
1999	9	−6.4%	39
2000	11	−6.6%	32
2001	13	−13.5%	53
2002	18	−11.9%	54
2003	9	−3.0%	17
2004	9	−3.7%	51
2005	10	−3.0%	37
2006	11	−2.0%	14
2007	8	−6.0%	33
2008	15	−17.0%	53
2009	10	−8.7%	15
2010	7	−3.1%	10
2011	11	−9.0%	53
2012	11	−4.0%	38
2013	7	−2.4%	15
2014	7	−2.5%	8
2015	12	−9.2%	44
2016	10	−2.7%	25
2017	11	−1.2%	18
2018	14	−5.8%	45
2019	7	−4.3%	32
2020	8	−19.0%	27
2021	7	−4.4%	38
2022	15	−7.8%	46
2023	8	−3.1%	21
2024	9	−3.8%	47
2025**	3	−7.1%	25
Average	**10**	**−6.0%**	**33**

*Over next 3 months, **Ending May 9, 2025*

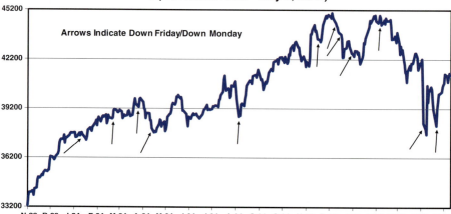

DOW JONES INDUSTRIALS (November 2023 - May 9, 2025)
Arrows Indicate Down Friday/Down Monday

Monday denotes first trading day of week, Friday denotes last trading day of week.

AUGUST 2026

August Worst Dow and Second Worst S&P Month 1988–2024
Harvesting Made August Best Dow Month 1901–1951

MONDAY
D 52.4
S 52.4
N 47.6
10

Successful investing is anticipating the anticipations of others.
— John Maynard Keynes (British economist, 1883–1946)

TUESDAY
D 38.1
S 42.9
N 42.9
11

Two signposts on the road to wisdom: 1. Nothing is the end of the world and, 2. Nobody gives a hoot what you think.
— Phil Pearlman (Founder, Pearl Institute, b. 1967)

WEDNESDAY
D 33.3
S 47.6
N 42.9
12

Banking establishments are more dangerous than standing armies; and that the principle of spending money to be paid by posterity, under the name of funding, is but swindling futurity on a large scale.
— Thomas Jefferson (3rd U.S. President, 1743–7/4/1826, 1816 letter to John Taylor of Caroline)

Mid-August Stronger Than Beginning and End

THURSDAY
D 61.9
S 47.6
N 57.1
13

A president is elected and tries to get rid of the dirty stuff in the economy as quickly as possible, so that by the time the next election comes around, he looks like a hero. The stock market is reacting to what the politicians are doing.
— Yale Hirsch (Creator of Stock Trader's Almanac, NY Times 10/10/2010, 1923–2021)

FRIDAY
D 66.7
S 57.1
N 61.9
14

All the features and achievements of modern civilization are, directly or indirectly, the products of the capitalist process.
— Joseph A. Schumpeter (Austrian-American economist, Theory of Economic Development, 1883–1950)

SATURDAY
15

SUNDAY
16

MARKET BEHAVIOR THREE DAYS BEFORE AND THREE DAYS AFTER HOLIDAYS

The *Stock Trader's Almanac* has tracked holiday seasonality annually since the first edition in 1968. Stocks used to rise on the day before holidays and sell off the day after, but nowadays each holiday moves to its own rhythm. Eight holidays are separated into five groups. Average percent changes for the Dow, S&P 500, NASDAQ, and Russell 2000 are shown.

The Dow and S&P consist of blue chips and the largest cap stocks, whereas NASDAQ represents tech stocks and the Russell 2000 would be more representative of smaller cap stocks. This is evident on the last day of the year with NASDAQ and the Russell 2000 having a field day, while their larger brethren in the Dow and S&P are showing losses on average.

Thanks to the Santa Claus Rally the three days before and after New Year's Day and Christmas are best. NASDAQ and the Russell 2000 average gains of 0.9% to 1.5% over the six-day spans. However, trading around the first day of the year has been mixed recently. Traders have been selling more the first trading day of the year, pushing gains and losses into the New Year.

Bullishness before Labor Day and after Memorial Day is often affected by strength the first day of September and June. The second worst day after a holiday is the day after Easter. Surprisingly, the following day is the best second day after a holiday, eclipsing the second day after New Year's Day.

Presidents' Day is the least bullish of all the holidays, bearish the day before and three days after. NASDAQ has dropped 23 of the last 36 days before Presidents' Day (Dow, 20 of 36; S&P 22 of 36; Russell 2000, 18 of 36).

HOLIDAYS: 3 DAYS BEFORE, 3 DAYS AFTER (Average % change 1980–April 2025)							
	−3	−2	−1		+1	+2	+3
S&P 500	−0.01	0.16	−0.11	**Mixed Before &**	0.16	0.22	0.03
DJIA	−0.01	0.11	−0.14	**Positive After**	0.27	0.20	0.15
NASDAQ	0.01	0.21	0.08	New Year's Day	0.16	0.41	0.10
Russell 2K	−0.05	0.35	0.28	1/1/26	0.01	0.18	0.09
S&P 500	0.35	−0.01	−0.11	**Negative Before & After**	−0.21	−0.07	−0.05
DJIA	0.30	−0.02	−0.04	Presidents'	−0.17	−0.08	−0.11
NASDAQ	0.54	0.21	−0.25	Day	−0.46	−0.07	0.03
Russell 2K	0.44	0.18	−0.04	2/16/26	−0.39	−0.17	−0.02
S&P 500	0.07	0.01	0.37	**Positive Before &**	−0.23	0.44	0.09
DJIA	0.05	0.01	0.26	**Negative After**	−0.19	0.40	0.09
NASDAQ	0.22	0.19	0.43	Good Friday	−0.29	0.50	0.18
Russell 2K	0.14	0.16	0.56	4/3/26	−0.40	0.39	0.05
S&P 500	0.09	0.06	0.11	**Positive Before**	0.22	0.10	0.25
DJIA	0.05	−0.02	0.02	**& After**	0.25	0.10	0.13
NASDAQ	0.18	0.24	0.21	Memorial Day	0.21	−0.03	0.43
Russell 2K	0.07	0.23	0.23	5/25/26	0.24	0.06	0.38
S&P 500	0.21	0.17	0.13	**Positive Before &**	−0.07	0.02	0.09
DJIA	0.18	0.13	0.12	**Negative After**	−0.05	0.01	0.06
NASDAQ	0.32	0.19	0.12	Independence Day	−0.0004	−0.11	0.27
Russell 2K	0.29	0.04	0.05	7/4/26	−0.23	−0.15	0.11
S&P 500	0.21	−0.21	0.10	Labor Day	−0.07	0.14	−0.09
DJIA	0.18	−0.23	0.10	9/7/26	−0.06	0.17	−0.13
NASDAQ	0.39	−0.07	0.10		−0.18	0.02	0.03
Russell 2K	0.48	0.02	0.12		−0.16	0.16	0.001
S&P 500	0.13	0.07	0.24	**Positive Before**	0.11	−0.36	0.25
DJIA	0.16	0.07	0.21	**& After**	0.08	−0.34	0.25
NASDAQ	0.04	−0.12	0.40	Thanksgiving	0.33	−0.32	0.11
Russell 2K	0.22	−0.03	0.38	11/26/26	0.20	−0.54	0.19
S&P 500	0.19	0.16	0.18	Christmas	0.29	−0.03	0.22
DJIA	0.24	0.19	0.19	12/25/26	0.32	0.001	0.18
NASDAQ	−0.02	0.30	0.34		0.27	−0.04	0.27
Russell 2K	0.28	0.29	0.32		0.31	−0.09	0.42

AUGUST 2026

Monday Before August Monthly Expiration, Dow Up 19 of Last 30, Average Gain 0.2%

MONDAY
D 57.1
S 66.7
N 57.1
17

Everything possible today was at one time impossible. Everything impossible today may at some time in the future be possible.
— Edward Lindaman (Apollo space project, president Whitworth College, 1920–1982)

TUESDAY
D 52.4
S 61.9
N 52.4
18

Major bottoms are usually made when analysts cut their earnings estimates and companies report earnings which are below expectations.
— Edward Babbitt, Jr. (Avatar Associates)

WEDNESDAY
D 61.9
S 61.9
N 57.1
19

We're not believers that the government is bigger than the business cycle.
— David Rosenberg (Economist, Merrill Lynch, *Barron's* 4/21/2008)

THURSDAY
D 52.4
S 47.6
N 47.6
20

The inherent vice of capitalism is the unequal sharing of blessings; the inherent virtue of socialism is the equal sharing of miseries.
— Winston Churchill (British statesman, 1874–1965)

August Monthly Expiration Day Less Bullish Lately, Dow Down 8 of Last 15 Dow Down 531 Points (3.1%) in 2015

FRIDAY
D 47.6
S 42.9
N 42.9
21

I've learned that only through focus can you do world-class things, no matter how capable you are.
— William H. Gates (Microsoft founder, *Fortune*, July 8, 2002)

SATURDAY
22

SUNDAY
23

FOURTH-QUARTER MARKET MAGIC

Examining market performance on a quarterly basis reveals several intriguing and helpful patterns. Fourth-quarter market gains have been magical, providing the greatest and most consistent gains over the years. First quarter performance runs a respectable second. This should not be surprising as cash inflows, trading volume, and buying bias are generally elevated during these two quarters.

Positive market psychology hits a fever pitch as the holiday season approaches and does not begin to wane until spring. Professionals drive the market higher as they make portfolio adjustments to maximize yearend numbers. Bonuses are paid and invested around the turn of the year.

The market's sweet spot of the Four-Year Cycle begins in the fourth quarter of the midterm year. The best two-quarter span runs from the fourth quarter of the midterm year through the first quarter of the pre-election year, averaging 13.8% for the Dow, 14.4% for the S&P 500 and an amazing 19.5% for NASDAQ. Pre-election Q2 is smoking too, the third best quarter of the cycle, creating a three-quarter sweet spot from midterm Q4 to pre-election Q2 (see page 46).

Quarterly strength fades in the latter half of the pre-election year, but stays impressively positive through the election year. Weakness is most consistent in the second and third quarters of midterm years. Post-election year Q1 has weakened recently.

QUARTERLY % CHANGES

	Q1	Q2	Q3	Q4	Year	Q2–Q3	Q4–Q1	Q4–Q2
Dow Jones Industrials (1949–March 2025)								
Average	1.9%	1.6%	0.6%	4.2%	8.6%	2.3%	6.4%	8.3%
Post Election	0.2%	1.9%	0.4%	4.3%	7.4%	2.3%	5.4%	3.4%
Midterm	0.9%	–1.9%	–0.2%	6.6%	5.2%	–2.0%	13.8%	19.3%
Pre-Election	6.9%	4.7%	0.8%	3.3%	16.1%	5.5%	3.2%	4.6%
Election	–0.2%	1.7%	1.5%	2.7%	5.8%	3.3%	3.1%	5.6%
S&P 500 (1949–March 2025)								
Average	2.1%	1.9%	0.8%	4.3%	9.5%	2.8%	6.6%	8.9%
Post Election	–0.2%	2.5%	0.8%	4.0%	8.0%	3.5%	4.8%	2.0%
Midterm	0.6%	–2.8%	0.2%	6.6%	4.6%	–1.5%	14.4%	20.2%
Pre-Election	7.4%	5.0%	0.4%	3.9%	17.2%	5.4%	4.7%	7.4%
Election	0.7%	2.8%	1.7%	2.5%	8.1%	4.7%	2.6%	5.8%
NASDAQ Composite (1971–March 2025)								
Average	3.9%	3.6%	0.5%	4.6%	13.6%	4.3%	8.6%	12.6%
Post Election	–1.6%	6.6%	2.2%	5.2%	13.2%	8.8%	6.3%	2.8%
Midterm	1.1%	–3.5%	–3.6%	5.8%	–0.5%	–6.6%	19.5%	29.4%
Pre-Election	13.4%	7.6%	0.5%	6.5%	30.3%	8.1%	9.4%	11.9%
Election	2.5%	3.3%	2.5%	1.0%	10.3%	6.4%	–0.1%	6.2%

AUGUST 2026

MONDAY 24
Week After August Monthly Expiration Mixed, Dow Down 10 of Last 20, Down 4.2% in 2022
D 61.9
S 57.1
N 57.1

In times of panic... these old fellows will be seen in Wall Street, hobbling down on their canes to their brokers' offices…. The panic usually rages until enough of these cash purchases of stock is made to afford a big rake in.
— Henry Clews (British-American financier, author, *Fifty Years in Wall Street*, 1888, 1834–1923)

TUESDAY 25
D 57.1
S 57.1
N 61.9

Become more humble as the market goes your way.
— Bernard Baruch (Financier, speculator, statesman, presidential adviser, 1870–1965)

WEDNESDAY 26
D 47.6
S 57.1
N 57.1

The way a young man spends his evenings is a part of that thin area between success and failure.
— Robert R. Young (U.S. financier and railroad tycoon, 1897–1958)

August's Third-to-Last Trading Day, S&P Up 19 Years in a Row 2003–2021, Down 0.7% in 2022, Up 1.5% in 2023, Down 0.6% in 2024

THURSDAY 27
D 90.5
S 90.5
N 81.0

We like what's familiar, and we dislike change. So, we push the familiar until it starts working against us big-time— a crisis. Then, MAYBE we can accept change.
— Kevin Cameron (Journalist, *Cycle World*, April 2013)

August's Next-to-Last Trading Day, S&P Down 19 of Last 29 Years

FRIDAY 28
D 42.9
S 42.9
N 57.1

Each day is a building block to the future. Who I am today is dependent on who I was yesterday.
— Matthew McConaughey (Actor, *Parade Magazine*)

SATURDAY 29

September Almanac Investor Sector Seasonalities: See Pages 94, 96, and 98

SUNDAY 30

SEPTEMBER ALMANAC

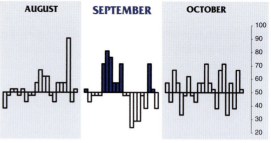

Market Probability Chart above is a graphic representation of the S&P 500 Recent Market Probability Calendar on page 126.

◆ Portfolio managers back after Labor Day tend to clean house in September ◆ Biggest % loser on the S&P, Dow and NASDAQ since 1950 (pages 52 & 60) ◆ Streak of four great Dow Septembers averaging 4.2% gains ended in 1999 with six losers in a row averaging –5.9% (page 156), up four straight 2005–2007, down 6% in 2008 and 2011, up 7.7% in 2010, down big in four of last five years ◆ Day after Labor Day Dow down 13 of last 16 ◆ S&P opened strong 18 of last 30 years but tends to close weak due to end-of-quarter mutual fund portfolio restructuring, last trading day: S&P down 18 of past 28 ◆ September Triple-Witching Week can be dangerous; week after is pitiful (page 108)

September Vital Statistics

	DJIA	S&P 500	NASDAQ	Russell 1K	Russell 2K
Rank	12	12	12	12	12
Up	30	33	28	22	24
Down	45	41	26	24	22
Average % Change	–0.8	–0.7	–0.9	–0.9	–0.8
Midterm Yr Avg % Chg	–1.2	–0.8	–1.6	–1.8	–1.6
Best & Worst September					
	% Change	% Change	% Change	% Change	% Change
Best	2010 7.7	2010 8.8	1998 13.0	2010 9.0	2010 12.3
Worst	2002 –12.4	1974 –11.9	2001 –17.0	2002 –10.9	2001 –13.6
Best & Worst September Weeks					
Best	9/28/01 7.4	9/28/01 7.8	9/16/11 6.3	9/28/01 7.6	9/28/01 6.9
Worst	9/21/01 –14.3	9/21/01 –11.6	9/21/01 –16.1	9/21/01 –11.7	9/21/01 –14.0
Best & Worst September Days					
Best	9/8/98 5.0	9/30/08 5.4	9/8/98 6.0	9/30/08 5.3	9/18/08 7.0
Worst	9/17/01 –7.1	9/29/08 –8.8	9/29/08 –9.1	9/29/08 –8.7	9/29/08 –6.7
First Trading Day of Monthly Options Expiration Week: 1980–2025					
Record (#Up–#Down)	30–15	26–19	18–27	26–19	22–23
Current streak	U5	U5	D1	U5	U6
Avg % Change	0.05	0.01	–0.17	–0.01	–0.05
Monthly Options Expiration Day: 1980–2025					
Record (#Up–#Down)	21–24	20–25	24–21	21–24	25–20
Current streak	U1	D7	D7	D7	D3
Avg % Change	–0.10	–0.03	–0.04	–0.05	0.01
Monthly Options Expiration Week: 1980–2025					
Record (#Up–#Down)	24–21	25–20	24–21	25–20	24–21
Current streak	U2	U1	U1	U1	U1
Avg % Change	–0.15	–0.03	–0.02	–0.03	0.13
Week After Monthly Options Expiration: 1980–2025					
Record (#Up–#Down)	16–29	14–31	20–25	14–30	15–30
Current streak	U1	U1	U1	U1	D3
Avg % Change	–0.74	–0.81	–0.90	–0.83	–1.44
First Trading Day Performance					
% of Time Up	58.7	60.0	53.7	54.3	50.0
Avg % Change	–0.02	–0.04	–0.09	–0.10	–0.07
Last Trading Day Performance					
% of Time Up	41.3	42.7	51.9	50.0	60.9
Avg % Change	–0.12	–0.06	0.02	0.02	0.20

Dow & S&P 1950–May 2, 2025; NASDAQ 1971–May 2, 2025; Russell 1K & 2K 1979–May 2, 2025.

*September is when leaves and stocks tend to fall;
On Wall Street it's the worst month of all.*

AUGUST/SEPTEMBER 2026

Last Trading Day in August, S&P Up 14 of Last 25 Years, But Down 6 of Last 10

MONDAY 31
D 47.6
S 52.4
N 52.4

Price is a fact. Earnings are an estimate.
— Ralph Acampora (Godfather of Technical Analysis, co-founder CMT Association, Altaira Wealth Management, b. 1941)

First Trading Day in September, S&P Up 18 of Last 30, but Down 10 of Last 17

TUESDAY 1
D 42.9
S 52.4
N 52.4

It is totally unproductive to think the world has been unfair to you. Every tough stretch is an opportunity.
— Charlie Munger (Vice-Chairman Berkshire Hathaway, 2007 Wesco Annual Meeting, 1924–2023)

WEDNESDAY 2
D 66.7
S 42.9
N 42.9

Entrepreneurs who believe they're in business to vanquish the competition are less successful than those who believe their goal is to maximize profits or increase their company's value.
— Kaihan Krippendorff (Business consultant, strategist, author, The Art of the Advantage, The Strategic Learning Center, b. 1971)

THURSDAY 3
D 52.4
S 47.6
N 52.4

At the end of the day, the most important thing is how good are you at risk control. Ninety-percent of any great trader is going to be the risk control.
— Paul Tudor Jones II (Founder Tudor Investment Corporation, b. 1954)

FRIDAY 4
D 47.6
S 47.6
N 52.4

When they stop joking with you is when they don't give a damn about you.
— Sammy Davis Jr. (American entertainer, 1925–1990)

SATURDAY 5

SUNDAY 6

BEST INVESTMENT BOOKS OF THE YEAR

Back by popular demand. After a five-year hiatus and countless requests from readers we present our picks for the Best Investment Books of the Year. This collection represents a broad range of approaches and asset classes. It also runs the gamut from sophisticated institutional level works and technical analysis trading manuals to books geared toward the retail investor. We hope you find these entertaining and beneficial.

How Not to Invest: The ideas, numbers, and behaviors that destroy wealth - and how to avoid them, Barry Ritholtz, Harriman House, $32.99. Ritholtz has done it again. Over the past decade, Barry has built one of the fastest growing RIAs in America. The OG financial blogger and self-proclaimed Director of Cognitive Dissonance shares the master plan he used to grow and manage his firm and his clients' assets. Irreverent, counterintuitive, insightful, engaging. Ritholtz illustrates how to avoid unforced errors, recognize fallacious data, and break bad habits that undermine investment success. The book lays out how to get rich in the markets through a simple, disciplined plan by focusing on what you can control that matters and how stick to it.

The Little Book of Bitcoin: What You Need to Know that Wall Street Has Already Figured Out, Anthony Scaramucci, Wiley, $27.95. A compelling bull thesis for a long and prosperous future for investors in Bitcoin, Scaramucci presents his journey from Bitcoin skeptic to champion. With entertaining stories and insights from early adopters and heavy hitters like Michael Saylor (who wrote the foreword), Peter Diamandis, and Larry Fink, *The Little Book of Bitcoin* is a comprehensive, yet engaging treatise on why Bitcoin is a vessel for innovation and disruption for the foreseeable future. Scaramucci explains the basics of how the blockchain, and coins work in lay terms and shares his views and recommendations on investing and trading in ETFs, futures or actual coins.

The Humble Investor: How to find a winning edge in a surprising world, Daniel Rasmussen, Harriman House, $37.99. Hedge fund manager Daniel Rasmussen breaks down his firm's investing philosophy and the strategies he uses to capture private equity-like returns in public markets. In the process he debunks a host of Wall Street dogma. He takes aim at deep-seated theories like efficient market hypothesis and outdated models like discounted cash flow. In clear, concise language Rasmussen reveals how to time markets and be a real contrarian by examining what works and what doesn't.

Dividend Investing: Dependable Income to Navigate All Market Environments, Jenny Harrington, Harriman House, $26.99. CNBC *Halftime Report* regular Jenny Harrington brings her dividend and income-focused investment philosophy to life. This is the strategy she uses as CEO and Portfolio Manager at Gilman Hill Asset Management to generate growth and income for the firm's clients. This book may be the new authority on dividend investing and how to construct and manage a portfolio of consistent, dependable dividend-paying stocks.

The Elements of Quantitative Investing, Giuseppe A. Paleologo, Wiley, $85.00. This one is heavy. For sophisticated investors and professionals who have no qualms about higher-level math and statistics. Considering Paleologo is currently Head of Quantitative Research at a Balyasny Asset Management with $21 billion AUM, has held senior quantitative research and risk management positions at three of the top four hedge fund platforms in the world and holds a Ph.D and two master's degrees from Stanford, this is a book for serious quants. However, it is accessible and relates what actually works in financial markets from the authors extensive real-world experience. It is a holistic and comprehensive guide to building strategies from modeling to testing to execution and post-trade analysis.

The Ultimate Moving Average Handbook: Bringing Science into the Art of Trend Following, Valeriy Zakamulin and Javier Giner, Palgrave Macmillan, $119.99. New technical analysis books are few and far between these days with many technicians turning to online education solutions. That said, Giner and Zakamulin, both finance professors at renowned European universities, have tackled the vast area of moving averages, arguably the most fundamental and widely used technical indicators. This quintessential guide applies a scientific rigor to trend following with evidence-based analysis that dispels myths and provides an objective framework for developing trend-based trading rules.

SEPTEMBER 2026

Labor Day *(Market Closed)*

MONDAY
7

Take care of your employees and they'll take care of your customers.
— John W. Marriott (Founder Marriott International, 1900–1985)

Day After Labor Day, Dow Up 16 of Last 31, but Down 12 of Last 15

D 57.1
S 47.6
N 52.4

TUESDAY
8

When the time comes to buy, you won't want to.
— Walter Deemer (Retired institutional market analyst 1963–2016, b. 1941)

WEDNESDAY
D 61.9
S 71.4
N 66.7

9

Our philosophy here is identifying change, anticipating change. Change is what drives earnings growth, and if you identify the underlying change, you recognize the growth before the market, and the deceleration of that growth.
— Peter Vermilye (Baring America Asset Management, 1987)

THURSDAY
D 81.0
S 81.0
N 71.4

10

The punishment of wise men who refuse to take part in the affairs of government is to live under the government of unwise men.
— Plato (Greek philosopher, 427–347 BC)

2001 4-Day Closing, Longest Since 9-Day Banking Moratorium in March 1933

D 66.7
S 76.2
N 66.7

FRIDAY
11

Writing a book is an adventure. To begin with it is a toy, an amusement; then it is a mistress, and then a master, and then a tyrant.
— Winston Churchill (British statesman, 1874–1965)

Rosh Hashanah

SATURDAY
12

SUNDAY
13

A CORRECTION FOR ALL SEASONS

While there's a rally for every season (page 76), almost always there's a decline or correction, too. Fortunately, corrections tend to be smaller than rallies, and that's what gives the stock market its long-term upward bias. In each season, the average bounce outdoes the average setback. On average the net gain between the rally and the correction is smallest in summer and fall.

The summer setback tends to be slightly outdone by the average correction in the fall. Tax selling and portfolio cleaning are the usual explanations—individuals sell to register a tax loss and institutions like to get rid of their losers before preparing year-end statements. The October jinx also plays a major part. Since 1964, there have been 20 fall declines of over 10%, and in 11 of them (1966, 1974, 1978, 1979, 1987, 1990, 1997, 2000, 2002, 2008, and 2018) much damage was done in October, where so many bear markets end. Recent October lows were also seen in 1998, 1999, 2004, 2005, 2011, and 2023. Most often, it has paid to buy after fourth-quarter or late third-quarter "waterfall declines" for a rally that may continue into January or even beyond. Covid-19 pandemic economic shutdown in late Q1/early Q2 of 2020 caused the worst winter and spring slumps since 1932. Easy monetary policy and strong corporate earnings spared Q1 2011 and 2012 from a seasonal slump. Tax cut expectations lifted the market in Q4 2017.

SEASONAL CORRECTIONS IN DOW JONES INDUSTRIALS

	WINTER SLUMP Nov/Dec High to Q1 Low	SPRING SLUMP Feb/Mar High to Q2 Low	SUMMER SLUMP May/Jun High to Q3 Low	FALL SLUMP Aug/Sep High to Q4 Low
1964	−0.1%	−2.4%	−1.0%	−2.1%
1965	−2.5	−7.3	−8.3	−0.9
1966	−6.0	−13.2	−17.7	−12.7
1967	−4.2	−3.9	−5.5	−9.9
1968	−8.8	−0.3	−5.5	+0.4
1969	−8.7	−8.7	−17.2	−8.1
1970	−13.8	−20.2	−8.8	−2.5
1971	−1.4	−4.8	−10.7	−13.4
1972	−0.5	−2.6	−6.3	−5.3
1973	−11.0	−12.8	−10.9	−17.3
1974	−15.3	−10.8	−29.8	−27.6
1975	−6.3	−5.5	−9.9	−6.7
1976	−0.2	−5.1	−4.7	−8.9
1977	−8.5	−7.2	−11.5	−10.2
1978	−12.3	−4.0	−7.0	−13.5
1979	−2.5	−5.8	−3.7	−10.9
1980	−10.0	−16.0	−1.7	−6.8
1981	−6.9	−5.1	−18.6	−12.9
1982	−10.9	−7.5	−10.6	−3.3
1983	−4.1	−2.8	−6.8	−3.6
1984	−11.9	−10.5	−8.4	−6.2
1985	−4.8	−4.4	−2.8	−2.3
1986	−3.3	−4.7	−7.3	−7.6
1987	−1.4	−6.6	−1.7	−36.1
1988	−6.7	−7.0	−7.6	−4.5
1989	−1.7	−2.4	−3.1	−6.6
1990	−7.9	−4.0	−17.3	−18.4
1991	−6.3	−3.6	−4.5	−6.3
1992	+0.1	−3.3	−5.4	−7.6
1993	−2.7	−3.1	−3.0	−2.0
1994	−4.4	−9.6	−4.4	−7.1
1995	−0.8	−0.1	−0.2	−2.0
1996	−3.5	−4.6	−7.5	+0.2
1997	−1.8	−9.8	−2.2	−13.3
1998	−7.0	−3.1	−18.2	−13.1
1999	−2.7	−1.7	−8.0	−11.5
2000	−14.8	−7.4	−4.1	−11.8
2001	−14.5	−13.6	−27.4	−16.2
2002	−5.1	−14.2	−26.7	−19.5
2003	−15.8	−5.3	−3.1	−2.1
2004	−3.9	−7.7	−6.3	−5.7
2005	−4.5	−8.5	−3.3	−4.5
2006	−2.4	−5.4	−7.8	−0.4
2007	−3.7	−3.2	−6.1	−8.4
2008	−14.5	−11.0	−20.6	−35.9
2009	−32.0	−6.3	−7.4	−3.5
2010	−6.1	−10.4	−13.1	−1.0
2011	+0.2	−4.0	−16.3	−12.2
2012	+0.5	−8.7	−5.3	−7.8
2013	−0.2	−0.3	−4.1	−5.7
2014	−7.3	−2.6	−3.4	−6.7
2015	−4.9	−3.8	−14.4	−7.6
2016	−12.6	−3.3	−0.9	−4.0
2017	−1.2	−3.4	−1.0	+0.6
2018	−5.3	−9.7	−4.5	−18.5
2019	−13.4	−4.9	−4.8	−4.2
2020	−35.1	−29.1	−6.8	−8.9
2021	−2.0	−0.1	−2.7	−4.6
2022	−10.6	−16.4	−15.7	−14.5
2023	−8.0	−4.3	−2.6	−9.0
2024	−1.2	−5.2	−3.3	−1.3
2025*	−9.3	−16.1*		
Totals	**−428.5%**	**−429.4%**	**−509.5%**	**−533.9%**
Average	**−6.9%**	**−6.9%**	**−8.4%**	**−8.8%**

*As of 5/9/25

SEPTEMBER 2026

Monday Before September Triple Witching, NASDAQ Down 15 of Last 26

MONDAY
D 61.9
S 57.1
N 66.7
14

What investors really get paid for is holding dogs. Small stocks tend to have higher average returns than big stocks, and value stocks tend to have higher average returns than growth stocks.
— Kenneth R. French (Economist, Dartmouth, NBER, b. 1954)

Monthly Expiration Week 2001, Dow Lost 1370 Points (14.3%)
15th Worst Weekly Point Loss Ever, 6th Worst Week Overall

TUESDAY
D 61.9
S 57.1
N 42.9
15

Leadership is the ability to hide your panic from others
— Lao Tzu (Chinese philosopher, Shaolin monk, founder of Taoism, 6th century BCE)

FOMC Meeting

WEDNESDAY
D 76.2
S 71.4
N 81.0
16

Nobody can be a great economist who is only an economist—and I am even tempted to add that the economist who is only an economist is likely to become a nuisance if not a positive danger.
— Friedrich Hayek (Austrian-British economist & philosopher, 1899–1992)

THURSDAY
D 47.6
S 47.6
N 42.9
17

Excellent firms don't believe in excellence—only in constant improvement and constant change.
— Tom Peters (*In Search Of Excellence*, b. 1942)

September Triple Witching, Dow Up 12 of Last 21, Down 9 of Last 13

FRIDAY
D 52.4
S 47.6
N 47.6
18

Some people are so boring they make you waste an entire day in five minutes.
— Jules Renard (French author, 1864–1910)

SATURDAY
19

SUNDAY
20

FIRST-TRADING-DAY-OF-THE-MONTH PHENOMENON

Dow Jones Industrial Average has gained 33626.96 points between September 2, 1997 (7622.42) and May 9, 2025 (41249.38), it is incredible that 9002.23 points were gained on the first trading days of these 333 months. The remaining 6633 trading days combined gained 24624.73 points during the period. This averages out to gains of 27.03 points on first days, in contrast to just 3.71 points on all others.

Note: September 1997 through October 2000 racked up a total gain of 2632.39 Dow points on the first trading days of these 38 months (winners except for seven occasions). But between November 2000 and September 2002, when the 2000–2002 bear markets did the bulk of their damage, frightened investors switched from pouring money into the market on that day to pulling it out, 14 months out of 23, netting a 404.80 Dow point loss. The 2007–2009 bear market lopped off 964.14 Dow points on first days in 17 months November 2007–March 2009. First days had their worst year in 2024, declining six times for a total loss of 865.32 Dow points.

First days of August have performed worst, declining 18 times in the last 27 years. July's first trading day is third best by points but best based upon frequency of gains with only six declines in the last 36 years. In rising market trends first days tend to perform much better as institutions are likely anticipating strong performance at each month's outset. S&P 500 and NASDAQ first days differ slightly from Dow's pattern. August's first trading day is worst for S&P 500. September is worst for NASDAQ while April, August, and October are also net point decliners.

DOW POINTS GAINED FIRST DAY OF MONTH
SEPTEMBER 1997–MAY 9, 2025

	Jan	Feb	Mar	Apr	May	Jun	Jul	Aug	Sep	Oct	Nov	Dec	Totals
1997									257.36	70.24	232.31	189.98	749.89
1998	56.79	201.28	4.73	68.51	83.70	22.42	96.65	−96.55	288.36	−210.09	114.05	16.99	646.84
1999	2.84	−13.13	18.20	46.35	225.65	36.52	95.62	−9.19	108.60	−63.95	−81.35	120.58	486.74
2000	−139.61	100.52	9.62	300.01	77.87	129.87	112.78	84.97	23.68	49.21	−71.67	−40.95	636.30
2001	−140.70	96.27	−45.14	−100.85	163.37	78.47	91.32	−12.80	47.74	−10.73	188.76	−87.60	268.11
2002	51.90	−12.74	262.73	−41.24	113.41	−215.46	−133.47	−229.97	−355.45	346.86	120.61	−33.52	−126.34
2003	265.89	56.01	−53.22	77.73	−25.84	47.55	55.51	−79.83	107.45	194.14	57.34	116.59	819.32
2004	−44.07	11.11	94.22	15.63	88.43	14.20	−101.32	39.45	−5.46	112.38	26.92	162.20	413.69
2005	−53.58	62.00	63.77	−99.46	59.19	82.39	28.47	−17.76	−21.97	−33.22	−33.30	106.70	143.23
2006	129.91	89.09	60.12	35.62	−23.85	91.97	77.80	−59.95	83.00	−8.72	−49.71	−27.80	397.48
2007	11.37	51.99	−34.29	27.95	73.23	40.47	126.81	150.38	91.12	191.92	−362.14	−57.15	311.66
2008	−220.86	92.83	−7.49	391.47	189.87	−134.50	32.25	−51.70	−26.63	−19.59	−5.18	−679.95	−439.48
2009	258.30	−64.03	−299.64	152.68	44.29	221.11	57.06	114.95	−185.68	−203.00	76.71	126.74	299.49
2010	155.91	118.20	78.53	70.44	143.22	−112.61	−41.49	208.44	254.75	41.63	6.13	249.76	1172.91
2011	93.24	148.23	−168.32	56.99	−3.18	−279.65	168.43	−10.75	−119.96	−258.08	−297.05	−25.65	−695.75
2012	179.82	83.55	28.23	52.45	65.69	−274.88	−8.70	−37.62	−54.90	77.98	136.16	−59.98	187.80
2013	308.41	149.21	35.17	−5.69	−138.85	138.46	65.36	128.48	23.65	62.03	69.80	−77.64	758.39
2014	−135.31	−326.05	−153.68	74.95	−21.97	26.46	129.47	−69.93	−30.89	−238.19	−24.28	−51.44	−820.86
2015	9.92	196.09	155.93	−77.94	185.54	29.69	138.40	−91.66	−469.68	−11.99	165.22	168.43	395.95
2016	−276.09	−17.12	348.58	107.66	117.52	2.47	19.38	−27.73	18.42	−54.30	−105.32	68.35	201.82
2017	119.16	26.85	303.31	−13.01	−27.05	135.53	129.64	72.80	39.46	152.51	57.77	−40.76	956.21
2018	104.79	37.32	−420.22	−458.92	−64.10	219.37	35.77	−81.37	−12.34	192.90	264.98	287.97	106.15
2019	18.78	64.22	110.32	329.74	−162.77	4.74	117.47	−280.85	−285.26	−343.79	301.13	−268.37	−394.64
2020	330.36	143.78	1293.96	−973.65	−622.03	91.91	−77.91	236.08	215.61	35.20	423.45	185.28	1282.04
2021	−382.59	229.29	603.14	171.66	238.38	45.86	131.02	−97.31	−48.20	482.54	94.28	−461.68	1006.39
2022	246.76	273.38	−597.65	139.92	84.29	−176.89	321.83	−46.73	145.99	765.38	−79.75	−194.76	881.77
2023	−10.88	6.92	5.14	327.00	−46.46	153.30	10.87	71.15	115.80	−74.15	221.71	294.61	1075.01
2024	25.50	369.54	91.49	−240.52	87.37	−115.29	50.66	−494.82	−626.15	−173.18	288.73	−128.65	−865.32
2025	−151.95	−122.25	−649.12	−11.80	83.60								−852.57
Totals	814.01	2051.86	1137.87	423.68	986.52	303.48	1729.68	−689.82	−421.58	1071.94	1736.31	−141.72	9002.23

SUMMARY FIRST DAYS VS. OTHER DAYS OF MONTH

	# of Days	Total Points Gained	Average Daily Point Gain
First days	333	9002.23	27.03
Other days	6633	24624.73	3.71

SEPTEMBER 2026

Yom Kippur

MONDAY
D 42.9
S 23.8
N 38.1
21

When margin clerks are told to sell, they sell immediately – at any price they can get. That's why so many bottoms are accompanied by some sort of forced selling.
— Walter Deemer (Retired institutional market analyst 1963–2016, b. 1941)

Week After September Triple Witching, Dow Down 26 of Last 35, Average Loss Since 1990, 1.1%

TUESDAY
D 38.1
S 28.6
N 28.6
22

Today's Ponzi-style acute fragility and speculative dynamics dictate that he who panics first panics best.
— Doug Noland (Prudent Bear Funds, *Credit Bubble Bulletin*, 10/26/07)

WEDNESDAY
D 28.6
S 28.6
N 38.1
23

We can guarantee cash benefits as far out and at whatever size you like, but we cannot guarantee their purchasing power.
— Alan Greenspan (Fed Chairman 1987–2006, on funding Social Security to Senate Banking Committee 2/15/05)

End of September Prone to Weakness
From End-of-Q3 Institutional Portfolio Restructuring

THURSDAY
D 47.6
S 47.6
N 52.4
24

Three billion new people will be active on the Internet within ten years, as wireless broadband becomes ubiquitous.
— John Mauldin (*Mauldin Economics*, Millennium Wave Advisors, 2/2/07)

FRIDAY
D 47.6
S 38.1
N 52.4
25

I was absolutely unemotional about numbers. Losses did not have an effect on me because I viewed them as purely probability-driven, which meant sometimes you came up with a loss. Bad days, bad weeks, bad months never impacted the way I approached markets the next day.
— James Leitner (Trader, hedge fund manager, Falcon Management Corp, b. 1953)

SATURDAY
26

October Almanac Investor Sector Seasonalities: See Pages 94, 96, and 98

SUNDAY
27

OCTOBER ALMANAC

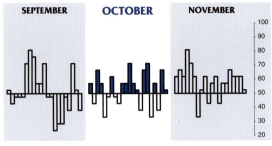

Market Probability Chart above is a graphic representation of the S&P 500 Recent Market Probability Calendar on page 126.

◆ Beware "Octoberphobia" from crashes in 1929, 1987, 554-point drop October 27, 1997, back-to-back massacres 1978 and 1979, Friday the 13th 1989 and the 2008 meltdown ◆ Yet October is a "Bear Killer" and turned the tide in 13 post-WWII bear markets: 1946, 1957, 1960, 1962, 1966, 1974, 1987, 1990, 1998, 2001, 2002, 2011, and 2022 ◆ First October Dow top in 2007 ◆ Worst six months of the year ends with October (page 54) ◆ No longer worst month (pages 52 & 60) ◆ Best Dow, S&P and NASDAQ month from 1993 to 2007 ◆ Midterm election year Octobers since 1950, #1 Dow (+3.2), #1 S&P (+3.0%) and #2 NASDAQ (+3.2%) ◆ October is a great time to buy ◆ Big October Dow gains five years 1999–2003 after atrocious Septembers ◆ Enter Best Six Months earlier using MACD (page 56) ◆ October 2022, best Dow month by points, up over 4000 (+14.0%)

October Vital Statistics

	DJIA		S&P 500		NASDAQ		Russell 1K		Russell 2K	
Rank	7		7		8		7		11	
Up	44		44		29		28		26	
Down	31		31		25		18		20	
Average % Change	0.7		0.9		0.7		0.9		–0.2	
Midterm Yr Avg % Chg	3.2		3.0		3.2		3.9		3.2	
Best & Worst October										
	% Change		% Change		% Change		% Change		% Change	
Best	2022	14.0	1974	16.3	1974	17.2	1982	11.3	2011	15.0
Worst	1987	–23.2	1987	–21.8	1987	–27.2	1987	–21.9	1987	–30.8
Best & Worst October Weeks										
Best	10/11/74	12.6	10/11/74	14.1	10/31/08	10.9	10/31/08	10.8	10/31/08	14.1
Worst	10/10/08	–18.2	10/10/08	–18.2	10/23/87	–19.2	10/10/08	–18.2	10/23/87	–20.4
Best & Worst October Days										
Best	10/13/08	11.1	10/13/08	11.6	10/13/08	11.8	10/13/08	11.7	10/13/08	9.3
Worst	10/19/87	–22.6	10/19/87	–20.5	10/19/87	–11.4	10/19/87	–19.0	10/19/87	–12.5
First Trading Day of Monthly Options Expiration Week: 1980–2025										
Record (#Up-#Down)	34–11		32–13		30–15		33–12		32–13	
Current streak	U3		U3		U3		U3		U3	
Avg % Change	0.66		0.66		0.59		0.64		0.44	
Monthly Options Expiration Day: 1980–2025										
Record (#Up-#Down)	23–22		24–21		25–20		23–22		17–28	
Current streak	U1		U1		U1		U1		D2	
Avg % Change	–0.05		–0.12		–0.07		–0.12		–0.18	
Monthly Options Expiration Week: 1980–2025										
Record (#Up-#Down)	32–13		33–12		27–18		32–13		27–18	
Current streak	U1		U1		U1		U1		U1	
Avg % Change	0.67		0.68		0.72		0.68		0.47	
Week After Monthly Options Expiration: 1980–2025										
Record (#Up-#Down)	22–23		20–25		24–21		20–25		21–24	
Current streak	D2		D2		U1		D2		D2	
Avg % Change	–0.27		–0.28		–0.28		–0.31		–0.51	
First Trading Day Performance										
% of Time Up	49.3		52.0		50.0		54.3		47.8	
Avg % Change	0.10		0.08		–0.08		0.23		–0.20	
Last Trading Day Performance										
% of Time Up	52.0		53.3		61.1		60.9		65.2	
Avg % Change	0.05		0.10		0.35		0.23		0.45	

Dow & S&P 1950–May 2, 2025; NASDAQ 1971–May 2, 2025; Russell 1K & 2K 1979–May 2, 2025.

October has killed many a bear;
Buy techs and small caps and soon wear a grin ear to ear.

SEPTEMBER/OCTOBER 2026

Start Looking for MACD BUY Signals on October 1 (Pages 56, 62, and 64)
Almanac Investor Subscribers Emailed when It Triggers (See Insert)

MONDAY
D 66.7
S 71.4
N 61.9
28

The task of leadership is not to put greatness into humanity, but to elicit it, for the greatness is already there.
— Sir John Buchan (Scottish author, Governor General of Canada 1935–1940, 1875–1940)

TUESDAY
D 57.1
S 52.4
N 38.1
29

You have to keep digging, keep asking questions, because otherwise you'll be seduced or brainwashed into the idea that it's somehow a great privilege, an honor, to report the lies they've been feeding you.
— David Halberstam (Amercian writer, war reporter, 1964 Pulitzer Prize, 1934–2007)

Last Day of Q3, S&P Down 18 of Last 28, But Up 6 of Last 10,
Massive 5.4% Rally in 2008

WEDNESDAY
D 42.9
S 38.1
N 52.4
30

Moses Shapiro (of General Instrument) told me, "Son, this is Talmudic wisdom. Always ask the question 'If not?' Few people have good strategies for when their assumptions are wrong." That's the best business advice I ever got.
— John Malone (CEO of cable giant TCI, Fortune, 2/16/98)

First Trading Day in October Mixed, Dow Down 11 of Last 21, Up 2.7% in 2022

THURSDAY
D 47.6
S 57.1
N 52.4
1

Financial markets will find and exploit hidden flaws, particularly in untested new innovations—and do so at a time that will inflict the most damage to the most people.
— Raymond F. DeVoe, Jr. (Market strategist Jesup & Lamont, The DeVoe Report, 3/30/07, 1929–2014)

October Ends Dow and S&P "Worst Six Months" (Pages 52, 54, 56, 64, and 149)
And NASDAQ "Worst Four Months" (Pages 60, 62, and 150)

FRIDAY
D 38.1
S 42.9
N 47.6
2

Far more money has been lost by investors in preparing for corrections, or anticipating corrections, than has been lost in the corrections themselves.
— Peter Lynch (Fidelity Investments, One Up On Wall Street, b. 1944)

SATURDAY
3

SUNDAY
4

SECTOR SEASONALITY: SELECTED PERCENTAGE PLAYS

Sector seasonality was featured in the first 1968 *Almanac*. A Merrill Lynch study showed that buying seven sectors around September or October and selling in the first few months of 1954–1964 tripled the gains of holding them for 10 years. Over the years we have honed this strategy significantly and now devote a significant portion of our time and resources to investing and trading during positive and negative seasonal periods for the different sector indexes below with highly correlated exchange-traded funds (ETFs).

Updated seasonalities appear in the table below. We specify whether the seasonality starts or finishes in the beginning third (B), middle third (M), or last third (E) of the month. These Selected Percentage Plays are geared to take advantage of the bulk of seasonal sector strength or weakness.

By design, entry points are in advance of the major seasonal moves, providing traders ample opportunity to accumulate positions at favorable prices. Conversely, exit points have been selected to capture the majority of the move.

From the major seasonalities in the table below, we created the Sector Index Seasonality Strategy Calendar on pages 96 and 98. Note the concentration of bullish sector seasonalities during the Best Six Months, November–April, and bearish sector seasonalities during the Worst Six Months, May–October.

Almanac Investor subscribers receive specific entry and exit points for highly correlated ETFs and detailed analysis in our *ETF Trades* email Issue. Visit *www.stocktradersalmanac.com* or see the insert for additional details and a special offer for new subscribers.

SECTOR INDEX SEASONALITY TABLE

			Seasonality				Average % Return[†]		
Ticker	Sector Index	Type	Start		Finish		25-Year	10-Year	5-Year
XCI	Computer Tech	Short	January	B	March	B	–5.13	–1.59	–3.52
XNG	Natural Gas	Long	February	E	June	B	16.19	17.82	22.56
S5INFT	InfoTech	Long	March	M	July	M	10.87	17.16	24.95
UTY	Utilities	Long	March	M	October	B	9.32	8.53	10.47
XCI	Computer Tech	Long	April	M	July	M	9.24	12.50	17.57
BKX	Banking	Short	May	B	July	B	–6.30	–4.39	–5.33
XAU	Gold & Silver	Short	May	M	June	E	–6.83	–7.24	–12.50
S5MATR	Materials	Short	May	M	October	M	–5.10	–2.03	–1.03
XOI	Oil	Short	June	B	August	E	–5.67	–8.98	–9.79
XNG	Natural Gas	Short	June	M	July	E	–6.96	–6.35	–5.36
XAU	Gold & Silver	Long	July	E	December	E	8.18	2.75	4.73
S5INDU	Industrials	Short	July	M	October	B	–3.61	–2.01	–1.77
DJT	Transports	Short	July	M	October	M	–4.72	–1.83	–1.21
BTK	Biotech	Long	August	B	March	B	11.18	4.02	3.83
S5INFT	InfoTech	Long	August	M	January	M	9.67	10.44	11.73
SOX	Semiconductor	Short	August	M	October	E	–7.69	–3.59	–8.39
BKX	Banking	Long	October	B	May	B	11.95	11.81	13.93
XBD	Broker/Dealer	Long	October	B	January	B	12.77	17.21	23.50
XCI	Computer Tech	Long	October	B	January	B	11.41	10.19	13.19
S5COND	Consumer Discretionary	Long	October	B	June	B	13.11	11.64	9.88
S5CONS	Consumer Staples	Long	October	B	June	B	8.47	8.62	9.92
S5HLTH	Healthcare	Long	October	B	May	B	8.74	8.85	12.58
S5INDU	Industrials	Long	October	E	May	M	11.30	10.07	11.37
S5MATR	Materials	Long	October	B	May	B	15.38	12.58	16.27
DRG	Pharmaceutical	Long	October	M	January	B	6.19	5.20	6.90
RMZ	Real Estate	Long	October	E	May	B	10.66	5.58	6.05
SOX	Semiconductor	Long	October	E	February	M	16.63	20.41	27.26
XTC	Telecom	Long	October	M	December	E	5.13	2.09	4.60
DJT	Transports	Long	October	B	May	B	14.74	8.59	11.12
XOI	Oil	Long	December	M	July	B	11.18	10.16	12.44

[†] Average % Return based on full seasonality completion through May 2, 2025

OCTOBER 2026

MONDAY
D 66.7
S 66.7
N 71.4
5

There's no trick to being a humorist when you have the whole government working for you.
— Will Rogers (American humorist and showman, 1879–1935)

TUESDAY
D 61.9
S 57.1
N 52.4
6

You try to be greedy when others are fearful, and fearful when others are greedy.
— Warren Buffett (CEO Berkshire Hathaway, investor and philanthropist, b. 1930)

October 2011, Second Dow Month to Gain 1000 Points

WEDNESDAY
D 33.3
S 33.3
N 42.9
7

The reading of all good books is indeed like a conversation with the noblest men of past centuries, in which they reveal to us the best of their thoughts.
— René Descartes (French philosopher, mathematician & scientist, 1596–1650)

THURSDAY
D 52.4
S 47.6
N 52.4
8

The first human who hurled an insult instead of a stone was the founder of civilization.
— Sigmund Freud (Austrian neurologist, psychiatrist, father of psychoanalysis, 1856–1939)

Dow Lost 18.2% (1874 points) on the Week Ending 10/10/2008
Worst Dow Week in the History of Wall Street

FRIDAY
D 66.7
S 61.9
N 61.9
9

If I had eight hours to chop down a tree, I'd spend six sharpening my axe.
— Abraham Lincoln (16th U.S. President, 1809–1865)

SATURDAY
10

SUNDAY
11

SECTOR INDEX SEASONALITY STRATEGY CALENDAR*

Index		Jan	Feb	Mar	Apr	May	Jun	Jul	Aug	Sep	Oct	Nov	Dec
BKX	L / S										→		
BTK	L / S						→						
S5COND & S5CONS	L / S										→		
S5INDU	L / S							→			→		
DJT	L / S							→			→		
DRG	S										→		
S5HLTH	L / S								→				
S5INFT	L / S			→									
RMZ	L / S										→		

*Graphic representation of the Sector Index Seasonality Percentage Plays on page 94.
L = Long Trade, S = Short Trade, → = Start of Trade

(continued on page 98)

OCTOBER 2026

Columbus Day *(Bond Market Closed)*
Monday Before October Monthly Expiration, Dow Up 33 of 43

MONDAY
D 47.6
S 47.6
N 47.6
12

I never met anyone, or heard of anyone, or read of anyone who was successful who was a pessimist. You have to be positive, or you'll never get anywhere.
— William J. O'Neil (Founder *Investors Business Daily,* investment adivisor, CANSLIM, *How to Make Money in Stocks,* 1933–2023)

TUESDAY
D 33.3
S 42.9
N 52.4
13

The higher a people's intelligence and moral strength, the lower will be the prevailing rate of interest.
— Eugen von Bohm-Bawerk (Austrian economist, *Capital and Interest,* 1851–1914)

WEDNESDAY
D 61.9
S 57.1
N 57.1
14

We all want progress, but if you're on the wrong road, progress means doing an about-turn and walking back to the right road; in that case, the man who turns back soonest is the most progressive.
— C. S. Lewis (Irish novelist, poet, academic, 1898–1963)

THURSDAY
D 52.4
S 57.1
N 57.1
15

If you torture the data long enough, it will confess to anything.
— Ronald Coase (British economist, 1991 Nobel Prize in Economics, 1910–2013)

October Monthly Expiration Day, Dow Down 6 Straight 2005–2010, But Up 10 of Last 14

FRIDAY
D 66.7
S 71.4
N 61.9
16

We were fairly arrogant, until we realized the Japanese were selling quality products for what it cost us to make them.
— Paul A. Allaire (former Chairman of Xerox)

SATURDAY
17

SUNDAY
18

(continued from page 96)

SECTOR INDEX SEASONALITY STRATEGY CALENDAR*

* Graphic representation of the Sector Index Seasonality Percentage Plays on page 94.
L = Long Trade, S = Short Trade, → = Start of Trade

OCTOBER 2026

Crash of October 19, 1987, Dow Down 22.6% in One Day

MONDAY
D 52.4
S 57.1
N 57.1
19

Most people have no idea of the giant capacity we can immediately command when we focus all of our resources on mastering a single area of our lives.
— Anthony Robbins (American author, coach, speaker, and philanthropist, b. 1960)

TUESDAY
D 47.6
S 52.4
N 42.9
20

The critical ingredient is getting off your butt and doing something. It's as simple as that. A lot of people have ideas, but there are few who decide to do something about them now. Not tomorrow. Not next week. But today. The true entrepreneur is a doer, not a dreamer.
— Nolan Bushnell (Founder Atari & Chuck E. Cheese's, b. 1943)

Late October Is Time to Buy Depressed Stocks Especially Techs and Small Caps

WEDNESDAY
D 28.6
S 38.1
N 38.1
21

Whatever method you use to pick stocks…, your ultimate success or failure will depend on your ability to ignore the worries of the world long enough to allow your investments to succeed. It isn't the head but the stomach that determines the fate of the stockpicker.
— Peter Lynch (Fidelity Investments, *Beating the Street*, 1994)

THURSDAY
D 52.4
S 66.7
N 71.4
22

When investment decisions need to consider the speed of light, something is seriously wrong.
— Frank M. Bifulco (Senior Portfolio Manager Alcott Capital Management, *Barron's Letters to the Editor*, 5/24/2010)

FRIDAY
D 57.1
S 71.4
N 66.7
23

If the market prefers a system that looks inefficient that's a good sign that its more efficient than it looks.
— Matt Levine (Bloomberg View columnist, former investment banker, lawyer & high-school Latin teacher)

SATURDAY
24

November Almanac Investor Sector Seasonalities: See Pages 94, 96, and 98

SUNDAY
25

NOVEMBER ALMANAC

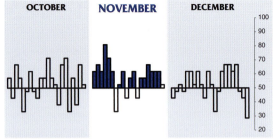

Market Probability Chart above is a graphic representation of the S&P 500 Recent Market Probability Calendar on page 126.

◆ #1 S&P and Dow month since 1950, #2 on NASDAQ since 1971 (pages 52 & 60) ◆ Start of the "Best Six Months" of the year (page 54), NASDAQ's Best Eight Months and Best Three (pages 149 & 150) ◆ Simple MACD timing indicator nearly triples "Best Six Months" strategy (page 56), about triples NASDAQ's Best Eight (page 62) ◆ Day before and after Thanksgiving Day combined, only 19 losses in 73 years (page 106) ◆ Week before Thanksgiving Dow up 21 of last 32, down 6 of last 8 ◆ Midterm election year Novembers rank #2 Dow (+2.6%), #2 S&P (+2.7%), NASDAQ #1 (+3.5%) ◆ NASDAQ down 22.9% in November 2000 (undecided election, tech bubble burst) (page 167)

November Vital Statistics

	DJIA	S&P 500	NASDAQ	Russell 1K	Russell 2K
Rank	1	1	2	1	1
Up	52	52	39	35	32
Down	23	23	15	11	14
Average % Change	1.9	1.9	2.1	2.2	2.6
Midterm Yr Avg % Chg	2.6	2.7	3.5	2.8	3.2
Best & Worst November					
	% Change	% Change	% Change	% Change	% Change
Best	2020 11.8	2020 10.8	2001 14.2	2020 11.6	2020 18.3
Worst	1973 −14.0	1973 −11.4	2000 −22.9	2000 −9.3	2008 −12.0
Best & Worst November Weeks					
Best	11/28/08 9.7	11/28/08 12.0	11/28/08 10.9	11/28/08 12.5	11/28/08 16.4
Worst	11/21/08 −5.3	11/21/08 −8.4	11/10/00 −12.2	11/21/08 −8.8	11/21/08 −11.0
Best & Worst November Days					
Best	11/13/08 6.7	11/13/08 6.9	11/10/22 7.4	11/13/08 7.0	11/13/08 8.5
Worst	11/20/08 −5.6	11/20/08 −6.7	11/19/08 −6.5	11/20/08 −6.9	11/19/08 −7.9
First Trading Day of Monthly Options Expiration Week: 1980–2025					
Record (#Up–#Down)	25–20	20–25	17–28	22–23	20–25
Current streak	U2	U1	U1	U1	D1
Avg % Change	−0.01	−0.07	−0.18	−0.07	−0.05
Monthly Options Expiration Day: 1980–2025					
Record (#Up–#Down)	28–17	26–19	24–21	26–19	26–18
Current streak	D1	D1	D1	D1	D1
Avg % Change	0.18	0.12	−0.01	0.12	0.14
Monthly Options Expiration Week: 1980–2025					
Record (#Up–#Down)	27–18	26–19	25–20	25–20	22–23
Current streak	D1	D1	D1	D1	D1
Avg % Change	0.23	0.07	0.04	0.06	−0.15
Week After Monthly Options Expiration: 1980–2025					
Record (#Up–#Down)	27–18	29–16	30–15	29–16	28–17
Current streak	U3	U3	U3	U3	U3
Avg % Change	0.60	0.58	0.65	0.60	0.80
First Trading Day Performance					
% of Time Up	65.3	65.3	66.7	73.9	65.2
Avg % Change	0.31	0.32	0.34	0.41	0.36
Last Trading Day Performance					
% of Time Up	56.0	53.3	61.1	47.8	65.2
Avg % Change	0.13	0.15	0.001	0.06	0.10

Dow & S&P 1950–May 2, 2025; NASDAQ 1971–May 2, 2025; Russell 1K & 2K 1979–May 2, 2025.

Astute investors always smile and remember,
When stocks seasonally start soaring, and salute November.

OCTOBER/NOVEMBER 2026

MONDAY
D 38.1
S 33.3
N 47.6
26

No profession requires more hard work, intelligence, patience, and mental discipline than successful speculation.
— Robert Rhea (Economist, trader, *The Dow Theory*, 1887–1952)

TUESDAY
D 66.7
S 57.1
N 52.4
27

Markets are constantly in a state of uncertainty and flux and money is made by discounting the obvious and betting on the unexpected.
— George Soros (Financier, philanthropist, political activist, author and philosopher, b. 1930)

FOMC Meeting

WEDNESDAY
D 38.1
S 38.1
N 57.1
28

Marketing is our No. 1 priority… A marketing campaign isn't worth doing unless it serves three purposes. It must grow the business, create news, and enhance our image.
— James Robinson III (American Express)

97th Anniversary of 1929 Crash, Dow Down 23.0% in Two Days, October 28 & 29

THURSDAY
D 61.9
S 66.7
N 66.7
29

Never bet on the end of the world, because it only happens once, and even if it does, who are you going to settle the trade with?
— Arthur D. Cashin, Jr. (Legendary NYSE floor trader, director of floor operations UBS Financial Services, 1941–2024)

FRIDAY
D 47.6
S 52.4
N 47.6
30

True wealth is created not by seeking the approval of others. True wealth is found when you make your own path.
— Anthony Scaramucci (American financier and broadcaster, Founder Skybridge Capital and SALT, *The Little Book of Bitcoin*, b. 1964)

Halloween

SATURDAY
31

Daylight Saving Time Ends

SUNDAY
1

MIDTERM ELECTION TIME UNUSUALLY BULLISH

Presidential election years tend to produce high drama and frenetic campaigns. Midterm years with only local or state candidates running are less stressful. Could this be the reason for the bullishness that seems to occur in the five days before and three days after midterm congressional elections? We don't think so.

So many bear markets seem to occur in midterm years, very often bottoming in October. Also, major military involvements began or were in their early stages in midterm years, such as World War II, Korea, Vietnam, Kuwait, and Iraq. Solidly bullish midterm years as 1954, 1958, 1986, 2006, 2010, and 2014 were exceptions.

With so many negative occurrences in midterm years, perhaps the opportunity for investors to make a change for the better by casting their votes translates into an inner bullish feeling before and after midterm elections.

An impressive 2.8% has been the average gain during the eight trading days surrounding midterm election days since 1934. This is equivalent to roughly 1200 Dow points at present levels. There was only one losing period in 1994 when the Republicans took control of both the House and the Senate for the first time in 40 years.

Five other midterm switches occurred in 1946, when control of Congress passed to the Republicans for just two years; in 1954, when Democrats took back control; in 2006 when Democrats regained control; in 2010, when Republicans reclaimed the House; in 2018 when Democrats recaptured the majority; and when Republicans reclaimed the House in 2022.

There were 12 occasions when the percentage of House seats lost by the president's party was in double digits. The average market gain during the eight-day trading period was 2.3%. In contrast, the average gain in the 10 occasions when there were no losses, or losses were in single digits, gains averaged 3.4%.

BULLS WIN BATTLE BETWEEN ELEPHANTS AND DONKEYS

Midterm Year	Dow Jones Industrials 5 Trading Days Before E. Day	Dow Jones Industrials 3 Trading Days After E. Day	% Change	President's Party % Seats Lost	President in Power
1934	93.36	99.02	6.1%	2.9%	Dem
1938	152.21	158.41	4.1	−21.3	Dem
1942	113.11	116.12	2.7	−16.9	Dem
1946	164.20	170.79	4.0	−22.6	**Dem***
1950	225.69	229.29	1.6	−11.0	Dem
1954	356.32	366.00	2.7	−8.1	**Rep***
1958	536.88	554.26	3.2	−23.9	Rep
1962	588.98	616.13	4.6	−1.5	Dem
1966	809.63	819.09	1.2	−15.9	Dem
1970	754.45	771.97	2.3	−6.3	Rep
1974	659.34	667.16	1.2	−25.0	Rep
1978	792.45	807.09	1.8	−5.1	Dem
1982	1006.07	1051.78	4.5	−13.5	Rep
1986	1845.47	1886.53	2.2	−2.7	Rep
1990	2448.02	2488.61	1.7	−4.6	Rep
1994	3863.37	3801.47	−1.6	−20.9	**Dem***
1998	8366.04	8975.46	7.3	2.4	Dem
2002	8368.94	8537.13	2.0	3.6	Rep
2006	12080.73	12108.43	0.2	−12.9	**Rep***
2010	11169.46	11444.08	2.5	−24.6	**Dem***
2014	17005.75	17573.93	3.3	−6.5	**Dem***
2018	24874.64	25989.30	4.5	−17.4	**Rep***
2022	32653.20	33747.86	3.4	− 3.2	**Dem***
		Total	65.5%		
		Average	2.8%	−11.1	

* Control switches to other party

NOVEMBER 2026

First Trading Day in November, Dow Up 12 of Last 16

MONDAY
D 61.9
S 61.9
N 61.9
2

No man's life, liberty, or property is safe while Congress is in session.
— Mark Twain (American novelist and satirist, pen name of Samuel Longhorne Clemens, 1835–1910)

Election Day

TUESDAY
D 61.9
S 66.7
N 61.9
3

Trending markets require different strategies than non-trending markets.
— Larry Williams (Legendary trader, author, politician, b. 1942)

November Begins Dow and S&P "Best Six Months" (Pages 52, 54, 56, 64, and 149) And NASDAQ "Best Eight Months" (Pages 60, 62, and 150)

WEDNESDAY
D 66.7
S 61.9
N 57.1
4

*If you don't make bold moves, you don't get f***ing anywhere. You've got to push the limits.*
— Keith Richards (Rolling Stones, *Life*, b. 1943)

THURSDAY
D 71.4
S 81.0
N 71.4
5

What lies behind us and what lies before us are tiny matters, compared to what lies within us.
— Ralph Waldo Emerson (American author, poet and philosopher, *Self-Reliance*, 1803–1882)

FRIDAY
D 76.2
S 71.4
N 76.2
6

Any fool can buy. It is the wise man who knows how to sell.
— Albert W. Thomas (Trader, investor, Over My Shoulder, mutualfundmagic.com, *If It Doesn't Go Up, Don't Buy It!*, b. 1927)

SATURDAY
7

SUNDAY
8

TRADERS FEAST ON SMALL STOCKS THANKSGIVING THROUGH SANTA CLAUS RALLY

Thanksgiving kicks off a run of solid bullish seasonal patterns. November–January is the year's best consecutive 3-month span (page 149). Then there's the January Effect (pages 112 & 114) of small caps outperforming large caps in January, which nowadays begins in mid-December.

And of course, the "Santa Claus Rally," (page 118) invented and named by our late founder Yale Hirsch in 1972 in the *Almanac* and often misunderstood, is the short, sweet rally that runs from the last five trading days of the year to the first two trading days of the New Year. Pop also coined the phrase: *"If Santa Claus should fail to call, bears may come to Broad and Wall."*

We have combined these seasonal occurrences into one trade: Buy the Tuesday before Thanksgiving and hold until the second trading day of the New Year. Our good friend and renowned technician and options guru Larry McMillan of the *Options Strategist* opened our eyes to this trade and runs it with options on iShares Russell 2000 (IWM) starting on the day before Thanksgiving.

We feature the Russell 2000 here as this trade produces a higher magnitude of returns for the small cap index with practically the same plurality of gains as the S&P. Since 1979 the Russell 2000 is up 76.1% of the time, 35 of 46 years, with an average gain of 3.1% from the Tuesday before Thanksgiving to the second trading day of the year. For comparison S&P 500 is up 78.7% of the time, 59 of 75 years, average gain 2.5% and NASDAQ is up 75.9% of the time, 41 of 54 years, average gain 2.9%.

RUSSELL 2000 THANKSGIVING–SANTA CLAUS RALLY TRADE

Year	Tuesday B4 Thanksgiving	2nd Trading Day New Year	% Change
1979	50.00	54.11	8.22%
1980	76.92	76.28	–0.83
1981	73.94	72.78	–1.57
1982	85.36	89.08	4.36
1983	113.40	113.66	0.23
1984	101.01	101.27	0.26
1985	123.42	130.88	6.04
1986	138.49	140.76	1.64
1987	115.58	126.13	9.13
1988	139.87	148.39	6.09
1989	166.62	170.79	2.50
1990	124.13	130.35	5.01
1991	175.50	192.09	9.45
1992	210.79	220.08	4.41
1993	248.12	256.97	3.57
1994	242.26	247.65	2.22
1995	301.12	315.21	4.68
1996	351.37	361.85	2.98
1997	426.91	437.06	2.38
1998	396.60	422.09	6.43
1999	454.45	478.38	5.27
2000	466.79	484.39	3.77
2001	453.90	495.51	9.17
2002	398.32	390.31	–2.01
2003	543.18	568.92	4.74
2004	624.53	628.54	0.64
2005	682.55	689.25	0.98
2006	792.17	789.95	–0.28
2007	749.33	745.01	–0.58
2008	443.18	505.03	13.96
2009	592.58	638.49	7.75
2010	719.92	785.83	9.16
2011	696.26	747.28	7.33
2012	793.81	872.60	9.93
2013	1134.53	1156.09	1.90
2014	1186.33	1181.35	–0.42
2015	1188.81	1110.44	–6.59
2016	1334.34	1387.95	4.02
2017	1518.89	1552.58	2.22
2018	1469.01	1330.83	–9.41
2019	1624.23	1660.87	2.26
2020	1853.53	1979.11	6.78
2021	2327.86	2268.87	–2.53
2022	1860.44	1772.54	–4.72
2023	1783.26	1959.20	9.87
2024	2424.31	2268.47	–6.43
		Average	3.13%
		Median	3.27%
		Up	35
		Down	11
		Win %	76.09%
		Avg Win	5.12%
		Avg Loss	–3.22%

© Hirsch Holdings Inc. & StockTradersAlmanac.com. All rights reserved.

NOVEMBER 2026

Week Before November Options Monthly Expiration, S&P 500 Up 11 of Last 16

MONDAY 9
D 66.7
S 61.9
N 66.7

We may face more inflation pressure than currently shows up in formal data.
— William Poole (Economist, president Federal Reserve Bank St. Louis 1998–2008, June 2006 speech, b. 1937)

TUESDAY 10
D 47.6
S 33.3
N 33.3

People won't have time for you if you're always angry or complaining.
— Professsor Stephen Hawking (English theoretical physicist, cosmologist, and author, 1942–2018)

Veterans' Day

WEDNESDAY 11
D 38.1
S 52.4
N 57.1

Complexity is the enemy of execution.
— Anthony Robbins (American author, coach, speaker, and philanthropist, b. 1960)

THURSDAY 12
D 66.7
S 61.9
N 61.9

If you are ready to give up everything else to study the whole history of the market as carefully as a medical student studies anatomy and you have the cool nerves of a great gambler, the sixth sense of a clairvoyant, and the courage of a lion, you have a ghost of a chance.
— Bernard Baruch (Financier, speculator, statesman, presidential adviser, 1870–1965)

FRIDAY 13
D 42.9
S 42.9
N 38.1

If banking institutions are protected by the taxpayer and they are given free reign to speculate, I may not live long enough to see the crisis, but my soul is going to come back and haunt you.
— Paul A. Volcker (Fed Chairman 1979–1987, Chair Economic Recovery Advisory Board, 2/2/2010, 1927–2019)

SATURDAY 14

SUNDAY 15

TRADING THE THANKSGIVING MARKET

For 35 years the "holiday spirit" gave Wednesday before Thanksgiving and Friday after a great track record, except for two occasions. Publishing it in the 1987 *Almanac* was the "kiss of death." Since 1988 Wednesday–Friday gained 21 of 37 times with a total Dow point gain of 81.85. The best strategy appears to be coming into the week long and exiting into strength before the holiday. Omicron Covid-19 variant cancelled Thanksgiving in 2021.

DOW JONES INDUSTRIALS BEFORE AND AFTER THANKSGIVING

	Tuesday Before	Wednesday Before		Friday After	Total Gain Dow Points	Dow Close	Next Monday
1952	−0.18	1.54		1.22	2.76	283.66	0.04
1953	1.71	0.65		2.45	3.10	280.23	1.14
1954	3.27	1.89		3.16	5.05	387.79	0.72
1955	4.61	0.71		0.26	0.97	482.88	−1.92
1956	−4.49	−2.16		4.65	2.49	472.56	−2.27
1957	−9.04	10.69		3.84	14.53	449.87	−2.96
1958	−4.37	8.63		8.31	16.94	557.46	2.61
1959	2.94	1.41		1.42	2.83	652.52	6.66
1960	−3.44	1.37		4.00	5.37	606.47	−1.04
1961	−0.77	1.10		2.18	3.28	732.60	−0.61
1962	6.73	4.31		7.62	11.93	644.87	−2.81
1963	32.03	−2.52		9.52	7.00	750.52	1.39
1964	−1.68	−5.21		−0.28	−5.49	882.12	−6.69
1965	2.56	N/C		−0.78	−0.78	948.16	−1.23
1966	−3.18	1.84		6.52	8.36	803.34	−2.18
1967	13.17	3.07		3.58	6.65	877.60	4.51
1968	8.14	−3.17	T	8.76	5.59	985.08	−1.74
1969	−5.61	3.23	H	1.78	5.01	812.30	−7.26
1970	5.21	1.98	A	6.64	8.62	781.35	12.74
1971	−5.18	0.66	N	17.96	18.62	816.59	13.14
1972	8.21	7.29	K	4.67	11.96	1025.21	−7.45
1973	−17.76	10.08	S	−0.98	9.10	854.00	−29.05
1974	5.32	2.03	G	−0.63	1.40	618.66	−15.64
1975	9.76	3.15	I	2.12	5.27	860.67	−4.33
1976	−6.57	1.66	V	5.66	7.32	956.62	−6.57
1977	6.41	0.78	I	1.12	1.90	844.42	−4.85
1978	−1.56	2.95	N	3.12	6.07	810.12	3.72
1979	−6.05	−1.80	G	4.35	2.55	811.77	16.98
1980	3.93	7.00		3.66	10.66	993.34	−23.89
1981	18.45	7.90	D	7.80	15.70	885.94	3.04
1982	−9.01	9.01	A	7.36	16.37	1007.36	−4.51
1983	7.01	−0.20	Y	1.83	1.63	1277.44	−7.62
1984	9.83	6.40		18.78	25.18	1220.30	−7.95
1985	0.12	18.92		−3.56	15.36	1472.13	−14.22
1986	6.05	4.64		−2.53	2.11	1914.23	−1.55
1987	40.45	−16.58		−36.47	−53.05	1910.48	−76.93
1988	11.73	14.58		−17.60	−3.02	2074.68	6.76
1989	7.25	17.49		18.77	36.26	2675.55	19.42
1990	−35.15	9.16		−12.13	−2.97	2527.23	5.94
1991	14.08	−16.10		−5.36	−21.46	2894.68	40.70
1992	25.66	17.56		15.94	33.50	3282.20	22.96
1993	3.92	13.41		−3.63	9.78	3683.95	−6.15
1994	−91.52	−3.36		33.64	30.28	3708.27	31.29
1995	40.46	18.06		7.23*	25.29	5048.84	22.04
1996	−19.38	−29.07		22.36*	−6.71	6521.70	N/C
1997	41.03	−14.17		28.35*	14.18	7823.13	189.98
1998	−73.12	13.13		18.80*	31.93	9333.08	−216.53
1999	−93.89	12.54		−19.26*	−6.72	10988.91	−40.99
2000	31.85	−95.18		70.91*	−24.27	10470.23	75.84
2001	−75.08	−66.70		125.03*	58.33	9959.71	23.04
2002	−172.98	255.26		−35.59*	219.67	8896.09	−33.52
2003	16.15	15.63	D	2.89*	18.52	9782.46	116.59
2004	3.18	27.71	A	1.92*	29.63	10522.23	−46.33
2005	51.15	44.66	Y	15.53*	60.19	10931.62	−40.90
2006	5.05	5.36		−46.78*	−41.42	12280.17	−158.46
2007	51.70	−211.10		181.84*	−29.26	12980.88	−237.44
2008	36.08	247.14		102.43*	349.57	8829.04	−679.95
2009	−17.24	30.69		−154.48*	−123.79	10309.92	34.92
2010	−142.21	150.91		−95.28*	55.63	11092.00	−39.51
2011	−53.59	−236.17		−25.77*	−261.94	11231.78	291.23
2012	−7.45	48.38		172.79*	221.17	13009.68	−42.31
2013	0.26	24.53		−10.92*	13.61	16086.41	−77.64
2014	−2.96	−2.69		15.99*	13.30	17828.24	−51.44
2015	19.51	1.20		−14.90*	−13.70	17798.49	−78.57
2016	67.18	59.31		68.96*	128.27	19152.14	−54.24
2017	160.50	−64.65		31.81*	−32.84	23557.99	22.79
2018	−551.80	−0.95		−178.74*	−179.69	24285.95	354.29
2019	55.21	42.32		−112.59*	−70.27	28051.41	−268.37
2020	454.97	−173.77		37.90*	−135.87	29910.37	−271.73
2021	194.55	−9.42		−905.04*	−914.46	34899.34	236.60
2022	397.82	95.96		152.97*	248.93	34347.03	−497.57
2023	−62.75	184.74		117.12*	301.86	35390.15	−56.68
2024	123.74	−138.28		188.62*	50.34	44910.65	−128.65

Shortened trading day

NOVEMBER 2026

Monday Before November Monthly Expiration, Dow Up 14 of Last 21, 2008 −2.6%, 2018 −2.3%

MONDAY
D 66.7
S 57.1
N 57.1
16

There are no secrets to success. Don't waste your time looking for them. Success is the result of perfection, hard work, learning from failure, loyalty to those for whom you work, and persistence.
— General Colin Powell (Chairman, Joint Chiefs 1989–1993, secretary of state 2001–2005, NY Times, 10/22/2008, b. 1937)

Week Before Thanksgiving, Dow Up 21 of Last 32, Down 6 of Last 8 2003 −1.4%, 2004 −0.8%, 2008 −5.3%, 2011 −2.9%, 2012 −1.8%, 2018 −2.2%

TUESDAY
D 57.1
S 61.9
N 66.7
17

In an uptrend, if a higher high is made but fails to carry through, and prices dip below the previous high, the trend is apt to reverse. The converse is true for downtrends.
— Victor Sperandeo (*Trader Vic—Methods of a Wall Street Master*)

Trading Thanksgiving Market: Long into Weakness Prior, Exit into Strength (Page 106)

WEDNESDAY
D 33.3
S 42.9
N 42.9
18

Change is the law of life. And those who look only to the past or present are certain to miss the future.
— John F. Kennedy (35th U.S. President, 1917–1963)

THURSDAY
D 52.4
S 57.1
N 57.1
19

It is a funny thing about life; if you refuse to accept anything but the best, you very often get it.
— W. Somerset Maugham (English writer, 1874–1965)

November Monthly Expiration Day, Dow Up 16 of Last 23 Dow Surged in 2008, Up 494 Points (6.5%)

FRIDAY
D 61.9
S 57.1
N 66.7
20

Anyone who has achieved excellence knows that it comes as a result of ceaseless concentration.
— Louise Brooks (Actress, 1906-1985)

SATURDAY
21

SUNDAY
22

AURA OF THE TRIPLE WITCH—4TH QUARTER MOST BULLISH: DOWN WEEKS TRIGGER MORE WEAKNESS WEEK AFTER

Options expire the third Friday of every month but in March, June, September, and December a powerful coven gathers. Since the S&P index futures began trading on April 21, 1982, stock options, index options, and index futures, all expire at the same time four times each year—known as Triple Witching. Traders have long sought to understand and master the magic of this quarterly phenomenon.

We have analyzed what the market does prior, during, and following Triple-Witching expirations in search of consistent trading patterns. Here are some of our findings of how the Dow Jones Industrials perform around Triple-Witching Week (TWW).

- Since 1991, TWW is most bullish in Q1 and Q4.
- Following weeks became more bearish. Since Q1 2000 only 43 of 100 were up, and 20 occurred in December, 12 in March, 7 in September, 4 in June.
- TWWs have tended to be down in flat periods and dramatically so during bear markets.
- Down weeks tend to follow down TWWs, creating an interesting pattern. Since 1991, of 50 down TWWs, 29 following weeks were also down. This is surprising inasmuch as the previous decade had an exactly opposite pattern: There were 13 down TWWs then, but 12 up weeks followed them.
- TWWs in Q2 and Q3 (Worst Six Months May–October) are much weaker and the weeks following, horrendous. But in Q1 and Q4 (Best Six Months November–April) only the week after Q1 expiration is negative.

Throughout the *Almanac* you will see notations on the performance of Mondays and Fridays of TWW as we place considerable significance on the beginnings and ends of weeks (pages 78 and 143–146).

TRIPLE-WITCHING WEEK AND WEEK AFTER DOW POINT CHANGES

	Expiration Week Q1	Week After	Expiration Week Q2	Week After	Expiration Week Q3	Week After	Expiration Week Q4	Week After
1991	−6.93	−89.36	−34.98	−58.81	33.54	−13.19	20.12	167.04
1992	40.48	−44.95	−69.01	−2.94	21.35	−76.73	9.19	12.97
1993	43.76	−31.60	−10.24	−3.88	−8.38	−70.14	10.90	6.15
1994	32.95	−120.92	3.33	−139.84	58.54	−101.60	116.08	26.24
1995	38.04	65.02	86.80	75.05	96.85	−33.42	19.87	−78.76
1996	114.52	51.67	55.78	−50.60	49.94	−15.54	179.53	76.51
1997	−130.67	−64.20	14.47	−108.79	174.30	4.91	−82.01	−76.98
1998	303.91	−110.35	−122.07	231.67	100.16	133.11	81.87	314.36
1999	27.20	−81.31	365.05	−303.00	−224.80	−524.30	32.73	148.33
2000	666.41	517.49	−164.76	−44.55	−293.65	−79.63	−277.95	200.60
2001	−821.21	−318.63	−353.36	−19.05	−1369.70	611.75	224.19	101.65
2002	34.74	−179.56	−220.42	−10.53	−326.67	−284.57	77.61	−207.54
2003	662.26	−376.20	83.63	−211.70	173.27	−331.74	236.06	46.45
2004	−53.48	26.37	6.31	−44.57	−28.61	−237.22	106.70	177.20
2005	−144.69	−186.80	110.44	−325.23	−36.62	−222.35	97.01	7.68
2006	203.31	0.32	122.63	−25.46	168.66	−52.67	138.03	−102.30
2007	−165.91	370.60	215.09	−279.22	377.67	75.44	110.80	−84.78
2008	410.23	−144.92	−464.66	−496.18	−33.55	−245.31	−50.57	−63.56
2009	54.40	497.80	−259.53	−101.34	214.79	−155.01	−142.61	191.21
2010	117.29	108.38	239.57	−306.83	145.08	252.41	81.59	81.58
2011	−185.88	362.07	52.45	−69.78	516.96	−737.61	−317.87	427.61
2012	310.60	−151.89	212.97	−126.39	−13.90	−142.34	55.83	−252.73
2013	117.04	−2.08	−270.78	110.20	75.03	−192.85	465.78	257.27
2014	237.10	20.29	171.34	−95.24	292.23	−166.59	523.97	248.91
2015	378.34	−414.99	117.11	−69.27	−48.51	−69.91	−136.66	423.62
2016	388.99	−86.57	−190.18	−274.41	38.35	137.65	86.56	90.40
2017	11.64	−317.90	112.31	10.48	470.55	81.25	322.58	102.32
2018	−389.23	−1413.31	−226.05	−509.59	588.83	−285.19	−1655.14	617.03
2019	398.63	−346.55	629.52	−119.17	−284.45	−114.82	319.71	190.17
2020	−4011.64	2462.80	265.92	−855.91	−8.22	−483.46	132.68	20.82
2021	−150.67	444.91	−1189.52	1143.76	−22.84	213.12	−605.55	585.12
2022	1810.74	106.31	−1504.01	1611.90	−1329.29	−1232.01	−556.00	283.47
2023	−47.66	375.55	422.34	−571.69	41.65	−654.40	1057.29	80.81
2024	−7.92	761.13	561.17	−31.47	669.58	249.64	−987.80	151.95
2025	497.16	−401.45						
Up	23	15	20	6	20	9	24	27
Down	12	20	14	28	14	25	10	7

NOVEMBER 2026

MONDAY
D 71.4
S 66.7
N 57.1
23

The worst trades are generally when people freeze and start to pray and hope rather than take some action.
— Robert Mnuchin (Partner Goldman Sachs)

TUESDAY
D 71.4
S 61.9
N 66.7
24

I hate to be wrong. That has aborted many a tempting error, but not all of them. But I hate much more to stay wrong.
— Paul A. Samuelson (American economist, 12/23/03 University of Kansas interview, 1915–2009)

WEDNESDAY
D 66.7
S 61.9
N 66.7
25

It is better to be out wishing you were in, than in wishing you were out.
— Albert W. Thomas (Trader, investor, Over My Shoulder, mutualfundmagic.com, If It Doesn't Go Up, Don't Buy It!, b. 1927)

Thanksgiving *(Market Closed)*

THURSDAY
26

Remember to look up at the stars and not down at your feet.
— Professsor Stephen Hawking (English theoretical physicist, cosmologist, and author, 1942–2018)

(Shortened Trading Day)

FRIDAY
D 61.9
S 61.9
N 57.1
27

There's no such thing as a loss, it's just an unmonetized lesson.
— Ted Weschler (Investment Manager at Berkshire Hathaway, b. 1962)

SATURDAY
28

December Almanac Investor Sector Seasonalities: See Pages 94, 96, and 98

SUNDAY
29

DECEMBER ALMANAC

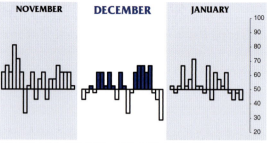

Market Probability Chart above is a graphic representation of the S&P 500 Recent Market Probability Calendar on page 126.

◆ #3 S&P (+1.4%) and Dow (+1.5%) month since 1950 (page 52), #3 NASDAQ (+1.5%) since 1971 ◆ 2018 worst December since 1931, Dow –8.7%, S&P –9.2%, NASDAQ –9.5% (pages 156, 162, & 166) ◆ "Free lunch" served on Wall Street before Christmas (page 116) ◆ Small caps start to outperform larger caps near middle of month (pages 112 and 114) ◆ "Santa Claus Rally" visible in graph above and on page 118 ◆ In 1998 was part of best fourth quarter since 1928 (page 180) ◆ Fourth quarter expiration week most bullish Triple-Witching Week, Dow up 24 of last 34 (page 108) ◆ Midterm election year December rankings: #5 Dow (+0.6%), #5 S&P (+0.8%) and #8 NASDAQ (–0.9%)

December Vital Statistics

	DJIA	S&P 500	NASDAQ	Russell 1K	Russell 2K
Rank	3	3	3	3	2
Up	52	55	33	34	34
Down	23	20	21	12	12
Average % Change	1.5	1.4	1.5	1.2	2.1
Midterm Yr Avg % Chg	0.6	0.8	–0.9	–0.5	–0.3
Best & Worst December					
	% Change	% Change	% Change	% Change	% Change
Best	1991 9.5	1991 11.2	1999 22.0	1991 11.2	1999 11.2
Worst	2018 –8.7	2018 –9.2	2002 –9.7	2018 –9.3	2018 –12.0
Best & Worst December Weeks					
Best	12/2/11 7.0	12/2/11 7.4	12/8/00 10.3	12/2/11 7.4	12/2/11 10.3
Worst	12/4/87 –7.5	12/6/74 –7.1	12/15/00 –9.1	12/21/18 –7.1	12/21/18 –8.4
Best & Worst December Days					
Best	12/26/18 5.0	12/16/08 5.1	12/5/00 10.5	12/16/08 5.2	12/16/08 6.7
Worst	12/1/08 –7.7	12/1/08 –8.9	12/1/08 –9.0	12/1/08 –9.1	12/1/08 –11.9
First Trading Day of Monthly Options Expiration Week: 1980–2025					
Record (#Up–#Down)	26–19	27–18	22–23	27–18	21–24
Current streak	D1	U3	U3	U3	U3
Avg % Change	0.12	0.10	–0.03	0.08	–0.18
Monthly Options Expiration Day: 1980–2025					
Record (#Up–#Down)	27–18	29–16	29–16	29–16	27–18
Current streak	U2	U1	U2	U1	U1
Avg % Change	0.15	0.22	0.22	0.21	0.31
Monthly Options Expiration Week: 1980–2025					
Record (#Up–#Down)	32–13	30–15	25–20	29–16	23–22
Current streak	D1	D1	D1	D1	D1
Avg % Change	0.45	0.47	0.08	0.43	0.39
Week After Monthly Options Expiration: 1980–2025					
Record (#Up–#Down)	34–10	29–16	31–14	29–16	32–13
Current streak	U12	U2	U2	U2	U2
Avg % Change	0.82	0.60	0.77	0.62	0.97
First Trading Day Performance					
% of Time Up	46.7	49.3	59.3	50.0	47.8
Avg % Change	–0.05	–0.02	0.10	–0.03	–0.11
Last Trading Day Performance					
% of Time Up	50.7	57.3	64.8	47.8	60.9
Avg % Change	0.06	0.08	0.22	–0.07	0.28

Dow & S&P 1950–May 2, 2025; NASDAQ 1971–May 2, 2025; Russell 1K & 2K 1979–May 2, 2025.

If Santa Claus should fail to call,
Bears may come to Broad and Wall.

NOVEMBER/DECEMBER 2026

Last Trading Day of November, S&P Down 16 of Last 27

MONDAY
30
D 57.1
S 52.4
N 47.6

In this age of instant information, investors can experience both fear and greed at the exact same moment.
— Sam Stovall (Chief Investment Strategist CFRA Research, October 2003)

First Trading Day in December, NASDAQ Up 25 of 38, But Down 7 of Last 13

TUESDAY
1
D 42.9
S 42.9
N 52.4

Taxes are what we pay for civilized society.
— Oliver Wendell Holmes Jr. (U.S. Supreme Court Justice 1902–1932, "The Great Dissenter," inscribed above IRS HQ entrance, 1841–1935)

WEDNESDAY
2
D 38.1
S 47.6
N 52.4

Buy when you are scared to death; sell when you are tickled to death.
— Market Maxim (*The Cabot Market Letter,* April 12, 2001)

THURSDAY
3
D 57.1
S 52.4
N 66.7

To me, the "tape" is the final arbiter of any investment decision. I have a cardinal rule: Never fight the tape!
— Martin Zweig (Fund manager, *Winning on Wall Street,* 1943–2013)

FRIDAY
4
D 47.6
S 47.6
N 57.1

The test of success is not what you do when you are on top. Success is how high you bounce when you hit bottom.
— General George S. Patton, Jr. (U.S. Army field commander WWII, 1885–1945)

Chanukah

SATURDAY
5

SUNDAY
6

MOST OF THE SO-CALLED JANUARY EFFECT TAKES PLACE IN THE LAST HALF OF DECEMBER

Over the years we reported annually on the fascinating January Effect, showing that small-cap stocks handily outperformed large-cap stocks during January 40 out of 43 years between 1953 and 1995. Readers saw that "Cats and Dogs" on average quadrupled the returns of blue chips in this period. Then, the January Effect disappeared over the next four years.

Looking at the graph on page 114, comparing the Russell 1000 index of large capitalization stocks to the Russell 2000 smaller capitalization stocks, shows small cap stocks beginning to outperform the blue chips in mid-December. Narrowing the comparison down to half-month segments was an inspiration and proved to be quite revealing, as you can see in the table below.

38-YEAR AVERAGE RATES OF RETURN (DEC 1987–FEB 2025)

Mid-Dec*	Russell 1000		Russell 2000	
	Change	Annualized	Change	Annualized
12/15–12/31	1.3%	34.4%	2.5%	76.1%
12/15–01/15	1.8	22.7	3.0	40.3
12/15–01/31	2.1	18.4	3.1	28.2
12/15–02/15	3.3	21.5	5.1	34.8
12/15–02/28	2.4	12.7	4.3	23.6
End-Dec*				
12/31–01/15	0.4	8.7	0.5	11.0
12/31–01/31	0.7	8.7	0.6	7.4
12/31–02/15	2.0	16.9	2.5	21.5
12/31–02/28	0.9	5.8	1.7	11.2

46-YEAR AVERAGE RATES OF RETURN (DEC 1979–FEB 2025)

Mid-Dec*	Russell 1000		Russell 2000	
	Change	Annualized	Change	Annualized
12/15–12/31	1.3%	34.4%	2.4%	72.2%
12/15–01/15	2.0	25.5	3.5	48.3
12/15–01/31	2.3	20.3	3.7	34.4
12/15–02/15	3.5	22.9	5.5	37.9
12/15–02/28	2.6	13.8	4.9	27.3
End-Dec*				
12/31–01/15	0.7	15.8	1.1	25.8
12/31–01/31	1.1	14.0	1.3	16.8
12/31–02/15	2.2	18.7	3.1	27.2
12/31–02/28	1.4	9.2	2.4	16.1

* Mid-month dates are the 11th trading day of the month, month end dates are monthly closes.

Small-cap strength in the last half of December became even more magnified after the 1987 market crash. Note the dramatic shift in gains in the last half of December during the 38-year period starting in 1987, versus the 46 years from 1979 to 2025. With all the beaten-down small stocks being dumped for tax loss purposes, it generally pays to get a head start on the January Effect in mid-December. You don't have to wait until December either; the small-cap sector often begins to turn around near the end of October (page 114).

DECEMBER 2025

MONDAY
7
D 66.7
S 61.9
N 57.1

Some men see things as they are and say "why?" I dream things that never were and say "why not?"
— George Bernard Shaw (Irish dramatist, 1856–1950)

TUESDAY
8
D 61.9
S 61.9
N 66.7

My grandfather always said, in low interest rate environments, borrow as little as you need. In high interest rate environments, borrow as much as you can afford.
— Anthony E. Malkin (Chairman & CEO Empire State Realty Trust, b. 1962)

FOMC Meeting

WEDNESDAY
9
D 47.6
S 52.4
N 57.1

Success is going from failure to failure without loss of enthusiasm.
— Winston Churchill (British statesman, 1874–1965)

Small Cap Strength Starts in Mid-December (Pages 112 and 114)

THURSDAY
10
D 57.1
S 61.9
N 57.1

In all recorded history, there has not been one economist who has had to worry about where the next meal would come from.
— Peter Drucker (Austrian-born pioneer management theorist, 1909–2005)

FRIDAY
11
D 61.9
S 52.4
N 42.9

Every truth passes through three stages before it is recognized. In the first it is ridiculed; in the second it is opposed; in the third it is regarded as self evident.
— Arthur Schopenhauer (German philosopher, 1788–1860)

SATURDAY
12

SUNDAY
13

JANUARY EFFECT NOW STARTS IN MID-DECEMBER

Small-cap stocks tend to outperform big caps in January. Known as the "January Effect," the tendency is clearly revealed by the graph below. Daily data for the Russell 2000 index of smaller companies are divided by the Russell 1000 index of largest companies since July 1, 1979, and then compressed into a single year to show an idealized yearly pattern. When the graph is descending, big blue chips are outperforming smaller companies; when the graph is rising, smaller companies are moving up faster than their larger brethren.

In a typical year the smaller fry stay on the sidelines while the big boys are on the field. Then, around early November, small stocks begin to wake up and in mid-December, they take off. Anticipated year-end dividends, payouts, and bonuses could be a factor. Other major moves are quite evident around Labor Day—possibly because individual investors are back from vacations and from mid-April through early June. Small caps tend to hold the lead through early June, though the bulk of the move is usually complete by early March.

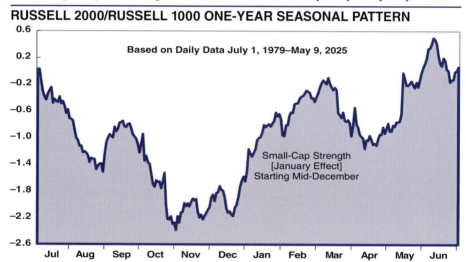

The bottom graph shows the actual ratio of the Russell 2000 divided by the Russell 1000 from 1979. Smaller companies had the upper hand for five years into 1983 as the last major bear trend wound to a close and the nascent bull market logged its first year. After falling behind for about eight years, they came back after the Persian Gulf War bottom in 1990, moving up until 1994 when big caps ruled the latter stages of the millennial bull. For six years the picture was bleak for small fry as the blue chips and tech stocks moved to stratospheric PE ratios. Small caps spiked in late 2020 and early 2021 and have been in retreat since. Note how the small cap advantage has waned during major bull moves and intensified during periods of uncertainty as traders may begin bargain hunting early.

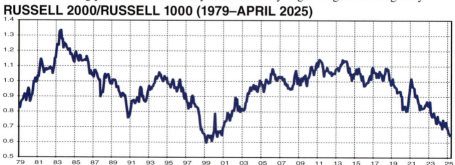

DECEMBER 2026

Monday Before December Triple Witching, S&P Up 16 of Last 25, 2018 Down 2.1%

MONDAY 14
D 47.6
S 42.9
N 52.4

Good luck is what happens when preparation meets opportunity, bad luck is what happens when lack of preparation meets a challenge.
— Paul Krugman (Economist, *NY Times* 3/3/2006)

TUESDAY 15
D 61.9
S 61.9
N 66.7

One of the more prolonged and extreme periods favoring large-cap stocks was 1994–1999. The tide turned in 2000. A cycle has begun of investors favoring small-cap stocks, which is likely to continue through the next several years.
— Jim Oberweis (*The Oberweis Report,* February 2001)

December Triple-Witching Week, S&P Up 29 of Last 41, 2018 Down 7.1%

WEDNESDAY 16
D 42.9
S 52.4
N 52.4

The investor who concentrated on the 50 stocks in the S&P 500 that are followed by the fewest Wall Street analysts wound up with a rousing 24.6% gain in [2006 versus] 13.6% [for] the S&P 500.
— Rich Bernstein (Chief Investment Strategist, Merrill Lynch, Barron's 1/8/07)

THURSDAY 17
D 28.6
S 33.3
N 38.1

Another factor contributing to productivity is technology, particularly the rapid introduction of new microcomputers based on single-chip circuits.... The results over the next decade will be a second industrial revolution.
— Yale Hirsch (Creator of *Stock Trader's Almanac, Smart Money Newsletter* 9/22/1976, 1923–2021)

December Triple-Witching Day, S&P Up 27 of Last 43, But Down 7 of Last 10, 2018 -2.1%

FRIDAY 18
D 52.4
S 47.6
N 42.9

Stock market seasonality is a powerful force. When it fails to materialize in any given year, it is an indication that other more powerful forces are at work and when the seasonal period ends, those forces often have a more intense impact.
— Jeffrey A. Hirsch (Editor, *Stock Trader's Almanac,* b. 1966)

The Only FREE LUNCH on Wall Street Is Served (Page 116)
Almanac Investors Emailed Before the Open, Monday (See Insert)

SATURDAY 19

SUNDAY 20

WALL STREET'S ONLY "FREE LUNCH" SERVED BEFORE CHRISTMAS

Investors tend to get rid of their losers near year-end for tax purposes, often hammering these stocks down to bargain levels. Over the years, the *Almanac* has shown that NYSE stocks selling at their lows on December 15 will usually outperform the market by February 15 in the following year. Preferred stocks, closed-end funds, splits, and new issues are eliminated.

BARGAIN STOCKS VS. THE MARKET*

Short Span* Late Dec–Jan/Feb	New Lows Late Dec	% Change Jan/Feb	% Change NYSE Composite	Bargain Stocks Advantage
1974–75	112	48.9%	22.1%	26.8%
1975–76	21	34.9	14.9	20.0
1976–77	2	1.3	−3.3	4.6
1977–78	15	2.8	−4.5	7.3
1978–79	43	11.8	3.9	7.9
1979–80	5	9.3	6.1	3.2
1980–81	14	7.1	−2.0	9.1
1981–82	21	−2.6	−7.4	4.8
1982–83	4	33.0	9.7	23.3
1983–84	13	−3.2	−3.8	0.6
1984–85	32	19.0	12.1	6.9
1985–86	4	−22.5	3.9	−26.4
1986–87	22	9.3	12.5	−3.2
1987–88	23	13.2	6.8	6.4
1988–89	14	30.0	6.4	23.6
1989–90	25	−3.1	−4.8	1.7
1990–91	18	18.8	12.6	6.2
1991–92	23	51.1	7.7	43.4
1992–93	9	8.7	0.6	8.1
1993–94	10	−1.4	2.0	−3.4
1994–95	25	14.6	5.7	8.9
1995–96	5	−11.3	4.5	−15.8
1996–97	16	13.9	11.2	2.7
1997–98	29	9.9	5.7	4.2
1998–99	40	−2.8	4.3	−7.1
1999–00	26	8.9	−5.4	14.3
2000–01	51	44.4	0.1	44.3
2001–02	12	31.4	−2.3	33.7
2002–03	33	28.7	3.9	24.8
2003–04	15	16.7	2.3	14.4
2004–05	36	6.8	−2.8	9.6
2005–06	71	12.0	2.6	9.4
2006–07	43	5.1	−0.5	5.6
2007–08	71	−3.2	−9.4	6.2
2008–09	88	11.4	−2.4	13.8
2009–10	25	1.8	−3.0	4.8
2010–11	20	8.3	3.4	4.9
2011–12	65	18.1	6.1	12.0
2012–13	17	20.9	3.4	17.5
2013–14	18	25.7	1.7	24.0
2014–15	17	0.2	−0.4	0.6
2015–16	38	−9.2	5.6	−14.8
2016–17	19	2.8	0.6	2.2
2017–18	18	3.3	1.2	2.1
2018–19	23	24.9	15.1	9.8
2019–20	13	−1.1	−0.3	−0.7
2020–21	3	−4.9	3.6	−8.5
2021–22	26	−1.5	−0.02	−1.5
2022–23	38	−0.3	3.7	−4.0
2023–24	13	−0.4	4.0	−4.4
2024–25	26	−2.1	5.3	−7.4
51-Year Totals		539.5%	162.9%	376.5%
Average		10.6%	3.2%	7.4%

*Dec 15–Feb 15 (1974–1999), Dec 1999–2025 based on actual newsletter portfolio

In response to changing market conditions, we tweaked the strategy the last 26 years adding selections from NASDAQ and AMEX, and selling sooner in some years. We email the list of stocks to our *Almanac Investor* subscribers. Visit www.stocktradersalmanac.com or see the insert for additional details and a special offer for new subscribers.

We have concluded that the most prudent course of action is to compile our list from the stocks making new lows on Triple-Witching Friday before Christmas, capitalizing on the Santa Claus Rally (page 118). This also gives us the weekend to evaluate the stocks in greater depth and weed out any glaringly problematic ones. *Almanac Investor* subscribers will receive the list of stocks selected from the new lows made on December 19, 2025, and December 18, 2026, via email.

This "Free Lunch" strategy is an extremely short-term strategy reserved for the nimblest traders. It has performed better after market corrections and when there are more new lows to choose from. The object is to buy bargain stocks near their 52-week lows and sell any quick, generous gains, as these issues can be real dogs.

DECEMBER 2026

Week After December Triple-Witching Dow Up 27 of Last 34, Average Gain 0.8% Since 1991

MONDAY
D 71.4
S 61.9
N 61.9
21

It is the mark of many famous people that they cannot part with their brightest hour.
— Lillian Hellman (Playwright, *The Children's Hour* and *Little Foxes*, 1905–1984)

TUESDAY
D 66.7
S 66.7
N 66.7
22

When the public buys toilet paper, I buy stocks.
— Larry Williams (Legendary trader, author, politician, 3/16/2020, b. 1942)

WEDNESDAY
D 71.4
S 66.7
N 57.1
23

Never attribute to malevolence what is merely due to incompetence.
— Arthur C. Clarke (British sci-fi writer, *3001: The Final Odyssey*, 1917–2008)

(Shortened Trading Day)
Santa Claus Rally Begins (Page 118)
Last Trading Day Before Christmas, NASDAQ Up 14 of Last 18, 2018 Down 2.2%

THURSDAY
D 52.4
S 61.9
N 76.2
24

I look at the future from the standpoint of probabilities. It's like a branching stream of probabilities, and there are actions that we can take that affect those probabilities or that accelerate one thing or slow down another thing.
— Elon Musk (South African engineer & industrialist, CEO Tesla, Founder SpaceX, b. 1971)

Christmas Day *(Market Closed)*

FRIDAY
25

Love your enemies, for they tell you your faults.
— Benjamin Franklin (U.S. Founding Father, diplomat, inventor, 1706–1790)

SATURDAY
26

SUNDAY
27

IF SANTA CLAUS SHOULD FAIL TO CALL, BEARS MAY COME TO BROAD AND WALL

Santa Claus tends to come to Wall Street nearly every year, bringing a short, sweet, respectable rally within the last five days of the year and the first two in January. This has been good for an average 1.2% gain since 1969 (1.3% since 1950). Santa's failure to show tends to precede bear markets, or times stocks could be purchased later in the year at much lower prices. We discovered this phenomenon in 1972. See page 20 for more.

DAILY % CHANGE IN S&P 500 AT YEAR-END

	Trading Days Before Year-End					First Days in January			Rally % Change
	6	5	4	3	2	1	1	2	3	
1969	−0.4	1.1	0.8	−0.7	0.4	0.5	1.0	0.5	−0.7	3.6
1970	0.1	0.6	0.5	1.1	0.2	−0.1	−1.1	0.7	0.6	1.9
1971	−0.4	0.2	1.0	0.3	−0.4	0.3	−0.4	0.4	1.0	1.3
1972	−0.3	−0.7	0.6	0.4	0.5	1.0	0.9	0.4	−0.1	3.1
1973	−1.1	−0.7	3.1	2.1	−0.2	0.01	0.1	2.2	−0.9	6.7
1974	−1.4	1.4	0.8	−0.4	0.03	2.1	2.4	0.7	0.5	7.2
1975	0.7	0.8	0.9	−0.1	−0.4	0.5	0.8	1.8	1.0	4.3
1976	0.1	1.2	0.7	−0.4	0.5	0.5	−0.4	−1.2	−0.9	0.8
1977	0.8	0.9	N/C	0.1	0.2	0.2	−1.3	−0.3	−0.8	−0.3
1978	0.03	1.7	1.3	−0.9	−0.4	−0.2	0.6	1.1	0.8	3.3
1979	−0.6	0.1	0.1	0.2	−0.1	0.1	−2.0	−0.5	1.2	−2.2
1980	−0.4	0.4	0.5	−1.1	0.2	0.3	0.4	1.2	0.1	2.0
1981	−0.5	0.2	−0.2	−0.5	0.5	0.2	0.2	−2.2	−0.7	−1.8
1982	0.6	1.8	−1.0	0.3	−0.7	0.2	−1.6	2.2	0.4	1.2
1983	−0.2	−0.03	0.9	0.3	−0.2	0.05	−0.5	1.7	1.2	2.1
1984	−0.5	0.8	−0.2	−0.4	0.3	0.6	−1.1	−0.5	−0.5	−0.6
1985	−1.1	−0.7	0.2	0.9	0.5	0.3	−0.8	0.6	−0.1	1.1
1986	−1.0	0.2	0.1	−0.9	−0.5	−0.5	1.8	2.3	0.2	2.4
1987	1.3	−0.5	−2.6	−0.4	1.3	−0.3	3.6	1.1	0.1	2.2
1988	−0.2	0.3	−0.4	0.1	0.8	−0.6	−0.9	1.5	0.2	0.9
1989	0.6	0.8	−0.2	0.6	0.5	0.8	1.8	−0.3	−0.9	4.1
1990	0.5	−0.6	0.3	−0.8	0.1	0.5	−1.1	−1.4	−0.3	−3.0
1991	2.5	0.6	1.4	0.4	2.1	0.5	0.04	0.5	−0.3	5.7
1992	−0.3	0.2	−0.1	−0.3	0.2	−0.7	−0.1	−0.2	0.04	−1.1
1993	0.01	0.7	0.1	−0.1	−0.1	−0.5	−0.2	0.3	0.1	−0.1
1994	0.01	0.2	0.4	−0.3	0.1	−0.4	−0.03	0.3	−0.1	0.2
1995	0.8	0.2	0.4	0.04	−0.1	0.3	0.8	0.1	−0.6	1.8
1996	−0.3	0.5	0.6	0.1	−0.4	−1.7	−0.5	1.5	−0.1	0.1
1997	−1.5	−0.7	0.4	1.8	1.8	−0.04	0.5	0.2	−1.1	4.0
1998	2.1	−0.2	−0.1	1.3	−0.8	−0.2	−0.1	1.4	2.2	1.3
1999	1.6	−0.1	0.04	0.4	0.1	0.3	−1.0	−3.8	0.2	−4.0
2000	0.8	2.4	0.7	1.0	0.4	−1.0	−2.8	5.0	−1.1	5.7
2001	0.4	−0.02	0.4	0.7	0.3	−1.1	0.6	0.9	0.6	1.8
2002	0.2	−0.5	−0.3	−1.6	0.5	0.05	3.3	−0.05	2.2	1.2
2003	0.3	−0.2	0.2	1.2	0.01	0.2	−0.3	1.2	0.1	2.4
2004	0.1	−0.4	0.7	−0.01	0.01	−0.1	−0.8	−1.2	−0.4	−1.8
2005	0.4	0.04	−1.0	0.1	−0.3	−0.5	1.6	0.4	0.002	0.4
2006	−0.4	−0.5	0.4	0.7	−0.1	−0.5	−0.1	−0.6		0.003
2007	1.7	0.8	0.1	−1.4	0.1	−0.7	−1.4	N/C	−2.5	−2.5
2008	−1.0	0.6	0.5	−0.4	2.4	1.4	3.2	−0.5	0.8	7.4
2009	0.2	0.5	0.1	−0.1	0.02	−1.0	1.6	0.3	0.05	1.4
2010	−0.2	0.1	0.1	0.1	−0.2	−0.02	1.1	−0.1	0.5	1.1
2011	0.8	0.9	0.01	−1.3	1.1	−0.4	1.6	0.02	0.3	1.9
2012	−0.9	−0.2	−0.5	−0.1	−1.1	1.7	2.5	−0.2	0.5	2.0
2013	0.5	0.3	0.5	−0.03	−0.02	0.4	−0.9	−0.03	−0.3	0.2
2014	−0.01	−0.01	0.3	0.1	−0.5	−1.0	−0.03	−1.8	−0.9	−3.0
2015	1.2	−0.2	−0.2	1.1	−0.7	−0.9	−1.5	0.2	−1.3	−2.3
2016	−0.2	0.1	0.2	−0.8	−0.03	−0.5	0.9	0.6	−0.1	0.4
2017	0.2	−0.05	−0.1	0.1	0.2	−0.5	0.8	0.6	0.4	1.1
2018	−2.1	−2.7	5.0	0.9	−0.1	0.9	0.1	−2.5	3.4	1.3
2019	0.1	−0.02	0.5	0.003	−0.6	0.3	0.8	−0.7	0.4	0.3
2020	0.1	0.4	0.9	−0.2	0.1	0.6	−1.5	0.7	0.6	1.0
2021	0.6	1.4	−0.1	0.1	−0.3	−0.3	0.6	−0.1	−1.9	1.4
2022	−1.4	0.6	−0.4	−1.2	1.7	−0.3	−0.4	0.8	−1.2	0.8
2023	1.0	0.2	0.4	0.1	0.04	−0.3	−0.6	−0.8	−0.3	−0.9
2024	0.7	1.1	−0.04	−1.1	−1.1	−0.4	−0.2	1.3	0.6	−0.5
Avg	0.09	0.27	0.33	0.02	0.14	0.001	0.18	0.29	0.03	1.2

The couplet above was certainly on the mark in 1999, as the period suffered a horrendous 4.0% loss. On January 14, 2000, the Dow started its 33-month 37.8% slide to the October 2002 midterm election-year bottom. NASDAQ cracked eight weeks later falling 37.3% in 10 weeks, eventually dropping 77.9% by October 2002. Energy prices and Middle East terror woes may have grounded Santa in 2004. In 2007 the fourth-worst reading since 1950 was recorded as a full-blown financial crisis led to the second-worst bear market in history. In 2016, the period was hit again as global growth concerns escalated and the market digested the first interest rate hike in nearly a decade. Inflation, interest rate, and new administration concerns weighed down Santa in 2024 and 2025.

DECEMBER/JANUARY 2027

MONDAY
D 76.2
S 66.7
N 61.9
28

A man should always hold something in reserve, a surprise to spring when things get tight.
— Christy Mathewson (MLB Hall of Fame Pitcher, 1 of 1st 5 members, 3rd most wins, 1880–1925)

TUESDAY
D 42.9
S 47.6
N 38.1
29

Short-term volatility is greatest at turning points and diminishes as a trend becomes established.
— George Soros (Financier, philanthropist, political activist, author and philosopher, b. 1930)

WEDNESDAY
D 42.9
S 42.9
N 38.1
30

He who knows how will always work for he who knows why.
— David Lee Roth (Lead singer of Van Halen, b. 1954)

Last Trading Day of the Year, NASDAQ Down 19 of last 25
NASDAQ Was Up 29 Years in a Row 1971–1999

THURSDAY
D 33.3
S 28.6
N 28.6
31

Nothing gives one person so much advantage over another as to remain always cool and unruffled under all circumstances.
— Thomas Jefferson (3rd U.S. President, 1743–7/4/1826)

New Years Day *(Market Closed)*

FRIDAY
1

Absorb what is useful, discard what is useless, and add what is specifically your own.
— Bruce Lee (Hong Kong-American martial artist, actor, philosopher and filmmaker, founder of Jeet Kune Do, 1940–1973)

SATURDAY
2

January Almanac Investor Sector Seasonalities: See Pages 94, 96, and 98

SUNDAY
3

2027 STRATEGY CALENDAR
(Option expiration dates circled)

	MONDAY	TUESDAY	WEDNESDAY	THURSDAY	FRIDAY	SATURDAY	SUNDAY
JANUARY	28	29	30	31	**1 JANUARY** New Year's Day	2	3
	4	5	6	7	8	9	10
	11	12	13	14	(15)	16	17
	18 Martin Luther King Jr. Day	19	20	21	22	23	24
	25	26	27	28	29	30	31
FEBRUARY	1 FEBRUARY	2	3	4	5	6	7
	8	9	10 Ash Wednesday	11	12	13	14 ♥
	15 Presidents' Day	16	17	18	(19)	20	21
	22	23	24	25	26	27	28
MARCH	1 MARCH	2	3	4	5	6	7
	8	9	10	11	12	13	14 Daylight Saving Time Begins
	15	16	17 ♣ St. Patrick's Day	18	(19)	20	21
	22	23	24	25	26 Good Friday	27	28 Easter
	29	30	31	1 APRIL	2	3	4
APRIL	5	6	7	8	9	10	11
	12	13	14	15 Tax Deadline	(16)	17	18
	19	20	21	22 Passover	23	24	25
	26	27	28	29	30	1 MAY	2
MAY	3	4	5	6	7	8	9 Mother's Day
	10	11	12	13	14	15	16
	17	18	19	20	(21)	22	23
	24	25	26	27	28	29	30
JUNE	31 Memorial Day	1 JUNE	2	3	4	5	6
	7	8	9	10	11	12	13
	14	15	16	17	(18)	19 Juneteenth	20 Father's Day
	21	22	23	24	25	26	27
	28	29	30	1 JULY	2	3	4 Independence Day

Market closed on shaded weekdays; closes early when half-shaded.

2027 STRATEGY CALENDAR
(Option expiration dates circled)

MONDAY	TUESDAY	WEDNESDAY	THURSDAY	FRIDAY	SATURDAY	SUNDAY	
5	6	7	8	9	10	11	JULY
12	13	14	15	(16)	17	18	
19	20	21	22	23	24	25	
26	27	28	29	30	31	1 AUGUST	
2	3	4	5	6	7	8	AUGUST
9	10	11	12	13	14	15	
16	17	18	19	(20)	21	22	
23	24	25	26	27	28	29	
30	31	1 SEPTEMBER	2	3	4	5	SEPTEMBER
6 Labor Day	7	8	9	10	11	12	
13	14	15	16	(17)	18	19	
20	21	22	23	24	25	26	
27	28	29	30	1 OCTOBER	2 Rosh Hashanah	3	OCTOBER
4	5	6	7	8	9	10	
11 Yom Kippur Columbus Day	12	13	14	(15)	16	17	
18	19	20	21	22	23	24	
25	26	27	28	29	30	31	
1 NOVEMBER	2 Election Day	3	4	5	6	7 Daylight Saving Time Ends	NOVEMBER
8	9	10	11 Veterans' Day	12	13	14	
15	16	17	18	(19)	20	21	
22	23	24	25 Thanksgiving Day	26	27	28	
29	30	1 DECEMBER	2	3	4	5	DECEMBER
6	7	8	9	10	11	12	
13	14	15	16	(17)	18	19	
20	21	22	23	24	25 Chanukah Christmas	26	
27	28	29	30	31	1 JANUARY New Year's Day	2	

DIRECTORY OF TRADING PATTERNS AND DATABANK

CONTENTS

123	Dow Jones Industrials Market Probability Calendar 2026
124	Recent Dow Jones Industrials Market Probability Calendar 2026
125	S&P 500 Market Probability Calendar 2026
126	Recent S&P 500 Market Probability Calendar 2026
127	NASDAQ Composite Market Probability Calendar 2026
128	Recent NASDAQ Composite Market Probability Calendar 2026
129	Russell 1000 Index Market Probability Calendar 2026
130	Russell 2000 Index Market Probability Calendar 2026
131	Decennial Cycle: A Market Phenomenon
132	Presidential Election/Stock Market Cycle: The 192-Year Saga Continues
133	Dow Jones Industrials Bull and Bear Markets Since 1900
134	Standard & Poor's 500 Bull and Bear Markets Since 1929/NASDAQ Composite Since 1971
135	Dow Jones Industrials 10-Year Daily Point Changes: January and February
136	Dow Jones Industrials 10-Year Daily Point Changes: March and April
137	Dow Jones Industrials 10-Year Daily Point Changes: May and June
138	Dow Jones Industrials 10-Year Daily Point Changes: July and August
139	Dow Jones Industrials 10-Year Daily Point Changes: September and October
140	Dow Jones Industrials 10-Year Daily Point Changes: November and December
141	A Typical Day in the Market
142	Through the Week on a Half-Hourly Basis
143	Tuesday & Wednesday Best Days of Week
144	NASDAQ Strongest Last 3 Days of Week
145	S&P Daily Performance Each Year Since 1952
146	NASDAQ Daily Performance Each Year Since 1971
147	Monthly Cash Inflows into S&P Stocks
148	Monthly Cash Inflows into NASDAQ Stocks
149	November, December, and January: Year's Best Three-Month Span
150	November Through June: NASDAQ's Eight-Month Run
151	Dow Jones Industrials Annual Highs, Lows, & Closes Since 1901
153	S&P 500 Annual Highs, Lows, & Closes Since 1930
154	NASDAQ Annual Highs, Lows, & Closes Since 1971
155	Russell 1000 and 2000 Annual Highs, Lows, & Closes Since 1979
156	Dow Jones Industrials Monthly Percent Changes Since 1950
158	Dow Jones Industrials Monthly Point Changes Since 1950
160	Dow Jones Industrials Monthly Closing Prices Since 1950
162	Standard & Poor's 500 Monthly Percent Changes Since 1950
164	Standard & Poor's 500 Monthly Closing Prices Since 1950
166	NASDAQ Composite Monthly Percent Changes Since 1971
168	NASDAQ Composite Monthly Closing Prices Since 1971
170	Russell 1000 Index Monthly Percent Changes and Closing Prices Since 1979
172	Russell 2000 Index Monthly Percent Changes and Closing Prices Since 1979
174	10 Best Days by Percent and Point
175	10 Worst Days by Percent and Point
176	10 Best Weeks by Percent and Point
177	10 Worst Weeks by Percent and Point
178	10 Best Months by Percent and Point
179	10 Worst Months by Percent and Point
180	10 Best Quarters by Percent and Point
181	10 Worst Quarters by Percent and Point
182	10 Best Years by Percent and Point
183	10 Worst Years by Percent and Point

DOW JONES INDUSTRIALS MARKET PROBABILITY CALENDAR 2026

THE % CHANCE OF THE MARKET RISING ON ANY TRADING DAY OF THE YEAR*
(Based on the number of times the DJIA rose on a particular trading day during **January 1954–December 2024**)

Date	Jan	Feb	Mar	Apr	May	Jun	Jul	Aug	Sep	Oct	Nov	Dec
1	H	S	S	59.2	54.9	60.6	67.6	S	56.3	47.9	S	45.1
2	59.2	63.4	66.2	60.6	S	56.3	56.3	S	60.6	54.9	63.4	50.7
3	S	54.9	59.2	H	S	50.7	H	42.3	57.7	S	53.5	60.6
4	S	42.3	57.7	S	63.4	62.0	S	45.1	43.7	S	67.6	56.3
5	70.4	56.3	49.3	S	53.5	54.9	S	49.3	S	56.3	60.6	S
6	49.3	49.3	45.1	50.7	46.5	S	59.2	52.1	S	60.6	52.1	S
7	57.7	S	S	59.2	50.7	S	56.3	56.3	H	43.7	S	52.1
8	46.5	S	S	52.1	53.5	49.3	59.2	S	49.3	52.1	S	47.9
9	49.3	43.7	50.7	62.0	S	36.6	56.3	S	46.5	46.5	63.4	52.1
10	S	46.5	62.0	59.2	S	52.1	53.5	47.9	60.6	S	52.1	59.2
11	S	62.0	50.7	S	46.5	57.7	S	45.1	60.6	S	53.5	46.5
12	50.7	46.5	54.9	S	50.7	53.5	S	46.5	S	42.3	50.7	S
13	49.3	50.7	53.5	59.2	43.7	S	47.9	50.7	S	49.3	47.9	S
14	54.9	S	S	54.9	54.9	S	69.0	66.2	50.7	59.2	S	49.3
15	52.1	S	S	69.0	57.7	52.1	54.9	S	54.9	52.1	S	50.7
16	59.2	H	60.6	60.6	S	50.7	46.5	S	56.3	54.9	59.2	53.5
17	S	59.2	62.0	57.7	S	49.3	52.1	57.7	40.8	S	50.7	46.5
18	S	43.7	57.7	S	45.1	45.1	S	52.1	49.3	S	46.5	53.5
19	H	46.5	54.9	S	50.7	H	S	47.9	S	45.1	50.7	S
20	42.3	47.9	43.7	52.1	43.7	S	54.9	53.5	S	59.2	66.2	S
21	40.8	S	S	54.9	36.6	S	40.8	49.3	45.1	43.7	S	60.6
22	42.3	S	S	50.7	53.5	46.5	50.7	S	42.3	42.3	S	59.2
23	47.9	39.4	47.9	54.9	S	43.7	46.5	S	38.0	50.7	63.4	54.9
24	S	46.5	38.0	50.7	S	38.0	45.1	53.5	49.3	S	66.2	59.2
25	S	59.2	52.1	S	H	47.9	S	52.1	52.1	S	59.2	H
26	57.7	46.5	47.9	S	45.1	45.1	S	46.5	S	31.0	H	S
27	57.7	46.5	53.5	56.3	46.5	S	62.0	63.4	S	54.9	54.9	S
28	49.3	S	S	56.3	56.3	S	53.5	42.3	52.1	50.7	S	73.2
29	59.2		S	53.5	53.5	57.7	45.1	S	50.7	60.6	S	49.3
30	54.9		47.9	47.9	S	54.9	57.7	S	42.3	52.1	53.5	53.5
31	S		43.7		S		50.7	57.7		S		50.7

* See developing trends on pages 72, 90, 143–148
H = Holiday, S = Saturday/Sunday

RECENT DOW JONES INDUSTRIALS MARKET PROBABILITY CALENDAR 2026
THE % CHANCE OF THE MARKET RISING ON ANY TRADING DAY OF THE YEAR*
(Based on the number of times the DJIA rose on a particular trading day during **January 2004–December 2024****)

Date	Jan	Feb	Mar	Apr	May	Jun	Jul	Aug	Sep	Oct	Nov	Dec
1	H	S	S	66.7	57.1	71.4	81.0	S	42.9	47.6	S	42.9
2	66.7	85.7	66.7	71.4	S	66.7	38.1	S	66.7	38.1	61.9	38.1
3	S	57.1	33.3	H	S	33.3	H	38.1	52.4	S	61.9	57.1
4	S	47.6	52.4	S	66.7	71.4	S	42.9	47.6	S	66.7	47.6
5	61.9	66.7	47.6	S	52.4	61.9	S	57.1	S	66.7	71.4	S
6	47.6	61.9	47.6	47.6	38.1	S	57.1	47.6	S	61.9	76.2	S
7	61.9	S	S	57.1	66.7	S	57.1	52.4	H	33.3	S	66.7
8	42.9	S	S	47.6	66.7	71.4	52.4	S	57.1	52.4	S	61.9
9	52.4	47.6	38.1	66.7	S	38.1	61.9	S	61.9	66.7	66.7	47.6
10	S	52.4	66.7	47.6	S	33.3	57.1	52.4	81.0	S	47.6	57.1
11	S	61.9	47.6	S	38.1	57.1	S	38.1	66.7	S	38.1	61.9
12	61.9	57.1	52.4	S	57.1	52.4	S	33.3	S	47.6	66.7	S
13	52.4	47.6	66.7	47.6	28.6	S	76.2	61.9	S	33.3	42.9	S
14	47.6	S	S	52.4	57.1	S	76.2	66.7	61.9	61.9	S	47.6
15	42.9	S	S	61.9	66.7	57.1	71.4	S	61.9	52.4	S	61.9
16	57.1	H	61.9	52.4	S	52.4	52.4	S	76.2	66.7	66.7	42.9
17	S	71.4	61.9	61.9	S	52.4	66.7	57.1	47.6	S	57.1	28.6
18	S	61.9	61.9	S	47.6	52.4	S	52.4	52.4	S	33.3	52.4
19	H	42.9	61.9	S	38.1	H	S	61.9	S	52.4	52.4	S
20	42.9	38.1	52.4	47.6	38.1	S	76.2	52.4	S	47.6	61.9	S
21	52.4	S	S	66.7	47.6	S	28.6	47.6	42.9	28.6	S	71.4
22	42.9	S	S	61.9	47.6	38.1	52.4	S	38.1	52.4	S	66.7
23	47.6	47.6	42.9	66.7	S	47.6	52.4	S	28.6	57.1	71.4	71.4
24	S	47.6	42.9	52.4	S	28.6	38.1	61.9	47.6	S	71.4	52.4
25	S	57.1	61.9	S	H	47.6	S	57.1	47.6	S	66.7	H
26	57.1	42.9	47.6	S	57.1	47.6	S	47.6	S	38.1	H	S
27	57.1	28.6	47.6	52.4	52.4	S	66.7	90.7	S	66.7	61.9	S
28	52.4	S	S	66.7	66.7	S	52.4	42.9	66.7	38.1	S	76.2
29	47.6		S	71.4	28.6	61.9	42.9	S	57.1	61.9	S	42.9
30	38.1		66.7	28.6	S	57.1	52.4	S	42.9	47.6	57.1	42.9
31	S		47.6		S		38.1	47.6		S		33.3

* See developing trends on pages 72, 90, 143–148   ** Based on most recent 21-year period
H = Holiday, S = Saturday/Sunday

S&P 500 MARKET PROBABILITY CALENDAR 2026
THE % CHANCE OF THE MARKET RISING ON ANY TRADING DAY OF THE YEAR*
(Based on the number of times the S&P 500 rose on a particular trading day during **January 1954–December 2024**)

Date	Jan	Feb	Mar	Apr	May	Jun	Jul	Aug	Sep	Oct	Nov	Dec
1	H	S	S	63.4	56.3	57.7	74.6	S	59.2	50.7	S	46.5
2	49.3	63.4	62.0	62.0	S	64.8	56.3	S	52.1	62.0	63.4	50.7
3	S	60.6	56.3	H	S	52.1	H	43.7	56.3	S	57.7	57.7
4	S	47.9	60.6	S	64.8	57.7	S	45.1	43.7	S	67.6	54.9
5	66.2	53.5	47.9	S	54.9	46.5	S	49.3	S	57.7	60.6	S
6	52.1	50.7	46.5	52.1	43.7	S	56.3	53.5	S	60.6	50.7	S
7	53.5	S	S	56.3	49.3	S	59.2	56.3	H	45.1	S	47.9
8	46.5	S	S	53.5	50.7	49.3	60.6	S	49.3	49.3	S	52.1
9	52.1	47.9	53.5	62.0	S	40.8	57.7	S	54.9	43.7	62.0	53.5
10	S	45.1	60.6	60.6	S	54.9	54.9	46.5	60.6	S	54.9	52.1
11	S	60.6	50.7	S	49.3	62.0	S	50.7	66.2	S	56.3	47.9
12	56.3	54.9	60.6	S	53.5	56.3	S	47.9	S	46.5	49.3	S
13	53.5	49.3	43.7	53.5	42.3	S	52.1	47.9	S	50.7	49.3	S
14	57.7	S	S	52.1	52.1	S	71.8	64.8	52.1	53.5	S	42.3
15	59.2	S	S	60.6	56.3	57.7	53.5	S	53.5	52.1	S	50.7
16	57.7	H	59.2	60.6	S	49.3	45.1	S	56.3	59.2	52.1	56.3
17	S	57.7	63.4	59.2	S	53.5	47.9	63.4	46.5	S	52.1	43.7
18	S	39.4	56.3	S	49.3	43.7	S	56.3	52.1	S	50.7	45.1
19	H	47.9	52.1	S	52.1	H	S	53.5	S	43.7	54.9	S
20	50.7	40.8	47.9	50.7	40.8	S	53.5	52.1	S	63.4	62.0	S
21	50.7	S	S	53.5	43.7	S	40.8	46.5	43.7	45.1	S	52.1
22	49.3	S	S	54.9	53.5	50.7	43.7	S	45.1	43.7	S	56.3
23	59.2	40.8	42.3	49.3	S	45.1	47.9	S	35.2	49.3	63.4	52.1
24	S	42.3	50.7	50.7	S	35.2	46.5	52.1	47.9	S	66.2	60.6
25	S	57.7	45.1	S	H	43.7	S	50.7	47.9	S	59.2	H
26	54.9	49.3	49.3	S	52.1	49.3	S	47.9	S	33.8	H	S
27	50.7	52.1	53.5	54.9	49.3	S	57.7	63.4	S	57.7	57.7	S
28	43.7	S	S	50.7	57.7	S	52.1	46.5	59.2	53.5	S	70.4
29	60.6		S	52.1	56.3	60.6	46.5	S	49.3	60.6	S	53.5
30	60.6		42.3	53.5	S	53.5	62.0	S	43.7	53.5	50.7	59.2
31	S		43.7		S		60.6	62.0		S		57.7

* See developing trends on pages 72, 90, 143–148
H = Holiday, S = Saturday/Sunday

RECENT S&P 500 MARKET PROBABILITY CALENDAR 2026
THE % CHANCE OF THE MARKET RISING ON ANY TRADING DAY OF THE YEAR*
(Based on the number of times the S&P 500 rose on a particular trading day during **January 2004–December 2024****)

Date	Jan	Feb	Mar	Apr	May	Jun	Jul	Aug	Sep	Oct	Nov	Dec
1	H	S	S	66.7	61.9	66.7	90.5	S	52.4	57.1	S	42.9
2	52.4	81.0	66.7	76.2	S	76.2	47.6	S	42.9	42.9	61.9	47.6
3	S	71.4	38.1	H	S	38.1	H	38.1	47.6	S	66.7	52.4
4	S	38.1	57.1	S	52.4	61.9	S	47.6	47.6	S	61.9	47.6
5	47.6	71.4	52.4	S	47.6	38.1	S	52.4	S	66.7	81.0	S
6	52.4	57.1	47.6	52.4	42.9	S	66.7	52.4	S	57.1	71.4	S
7	66.7	S	S	57.1	66.7	S	57.1	47.6	H	33.3	S	61.9
8	52.4	S	S	47.6	52.4	71.4	57.1	S	47.6	47.6	S	61.9
9	57.1	61.9	38.1	61.9	S	38.1	66.7	S	71.4	61.9	61.9	52.4
10	S	57.1	61.9	52.4	S	38.1	66.7	52.4	81.0	S	33.3	61.9
11	S	57.1	57.1	S	47.6	61.9	S	42.9	76.2	S	52.4	52.4
12	71.4	71.4	57.1	S	57.1	61.9	S	47.6	S	47.6	61.9	S
13	52.4	61.9	42.9	57.1	28.6	S	66.7	47.6	S	42.9	42.9	S
14	52.4	S	S	57.1	47.6	S	66.7	57.1	57.1	57.1	S	42.9
15	47.6	S	S	57.1	57.1	66.7	47.6	S	57.1	57.1	S	61.9
16	66.7	H	47.6	57.1	S	52.4	52.4	S	71.4	71.4	57.1	52.4
17	S	71.4	66.7	66.7	S	52.4	61.9	66.7	47.6	S	61.9	33.3
18	S	52.4	61.9	S	52.4	52.4	S	61.9	47.6	S	42.9	47.6
19	H	38.1	52.4	S	38.1	H	S	61.9	S	57.1	57.1	S
20	42.9	33.3	52.4	47.6	42.9	S	71.4	47.6	S	52.4	57.1	S
21	61.9	S	S	52.4	47.6	S	33.3	42.9	23.8	38.1	S	61.9
22	57.1	S	S	66.7	52.4	42.9	47.6	S	28.6	66.7	S	66.7
23	52.4	38.1	38.1	61.9	S	52.4	57.1	S	28.6	71.4	66.7	66.7
24	S	52.4	47.6	61.9	S	23.8	52.4	57.1	47.6	S	61.9	61.9
25	S	61.9	57.1	S	H	57.1	S	57.1	38.1	S	61.9	H
26	61.9	47.6	47.6	S	71.4	47.6	S	57.1	S	33.3	H	S
27	47.6	28.6	47.6	47.6	61.9	S	57.1	90.5	S	57.1	61.9	S
28	42.9	S	S	57.1	71.4	S	47.6	42.9	71.4	38.1	S	66.7
29	47.6		S	71.4	42.9	61.9	38.1	S	52.4	66.7	S	47.6
30	42.9		61.9	33.3	S	57.1	61.9	S	38.1	52.4	52.4	42.9
31	S		47.6		S		42.9	52.4		S		28.6

* See developing trends on pages 72, 90, 143–148 ** Based on most recent 21-year period
H = Holiday, S = Saturday/Sunday

NASDAQ COMPOSITE MARKET PROBABILITY CALENDAR 2026
THE % CHANCE OF THE MARKET RISING ON ANY TRADING DAY OF THE YEAR*
(Based on the number of times the NASDAQ rose on a particular trading day during **January 1972–December 2024**)

Date	Jan	Feb	Mar	Apr	May	Jun	Jul	Aug	Sep	Oct	Nov	Dec
1	H	S	S	47.2	60.4	58.5	66.0	S	52.8	49.1	S	58.5
2	54.7	71.7	62.3	64.2	S	75.5	49.1	S	56.6	56.6	67.9	56.6
3	S	67.9	52.8	H	S	54.7	H	50.9	56.6	S	54.7	64.2
4	S	50.9	64.2	S	66.0	60.4	S	41.5	54.7	S	67.9	58.5
5	62.3	64.2	47.2	S	56.6	50.9	S	52.8	S	60.4	60.4	S
6	54.7	54.7	47.2	58.5	52.8	S	50.9	62.3	S	58.5	56.6	S
7	64.2	S	S	52.8	56.6	S	54.7	52.8	H	54.7	S	49.1
8	58.5	S	S	45.3	62.3	52.8	62.3	S	54.7	58.5	S	56.6
9	62.3	54.7	52.8	64.2	S	43.4	67.9	S	52.8	52.8	58.5	47.2
10	S	54.7	58.5	58.5	S	52.8	62.3	43.4	54.7	S	50.9	47.2
11	S	62.3	49.1	S	54.7	60.4	S	49.1	62.3	S	62.3	43.4
12	60.4	60.4	67.9	S	41.5	66.0	S	49.1	S	49.1	54.7	S
13	60.4	67.9	47.2	60.4	54.7	S	66.0	56.6	S	67.9	49.1	S
14	60.4	S	S	50.9	58.5	S	75.5	62.3	60.4	62.3	S	43.4
15	60.4	S	S	56.6	56.6	58.5	64.2	S	37.7	52.8	S	52.8
16	67.9	H	52.8	49.1	S	49.1	50.9	S	56.6	54.7	47.2	54.7
17	S	64.2	67.9	62.3	S	54.7	54.7	56.6	49.1	S	50.9	47.2
18	S	47.2	60.4	S	56.6	49.1	S	50.9	60.4	S	50.9	49.1
19	H	50.9	67.9	S	47.2	H	S	56.6	S	45.3	54.7	S
20	58.5	37.7	49.1	50.9	43.4	S	60.4	50.9	S	62.3	67.9	S
21	47.2	S	S	54.7	47.2	S	35.8	50.9	47.2	52.8	S	54.7
22	50.9	S	S	56.6	54.7	49.1	49.1	S	47.2	50.9	S	60.4
23	58.5	47.2	54.7	52.8	S	49.1	49.1	S	43.4	50.9	60.4	64.2
24	S	50.9	54.7	52.8	S	37.7	50.9	52.8	50.9	S	60.4	71.7
25	S	64.2	49.1	S	H	47.2	S	54.7	49.1	S	67.9	H
26	47.2	56.6	45.3	S	58.5	60.4	S	56.6	S	39.6	H	S
27	64.2	49.1	50.9	43.4	60.4	S	56.6	64.2	S	45.3	62.3	S
28	58.5	S	S	62.3	56.6	S	49.1	60.4	50.9	56.6	S	67.9
29	54.7		S	67.9	60.4	66.0	47.2	S	43.4	60.4	S	47.2
30	62.3		S	58.5	S	66.0	58.5	S	50.9	60.4	60.4	58.5
31	S		62.3		S		52.8	66.0		S		64.2

* See developing trends on pages 72, 90, 143–148
Based on NASDAQ composite, prior to Feb. 5, 1971 based on National Quotation Bureau indices. H = Holiday, S = Saturday/Sunday

RECENT NASDAQ COMPOSITE MARKET PROBABILITY CALENDAR 2026
THE % CHANCE OF THE MARKET RISING ON ANY TRADING DAY OF THE YEAR*
(Based on the number of times the NASDAQ rose on a particular trading day during **January 2004–December 2024****)

Date	Jan	Feb	Mar	Apr	May	Jun	Jul	Aug	Sep	Oct	Nov	Dec
1	H	S	S	61.9	61.9	61.9	85.7	S	52.4	52.4	S	52.4
2	61.9	81.0	61.9	71.4	S	71.4	47.6	S	42.9	47.6	61.9	52.4
3	S	66.7	42.9	H	S	42.9	H	52.4	52.4	S	61.9	66.7
4	S	33.3	47.6	S	57.1	61.9	S	42.9	52.4	S	57.1	57.1
5	38.1	61.9	38.1	S	42.9	42.9	S	57.1	S	71.4	71.4	S
6	47.6	57.1	33.3	57.1	47.6	S	66.7	57.1	S	52.4	76.2	S
7	61.9	S	S	52.4	57.1	S	61.9	38.1	H	42.9	S	57.1
8	71.4	S	S	33.3	66.7	61.9	61.9	S	52.4	52.4	S	66.7
9	66.7	61.9	42.9	66.7	S	38.1	76.2	S	66.7	61.9	66.7	57.1
10	S	61.9	57.1	47.6	S	42.9	66.7	47.6	71.4	S	33.3	57.1
11	S	57.1	42.9	S	52.4	57.1	S	42.9	66.7	S	57.1	42.9
12	71.4	71.4	61.9	S	42.9	71.4	S	42.9	S	47.6	61.9	S
13	61.9	81.0	47.6	61.9	52.4	S	52.4	57.1	S	52.4	38.1	S
14	47.6	S	S	47.6	57.1	S	71.4	61.9	66.7	57.1	S	52.4
15	42.9	S	S	42.9	47.6	66.7	57.1	S	42.9	57.1	S	66.7
16	66.7	H	47.6	42.9	S	52.4	57.1	S	81.0	61.9	57.1	52.4
17	S	71.4	71.4	66.7	S	61.9	66.7	57.1	42.9	S	66.7	38.1
18	S	42.9	71.4	S	57.1	47.6	S	52.4	47.6	S	42.9	42.9
19	H	38.1	76.2	S	38.1	H	S	57.1	S	57.1	57.1	S
20	47.6	33.3	61.9	33.3	42.9	S	71.4	47.6	S	42.9	66.7	S
21	47.6	S	S	57.1	47.6	S	19.0	42.9	38.1	38.1	S	61.9
22	52.4	S	S	61.9	47.6	47.6	57.1	S	28.6	71.4	S	66.7
23	66.7	42.9	42.9	52.4	S	47.6	52.4	S	38.1	66.7	57.1	57.1
24	S	42.9	52.4	61.9	S	19.0	47.6	57.1	52.4	S	66.7	76.2
25	S	76.2	66.7	S	H	57.1	S	61.9	52.4	S	66.7	H
26	57.1	61.9	38.1	S	71.4	61.9	S	57.1	S	47.6	H	S
27	61.9	33.3	47.6	33.3	66.7	S	52.4	81.0	S	52.4	57.1	S
28	57.1	S	S	52.4	66.7	S	47.6	57.1	61.9	57.1	S	61.9
29	42.9		S	81.0	42.9	61.9	42.9	S	38.1	66.7	S	38.1
30	52.4		71.4	28.6	S	52.4	71.4	S	52.4	47.6	47.6	38.1
31	S		52.4		S		42.9	52.4		S		28.6

* See developing trends on pages 72, 90, 143–148   ** Based on most recent 21-year period
H = Holiday, S = Saturday/Sunday

RUSSELL 1000 INDEX MARKET PROBABILITY CALENDAR 2026

THE % CHANCE OF THE MARKET RISING ON ANY TRADING DAY OF THE YEAR*
(Based on the number of times the Russell 1000 rose on a particular trading day during **January 1980–December 2024**)

Date	Jan	Feb	Mar	Apr	May	Jun	Jul	Aug	Sep	Oct	Nov	Dec
1	H	S	S	60.0	57.8	60.0	80.0	S	55.6	55.6	S	51.1
2	44.4	68.9	60.0	62.2	S	64.4	44.4	S	48.9	53.3	73.3	51.1
3	S	64.4	46.7	H	S	48.9	H	40.0	48.9	S	57.8	57.8
4	S	55.6	57.8	S	60.0	57.8	S	40.0	40.0	S	62.2	42.2
5	55.6	55.6	42.2	S	51.1	40.0	S	48.9	S	57.8	66.7	S
6	55.6	55.6	42.2	51.1	40.0	S	48.9	51.1	S	55.6	53.3	S
7	55.6	S	S	57.8	51.1	S	57.8	53.3	H	40.0	S	51.1
8	53.3	S	S	48.9	53.3	51.1	57.8	S	48.9	53.3	S	51.1
9	62.2	53.3	51.1	71.1	S	40.0	55.6	S	60.0	42.2	60.0	51.1
10	S	46.7	57.8	55.6	S	48.9	62.2	53.3	64.4	S	44.4	51.1
11	S	71.1	44.4	S	55.6	57.8	S	44.4	68.9	S	55.6	44.4
12	60.0	64.4	57.8	S	53.3	57.8	S	46.7	S	44.4	55.6	S
13	55.6	53.3	42.2	51.1	48.9	S	64.4	44.4	S	60.0	53.3	S
14	55.6	S	S	51.1	55.6	S	77.8	62.2	57.8	62.2	S	37.8
15	62.2	S	S	55.6	57.8	60.0	51.1	S	53.3	57.8	S	57.8
16	64.4	H	55.6	62.2	S	53.3	53.3	S	53.3	60.0	53.3	57.8
17	S	66.7	62.2	57.8	S	57.8	51.1	64.4	46.7	S	51.1	46.7
18	S	42.2	55.6	S	53.3	40.0	S	62.2	44.4	S	55.6	42.2
19	H	40.0	53.3	S	48.9	H	S	60.0	S	44.8	53.3	S
20	44.4	37.8	48.9	46.7	46.7	S	62.2	62.2	S	66.7	60.0	S
21	42.2	S	S	51.1	42.2	S	37.8	48.9	35.6	46.7	S	53.3
22	51.1	S	S	53.3	60.0	51.1	42.2	S	42.2	48.9	S	66.7
23	51.1	44.4	42.2	55.6	S	44.4	48.9	S	37.8	48.9	66.7	62.2
24	S	46.7	46.7	51.1	S	33.3	42.2	55.6	42.2	S	66.7	62.2
25	S	60.0	53.3	S	H	44.4	S	48.9	44.4	S	68.9	H
26	53.3	55.6	42.2	S	60.0	51.1	S	55.6	S	35.6	H	S
27	57.8	46.7	48.9	51.1	57.8	S	71.1	62.2	S	53.3	64.4	S
28	51.1	S	S	57.8	57.8	S	51.1	51.1	64.4	48.9	S	66.7
29	57.8		S	62.2	51.1	62.2	44.4	S	53.3	64.4	S	55.6
30	57.8		48.9	51.1	S	55.6	62.2	S	51.1	62.2	48.9	60.0
31	S		51.1		S		57.8	55.6		S		46.7

* See developing trends on pages 72, 90, 143–148
H = Holiday, S = Saturday/Sunday

RUSSELL 2000 INDEX MARKET PROBABILITY CALENDAR 2026
THE % CHANCE OF THE MARKET RISING ON ANY TRADING DAY OF THE YEAR*
(Based on the number of times the Russell 2000 rose on a particular trading day during January 1980–December 2024)

Date	Jan	Feb	Mar	Apr	May	Jun	Jul	Aug	Sep	Oct	Nov	Dec
1	H	S	S	48.9	62.2	64.4	68.9	S	51.1	48.9	S	48.9
2	44.4	71.1	66.7	57.8	S	71.1	46.7	S	57.8	46.7	64.4	60.0
3	S	60.0	55.6	H	S	48.9	H	42.2	48.9	S	71.1	60.0
4	S	53.3	60.0	S	64.4	55.6	S	42.2	55.6	S	64.4	57.8
5	60.0	66.7	51.1	S	57.8	60.0	S	46.7	S	53.3	62.2	S
6	55.6	60.0	55.6	44.4	55.6	S	44.4	51.1	S	62.2	55.6	S
7	60.0	S	S	53.3	60.0	S	55.6	51.1	H	40.0	S	48.9
8	57.8	S	S	46.7	51.1	44.4	51.1	S	55.6	48.9	S	55.6
9	60.0	60.0	48.9	62.2	S	40.0	60.0	S	60.0	51.1	55.6	46.7
10	S	51.1	55.6	57.8	S	51.1	57.8	46.7	62.2	S	48.9	46.7
11	S	68.9	42.2	S	57.8	55.6	S	51.1	60.0	S	64.4	42.2
12	60.0	64.4	60.0	S	48.9	57.8	S	44.4	S	48.9	48.9	S
13	62.2	66.7	48.9	62.2	51.1	S	60.0	48.9	S	62.2	46.7	S
14	62.2	S	S	51.1	51.1	S	64.4	66.7	57.8	55.6	S	37.8
15	60.0	S	S	55.6	51.1	60.0	55.6	S	42.2	64.4	S	44.4
16	68.9	H	51.1	57.8	S	51.1	51.1	S	51.1	51.1	51.1	51.1
17	S	60.0	62.2	60.0	S	42.2	51.1	57.8	44.4	S	31.1	60.0
18	S	53.3	64.4	S	55.6	46.7	S	57.8	40.0	S	57.8	55.6
19	H	42.2	57.8	S	48.9	H	S	55.6	S	46.7	51.1	S
20	64.4	40.0	44.4	48.9	57.8	S	53.3	46.7	S	60.0	64.4	S
21	37.8	S	S	53.3	53.3	S	35.6	46.7	40.0	48.9	S	64.4
22	51.1	S	S	60.0	60.0	44.4	48.9	S	46.7	48.9	S	66.7
23	55.6	51.1	55.6	55.6	S	51.1	44.4	S	35.6	48.9	66.7	66.7
24	S	53.3	48.9	51.1	S	42.2	46.7	62.2	46.7	S	62.2	75.6
25	S	60.0	57.8	S	H	51.1	S	62.2	40.0	S	57.8	H
26	48.9	64.4	48.9	S	51.1	51.1	S	55.6	S	35.6	H	S
27	64.4	55.6	51.1	55.6	64.4	S	64.4	66.7	S	42.2	68.9	S
28	53.3	S	S	66.7	64.4	S	60.0	62.2	55.6	51.1	S	64.4
29	51.1		S	60.0	57.8	68.9	46.7	S	51.1	55.6	S	51.1
30	71.1		55.6	57.8	S	66.7	57.8	S	62.2	66.7	64.4	57.8
31	S		80.0		S		62.2	64.4		S		60.0

* See new trends developing on pages 72, 90, 143–148
H = Holiday, S = Saturday/Sunday

DECENNIAL CYCLE: A MARKET PHENOMENON

By arranging each year's market gain or loss so the first and succeeding years of each decade fall into the same column, certain interesting patterns emerge—strong fifth and eighth years; weak second, seventh, and zero years.

This fascinating phenomenon was first presented by Edgar Lawrence Smith in *Common Stocks and Business Cycles* (William-Frederick Press, 1959). Anthony Gaubis co-pioneered the decennial pattern with Smith.

When Smith first cut graphs of market prices into 10-year segments and placed them above one another, he observed that each decade tended to have three bull market cycles and that the longest and strongest bull markets seem to favor the middle years of a decade.

Don't place too much emphasis on the decennial cycle nowadays, other than the extraordinary fifth and zero years, as the stock market is more influenced by the quadrennial presidential election cycle, shown on page 132. Also, the last half-century, which has been the most prosperous in U.S. history, has distributed the returns among most years of the decade. Interestingly, NASDAQ suffered its worst bear market ever in a zero year.

Sixth years are fifth best in the decennial cycle with an average gain of +7.2% which is modestly better than the +6.9% average gain of all years. 2026 is a midterm-election year which has the second weakest record in the four-year-presidential-election cycle since 1833, but the weakest since 1949. The last six years ending in six that were also midterm-election years (2006, 1986, 1966, 1946, 1926, and 1906) were mixed and averaged just +1.7%.

THE 10-YEAR STOCK MARKET CYCLE
Annual % Change in Dow Jones Industrial Average

					Year of Decade					
DECADES	1st	2nd	3rd	4th	5th	6th	7th	8th	9th	10th
1881–1890	3.0%	−2.9%	−8.5%	−18.8%	20.1%	12.4%	−8.4%	4.8%	5.5%	−14.1%
1891–1900	17.6	−6.6	−24.6	−0.6	2.3	−1.7	21.3	22.5	9.2	7.0
1901–1910	−8.7	−0.4	−23.6	41.7	38.2	−1.9	−37.7	46.6	15.0	−17.9
1911–1920	0.4	7.6	−10.3	−5.4	81.7	−4.2	−21.7	10.5	30.5	−32.9
1921–1930	12.7	21.7	−3.3	26.2	30.0	0.3	28.8	48.2	−17.2	−33.8
1931–1940	−52.7	−23.1	66.7	4.1	38.5	24.8	−32.8	28.1	−2.9	−12.7
1941–1950	−15.4	7.6	13.8	12.1	26.6	−8.1	2.2	−2.1	12.9	17.6
1951–1960	14.4	8.4	−3.8	44.0	20.8	2.3	−12.8	34.0	16.4	−9.3
1961–1970	18.7	−10.8	17.0	14.6	10.9	−18.9	15.2	4.3	−15.2	4.8
1971–1980	6.1	14.6	−16.6	−27.6	38.3	17.9	−17.3	−3.1	4.2	14.9
1981–1990	−9.2	19.6	20.3	−3.7	27.7	22.6	2.3	11.8	27.0	−4.3
1991–2000	20.3	4.2	13.7	2.1	33.5	26.0	22.6	16.1	25.2	−6.2
2001–2010	−7.1	−16.8	25.3	3.1	−0.6	16.3	6.4	−33.8	18.8	11.0
2011–2020	5.5	7.3	26.5	7.5	−2.2	13.4	25.1	−5.6	22.3	7.2
2021–2030	18.7	−8.8	13.7	12.9						
Total % Change	24.3%	21.6%	106.3%	112.3%	365.8%	101.2%	−6.8%	182.3%	151.7%	−68.7%
Avg % Change	1.6%	1.4%	6.6%	7.5%	26.1%	7.2%	−0.5%	13.0%	10.8%	−4.9%
Up Years	10	8	8	10	12	9	8	10	11	6
Down Years	5	7	7	5	2	5	6	4	3	8

Based on annual close; Cowles indices 1881–1885; 12 Mixed Stocks, 10 Rails, 2 Inds 1886–1889;
20 Mixed Stocks, 18 Rails, 2 Inds 1890–1896; Railroad average 1897 (First industrial average published May 26, 1896).

PRESIDENTIAL ELECTION/STOCK MARKET CYCLE: THE 192-YEAR SAGA CONTINUES

It is no mere coincidence that the last two years (pre-election year and election year) of the 48 presidential terms since 1833 produced a total net market gain of 798.6%, dwarfing the 336.5% gain of the first two years of these terms.

Presidential elections every four years have a profound impact on the economy and the stock market. Wars, recessions and bear markets tend to start or occur in the first half of the term (2022 Russia-Ukraine War and bear market); prosperous times and bull markets, in the latter half. A millennial bull market, financial crisis, and a global pandemic had temporarily overridden the four-year cycle in recent decades, but the four-year cycle continues to reassert its overarching domination of market behavior as incumbents incessantly seek re-election or to keep the party in power.

STOCK MARKET ACTION SINCE 1833
Annual % Change in Dow Jones Industrial Average[1]

4-Year Cycle Beginning	President Elected	Post-Election Year	Midterm Year	Pre-Election Year	Election Year
1833	Jackson (D)	−0.9	13.0	3.1	−11.7
1837	Van Buren (D)	−11.5	1.6	−12.3	5.5
1841*	W.H. Harrison (W)**	−13.3	−18.1	45.0	15.5
1845*	Polk (D)	8.1	−14.5	1.2	−3.6
1849*	Taylor (W)	N/C	18.7	−3.2	19.6
1853*	Pierce (D)	−12.7	−30.2	1.5	4.4
1857	Buchanan (D)	−31.0	14.3	−10.7	14.0
1861*	Lincoln (R)	−1.8	55.4	38.0	6.4
1865	Lincoln (R)**	−8.5	3.6	1.6	10.8
1869	Grant (R)	1.7	5.6	7.3	6.8
1873	Grant (R)	−12.7	2.8	−4.1	−17.9
1877	Hayes (R)	−9.4	6.1	43.0	18.7
1881	Garfield (R)**	3.0	−2.9	−8.5	−18.8
1885*	Cleveland (D)	20.1	12.4	−8.4	4.8
1889*	B. Harrison (R)	5.5	−14.1	17.6	−6.6
1893*	Cleveland (D)	−24.6	−0.6	2.3	−1.7
1897*	McKinley (R)	21.3	22.5	9.2	7.0
1901	McKinley (R)**	−8.7	−0.4	−23.6	41.7
1905	T. Roosevelt (R)	38.2	−1.9	−37.7	46.6
1909	Taft (R)	15.0	−17.9	0.4	7.6
1913*	Wilson (D)	−10.3	−5.4	81.7	−4.2
1917	Wilson (D)	−21.7	10.5	30.5	−32.9
1921*	Harding (R)**	12.7	21.7	−3.3	26.2
1925	Coolidge (R)	30.0	0.3	28.8	48.2
1929	Hoover (R)	−17.2	−33.8	−52.7	−23.1
1933*	F. Roosevelt (D)	66.7	4.1	38.5	24.8
1937	F. Roosevelt (D)	−32.8	28.1	−2.9	−12.7
1941	F. Roosevelt (D)	−15.4	7.6	13.8	12.1
1945	F. Roosevelt (D)**	26.6	−8.1	2.2	−2.1
1949	Truman (D)	12.9	17.6	14.4	8.4
1953*	Eisenhower (R)	−3.8	44.0	20.8	2.3
1957	Eisenhower (R)	−12.8	34.0	16.4	−9.3
1961*	Kennedy (D)**	18.7	−10.8	17.0	14.6
1965	Johnson (D)	10.9	−18.9	15.2	4.3
1969*	Nixon (R)	−15.2	4.8	6.1	14.6
1973	Nixon (R)***	−16.6	−27.6	38.3	17.9
1977*	Carter (D)	−17.3	−3.1	4.2	14.9
1981*	Reagan (R)	−9.2	19.6	20.3	−3.7
1985	Reagan (R)	27.7	22.6	2.3	11.8
1989	G. H. W. Bush (R)	27.0	−4.3	20.3	4.2
1993*	Clinton (D)	13.7	2.1	33.5	26.0
1997	Clinton (D)	22.6	16.1	25.2	−6.2
2001*	G. W. Bush (R)	−7.1	−16.8	25.3	3.1
2005	G. W. Bush (R)	−0.6	16.3	6.4	−33.8
2009*	Obama (D)	18.8	11.0	5.5	7.3
2013	Obama (D)	26.5	7.5	−2.2	13.4
2017*	Trump (R)	25.1	−5.6	22.3	7.2
2021*	Biden (D)	18.7	−8.8	13.7	12.9
Total % Gain		156.4%	180.1%	503.3%	295.3%
Average % Gain		3.3%	3.8%	10.5%	6.2%
# Up		23	28	36	33
# Down		24	20	12	15

*Party in power ousted   **Died in office   ***Resigned   D–Democrat, W–Whig, R–Republican

[1] Based on annual close; prior to 1886 based on Cowles and other indices; 12 Mixed Stocks, 10 Rails, 2 Inds 1886–1889; 20 Mixed Stocks, 18 Rails, 2 Inds 1890–1896; Railroad average 1897 (First industrial average published May 26, 1896).

DOW JONES INDUSTRIALS BULL AND BEAR MARKETS SINCE 1900

Bear markets begin at the end of one bull market and end at the start of the next bull market (1/4/2022 to 9/30/2022 as an example). The longest bull market on record ended on 7/17/98, and the shortest bear market on record ended on 3/23/2020, when the new bull market began. The greatest bull super cycle in history that began 8/12/82 ended in 2000 after the Dow gained 1409% and NASDAQ climbed 3072%. The Dow gained only 497% in the eight-year super bull from 1921 to the top in 1929. NASDAQ suffered its worst loss ever from the 2000 top to the 2002 bottom, down 77.9%, nearly as much as the 89.2% drop in the Dow from the 1929 top to the 1932 bottom. The third longest Dow bull since 1900 that began 10/9/02 ended on its fifth anniversary. The ensuing bear market was the second worst bear market since 1900, slashing the Dow 53.8%. At press time, Dow is currently in a bull market, trading around 43,000, rebounding after a pullback from all-time highs due to tariff, economic, and interest rate uncertainty. (See page 134 for S&P 500 and NASDAQ bulls and bears.)

DOW JONES INDUSTRIALS BULL AND BEAR MARKETS SINCE 1900

— Beginning —		— Ending —		Bull		Bear	
Date	DJIA	Date	DJIA	% Gain	Days	% Change	Days
9/24/00	38.80	6/17/01	57.33	47.8%	266	−46.1%	875
11/9/03	30.88	1/19/06	75.45	144.3	802	−48.5	665
11/15/07	38.83	11/19/09	73.64	89.6	735	−27.4	675
9/25/11	53.43	9/30/12	68.97	29.1	371	−24.1	668
7/30/14	52.32	11/21/16	110.15	110.5	845	−40.1	393
12/19/17	65.95	11/3/19	119.62	81.4	684	−46.6	660
8/24/21	63.90	3/20/23	105.38	64.9	573	−18.6	221
10/27/23	85.76	9/3/29	381.17	344.5	2138	−47.9	71
11/13/29	198.69	4/17/30	294.07	48.0	155	−86.0	813
7/8/32	41.22	9/7/32	79.93	93.9	61	−37.2	173
2/27/33	50.16	2/5/34	110.74	120.8	343	−22.8	171
7/26/34	85.51	3/10/37	194.40	127.3	958	−49.1	386
3/31/38	98.95	11/12/38	158.41	60.1	226	−23.3	147
4/8/39	121.44	9/12/39	155.92	28.4	157	−40.4	959
4/28/42	92.92	5/29/46	212.50	128.7	1492	−23.2	133
10/9/46	163.12	6/15/48	193.16	18.4	615	−16.3	363
6/13/49	161.60	1/5/53	293.79	81.8	1302	−13.0	252
9/14/53	255.49	4/6/56	521.05	103.9	935	−19.4	564
10/22/57	419.79	1/5/60	685.47	63.3	805	−17.4	294
10/25/60	566.05	12/13/61	734.91	29.8	414	−27.1	195
6/26/62	535.76	2/9/66	995.15	85.7	1324	−25.2	240
10/7/66	744.32	12/3/68	985.21	32.4	788	−35.9	539
5/26/70	631.16	4/28/71	950.82	50.6	337	−16.1	209
11/23/71	797.97	1/11/73	1051.70	31.8	415	−45.1	694
12/6/74	577.60	9/21/76	1014.79	75.7	655	−26.9	525
2/28/78	742.12	9/8/78	907.74	22.3	192	−16.4	591
4/21/80	759.13	4/27/81	1024.05	34.9	371	−24.1	472
8/12/82	776.92	11/29/83	1287.20	65.7	474	−15.6	238
7/24/84	1086.57	8/25/87	2722.42	150.6	1127	−36.1	55
10/19/87	1738.74	7/17/90	2999.75	72.5	1002	−21.2	86
10/11/90	2365.10	7/17/98	9337.97	294.8	2836	−19.3	45
8/31/98	7539.07	1/14/00	11722.98	55.5	501	−29.7	616
9/21/01	8235.81	3/19/02	10635.25	29.1	179	−31.5	204
10/9/02	7286.27	10/9/07	14164.53	94.4	1826	−53.8	517
3/9/09	6547.05	4/29/11	12810.54	95.7	781	−16.8	157
10/3/11	10655.30	5/19/15	18312.39	71.9	1324	−14.5	268
2/11/16	15660.18	2/12/20	29551.42	88.7	1462	−37.1	40
3/23/20	18591.93	1/4/22	36799.65	97.9	652	−21.9	269
9/30/22	28725.51	12/4/24	45014.04	56.7%*	796*		
				*As of May 2, 2025—not in averages			
			Average	86.0%	793	−30.6%	380

Based on Dow Jones Industrial Average.
1900–2000 Data: Ned Davis Research
The NYSE was closed from 7/31/1914 to 12/11/1914 due to World War I.
DJIA figures were then adjusted back to reflect the composition change from 12 to 20 stocks in September 1916.

STANDARD & POOR'S 500 BULL AND BEAR MARKETS SINCE 1929
NASDAQ COMPOSITE SINCE 1971

A constant debate of the definition and timing of bull and bear markets permeates Wall Street like the bell that signals the open and close of every trading day. We have relied on the Ned Davis Research parameters for years to track bulls and bears on the Dow (see page 133). Standard & Poor's 500 index has been a stalwart indicator for decades and at times marched to a slightly different beat than the Dow. The moves of the S&P 500 and NASDAQ have been correlated to the bull & bear dates on page 133. Many dates line up for the three indices, but you will notice quite a lag or lead on several occasions, especially NASDAQ's independent cadence from 1975 to 1980. The 2022 bear market ended on different days for the three indices.

STANDARD & POOR'S 500 BULL AND BEAR MARKETS

— Beginning —		— Ending —		Bull		Bear	
Date	S&P 500	Date	S&P 500	% Gain	Days	% Change	Days
11/13/29	17.66	4/10/30	25.92	46.8%	148	–83.0%	783
6/1/32	4.40	9/7/32	9.31	111.6	98	–40.6	173
2/27/33	5.53	2/6/34	11.82	113.7	344	–31.8	401
3/14/35	8.06	3/6/37	18.68	131.8	723	–49.0	390
3/31/38	8.50	11/9/38	13.79	62.2	223	–26.2	150
4/8/39	10.18	10/25/39	13.21	29.8	200	–43.5	916
4/28/42	7.47	5/29/46	19.25	157.7	1492	–28.8	353
5/17/47	13.71	6/15/48	17.06	24.4	395	–20.6	363
6/13/49	13.55	1/5/53	26.66	96.8	1302	–14.8	252
9/14/53	22.71	8/2/56	49.74	119.0	1053	–21.6	446
10/22/57	38.98	8/3/59	60.71	55.7	650	–13.9	449
10/25/60	52.30	12/12/61	72.64	38.9	413	–28.0	196
6/26/62	52.32	2/9/66	94.06	79.8	1324	–22.2	240
10/7/66	73.20	11/29/68	108.37	48.0	784	–36.1	543
5/26/70	69.29	4/28/71	104.77	51.2	337	–13.9	209
11/23/71	90.16	1/11/73	120.24	33.4	415	–48.2	630
10/3/74	62.28	9/21/76	107.83	73.1	719	–19.4	531
3/6/78	86.90	9/12/78	106.99	23.1	190	–8.2	562
3/27/80	98.22	11/28/80	140.52	43.1	246	–27.1	622
8/12/82	102.42	10/10/83	172.65	68.6	424	–14.4	288
7/24/84	147.82	8/25/87	336.77	127.8	1127	–33.5	101
12/4/87	223.92	7/16/90	368.95	64.8	955	–19.9	87
10/11/90	295.46	7/17/98	1186.75	301.7	2836	–19.3	45
8/31/98	957.28	3/24/00	1527.46	59.6	571	–36.8	546
9/21/01	965.80	1/4/02	1172.51	21.4	105	–33.8	278
10/9/02	776.76	10/9/07	1565.15	101.5	1826	–56.8	517
3/9/09	676.53	4/29/11	1363.61	101.6	781	–19.4	157
10/3/11	1099.23	5/21/15	2130.82	93.8	1326	–14.2	266
2/11/16	1829.08	2/19/20	3386.15	85.1	1469	–33.9	33
3/23/20	2237.40	1/3/22	4796.56	114.4	651	–25.4	282
10/12/22	3577.03	2/19/25	6144.15	71.8%*	861*	*As of May 2, 2025—not in averages	
		Average		82.7%	771	–29.7%	360

NASDAQ COMPOSITE BULL AND BEAR MARKETS

— Beginning —		— Ending —		Bull		Bear	
Date	NASDAQ	Date	NASDAQ	% Gain	Days	% Change	Days
11/23/71	100.31	1/11/73	136.84	36.4%	415	–59.9%	630
10/3/74	54.87	7/15/75	88.00	60.4	285	–16.2	63
9/16/75	73.78	9/13/78	139.25	88.7	1093	–20.4	62
11/14/78	110.88	2/8/80	165.25	49.0	451	–24.9	48
3/27/80	124.09	5/29/81	223.47	80.1	428	–28.8	441
8/13/82	159.14	6/24/83	328.91	106.7	315	–31.5	397
7/25/84	225.30	8/26/87	455.26	102.1	1127	–35.9	63
10/28/87	291.88	10/9/89	485.73	66.4	712	–33.0	372
10/16/90	325.44	7/20/98	2014.25	518.9	2834	–29.5	80
10/8/98	1419.12	3/10/00	5048.62	255.8	519	–71.8	560
9/21/01	1423.19	1/4/02	2059.38	44.7	105	–45.9	278
10/9/02	1114.11	10/31/07	2859.12	156.6	1848	–55.6	495
3/9/09	1268.64	4/29/11	2873.54	126.5	781	–18.7	157
10/3/11	2335.83	7/20/15	5218.86	123.4	1386	–18.2	206
2/11/16	4266.84	2/19/20	9817.18	130.1	1469	–30.1	33
3/23/20	6860.67	11/19/21	16057.44	134.1	606	–36.4	404
12/28/22	10213.29	12/16/24	20173.89	97.5%*	719*	*As of May 2, 2025—not in averages	
		Average		130.0%	898	–34.8%	268

JANUARY DAILY POINT CHANGES DOW JONES INDUSTRIALS

	2016	2017	2018	2019	2020	2021	2022	2023	2024	2025
Previous Month Close	17425.03	19762.60	24719.22	23327.46	28538.44	30606.48	36338.30	33147.25	37689.54	42544.22
1	H	S	H	H	H	H	S	S	H	H
2	S	H	104.79	18.78	330.36	S	S	H	25.50	−151.95
3	S	119.16	98.67	−660.02	−233.92	S	246.76	−10.88	−284.85	339.86
4	−276.09	60.40	152.45	746.94	S	−382.59	214.59	133.40	10.15	S
5	9.72	−42.87	220.74	S	S	167.71	−392.54	−339.69	25.77	S
6	−252.15	64.51	S	S	68.50	437.80	−170.64	700.53	S	−25.57
7	−392.41	S	S	98.19	−119.70	211.73	−4.81	S	S	−178.20
8	−167.65	S	−12.87	256.10	161.41	56.84	S	S	216.90	106.84
9	S	−76.42	102.80	91.67	211.81	S	S	−112.96	−157.85	H*
10	S	−31.85	−16.67	122.80	−133.13	S	−162.79	186.45	170.57	−696.75
11	52.12	98.75	205.60	−5.97	S	−89.28	183.15	268.91	15.29	S
12	117.65	−63.28	228.46	S	60.00	38.30	216.96	−118.04	S
13	−364.81	−5.27	S	S	83.28	−8.22	−176.70	112.64	S	358.67
14	227.64	S	S	−86.11	32.62	−68.95	−201.81	S	S	221.16
15	−390.97	S	H	155.75	90.55	−177.26	S	S	H	703.27
16	S	H	−10.33	141.57	267.42	S	S	H	−231.86	−68.42
17	S	−58.96	322.79	162.94	50.46	S	H	−391.76	−94.45	334.70
18	H	−22.05	−97.84	336.25	S	S	H	−543.34	−613.89	201.94	S
19	27.94	−72.32	53.91	S	S	H	116.26	−339.82	−252.40	395.19	S
20	−249.28	94.85	S	S	H	257.86	−313.26	330.93	S	H
21	115.94	S	S	H	−152.06	−12.37	−450.02	S	S	537.98
22	210.83	S	142.88	−301.87	−9.77	−179.03	S	138.01	130.92
23	S	−27.40	−3.79	171.14	−26.18	S	S	254.07	−96.36	408.34
24	S	112.86	41.31	−22.38	−170.36	S	99.13	104.40	−99.06	−140.82
25	−208.29	155.80	140.67	183.96	S	−36.98	−66.77	9.88	242.74	S
26	282.01	32.40	223.92	S	S	−22.96	−129.64	205.57	60.30	S
27	−222.77	−7.13	S	S	−453.93	−633.87	−7.31	28.67	S	289.33
28	125.18	S	S	−208.98	187.05	300.19	564.69	S	S	136.77
29	396.66	S	−177.23	51.74	11.60	−620.74	S	S	224.02	−136.83
30	S	−122.65	−362.59	434.90	124.99	S	S	−260.99	133.86	168.61
31	S	−107.04	72.50	−15.19	−603.41	S	406.39	368.95	−317.01	−337.47
Close	16466.30	19864.09	26149.39	24999.67	28256.03	29982.62	35131.86	34086.04	38150.30	44544.66
Change	−958.73	101.49	1430.17	1672.21	−282.41	−623.86	−1206.44	938.79	460.76	2000.44

FEBRUARY DAILY POINT CHANGES DOW JONES INDUSTRIALS

	2016	2017	2018	2019	2020	2021	2022	2023	2024	2025
Previous Month Close	16466.30	19864.09	26149.39	24999.67	28256.03	29982.62	35131.86	34086.04	38150.30	44544.66
1	−17.12	26.85	37.32	64.22	S	229.29	273.38	6.92	369.54	S
2	−295.64	−6.03	−665.75	S	S	475.57	224.09	−39.02	134.58	S
3	183.12	186.55	S	S	143.78	36.12	−518.17	−127.93	S	−122.75
4	79.92	S	S	175.48	407.82	332.26	−21.42	S	S	134.13
5	−211.61	S	−1175.21	172.15	483.22	92.38	S	S	−274.30	317.24
6	S	−19.04	567.02	−21.22	88.92	S	S	−34.99	141.24	−125.65
7	S	37.87	−19.42	−220.77	−277.26	S	1.39	265.67	156.00	−444.23
8	−177.92	−35.95	−1032.89	−63.20	S	237.52	371.65	−207.68	48.97	S
9	−12.67	118.06	330.44	S	S	−9.93	305.28	−249.13	−54.64	S
10	−99.64	96.97	S	S	174.31	61.97	−526.47	169.39	S	167.01
11	−254.56	S	S	−53.22	−0.48	−7.10	−503.53	S	S	123.24
12	313.66	S	410.37	372.65	275.08	27.70	S	S	125.69	−225.09
13	S	142.79	39.18	117.51	−128.11	S	S	376.66	−524.63	342.87
14	S	92.25	253.04	−103.88	−25.23	S	−171.89	−156.66	151.52	−165.35
15	H	107.45	306.88	443.86	S	H	422.67	38.78	348.85	S
16	222.57	7.91	19.01	S	S	64.35	−54.57	−431.20	−145.13	S
17	257.42	4.28	S	S	H	90.27	−622.24	129.84	S	H
18	−40.40	S	S	H	−165.89	−119.68	−232.85	S	S	10.26
19	−21.44	S	H	8.07	115.84	0.98	S	S	H	71.25
20	S	H	−254.63	63.12	−128.05	S	S	H	−64.19	−450.94
21	S	118.95	−166.97	−103.81	−227.57	S	H	−697.10	48.44	−748.63
22	228.67	32.60	164.70	181.18	S	27.37	−482.57	−84.50	456.87	S
23	−188.88	34.72	347.51	S	S	15.66	−464.85	108.82	62.42	S
24	53.21	11.44	S	S	−1031.61	424.51	92.07	−336.99	S	33.19
25	212.30	S	S	60.14	−879.44	−559.85	834.92	S	S	159.95
26	−57.32	S	399.28	−33.97	−123.77	−469.64	S	S	−62.30	−188.04
27	S	15.68	−299.24	−72.82	−1190.95	S	S	72.17	−96.82	−193.62
28	S	−25.20	−380.83	−69.16	−357.28	S	−166.15	−232.39	−23.39	601.41
29	−123.47	—	—	—	—	—	—	—	47.37	—
Close	16516.50	20812.24	25029.20	25916.00	25409.36	30932.37	33892.60	32656.70	38996.39	43840.91
Change	50.20	948.15	−1120.19	916.33	−2846.67	949.75	−1239.26	−1429.34	846.09	−703.75

* President Carter Funeral

135

MARCH DAILY POINT CHANGES DOW JONES INDUSTRIALS

	2016	2017	2018	2019	2020	2021	2022	2023	2024	2025
Previous Month Close	16516.50	20812.24	25029.20	25916.00	25409.36	30932.37	33892.60	32656.70	38996.39	43840.91
1	348.58	303.31	– 420.22	110.32	S	603.14	– 597.65	5.14	90.99	S
2	34.24	– 112.58	– 70.92	S	1293.96	– 143.99	596.40	341.73	S	S
3	44.58	2.74	S	S	– 785.91	– 121.43	– 96.69	387.40	S	– 649.67
4	62.87	S	S	– 206.67	1173.45	– 345.95	– 179.86	S	– 97.55	– 670.25
5	S	S	336.70	– 13.02	– 969.58	572.16	S	S	– 404.64	485.60
6	S	– 51.37	9.36	– 133.17	– 256.50	S	S	40.47	75.86	– 427.51
7	67.18	– 29.58	– 82.76	– 200.23	S	S	– 797.42	– 574.98	130.30	222.64
8	– 109.85	– 69.03	93.85	– 22.99	S	306.14	– 184.74	– 58.06	– 68.66	S
9	36.26	2.46	440.53	S	– 2013.76	30.30	653.61	– 543.54	S	S
10	– 5.23	44.79	S	S	1167.14	464.28	– 112.18	– 345.22	S	– 890.01
11	218.18	S	S	200.64	– 1464.94	188.57	– 229.88	S	46.97	– 478.23
12	S	S	– 157.13	– 96.22	– 2352.60	293.05	S	S	235.83	– 82.55
13	S	– 21.50	– 171.58	148.23	1985.00	S	S	– 90.50	37.83	– 537.36
14	15.82	– 44.11	– 248.91	7.05	S	S	1.05	336.26	– 137.66	674.62
15	22.40	112.73	115.54	138.93	S	174.82	599.10	– 280.83	– 190.89	S
16	74.23	– 15.55	72.85	S	– 2997.10	– 127.51	518.76	371.98	S	S
17	155.73	– 19.93	S	S	1048.86	189.42	417.66	– 384.57	S	353.44
18	120.81	S	S	65.23	– 1338.46	– 153.07	274.17	S	75.66	– 260.32
19	S	S	– 335.60	– 26.72	188.27	– 234.33	S	S	320.33	383.32
20	S	– 8.76	116.36	– 141.71	– 913.21	S	S	382.60	401.37	– 11.31
21	21.57	– 237.85	– 44.96	216.84	S	S	– 201.94	316.02	269.24	32.03
22	– 41.30	– 6.71	– 724.42	– 460.19	S	103.23	254.47	– 530.49	– 305.47	S
23	– 79.98	– 4.72	– 424.69	S	– 582.05	– 308.05	– 448.96	75.14	S	S
24	13.14	– 59.86	S	S	2112.98	– 3.09	349.44	132.28	S	597.97
25	H	S	S	14.51	495.64	199.42	153.30	S	– 162.26	4.18
26	S	S	669.40	140.90	1351.62	453.40	S	S	– 31.31	– 132.71
27	S	– 45.74	– 344.89	– 32.14	– 915.39	S	S	194.55	477.75	– 155.09
28	19.66	150.52	– 9.29	91.87	S	S	94.65	– 37.83	47.29	– 715.80
29	97.72	– 42.18	254.69	211.22	S	98.49	338.30	323.35	H	S
30	83.55	69.17	H	S	690.70	– 104.41	– 65.38	141.43	S	S
31	– 31.57	– 65.27	S	S	– 410.32	– 85.41	– 550.46	415.12	S	417.86
Close	17685.09	20663.22	24103.11	25928.68	21917.16	32981.55	34678.35	33274.15	39807.37	42001.76
Change	1168.59	– 149.02	– 926.09	12.68	– 3492.20	2049.18	785.75	617.45	810.98	– 1839.15

APRIL DAILY POINT CHANGES DOW JONES INDUSTRIALS

	2016	2017	2018	2019	2020	2021	2022	2023	2024	2025
Previous Month Close	17685.09	20663.22	24103.11	25928.68	21917.16	32981.55	34678.35	33274.15	39807.37	42001.76
1	107.66	S	S	329.74	– 973.65	171.66	139.92	S	– 240.52	– 11.80
2	S	S	– 458.92	– 79.29	469.93	H	S	S	– 396.61	235.36
3	S	– 13.01	389.17	39.00	– 360.91	S	S	327.00	– 43.10	– 1679.39
4	– 55.75	39.03	230.94	166.50	S	S	103.61	– 198.77	– 530.16	– 2231.07
5	– 133.68	– 41.09	240.92	40.36	S	373.98	– 280.70	80.34	307.06	S
6	112.73	14.80	– 572.46	S	1627.46	– 96.95	– 144.67	2.57	S	S
7	– 174.09	– 6.85	S	S	– 26.13	16.02	87.06	H	S	– 349.26
8	35.00	S	S	– 83.97	779.71	57.31	137.55	S	– 11.24	– 320.01
9	S	S	46.34	– 190.44	285.80	297.03	S	S	– 9.13	2962.86
10	S	1.92	428.90	6.58	H	S	S	101.23	– 422.16	– 1014.79
11	– 20.55	– 6.72	– 218.55	– 14.11	S	S	– 413.04	98.27	– 2.43	619.05
12	164.84	– 59.44	293.60	269.25	S	– 55.20	– 87.72	– 38.29	– 475.84	S
13	187.03	– 138.61	– 122.91	S	– 328.60	– 68.13	344.23	383.19	S	S
14	18.15	H	S	S	558.99	53.62	– 113.36	– 143.22	S	312.08
15	– 28.97	S	S	– 27.53	– 445.41	305.10	H	S	– 248.13	– 155.83
16	S	S	212.90	67.89	33.33	164.68	S	S	63.86	– 699.57
17	S	183.67	213.59	– 3.12	704.81	S	S	100.71	– 45.66	– 527.16
18	106.70	– 113.64	– 38.56	110.00	S	S	– 39.54	– 10.55	22.07	H
19	49.44	– 118.79	– 83.18	H	S	– 123.04	499.51	– 79.62	211.02	S
20	42.67	174.22	– 201.95	S	– 592.05	– 256.33	249.59	– 110.39	S	S
21	– 113.75	– 30.95	S	S	– 631.56	316.01	– 368.03	22.34	S	– 971.82
22	21.23	S	S	– 48.49	456.94	– 321.41	– 981.36	S	253.58	1016.57
23	S	S	– 14.25	145.34	39.44	227.59	S	S	263.71	419.59
24	S	216.13	– 424.56	– 59.34	260.01	S	S	66.44	– 42.77	486.83
25	– 26.51	232.23	59.70	– 134.97	S	S	238.06	– 344.57	– 375.12	20.10
26	13.08	– 21.03	238.51	81.25	S	– 61.92	– 809.28	– 228.96	153.86	S
27	51.23	6.24	– 11.15	S	358.51	3.36	61.75	524.29	S	S
28	– 210.79	– 40.82	S	S	– 32.23	– 164.55	614.46	272.00	S	114.09
29	– 57.12	S	S	11.06	532.31	239.98	– 939.18	S	146.43	300.03
30	S	S	– 148.04	38.52	– 288.14	– 185.51	S	S	– 570.17	141.74
Close	17773.64	20940.51	24163.15	26592.91	24345.72	33874.85	32977.21	34098.16	37815.92	40669.36
Change	88.55	277.29	60.04	664.23	2428.56	893.30	– 1701.14	824.01	– 1991.45	– 1332.40

MAY DAILY POINT CHANGES DOW JONES INDUSTRIALS

Previous Month Close	2015	2016	2017	2018	2019	2020	2021	2022	2023	2024
	17840.52	17773.64	20940.51	24163.15	26592.91	24345.72	33874.85	32977.21	34098.16	37815.92
1	183.54	S	−27.05	−64.10	−162.77	−622.03	S	S	−46.46	87.37
2	S	117.52	36.43	−174.07	−122.35	S	S	84.29	−367.17	322.37
3	S	−140.25	8.01	5.17	197.16	S	238.38	67.29	−270.29	450.02
4	46.34	−99.65	−6.43	332.36	S	26.07	19.80	932.27	−286.50	S
5	−142.20	9.45	55.47	S	S	133.33	97.31	−1063.09	546.64	S
6	−86.22	79.92	S	S	−66.47	−218.45	318.19	−98.60	S	176.59
7	82.08	S	S	94.81	−473.39	211.25	229.23	S	S	31.99
8	267.05	S	5.34	2.89	2.24	455.43	S	S	−55.69	172.13
9	S	−34.72	−36.50	182.33	−138.97	S	S	−653.67	−56.88	331.37
10	S	222.44	−32.67	196.99	114.01	S	−34.94	−84.96	−30.48	125.08
11	−85.94	−217.23	−23.69	91.64	S	−109.33	−473.66	−326.63	−221.82	S
12	−36.94	9.38	−22.81	S	S	−457.21	−681.50	−103.81	−8.89	S
13	−7.74	−185.18	S	S	−617.38	−516.81	433.79	466.36	S	−81.33
14	191.75	S	S	68.24	207.06	377.37	360.68	S	S	126.60
15	20.32	S	85.33	−193.00	115.97	60.08	S	S	47.98	349.89
16	S	175.39	−2.19	62.52	214.66	S	S	26.76	−336.46	−38.62
17	S	−180.73	−372.82	−54.95	−98.68	S	−54.34	431.17	408.63	134.21
18	26.32	−3.36	56.09	1.11	S	911.95	−267.13	−1164.52	115.14	S
19	13.51	−91.22	141.82	S	S	−390.51	−164.62	−236.94	−109.28	S
20	−26.99	65.54	S	S	−84.10	369.04	188.11	8.77	S	−196.82
21	0.34	S	S	298.20	197.43	−101.78	123.69	S	S	66.22
22	−53.72	S	89.99	−178.88	−100.72	−8.96	S	S	−140.05	−201.95
23	S	−8.01	43.08	52.40	−286.14	S	S	618.34	−231.07	−605.78
24	S	213.12	74.51	−75.05	95.22	S	186.14	58.38	−255.59	4.33
25	H	145.46	70.53	−58.67	S	H	−81.52	181.66	−35.27	S
26	−190.48	−23.22	−2.67	S	S	529.95	10.59	516.91	328.69	H
27	121.45	44.93	S	S	H	553.16	141.59	575.77	S	H
28	−36.87	S	S	H	−237.92	−147.63	64.81	S	S	−216.73
29	−115.44	S	H	−391.64	−221.36	−17.53	S	S	H	−411.32
30	S	H	−50.81	306.33	43.47	S	S	H	−50.56	−330.06
31	S	−86.02	−20.82	−251.94	−354.84	S	H	−222.84	−134.51	574.84
Close	18010.68	17787.20	21008.65	24415.84	24815.04	25383.11	34529.45	32990.12	32908.27	38686.32
Change	170.16	13.56	68.14	252.69	−1777.87	1037.39	654.60	12.91	−1189.89	870.40

JUNE DAILY POINT CHANGES DOW JONES INDUSTRIALS

Previous Month Close	2015	2016	2017	2018	2019	2020	2021	2022	2023	2024
	18010.68	17787.20	21008.65	24415.84	24815.04	25383.11	34529.45	32990.12	32908.27	38686.32
1	29.69	2.47	135.53	219.37	S	91.91	45.86	−176.89	153.30	S
2	−28.43	48.89	62.11	S	S	267.63	25.07	435.05	701.19	S
3	64.33	−31.50	S	S	4.74	527.24	−23.34	−348.58	S	−115.29
4	−170.69	S	S	178.48	512.40	11.93	179.35	S	S	140.26
5	−56.12	S	−22.25	−13.71	207.39	829.16	S	S	−199.90	96.04
6	S	113.27	−47.81	346.41	181.09	S	S	16.08	10.42	78.84
7	S	17.95	37.46	95.02	263.28	S	−126.15	264.36	91.74	−87.18
8	−82.91	66.77	8.84	75.12	S	461.46	−30.42	−269.24	168.59	S
9	−2.51	−19.86	89.44	S	S	−300.14	−152.68	−638.11	43.17	S
10	236.36	−119.85	S	S	78.74	−282.31	19.10	−880.00	S	69.05
11	38.97	S	S	5.78	−14.17	−1861.82	13.36	S	S	−120.62
12	−140.53	S	−36.30	−1.58	−43.68	477.37	S	S	189.55	−35.21
13	S	−132.86	92.80	−119.53	101.94	S	S	−876.05	145.79	−65.11
14	S	−57.66	46.09	−25.89	−17.16	S	−85.85	−151.91	−232.79	−57.94
15	−107.67	−34.65	−14.66	−84.83	S	157.62	−94.42	303.70	428.73	S
16	113.31	92.93	24.38	S	S	526.82	−265.66	−741.46	−108.94	S
17	31.26	−57.94	S	S	22.92	−170.37	−210.22	−38.29	S	188.94
18	180.10	S	S	−103.01	353.01	−39.51	−533.37	S	S	56.76
19	−99.89	S	144.71	−287.26	38.46	−208.64	S	S	H	H
20	S	129.71	−61.85	−42.41	249.17	S	S	S	H	−245.25	299.90
21	S	24.86	−57.11	−196.10	−34.04	S	586.89	641.47	−102.35	15.57
22	103.83	−48.90	−12.74	119.19	S	153.50	68.61	−47.12	−4.81	S
23	24.29	230.24	−2.53	S	S	131.14	−71.34	194.23	−219.28	S
24	−178.00	−610.32	S	S	8.41	−710.16	322.58	823.32	S	260.88
25	−75.71	S	S	−328.09	−179.32	299.66	237.02	S	S	−299.05
26	56.32	S	14.79	30.31	−11.40	−730.05	S	S	−12.72	15.64
27	S	−260.51	−98.89	−165.52	−10.24	S	S	−62.42	212.03	36.26
28	S	269.48	143.95	98.46	73.38	S	−150.57	−491.27	−74.08	−45.20
29	−350.33	284.96	−167.58	55.36	S	580.25	9.02	82.32	269.76	S
30	23.16	235.31	62.60	S	S	217.08	210.22	−253.88	285.18	S
Close	17619.51	17929.99	21349.63	24271.41	26599.96	25812.88	34502.51	30775.43	34407.60	39118.86
Change	−391.17	142.79	340.98	−144.43	1784.92	429.77	−26.94	−2214.69	1499.33	432.54

JULY DAILY POINT CHANGES DOW JONES INDUSTRIALS

Previous Month Close	2015	2016	2017	2018	2019	2020	2021	2022	2023	2024
	17619.51	17929.99	21349.63	24271.41	26599.96	25812.88	34502.51	30775.43	34407.60	39118.86
1	138.40	19.38	S	S	117.47	−77.91	131.02	321.83	S	50.66
2	−27.80	S	S	35.77	69.25	92.39	152.82	S	S	162.33
3	H	S	129.64*	−132.36*	179.32*	H	S	S	10.87*	−23.85*
4	S	H	H	H	H	H	S	H	H	H
5	S	−108.75	−1.10	181.92	−43.88	S	H	−129.44	−129.83	67.87
6	−46.53	78.00	−158.13	99.74	S	459.67	−208.98	69.86	−366.38	S
7	93.33	−22.74	94.30	S	S	−396.85	104.42	346.87	−187.38	S
8	−261.49	250.86	S	S	−115.98	177.10	−259.86	−46.40	S	−31.08
9	33.20	S	S	320.11	−22.65	−361.19	448.23	S	S	−52.82
10	211.79	S	−5.82	143.07	76.71	369.21	S	S	209.52	429.39
11	S	80.19	0.55	−219.21	227.88	S	S	−164.31	317.02	32.39
12	S	120.74	123.07	224.44	243.95	S	126.02	−192.51	86.01	247.15
13	217.27	24.45	20.95	94.52	S	10.50	−107.39	−208.54	47.71	S
14	75.90	134.29	84.65	S	S	556.79	44.44	−142.62	113.89	S
15	−3.41	10.14	S	S	27.13	227.51	53.79	658.09	S	210.82
16	70.08	S	S	44.95	−23.53	−135.39	−299.17	S	S	742.76
17	−33.80	S	−8.02	55.53	−115.78	−62.76	S	S	76.32	243.60
18	S	16.50	−54.99	79.40	3.12	S	S	−215.65	366.58	−533.06
19	S	25.96	66.02	−134.79	−68.77	S	−725.81	754.44	109.28	−377.49
20	13.96	36.02	−28.97	−6.38	S	8.92	549.95	47.79	163.97	S
21	−181.12	−77.80	−31.71	S	S	159.53	286.01	162.06	2.51	S
22	−68.25	53.62	S	S	17.70	165.44	25.35	−137.61	S	127.91
23	−119.12	S	S	−13.83	177.29	−353.51	238.20	S	S	−57.35
24	−163.39	S	−66.90	197.65	−79.22	−182.44	S	S	183.55	−504.22
25	S	−77.79	100.26	172.16	−128.99	S	S	90.75	26.83	81.20
26	S	−19.31	97.58	112.97	51.47	S	82.76	−228.50	82.05	654.27
27	−127.94	−1.58	85.54	−76.01	S	114.88	−85.79	436.05	−237.40	S
28	189.68	−15.82	33.76	S	S	−205.49	−127.59	332.04	176.57	S
29	121.12	−24.11	S	S	28.90	160.29	153.60	315.50	S	−49.41
30	−5.41	S	S	−144.23	−23.33	−225.92	−149.06	S	S	203.40
31	−56.12	S	60.81	108.36	−333.75	114.67	S	S	100.24	99.46
Close	17689.86	18432.24	21891.12	25415.19	26864.27	26428.32	34935.47	32845.13	35559.53	40842.79
Change	70.35	502.25	541.49	1143.78	264.31	615.44	432.96	2069.70	1151.93	1723.93

*Shortened trading day

AUGUST DAILY POINT CHANGES DOW JONES INDUSTRIALS

Previous Month Close	2015	2016	2017	2018	2019	2020	2021	2022	2023	2024
	17689.86	18432.24	21891.12	25415.19	26864.27	26428.32	34935.47	32845.13	35559.53	40842.79
1	S	−27.73	72.80	−81.37	−280.85	S	S	−46.73	71.15	−494.82
2	S	−90.74	52.32	−7.66	−98.41	S	−97.31	−402.23	−348.16	−610.71
3	−91.66	41.23	9.86	136.42	S	236.08	278.24	416.33	−66.63	S
4	−47.51	−2.95	66.71	S	S	164.07	−323.73	−85.68	−150.27	S
5	−10.22	191.48	S	S	−767.27	373.05	271.58	76.65	S	−1033.99
6	−120.72	S	S	39.60	311.78	185.46	144.26	S	S	294.39
7	−46.37	S	25.61	126.73	−22.45	46.50	S	S	407.51	−234.21
8	S	−14.24	−33.08	−45.16	371.12	S	S	29.07	−158.64	683.04
9	S	3.76	−36.64	−74.52	−90.75	S	−106.66	−58.13	−191.13	51.05
10	241.79	−37.39	−204.69	−196.09	S	357.96	162.82	535.10	52.79	S
11	−212.33	117.86	14.31	S	S	−104.53	220.30	27.16	105.25	S
12	−0.33	−37.05	S	S	−380.07	289.93	14.88	424.38	S	−140.53
13	5.74	S	S	−125.44	372.54	−80.12	15.53	S	S	408.63
14	69.15	S	135.39	112.22	−800.49	34.30	S	S	26.23	242.75
15	S	59.58	5.28	−137.51	99.97	S	S	151.39	−361.24	554.67
16	S	−84.03	25.88	396.32	306.62	S	110.02	239.57	−180.65	96.70
17	67.78	21.92	−274.14	110.59	S	−86.11	−282.12	−171.69	−290.91	S
18	−33.84	23.76	−76.22	S	S	−66.84	−382.59	18.72	25.83	S
19	−162.61	−45.13	S	S	249.78	−85.19	−66.57	−292.30	S	236.77
20	−358.04	S	S	89.37	−173.35	46.85	225.96	S	S	−61.56
21	−530.94	S	29.24	63.60	240.29	190.60	S	S	−36.97	55.52
22	S	−23.15	196.14	−88.69	49.51	S	S	−643.13	−174.86	−177.71
23	S	17.88	−87.80	−76.62	−623.34	S	215.63	−154.02	184.15	462.30
24	−588.40	−65.82	−28.69	133.37	S	378.13	30.55	59.64	−373.56	S
25	−204.91	−33.07	30.27	S	S	−60.02	39.24	322.55	247.48	S
26	619.07	−53.01	S	S	269.93	83.48	−192.38	−1008.38	S	65.44
27	369.26	S	S	259.29	−120.93	160.35	242.68	S	S	9.98
28	−11.76	S	−5.27	14.38	258.20	161.60	S	S	213.08	−159.08
29	S	107.59	56.97	60.55	326.15	S	S	−184.41	292.69	243.63
30	S	−48.69	27.06	−137.65	41.03	S	−55.96	−308.12	37.57	228.03
31	−114.98	−53.42	55.67	−22.10	S	−223.82	−39.11	−280.44	−168.33	S
Close	16528.03	18400.88	21948.10	25964.82	26403.28	28430.05	35360.73	31510.43	34721.91	41563.08
Change	−1161.83	−31.36	56.98	549.63	−460.99	2001.73	425.26	−1334.70	−837.62	720.29

SEPTEMBER DAILY POINT CHANGES DOW JONES INDUSTRIALS

Previous Month Close	2015	2016	2017	2018	2019	2020	2021	2022	2023	2024
	16528.03	18400.88	21948.10	25964.82	26403.28	28430.05	35360.73	31510.43	34721.91	41563.08
1	−469.68	18.42	39.46	S	S	215.61	−48.20	145.99	115.80	S
2	293.03	72.66	S	S	H	454.84	131.29	−337.98	S	H
3	23.38	S	S	H	−285.26	−807.77	−74.73	S	S	−626.15
4	−272.38	S	H	−12.34	237.45	−159.42	S	S	H	38.04
5	S	H	−234.25	22.51	372.68	S	S	H	−195.74	−219.22
6	S	46.16	54.33	20.88	69.31	S	S	H	−198.78	−410.34
7	H	−11.98	−22.86	−79.33	S	H	−269.09	435.98	57.54	S
8	390.30	−46.23	13.01	S	S	−632.42	−68.93	193.24	75.86	S
9	−239.11	−394.46	S	S	38.05	439.58	−151.69	377.19	S	484.18
10	76.83	S	S	−59.47	73.92	−405.89	−271.66	S	S	−92.63
11	102.69	S	259.58	113.99	227.61	131.06	S	S	87.13	124.75
12	S	239.62	61.49	27.86	45.41	S	S	229.63	−17.73	235.06
13	S	−258.32	39.32	147.07	37.07	S	261.91	−1276.37	−70.46	297.01
14	−62.13	−31.98	45.30	8.68	S	327.69	−312.06	30.12	331.58	S
15	228.89	177.71	64.86	S	S	2.27	256.82	−173.27	−288.87	S
16	140.10	−88.68	S	S	−142.70	36.78	−63.07	−139.40	S	228.30
17	−65.21	S	S	−92.55	33.98	−130.40	−166.44	S	S	−15.90
18	−290.16	S	S	184.84	36.28	−244.56	S	S	6.06	−103.08
19	S	−3.63	39.45	158.80	−52.29	S	S	197.26	−106.57	522.09
20	S	9.79	41.79	251.22	−159.72	S	−614.41	−313.45	−76.85	38.17
21	125.61	163.74	−53.36	86.52	S	−509.72	−50.63	−522.45	−370.46	S
22	−179.72	98.76	−9.64	S	S	140.48	338.48	−107.10	−106.58	S
23	−50.58	−131.01	S	S	14.92	−525.05	506.50	−486.27	S	61.29
24	−78.57	S	S	−181.45	−142.22	52.31	33.18	S	S	83.57
25	113.35	S	−53.50	−69.84	162.94	358.52	S	S	43.04	−293.47
26	S	−166.62	−11.77	−106.93	−79.59	S	S	−329.60	−388.00	260.36
27	S	133.47	56.39	54.65	−70.87	S	71.37	−125.82	−68.61	137.89
28	−312.78	110.94	40.49	18.38	S	410.10	−569.38	548.75	116.07	S
29	47.24	−195.79	23.89	S	S	−131.40	90.73	−458.13	−158.84	S
30	234.87	164.70	S	S	96.58	329.04	−546.80	−500.10	S	17.15
Close	16284.00	18308.15	22405.09	26458.31	26916.83	27781.70	33843.92	28725.51	33507.50	42330.15
Change	−244.03	−92.73	456.99	493.49	513.55	−648.35	−1516.81	−2784.92	−1214.41	767.07

OCTOBER DAILY POINT CHANGES DOW JONES INDUSTRIALS

Previous Month Close	2015	2016	2017	2018	2019	2020	2021	2022	2023	2024
	16284.00	18308.15	22405.09	26458.31	26916.83	27781.70	33843.92	28725.51	33507.50	42330.15
1	−11.99	S	S	192.90	−343.79	35.20	482.54	S	S	−173.18
2	200.36	S	152.51	122.73	−494.42	−134.09	S	S	−74.15	39.55
3	S	−54.30	84.07	54.45	122.42	S	S	765.38	−430.97	−184.93
4	S	−85.40	19.97	−200.91	372.68	S	−323.54	825.43	127.17	341.16
5	304.06	112.58	113.75	−180.43	S	465.83	311.75	−42.45	−9.98	S
6	13.76	−12.53	−1.72	S	S	−375.88	102.32	−346.93	288.01	S
7	122.10	−28.01	S	S	−95.70	530.70	337.95	−630.15	S	−398.51
8	138.46	S	S	39.73	−313.98	122.05	−8.69	S	S	126.13
9	33.74	S	−12.60	−56.21	181.97	161.39	S	S	197.07	431.63
10	S	88.55	69.61	−831.83	150.66	S	S	−93.91	134.65	−57.88
11	S	−200.38	42.21	−545.91	319.92	S	−250.19	36.31	65.57	409.74
12	47.37	15.54	−31.88	287.16	S	250.62	−117.72	−28.34	−173.73	S
13	−49.97	−45.26	30.71	S	S	−157.71	−0.53	827.87	39.15	S
14	−157.14	39.44	S	S	−29.23	−165.81	534.75	−403.89	S	201.36
15	217.00	S	S	−89.44	237.44	−19.80	382.20	S	S	−324.80
16	74.22	S	85.24	547.87	−22.82	112.11	S	S	314.25	337.28
17	S	−51.98	40.48	−91.74	23.90	S	S	550.99	13.11	161.35
18	S	75.54	160.16	−327.23	−255.68	S	−36.15	337.98	−332.57	36.86
19	14.57	40.68	5.44	64.89	S	−410.89	198.70	−99.99	−250.91	S
20	−13.43	−40.27	165.59	S	S	113.37	152.03	−90.22	−286.89	S
21	−48.50	−16.64	S	S	57.44	−97.97	−6.26	748.97	S	−344.31
22	320.55	S	S	−126.93	−39.54	152.84	73.94	S	S	−6.71
23	157.54	S	−54.67	−125.98	45.85	−28.09	S	S	−190.87	−409.94
24	S	77.32	167.80	−608.01	−28.42	S	S	417.06	204.97	−140.59
25	S	−53.76	−112.30	401.13	152.53	S	64.13	337.12	−105.45	−259.96
26	−23.65	30.06	71.40	−296.24	S	−650.19	15.73	2.37	−251.63	S
27	−41.62	−29.65	33.33	S	S	−222.19	−266.19	194.17	−366.71	S
28	198.09	−8.49	S	S	132.66	−943.24	239.79	828.52	S	273.17
29	−23.72	S	S	−245.39	−19.26	139.16	89.08	S	S	−154.52
30	−92.26	S	−85.45	431.72	115.23	−157.51	S	S	511.37	−91.51
31	S	−18.77	28.50	241.12	−140.46	S	S	−128.85	123.91	−378.08
Close	17663.54	18142.42	23377.24	25115.76	27046.23	26501.60	35819.56	32732.95	33052.87	41763.46
Change	1379.54	−165.73	972.15	−1342.55	129.40	−1280.10	1975.64	4007.44	−454.63	−566.69

NOVEMBER DAILY POINT CHANGES DOW JONES INDUSTRIALS

	2015	2016	2017	2018	2019	2020	2021	2022	2023	2024
Previous Month Close	17663.54	18142.42	23377.24	25115.76	27046.23	26501.60	35819.56	32732.95	33052.87	41763.46
1	S	− 105.32	57.77	264.98	301.13	S	94.28	− 79.75	221.71	288.73
2	165.22	− 77.46	81.25	− 109.91	S	423.45	138.79	− 505.44	564.50	S
3	89.39	− 28.97	22.93	S	S	554.98	104.95	− 146.51	222.24	S
4	− 50.57	− 42.39	S	S	114.75	367.63	− 33.35	401.97	S	− 257.59
5	− 4.15	S	S	190.87	30.52	542.52	203.72	S	S	427.28
6	46.90	S	9.23	173.31	− 0.07	− 66.78	S	S	34.54	1508.05
7	S	371.32	8.81	545.29	182.24	S	S	423.78	56.74	− 0.59
8	S	73.14	6.13	10.92	6.44	S	104.27	333.83	− 40.33	259.65
9	− 179.85	256.95	− 101.42	− 201.92	S	834.57	− 112.24	− 646.89	− 220.33	S
10	27.73	218.19	− 39.73	S	S	262.95	− 240.04	1201.43	391.16	S
11	− 55.99	39.78	S	S	10.25	− 23.29	− 158.71	32.49	S	304.14
12	− 254.15	S	S	− 602.12	0.00	− 317.46	179.08	S	S	− 382.15
13	− 202.83	S	17.49	− 100.69	92.10	399.64	S	S	54.77	47.21
14	S	21.03	− 30.23	− 205.99	− 1.63	S	S	− 211.16	489.83	− 207.33
15	S	54.37	− 138.19	208.77	222.93	S	− 12.86	56.22	163.51	− 305.87
16	237.77	− 54.92	187.08	123.95	S	470.63	54.77	− 39.09	− 45.74	S
17	6.49	35.68	− 100.12	S	S	− 167.09	− 211.17	− 7.51	1.81	S
18	247.66	− 35.89	S	S	31.33	− 344.93	− 60.10	199.37	S	− 55.39
19	− 4.41	S	S	− 395.78	− 102.20	44.81	− 268.97	S	S	− 120.66
20	91.06	S	72.09	− 551.80	− 112.93	− 219.75	S	S	203.76	139.53
21	S	88.76	160.50	− 0.95	− 54.80	S	S	− 45.41	− 62.75	461.88
22	S	67.18	− 64.65	H	109.33	S	17.27	397.82	184.74	426.16
23	− 31.13	59.31	H	− 178.74*	S	327.79	194.55	95.96	H	S
24	19.51	H	31.81*	S	S	454.97	− 9.42	H	117.12*	S
25	1.20	68.96*	S	S	190.85	− 173.77	H	152.97*	S	440.06
26	H	S	S	354.29	55.21	H	− 905.04*	S	S	123.74
27	− 14.90*	S	22.79	108.49	42.32	37.90*	S	S	− 56.68	− 138.28
28	S	− 54.24	255.93	617.70	H	S	S	− 497.57	83.51	H
29	S	23.70	103.97	− 27.59	− 112.59*	S	236.60	3.07	13.44	188.62*
30	− 78.57	1.98	331.67	199.62	S	− 271.73	− 652.22	737.24	520.47	S
Close	17719.92	19123.58	24272.35	25538.46	28051.41	29638.64	34483.72	34589.77	35950.89	44910.65
Change	56.38	981.16	895.11	422.70	1005.18	3137.04	− 1335.84	1856.82	2898.02	3147.19

*Shortened trading day

DECEMBER DAILY POINT CHANGES DOW JONES INDUSTRIALS

	2015	2016	2017	2018	2019	2020	2021	2022	2023	2024
Previous Month Close	17719.92	19123.58	24272.35	25538.46	28051.41	29638.64	34483.72	34589.77	35950.89	44910.65
1	168.43	68.35	− 40.76	S	S	185.28	− 461.68	− 194.76	294.61	S
2	− 158.67	− 21.51	S	S	− 268.37	59.87	617.75	34.87	S	− 128.65
3	− 252.01	S	S	287.97	− 280.23	85.73	− 59.71	S	S	− 76.47
4	369.96	S	58.46	− 799.36	146.97	248.74	S	S	− 41.06	308.51
5	S	45.82	− 109.41	H**	28.01	S	S	− 482.78	− 79.88	− 248.33
6	S	35.54	− 39.73	− 79.40	337.27	S	646.95	− 350.76	− 70.13	− 123.19
7	− 117.12	297.84	70.57	− 558.72	S	− 148.47	492.40	1.58	62.95	S
8	− 162.51	65.19	117.68	S	S	104.09	35.32	183.56	130.49	S
9	− 75.70	142.04	S	S	− 105.46	− 105.07	− 0.06	− 305.02	S	− 240.59
10	82.45	S	S	34.31	− 27.88	− 69.55	216.30	S	S	− 154.10
11	− 309.54	S	56.87	− 53.02	29.58	47.11	S	S	157.06	− 99.27
12	S	39.58	118.77	157.03	220.75	S	S	528.58	173.01	− 234.44
13	S	114.78	80.63	70.11	3.33	S	− 320.04	103.60	512.30	− 86.06
14	103.29	− 118.68	− 76.77	− 496.87	S	− 184.82	− 106.77	− 142.29	158.11	S
15	156.41	59.71	143.08	S	S	337.76	383.25	− 764.13	56.81	S
16	224.18	− 8.83	S	S	100.51	− 44.77	− 29.79	− 281.76	S	− 110.58
17	− 253.25	S	S	− 507.53	31.27	148.83	− 532.20	S	S	− 267.58
18	− 367.29	S	140.46	82.66	− 27.88	− 124.32	S	S	0.86	− 1123.03
19	S	39.65	− 37.45	− 351.98	137.68	S	S	− 162.92	251.90	15.37
20	S	91.56	− 28.10	− 464.06	78.13	S	− 433.28	92.20	− 475.92	498.02
21	123.07	− 32.66	55.64	− 414.23	S	37.40	560.54	526.74	322.35	S
22	165.65	− 23.08	− 28.23	S	S	− 200.94	261.19	− 348.99	− 18.38	S
23	185.34	14.93	S	S	96.44	114.32	196.67	176.44	S	66.69
24	− 50.44*	S	S	− 653.17*	− 36.08*	70.04*	H	S	S	390.08*
25	H	S	H	H	H	H	S	S	H	H
26	S	H	− 7.85	1086.25	105.94	S	S	H	159.36	28.77
27	S	11.23	28.09	260.37	23.87	S	351.82	37.63	111.19	− 333.59
28	− 23.90	− 111.36	63.21	− 76.42	S	204.10	95.83	− 365.85	53.58	S
29	192.71	− 13.90	− 118.29	S	S	− 68.30	90.42	345.09	− 20.56	S
30	− 117.11	− 57.18	S	S	− 183.12	73.89	− 90.55	− 73.55	S	− 418.48
31	− 178.84	S	S	265.06	76.30	196.92	− 59.78	S	S	− 29.51
Close	17425.03	19762.60	24719.22	23327.46	28538.44	30606.48	36338.30	33147.25	37689.54	42544.22
Change	− 294.89	639.02	446.87	− 2211.00	487.03	967.84	1854.58	− 1442.52	1738.65	− 2366.43

* Shortened trading day, ** President H.W. Bush Funeral

A TYPICAL DAY IN THE MARKET

Half-hourly data became available for the Dow Jones Industrial Average starting in January 1987. The NYSE switched 10:00 a.m. openings to 9:30 a.m. in October 1985. Below is the comparison between half-hourly performance 1987–May 2, 2025, and hourly November 1963 to June 1985. Stronger closings in a more bullish climate are evident. Morning and afternoon weaknesses appear an hour earlier.

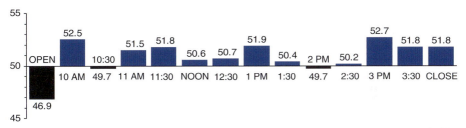

Based on the number of times the Dow Jones Industrial Average increased over the previous half-hour

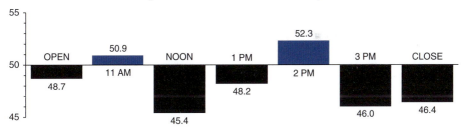

Based on the number of times the Dow Jones Industrial Average increased over the previous hour

On the next page, half-hourly movements since January 1987 are separated by day of the week. From 1953 to 1989 Monday was the worst day of the week, especially during long bear markets, but times changed. Monday was the best day of the week and on the plus side eleven years in a row from 1990 to 2000. Since the 2000 top Monday has been the worst day.

During the last 15 years (2010–May 2, 2025) Monday is the weakest day of the week and Tuesday is the best. On all days stocks do tend to firm up near the close with weakness early morning and from 1:30 to 2:30 frequently.

THROUGH THE WEEK ON A HALF-HOURLY BASIS

From the chart showing the percentage of times the Dow Jones Industrial Average rose over the preceding half-hour (January 1987 to May 2, 2025*), the typical week unfolds.

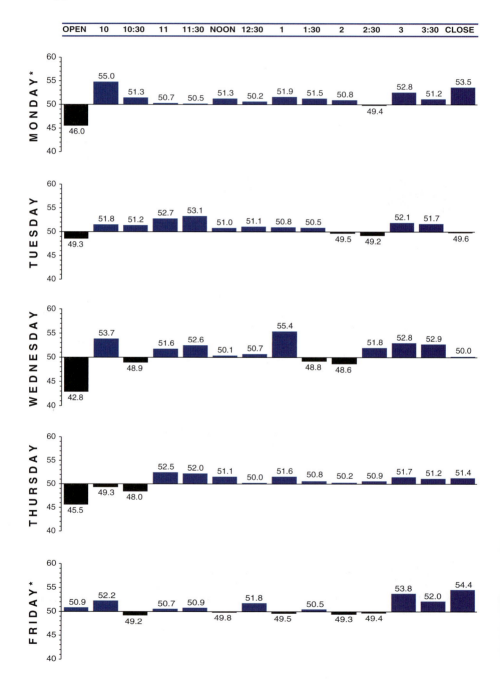

* Monday denotes first trading day of week, Friday denotes last trading day of week

TUESDAY & WEDNESDAY, BEST DAYS OF WEEK

Between 1952 and 1989, Monday was the worst trading day of the week. The first trading day of the week (including Tuesday when Monday is a holiday) rose only 44.3% of the time, while the other trading days closed higher 54.8% of the time. (NYSE Saturday trading was discontinued in June 1952.)

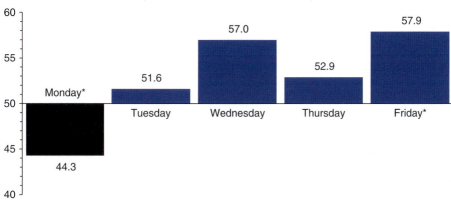

A dramatic reversal occurred in 1990—Monday became the most powerful day of the week. However, during the last 24 and a half years Tuesday has produced the most gains and Wednesday has the greatest frequency of advances. Weakness on Friday and/or Monday is common during uncertain market times. Monday was the worst day during the 2007–2009 bear and only Tuesday and Friday were net gainers. Since 2010, Wednesday is best. See pages 78 and 145.

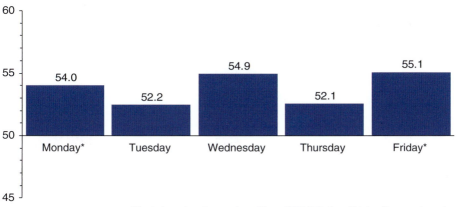

Charts based on the number of times S&P 500 closed higher than previous day
* Monday denotes first trading day of week, Friday denotes last trading day of week

NASDAQ STRONGEST LAST 3 DAYS OF WEEK

Despite 20 years less data, daily trading patterns on NASDAQ through 1989 appear to be fairly similar to the S&P on page 143 except for more bullishness on Thursdays. During the mostly flat markets of the 1970s and early 1980s, it would appear that apprehensive investors decided to throw in the towel over weekends and sell on Mondays and Tuesdays.

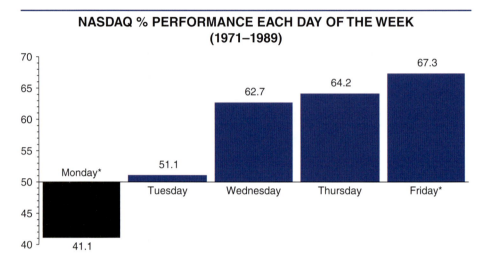

Notice the modest difference in the daily trading pattern between NASDAQ and S&P from January 1, 1990, to recent times. NASDAQ's weekly patterns are beginning to move in step with the rest of the market as technology continues to take an ever-increasing role throughout the economy. Notice the similarities to the S&P since 2001 on pages 145 and 146, Monday and/or Friday weakness, mid-week strength during bear markets.

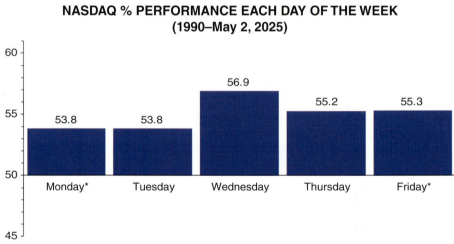

Based on NASDAQ composite, prior to Feb. 5, 1971 based on National Quotation Bureau indices
* Monday denotes first trading day of week, Friday denotes last trading day of week

S&P DAILY PERFORMANCE EACH YEAR SINCE 1952

To determine if market trend alters performance of different days of the week, we separated 24 bear years—1953, '56, '57, '60, '62, '66, '69, '70, '73, '74, '77, '78, '81, '84, '87, '90, '94, 2000, '01, '02, '08, '11, '15, '22, and '24 from 49 bull market years. While Tuesdays and Thursdays did not vary much between bull and bear years, Mondays and Fridays were sharply affected. There was a swing of 10.8 percentage points in Monday's performance and 9.9 in Friday's.

PERCENTAGE OF TIMES MARKET CLOSED HIGHER THAN PREVIOUS DAY
(JUNE 1952–MAY 2, 2025)

	Monday*	Tuesday	Wednesday	Thursday	Friday**
1952	48.4%	55.6%	58.1%	51.9%	66.7%
1953	32.7	50.0	54.9	57.5	56.6
1954	50.0	57.5	63.5	59.2	73.1
1955	50.0	45.7	63.5	60.0	78.9
1956	36.5	39.6	46.9	50.0	59.6
1957	25.0	54.0	66.7	48.9	44.2
1958	59.6	52.0	59.6	68.1	72.6
1959	42.3	53.1	55.8	48.9	69.8
1960	34.6	50.0	44.2	54.0	59.6
1961	52.9	54.4	64.7	56.0	67.3
1962	28.3	52.1	54.0	51.0	50.0
1963	46.2	63.3	51.0	57.5	69.2
1964	40.4	48.0	61.5	58.7	77.4
1965	44.2	57.5	55.8	51.0	71.2
1966	36.5	47.8	53.9	42.0	57.7
1967	38.5	50.0	60.8	64.0	69.2
1968†	49.1	57.5	64.3	42.6	54.9
1969	30.8	45.8	50.0	67.4	50.0
1970	38.5	46.0	63.5	48.9	52.8
1971	44.2	64.6	57.7	55.1	51.9
1972	38.5	60.9	57.7	51.0	67.3
1973	32.1	51.1	52.9	44.4	44.2
1974	32.7	57.1	51.0	36.7	30.8
1975	53.9	38.8	61.5	56.3	55.8
1976	55.8	55.3	55.8	40.8	58.5
1977	40.4	40.4	46.2	53.1	53.9
1978	51.9	43.5	59.6	54.0	48.1
1979	54.7	53.2	58.8	66.0	44.2
1980	55.8	54.2	71.7	35.4	59.6
1981	44.2	38.8	55.8	53.2	47.2
1982	46.2	39.6	44.2	44.9	50.0
1983	55.8	46.8	61.5	52.0	55.8
1984	39.6	63.8	31.4	46.0	44.2
1985	44.2	61.2	54.9	56.3	53.9
1986	51.9	44.9	67.3	58.3	55.8
1987	51.9	57.1	63.5	61.7	49.1
1988	51.9	61.7	51.9	48.0	59.6
1989	51.9	47.8	69.2	58.0	69.2
1990	67.9	53.2	52.9	40.0	51.9
1991	44.2	46.9	52.9	49.0	51.9
1992	51.9	49.0	53.9	56.3	45.3
1993	65.4	41.7	55.8	44.9	48.1
1994	55.8	46.8	52.9	48.0	59.6
1995	63.5	56.5	63.5	62.0	63.5
1996	54.7	44.9	51.0	57.1	63.5
1997	67.3	67.4	42.3	41.7	57.7
1998	57.7	62.5	57.7	38.3	60.4
1999	46.2	29.8	67.3	53.1	57.7
2000	51.9	43.5	40.4	56.0	46.2
2001	45.3	51.1	44.0	59.2	43.1
2002	40.4	37.5	56.9	38.8	48.1
2003	59.6	62.5	42.3	58.3	50.0
2004	51.9	61.7	59.6	52.1	52.8
2005	59.6	47.8	59.6	56.0	55.8
2006	55.8	55.6	67.3	52.0	48.1
2007	47.2	50.0	64.0	50.0	61.5
2008	42.3	50.0	41.5	60.4	55.8
2009	53.9	50.0	57.7	63.8	52.8
2010	61.5	57.5	55.8	53.1	57.7
2011	48.1	56.5	55.8	56.0	57.7
2012	52.8	48.9	50.0	58.0	53.9
2013	51.9	60.4	54.9	59.2	65.4
2014	53.9	56.3	57.7	56.3	61.5
2015	51.9	43.8	44.2	53.2	43.4
2016	50.0	58.7	55.8	50.0	46.2
2017	55.8	55.6	61.5	50.0	61.5
2018	52.8	60.9	50.0	46.0	53.9
2019	50.0	54.2	60.8	65.3	67.3
2020	63.5	54.2	61.5	52.1	54.7
2021	51.9	44.7	61.5	65.3	59.6
2022	38.5	48.9	46.2	38.0	44.2
2023	61.5	54.6	44.2	52.0	65.4
2024	58.5	62.5	56.0	44.9	61.5
2025‡	58.8	53.3	76.5	37.5	55.6
Average	**48.9%**	**51.9%**	**55.7%**	**52.7%**	**56.5%**
49 Bull Years	**52.4%**	**53.4%**	**57.9%**	**53.6%**	**59.8%**
24 Bear Years	**41.6%**	**48.7%**	**51.2%**	**50.8%**	**49.9%**

Based on S&P 500

† Most Wednesdays closed last 7 months of 1968   ‡ Through 5/2/2025 only, not included in averages
*Monday denotes first trading day of week, Friday denotes last trading day of week.

NASDAQ DAILY PERFORMANCE EACH YEAR SINCE 1971

After dropping a hefty 77.9% from its 2000 high (versus –37.8% on the Dow and –49.1% on the S&P 500), NASDAQ tech stocks still lead. From January 1, 1971, through May 2, 2025, NASDAQ moved up an impressive 19962%. The Dow (up 4825%) and the S&P (up 6071%) gained less than a quarter and third as much, respectively.

Monday's performance on NASDAQ was lackluster during the three-year bear market of 2000–2002. As NASDAQ rebounded (up 50% in 2003), strength returned to Monday during 2003–2006. During the bear market from late 2007 to early 2009, weakness was most consistent on Monday and Friday. At press time, Wednesday has been best day of 2025 followed by Friday.

PERCENTAGE OF TIMES NASDAQ CLOSED HIGHER THAN PREVIOUS DAY
(1971–MAY 2, 2025)

	Monday*	Tuesday	Wednesday	Thursday	Friday**
1971	51.9%	52.1%	59.6%	65.3%	71.2%
1972	30.8	60.9	63.5	57.1	78.9
1973	34.0	48.9	52.9	53.1	48.1
1974	30.8	44.9	52.9	51.0	42.3
1975	44.2	42.9	63.5	64.6	63.5
1976	50.0	63.8	67.3	59.2	58.5
1977	51.9	40.4	53.9	63.3	73.1
1978	48.1	47.8	73.1	72.0	84.6
1979	45.3	53.2	64.7	86.0	82.7
1980	46.2	64.6	84.9	52.1	73.1
1981	42.3	32.7	67.3	76.6	69.8
1982	34.6	47.9	59.6	51.0	63.5
1983	42.3	44.7	67.3	68.0	73.1
1984	22.6	53.2	35.3	52.0	51.9
1985	36.5	59.2	62.8	68.8	66.0
1986	38.5	55.1	65.4	72.9	75.0
1987	42.3	49.0	65.4	68.1	66.0
1988	50.0	55.3	61.5	66.0	63.5
1989	38.5	54.4	71.2	72.0	75.0
1990	54.7	42.6	60.8	46.0	55.8
1991	51.9	59.2	66.7	65.3	51.9
1992	44.2	53.1	59.6	60.4	45.3
1993	55.8	56.3	69.2	57.1	67.3
1994	51.9	46.8	54.9	52.0	55.8
1995	50.0	52.2	63.5	64.0	63.5
1996	50.9	57.1	64.7	61.2	63.5
1997	65.4	59.2	53.9	52.1	55.8
1998	59.6	58.3	65.4	44.7	58.5
1999	61.5	40.4	63.5	57.1	65.4
2000	40.4	41.3	42.3	60.0	57.7
2001	41.5	57.8	52.0	55.1	47.1
2002	44.2	37.5	56.9	46.9	46.2
2003	57.7	60.4	40.4	60.4	46.2
2004	57.7	59.6	53.9	50.0	50.9
2005	61.5	47.8	51.9	48.0	59.6
2006	55.8	51.1	65.4	50.0	44.2
2007	47.2	63.0	66.0	56.0	57.7
2008	34.6	52.1	49.1	54.2	42.3
2009	51.9	54.2	63.5	63.8	50.9
2010	61.5	53.2	61.5	55.1	61.5
2011	50.0	56.5	50.0	64.0	53.9
2012	49.1	53.3	50.0	54.0	51.9
2013	57.7	60.4	52.9	59.2	67.3
2014	57.7	58.3	57.7	52.1	59.6
2015	55.8	39.6	53.9	59.6	49.1
2016	51.9	52.2	55.8	50.0	57.7
2017	59.6	62.2	67.3	50.0	67.3
2018	54.7	69.6	50.0	46.0	50.0
2019	50.0	58.3	62.8	59.2	59.6
2020	69.2	58.3	67.3	60.4	54.7
2021	55.8	44.7	48.1	67.4	63.5
2022	40.4	51.1	44.2	44.0	42.3
2023	67.3	52.3	53.9	54.0	53.9
2024	64.2	64.6	52.0	51.0	59.6
2025†	47.1	40.0	70.6	37.5	55.6
Average	**49.3%**	**52.6%**	**59.2%**	**57.9%**	**59.5%**
40 Bull Years	**52.0%**	**55.0%**	**61.1%**	**59.2%**	**62.2%**
14 Bear Years	**41.8%**	**46.7%**	**52.7%**	**55.9%**	**52.0%**

Based on NASDAQ composite; prior to Feb. 5, 1971 based on National Quotation Bureau indices
† Through 5/2/2025 only, not included in averages
*Monday denotes first trading day of week, Friday denotes last trading day of week

MONTHLY CASH INFLOWS INTO S&P STOCKS

For many years, the last trading day of the month, plus the first four of the following month, were the best market days of the month. This pattern is quite clear in the first chart, showing these five consecutive trading days towering above the other 16 trading days of the average month in the 1953–1981 period. The rationale was that individuals and institutions tended to operate similarly, causing a massive flow of cash into stocks near beginnings of months.

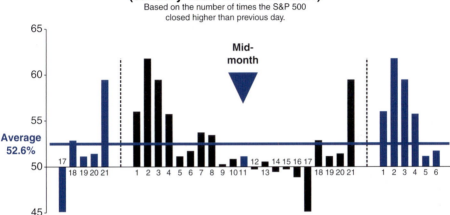

Clearly "front-running" traders took advantage of this phenomenon, drastically altering the previous pattern. The second chart from 1982 onward shows the trading shift caused by these "anticipators" to the end of the month plus the first two. Another development shows the ninth, 10th, 11th, and 12th trading days rising as well. Growth of 401(k) retirement plans, IRAs, and similar plans (participants' salaries are usually paid twice monthly) are likely responsible for this mid-month bulge. First trading days of the month have produced the greatest gains in recent years (see page 90). Last trading day of the month strength has faded substantially over the last 25 years.

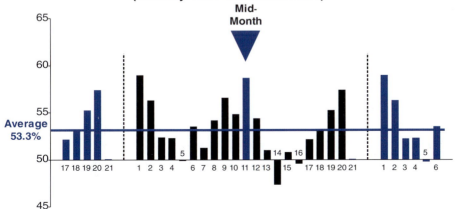

Trading days (excluding Saturdays, Sundays, and holidays).

MONTHLY CASH INFLOWS INTO NASDAQ STOCKS

NASDAQ stocks moved up 58.1% of the time through 1981 compared to 52.6% for the S&P on page 147. Ends and beginnings of the month are fairly similar, specifically the last plus the first four trading days. But notice how investors piled into NASDAQ stocks until midmonth. NASDAQ rose 118.6% from January 1, 1971, to December 31, 1981, compared to 33.0% for the S&P.

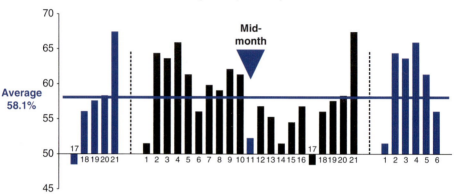

After the air was let out of the tech market in 2000–2002, S&P's 4699% gain over the last 43 years is less unevenly matched with NASDAQ's 9760% gain. Last three, first four, and middle ninth, 10th, 11th and 12th days rose the most. Where the S&P now has three days of the month that go down more often than up, NASDAQ has one. NASDAQ exhibits the most strength on the first trading day of the month. Over the past 25 years, last days have weakened considerably, down more frequently than not.

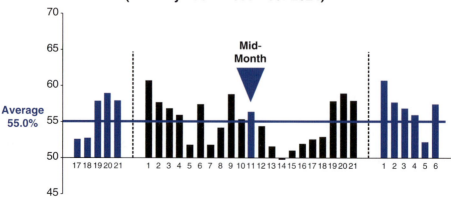

Trading days (excluding Saturdays, Sundays, and holidays).
Based on NASDAQ composite, prior to February 5, 1971, based on National Quotation Bureau indices.

NOVEMBER, DECEMBER, AND JANUARY: YEAR'S BEST THREE-MONTH SPAN

The most important observation to be made from a chart showing the average monthly percent change in market prices since 1950 is that institutions (mutual funds, pension funds, banks, etc.) determine the trading patterns in today's market.

The "investment calendar" reflects the annual, semiannual, and quarterly operations of institutions during January, April, and July. October, besides being the last campaign month before elections, is also the time when most bear markets seem to end, as in 1946, 1957, 1960, 1966, 1974, 1987, 1990, 1998, 2002, and 2022. (August and September tend to combine to make the worst consecutive two-month period.)

Average month-to-month % change in S&P 500.
(Based on monthly closing prices.)

Unusual year-end strength comes from corporate and private pension funds, producing a 4.4% gain on average between November 1 and January 31. In 2007–2008, these three months were all down for the fourth time since 1930; previously in 1931–1932, 1940–1941 and 1969–1970, also bear markets. September's dismal performance makes it the worst month of the year. However, in the last 21 years, it has been up 12 times after being down five in a row 1999–2003, but down seven of the last 11.

In midterm-election years since 1950, October is the best month +3.0% (up 14, down 5). November is second best with an average 2.7% gain. February, March, July, and December are also positive. June is the worst month in midterm-election years, average loss –2.1% (up 7, down 12). January, April, May, August, and September are also net decliners.

See page 52 for monthly performance tables for the S&P 500 and the Dow Jones industrials. See pages 54, 56, 62, and 64 for unique switching strategies.

On page 68, you can see how the first month of the first three quarters far outperforms the second and third months since 1950, and note the improvement in May's and October's performance since 1991.

NOVEMBER THROUGH JUNE: NASDAQ'S EIGHT-MONTH RUN

The two-and-a-half-year plunge of 77.9% in NASDAQ stocks, between March 10, 2000, and October 9, 2002, brought several horrendous monthly losses (the two greatest were November 2000, −22.9% and February 2001, −22.4%), which trimmed average monthly performance over the 54^1/$_3$-year period. Ample Octobers in 17 of the last 27 years, including three huge turnarounds in 2001 (+12.8%), 2002 (+13.5%) and 2011 (+11.1%) have put bear-killing October in the number two spot since 1998. January's 2.6% average gain is still awesome, and more than twice S&P's 1.1% January average since 1971.

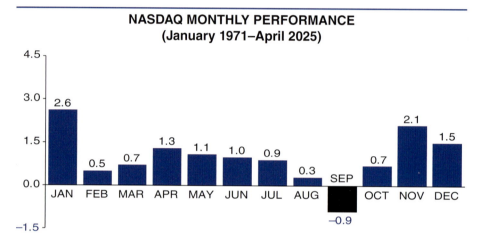

Average month-to-month % change in NASDAQ composite, prior to February 5, 1971, based on National Quotation Bureau indices.
(Based on monthly closing prices.)

Bear in mind, when comparing NASDAQ to the S&P on page 149, that there are 23 fewer years of data here. During this 54^1/$_3$-year (1971–April 2025) period, NASDAQ gained 19369%, while the S&P and the Dow rose only 5943% and 4748%, respectively. On page 60, you can see a statistical monthly comparison between NASDAQ and the Dow.

Year-end strength is even more pronounced in NASDAQ, producing a 6.2% gain on average between November 1 and January 31—nearly 1.5 times greater than that of the S&P 500 on page 149. September is the worst month of the year for the over-the-counter index as well, posting an average loss of −0.9%. These extremes underscore NASDAQ's higher volatility—and moves of greater magnitude.

In midterm-election years since 1971, November is best with an average gain of 3.5% (up 9, down 4). February, March, and October are also positive. June is the worst month in midterm-election years, −1.9% (down 7, up 6). January, April, May, July, August, September, and December also are negative on average.

DOW JONES INDUSTRIALS ANNUAL HIGHS, LOWS, & CLOSES SINCE 1901

YEAR	HIGH DATE	HIGH CLOSE	LOW DATE	LOW CLOSE	YEAR CLOSE	YEAR	HIGH DATE	HIGH CLOSE	LOW DATE	LOW CLOSE	YEAR CLOSE
1901	6/17	57.33	12/24	45.07	47.29	1933	7/18	108.67	2/27	50.16	99.90
1902	4/24	50.14	12/15	43.64	47.10	1934	2/5	110.74	7/26	85.51	104.04
1903	2/16	49.59	11/9	30.88	35.98	1935	11/19	148.44	3/14	96.71	144.13
1904	12/5	53.65	3/12	34.00	50.99	1936	11/17	184.90	1/6	143.11	179.90
1905	12/29	70.74	1/25	50.37	70.47	1937	3/10	194.40	11/24	113.64	120.85
1906	1/19	75.45	7/13	62.40	69.12	1938	11/12	158.41	3/31	98.95	154.76
1907	1/7	70.60	11/15	38.83	43.04	1939	9/12	155.92	4/8	121.44	150.24
1908	11/13	64.74	2/13	42.94	63.11	1940	1/3	152.80	6/10	111.84	131.13
1909	11/19	73.64	2/23	58.54	72.56	1941	1/10	133.59	12/23	106.34	110.96
1910	1/3	72.04	7/26	53.93	59.60	1942	12/26	119.71	4/28	92.92	119.40
1911	6/19	63.78	9/25	53.43	59.84	1943	7/14	145.82	1/8	119.26	135.89
1912	9/30	68.97	2/10	58.72	64.37	1944	12/16	152.53	2/7	134.22	152.32
1913	1/9	64.88	6/11	52.83	57.71	1945	12/11	195.82	1/24	151.35	192.91
1914	3/20	61.12	7/30	52.32	54.58	1946	5/29	212.50	10/9	163.12	177.20
1915	12/27	99.21	2/24	54.22	99.15	1947	7/24	186.85	5/17	163.21	181.16
1916	11/21	110.15	4/22	84.96	95.00	1948	6/15	193.16	3/16	165.39	177.30
1917	1/3	99.18	12/19	65.95	74.38	1949	12/30	200.52	6/13	161.60	200.13
1918	10/18	89.07	1/15	73.38	82.20	1950	11/24	235.47	1/13	196.81	235.41
1919	11/3	119.62	2/8	79.15	107.23	1951	9/13	276.37	1/3	238.99	269.23
1920	1/3	109.88	12/21	66.75	71.95	1952	12/30	292.00	5/1	256.35	291.90
1921	12/15	81.50	8/24	63.90	81.10	1953	1/5	293.79	9/14	255.49	280.90
1922	10/14	103.43	1/10	78.59	98.73	1954	12/31	404.39	1/11	279.87	404.39
1923	3/20	105.38	10/27	85.76	95.52	1955	12/30	488.40	1/17	388.20	488.40
1924	12/31	120.51	5/20	88.33	120.51	1956	4/6	521.05	1/23	462.35	499.47
1925	11/6	159.39	3/30	115.00	156.66	1957	7/12	520.77	10/22	419.79	435.69
1926	8/14	166.64	3/30	135.20	157.20	1958	12/31	583.65	2/25	436.89	583.65
1927	12/31	202.40	1/25	152.73	202.40	1959	12/31	679.36	2/9	574.46	679.36
1928	12/31	300.00	2/20	191.33	300.00	1960	1/5	685.47	10/25	566.05	615.89
1929	9/3	381.17	11/13	198.69	248.48	1961	12/13	734.91	1/3	610.25	731.14
1930	4/17	294.07	12/16	157.51	164.58	1962	1/3	726.01	6/26	535.76	652.10
1931	2/24	194.36	12/17	73.79	77.90	1963	12/18	767.21	1/2	646.79	762.95
1932	3/8	88.78	7/8	41.22	59.93	1964	11/18	891.71	1/2	766.08	874.13

continued

DOW JONES INDUSTRIALS ANNUAL HIGHS, LOWS, & CLOSES SINCE 1901 (continued)

YEAR	HIGH DATE	HIGH CLOSE	LOW DATE	LOW CLOSE	YEAR CLOSE	YEAR	HIGH DATE	HIGH CLOSE	LOW DATE	LOW CLOSE	YEAR CLOSE
1965	12/31	969.26	6/28	840.59	969.26	1996	12/27	6560.91	1/10	5032.94	6448.27
1966	2/9	995.15	10/7	744.32	785.69	1997	8/6	8259.31	4/11	6391.69	7908.25
1967	9/25	943.08	1/3	786.41	905.11	1998	11/23	9374.27	8/31	7539.07	9181.43
1968	12/3	985.21	3/21	825.13	943.75	1999	12/31	11497.12	1/22	9120.67	11497.12
1969	5/14	968.85	12/17	769.93	800.36	2000	1/14	11722.98	3/7	9796.03	10786.85
1970	12/29	842.00	5/26	631.16	838.92	2001	5/21	11337.92	9/21	8235.81	10021.50
1971	4/28	950.82	11/23	797.97	890.20	2002	3/19	10635.25	10/9	7286.27	8341.63
1972	12/11	1036.27	1/26	889.15	1020.02	2003	12/31	10453.92	3/11	7524.06	10453.92
1973	1/11	1051.70	12/5	788.31	850.86	2004	12/28	10854.54	10/25	9749.99	10783.01
1974	3/13	891.66	12/6	577.60	616.24	2005	3/4	10940.55	4/20	10012.36	10717.50
1975	7/15	881.81	1/2	632.04	852.41	2006	12/27	12510.57	1/20	10667.39	12463.15
1976	9/21	1014.79	1/2	858.71	1004.65	2007	10/9	14164.53	3/5	12050.41	13264.82
1977	1/3	999.75	11/2	800.85	831.17	2008	5/2	13058.20	11/20	7552.29	8776.39
1978	9/8	907.74	2/28	742.12	805.01	2009	12/30	10548.51	3/9	6547.05	10428.05
1979	10/5	897.61	11/7	796.67	838.74	2010	12/29	11585.38	7/2	9686.48	11577.51
1980	11/20	1000.17	4/21	759.13	963.99	2011	4/29	12810.54	10/3	10655.30	12217.56
1981	4/27	1024.05	9/25	824.01	875.00	2012	10/5	13610.15	6/4	12101.46	13104.14
1982	12/27	1070.55	8/12	776.92	1046.54	2013	12/31	16576.66	1/8	13328.85	16576.66
1983	11/29	1287.20	1/3	1027.04	1258.64	2014	12/26	18053.71	2/3	15372.80	17823.07
1984	1/6	1286.64	7/24	1086.57	1211.57	2015	5/19	18312.39	8/25	15666.44	17425.03
1985	12/16	1553.10	1/4	1184.96	1546.67	2016	12/20	19974.62	2/11	15660.18	19762.60
1986	12/2	1955.57	1/22	1502.29	1895.95	2017	12/28	24837.51	1/19	19732.40	24719.22
1987	8/25	2722.42	10/19	1738.74	1938.83	2018	10/3	26828.39	12/24	21792.20	23327.46
1988	10/21	2183.50	1/20	1879.14	2168.57	2019	12/27	28645.26	1/3	22686.22	28538.44
1989	10/9	2791.41	1/3	2144.64	2753.20	2020	12/31	30606.48	3/23	18591.93	30606.48
1990	7/17	2999.75	10/11	2365.10	2633.66	2021	12/29	36488.63	1/29	29982.62	36338.30
1991	12/31	3168.83	1/9	2470.30	3168.83	2022	1/4	36799.65	9/30	28725.51	33147.25
1992	6/1	3413.21	10/9	3136.58	3301.11	2023	12/28	37710.10	3/13	31819.14	37689.54
1993	12/29	3794.33	1/20	3241.95	3754.09	2024	12/4	45014.04	1/17	37266.67	42544.22
1994	1/31	3978.36	4/4	3593.35	3834.44	2025*	1/30	44882.13	4/8	37645.59	At press time
1995	12/13	5216.47	1/30	3832.08	5117.12						

*Through May 2, 2025

S&P 500 ANNUAL HIGHS, LOWS, & CLOSES SINCE 1930

YEAR	HIGH DATE	HIGH CLOSE	LOW DATE	LOW CLOSE	YEAR CLOSE	YEAR	HIGH DATE	HIGH CLOSE	LOW DATE	LOW CLOSE	YEAR CLOSE
1930	4/10	25.92	12/16	14.44	15.34	1978	9/12	106.99	3/6	86.90	96.11
1931	2/24	18.17	12/17	7.72	8.12	1979	10/5	111.27	2/27	96.13	107.94
1932	9/7	9.31	6/1	4.40	6.89	1980	11/28	140.52	3/27	98.22	135.76
1933	7/18	12.20	2/27	5.53	10.10	1981	1/6	138.12	9/25	112.77	122.55
1934	2/6	11.82	7/26	8.36	9.50	1982	11/9	143.02	8/12	102.42	140.64
1935	11/19	13.46	3/14	8.06	13.43	1983	10/10	172.65	1/3	138.34	164.93
1936	11/9	17.69	1/2	13.40	17.18	1984	11/6	170.41	7/24	147.82	167.24
1937	3/6	18.68	11/24	10.17	10.55	1985	12/16	212.02	1/4	163.68	211.28
1938	11/9	13.79	3/31	8.50	13.21	1986	12/2	254.00	1/22	203.49	242.17
1939	1/4	13.23	4/8	10.18	12.49	1987	8/25	336.77	12/4	223.92	247.08
1940	1/3	12.77	6/10	8.99	10.58	1988	10/21	283.66	1/20	242.63	277.72
1941	1/10	10.86	12/29	8.37	8.69	1989	10/9	359.80	1/3	275.31	353.40
1942	12/31	9.77	4/28	7.47	9.77	1990	7/16	368.95	10/11	295.46	330.22
1943	7/14	12.64	1/2	9.84	11.67	1991	12/31	417.09	1/9	311.49	417.09
1944	12/16	13.29	2/7	11.56	13.28	1992	12/18	441.28	4/8	394.50	435.71
1945	12/10	17.68	1/23	13.21	17.36	1993	12/28	470.94	1/8	429.05	466.45
1946	5/29	19.25	10/9	14.12	15.30	1994	2/2	482.00	4/4	438.92	459.27
1947	2/8	16.20	5/17	13.71	15.30	1995	12/13	621.69	1/3	459.11	615.93
1948	6/15	17.06	2/14	13.84	15.20	1996	11/25	757.03	1/10	598.48	740.74
1949	12/30	16.79	6/13	13.55	16.76	1997	12/5	983.79	1/2	737.01	970.43
1950	12/29	20.43	1/14	16.65	20.41	1998	12/29	1241.81	1/9	927.69	1229.23
1951	10/15	23.85	1/3	20.69	23.77	1999	12/31	1469.25	1/14	1212.19	1469.25
1952	12/30	26.59	2/20	23.09	26.57	2000	3/24	1527.46	12/20	1264.74	1320.28
1953	1/5	26.66	9/14	22.71	24.81	2001	2/1	1373.47	9/21	965.80	1148.08
1954	12/31	35.98	1/11	24.80	35.98	2002	1/4	1172.51	10/9	776.76	879.82
1955	11/14	46.41	1/17	34.58	45.48	2003	12/31	1111.92	3/11	800.73	1111.92
1956	8/2	49.74	1/23	43.11	46.67	2004	12/30	1213.55	8/12	1063.23	1211.92
1957	7/15	49.13	10/22	38.98	39.99	2005	12/14	1272.74	4/20	1137.50	1248.29
1958	12/31	55.21	1/2	40.33	55.21	2006	12/15	1427.09	6/13	1223.69	1418.30
1959	8/3	60.71	2/9	53.58	59.89	2007	10/9	1565.15	3/5	1374.12	1468.36
1960	1/5	60.39	10/25	52.30	58.11	2008	1/2	1447.16	11/20	752.44	903.25
1961	12/12	72.64	1/3	57.57	71.55	2009	12/28	1127.78	3/9	676.53	1115.10
1962	1/3	71.13	6/26	52.32	63.10	2010	12/29	1259.78	7/2	1022.58	1257.64
1963	12/31	75.02	1/2	62.69	75.02	2011	4/29	1363.61	10/3	1099.23	1257.60
1964	11/20	86.28	1/2	75.43	84.75	2012	9/14	1465.77	1/3	1277.06	1426.19
1965	11/15	92.63	6/28	81.60	92.43	2013	12/31	1848.36	1/8	1457.15	1848.36
1966	2/9	94.06	10/7	73.20	80.33	2014	12/29	2090.57	2/3	1741.89	2058.90
1967	9/25	97.59	1/3	80.38	96.47	2015	5/21	2130.82	8/25	1867.61	2043.94
1968	11/29	108.37	3/5	87.72	103.86	2016	12/13	2271.72	2/11	1829.08	2238.83
1969	5/14	106.16	12/17	89.20	92.06	2017	12/18	2690.16	1/3	2257.83	2673.61
1970	1/5	93.46	5/26	69.29	92.15	2018	9/20	2930.75	12/24	2351.10	2506.85
1971	4/28	104.77	11/23	90.16	102.09	2019	12/27	3240.02	1/3	2447.89	3230.78
1972	12/11	119.12	1/3	101.67	118.05	2020	12/31	3756.07	3/23	2237.40	3756.07
1973	1/11	120.24	12/5	92.16	97.55	2021	12/29	4793.06	1/4	3700.65	4766.18
1974	1/3	99.80	10/3	62.28	68.56	2022	1/3	4796.56	10/12	3577.03	3839.50
1975	7/15	95.61	1/8	70.04	90.19	2023	12/28	4783.35	1/5	3808.10	4769.83
1976	9/21	107.83	1/2	90.90	107.46	2024	12/6	6090.27	1/4	4688.68	5881.63
1977	1/3	107.00	11/2	90.71	95.10	2025*	2/19	6144.15	4/8	4982.77	At press time

*Through May 2, 2025

NASDAQ ANNUAL HIGHS, LOWS, & CLOSES SINCE 1971

YEAR	HIGH DATE	HIGH CLOSE	LOW DATE	LOW CLOSE	YEAR CLOSE
1971	12/31	114.12	1/5	89.06	114.12
1972	12/8	135.15	1/3	113.65	133.73
1973	1/11	136.84	12/24	88.67	92.19
1974	3/15	96.53	10/3	54.87	59.82
1975	7/15	88.00	1/2	60.70	77.62
1976	12/31	97.88	1/2	78.06	97.88
1977	12/30	105.05	4/5	93.66	105.05
1978	9/13	139.25	1/11	99.09	117.98
1979	10/5	152.29	1/2	117.84	151.14
1980	11/28	208.15	3/27	124.09	202.34
1981	5/29	223.47	9/28	175.03	195.84
1982	12/8	240.70	8/13	159.14	232.41
1983	6/24	328.91	1/3	230.59	278.60
1984	1/6	287.90	7/25	225.30	247.35
1985	12/16	325.16	1/2	245.91	324.93
1986	7/3	411.16	1/9	323.01	349.33
1987	8/26	455.26	10/28	291.88	330.47
1988	7/5	396.11	1/12	331.97	381.38
1989	10/9	485.73	1/3	378.56	454.82
1990	7/16	469.60	10/16	325.44	373.84
1991	12/31	586.34	1/14	355.75	586.34
1992	12/31	676.95	6/26	547.84	676.95
1993	10/15	787.42	4/26	645.87	776.80
1994	3/18	803.93	6/24	693.79	751.96
1995	12/4	1069.79	1/3	743.58	1052.13
1996	12/9	1316.27	1/15	988.57	1291.03
1997	10/9	1745.85	4/2	1201.00	1570.35
1998	12/31	2192.69	10/8	1419.12	2192.69
1999	12/31	4069.31	1/4	2208.05	4069.31
2000	3/10	5048.62	12/20	2332.78	2470.52
2001	1/24	2859.15	9/21	1423.19	1950.40
2002	1/4	2059.38	10/9	1114.11	1335.51
2003	12/30	2009.88	3/11	1271.47	2003.37
2004	12/30	2178.34	8/12	1752.49	2175.44
2005	12/2	2273.37	4/28	1904.18	2205.32
2006	11/22	2465.98	7/21	2020.39	2415.29
2007	10/31	2859.12	3/5	2340.68	2652.28
2008	1/2	2609.63	11/20	1316.12	1577.03
2009	12/30	2291.28	3/9	1268.64	2269.15
2010	12/22	2671.48	7/2	2091.79	2652.87
2011	4/29	2873.54	10/3	2335.83	2605.15
2012	9/14	3183.95	1/4	2648.36	3019.51
2013	12/31	4176.59	1/8	3091.81	4176.59
2014	12/29	4806.91	2/3	3996.96	4736.05
2015	7/20	5218.86	8/25	4506.49	5007.41
2016	12/27	5487.44	2/11	4266.84	5383.12
2017	12/18	6994.76	1/3	5429.08	6903.39
2018	8/29	8109.69	12/24	6192.92	6635.28
2019	12/26	9022.39	1/3	6463.50	8972.60
2020	12/28	12899.42	3/23	6860.67	12888.28
2021	11/29	16057.44	3/8	12609.16	15644.97
2022	1/3	15832.80	12/28	10213.29	10466.48
2023	12/27	15099.18	1/5	10305.24	15011.35
2024	12/16	20173.89	1/4	14510.30	19310.79
2025*	2/19	20056.25	4/8	15267.91	At press time

*Through May 2, 2025

RUSSELL 1000 ANNUAL HIGHS, LOWS, & CLOSES SINCE 1979

YEAR	HIGH DATE	HIGH CLOSE	LOW DATE	LOW CLOSE	YEAR CLOSE	YEAR	HIGH DATE	HIGH CLOSE	LOW DATE	LOW CLOSE	YEAR CLOSE
1979	10/5	61.18	2/27	51.83	59.87	2003	12/31	594.56	3/11	425.31	594.56
1980	11/28	78.26	3/27	53.68	75.20	2004	12/30	651.76	8/13	566.06	650.99
1981	1/6	76.34	9/25	62.03	67.93	2005	12/14	692.09	4/20	613.37	679.42
1982	11/9	78.47	8/12	55.98	77.24	2006	12/15	775.05	6/13	665.81	770.08
1983	10/10	95.07	1/3	76.04	90.38	2007	10/9	852.32	3/5	749.85	799.82
1984	1/6	92.80	7/24	79.49	90.31	2008	1/2	788.62	11/20	402.91	487.77
1985	12/16	114.97	1/4	88.61	114.39	2009	12/28	619.22	3/9	367.55	612.01
1986	7/2	137.87	1/22	111.14	130.00	2010	12/29	698.11	7/2	562.58	696.90
1987	8/25	176.22	12/4	117.65	130.02	2011	4/29	758.45	10/3	604.42	693.36
1988	10/21	149.94	1/20	128.35	146.99	2012	9/14	809.01	1/4	703.72	789.90
1989	10/9	189.93	1/3	145.78	185.11	2013	12/31	1030.36	1/8	807.95	1030.36
1990	7/16	191.56	10/11	152.36	171.22	2014	12/29	1161.45	2/3	972.95	1144.37
1991	12/31	220.61	1/9	161.94	220.61	2015	5/21	1189.55	8/25	1042.77	1131.88
1992	12/18	235.06	4/8	208.87	233.59	2016	12/13	1260.06	2/11	1005.89	1241.66
1993	10/15	252.77	1/8	229.91	250.71	2017	12/18	1490.06	1/3	1252.11	1481.81
1994	2/1	258.31	4/4	235.38	244.65	2018	9/20	1624.28	12/24	1298.02	1384.26
1995	12/13	331.18	1/3	244.41	328.89	2019	12/26	1789.56	1/3	1351.87	1784.21
1996	12/2	401.21	1/10	318.24	393.75	2020	12/31	2120.87	3/23	1224.45	2120.87
1997	12/5	519.72	4/11	389.03	513.79	2021	12/27	2660.44	1/4	2089.72	2645.91
1998	12/29	645.36	1/9	490.26	642.87	2022	1/3	2660.78	10/12	1969.25	2105.90
1999	12/31	767.97	2/9	632.53	767.97	2023	12/28	2631.33	1/5	2089.03	2622.14
2000	9/1	813.71	12/20	668.75	700.09	2024	12/6	3350.31	1/4	2573.83	3221.05
2001	1/30	727.35	9/21	507.98	604.94	2025*	2/19	3370.65	4/8	2719.99	At press time
2002	3/19	618.74	10/9	410.52	466.18						

RUSSELL 2000 ANNUAL HIGHS, LOWS, & CLOSES SINCE 1979

YEAR	HIGH DATE	HIGH CLOSE	LOW DATE	LOW CLOSE	YEAR CLOSE	YEAR	HIGH DATE	HIGH CLOSE	LOW DATE	LOW CLOSE	YEAR CLOSE
1979	12/31	55.91	1/2	40.81	55.91	2003	12/30	565.47	3/12	345.94	556.91
1980	11/28	77.70	3/27	45.36	74.80	2004	12/28	654.57	8/12	517.10	651.57
1981	6/15	85.16	9/25	65.37	73.67	2005	12/2	690.57	4/28	575.02	673.22
1982	12/8	91.01	8/12	60.33	88.90	2006	12/27	797.73	7/21	671.94	787.66
1983	6/24	126.99	1/3	88.29	112.27	2007	7/13	855.77	11/26	735.07	766.03
1984	1/12	116.69	7/25	93.95	101.49	2008	6/5	763.27	11/20	385.31	499.45
1985	12/31	129.87	1/2	101.21	129.87	2009	12/24	634.07	3/9	343.26	625.39
1986	7/3	155.30	1/9	128.23	135.00	2010	12/27	792.35	2/8	586.49	783.65
1987	8/25	174.44	10/28	106.08	120.42	2011	4/29	865.29	10/3	609.49	740.92
1988	7/15	151.42	1/12	121.23	147.37	2012	9/14	864.70	6/4	737.24	849.35
1989	10/9	180.78	1/3	146.79	168.30	2013	12/31	1163.64	1/3	872.60	1163.64
1990	6/15	170.90	10/30	118.82	132.16	2014	12/29	1219.11	10/13	1049.30	1204.70
1991	12/31	189.94	1/15	125.25	189.94	2015	6/23	1295.80	9/29	1083.91	1135.89
1992	12/31	221.01	7/8	185.81	221.01	2016	12/9	1388.07	2/11	953.72	1357.13
1993	11/2	260.17	2/23	217.55	258.59	2017	12/28	1548.93	4/13	1345.24	1535.51
1994	3/18	271.08	12/9	235.16	250.36	2018	8/31	1740.75	12/24	1266.92	1348.56
1995	9/14	316.12	1/30	246.56	315.97	2019	12/24	1678.01	1/3	1330.83	1668.47
1996	5/22	364.61	1/16	301.75	362.61	2020	12/23	2007.10	3/18	991.16	1974.86
1997	10/13	465.21	4/25	335.85	437.02	2021	11/8	2442.74	1/4	1945.91	2245.31
1998	4/21	491.41	10/8	310.28	421.96	2022	1/3	2272.56	6/16	1649.84	1761.25
1999	12/31	504.75	3/23	383.37	504.75	2023	12/27	2066.21	10/27	1636.94	2027.07
2000	3/9	606.05	12/20	443.80	483.53	2024	11/25	2442.03	1/17	1913.17	2230.16
2001	5/22	517.23	9/21	378.89	488.50	2025*	1/21	2317.97	4/8	1760.71	At press time
2002	4/16	522.95	10/9	327.04	383.09						

*Through May 2, 2025

DOW JONES INDUSTRIALS MONTHLY PERCENT CHANGES SINCE 1950

	Jan	Feb	Mar	Apr	May	Jun	Jul	Aug	Sep	Oct	Nov	Dec	Year
1950	0.8	0.8	1.3	4.0	4.2	−6.4	0.1	3.6	4.4	−0.6	1.2	3.4	17.6
1951	5.7	1.3	−1.6	4.5	−3.7	−2.8	6.3	4.8	0.3	−3.2	−0.4	3.0	14.4
1952	0.5	−3.9	3.6	−4.4	2.1	4.3	1.9	−1.6	−1.6	−0.5	5.4	2.9	8.4
1953	−0.7	−1.9	−1.5	−1.8	−0.9	−1.5	2.7	−5.1	1.1	4.5	2.0	−0.2	−3.8
1954	4.1	0.7	3.0	5.2	2.6	1.8	4.3	−3.5	7.3	−2.3	9.8	4.6	44.0
1955	1.1	0.7	−0.5	3.9	−0.2	6.2	3.2	0.5	−0.3	−2.5	6.2	1.1	20.8
1956	−3.6	2.7	5.8	0.8	−7.4	3.1	5.1	−3.0	−5.3	1.0	−1.5	5.6	2.3
1957	−4.1	−3.0	2.2	4.1	2.1	−0.3	1.0	−4.8	−5.8	−3.3	2.0	−3.2	−12.8
1958	3.3	−2.2	1.6	2.0	1.5	3.3	5.2	1.1	4.6	2.1	2.6	4.7	34.0
1959	1.8	1.6	−0.3	3.7	3.2	−0.03	4.9	−1.6	−4.9	2.4	1.9	3.1	16.4
1960	−8.4	1.2	−2.1	−2.4	4.0	2.4	−3.7	1.5	−7.3	0.04	2.9	3.1	−9.3
1961	5.2	2.1	2.2	0.3	2.7	−1.8	3.1	2.1	−2.6	0.4	2.5	1.3	18.7
1962	−4.3	1.1	−0.2	−5.9	−7.8	−8.5	6.5	1.9	−5.0	1.9	10.1	0.4	−10.8
1963	4.7	−2.9	3.0	5.2	1.3	−2.8	−1.6	4.9	0.5	3.1	−0.6	1.7	17.0
1964	2.9	1.9	1.6	−0.3	1.2	1.3	1.2	−0.3	4.4	−0.3	0.3	−0.1	14.6
1965	3.3	0.1	−1.6	3.7	−0.5	−5.4	1.6	1.3	4.2	3.2	−1.5	2.4	10.9
1966	1.5	−3.2	−2.8	1.0	−5.3	−1.6	−2.6	−7.0	−1.8	4.2	−1.9	−0.7	−18.9
1967	8.2	−1.2	3.2	3.6	−5.0	0.9	5.1	−0.3	2.8	−5.1	−0.4	3.3	15.2
1968	−5.5	−1.7	0.02	8.5	−1.4	−0.1	−1.6	1.5	4.4	1.8	3.4	−4.2	4.3
1969	0.2	−4.3	3.3	1.6	−1.3	−6.9	−6.6	2.6	−2.8	5.3	−5.1	−1.5	−15.2
1970	−7.0	4.5	1.0	−6.3	−4.8	−2.4	7.4	4.1	−0.5	−0.7	5.1	5.6	4.8
1971	3.5	1.2	2.9	4.1	−3.6	−1.8	−3.7	4.6	−1.2	−5.4	−0.9	7.1	6.1
1972	1.3	2.9	1.4	1.4	0.7	−3.3	−0.5	4.2	−1.1	0.2	6.6	0.2	14.6
1973	−2.1	−4.4	−0.4	−3.1	−2.2	−1.1	3.9	−4.2	6.7	1.0	−14.0	3.5	−16.6
1974	0.6	0.6	−1.6	−1.2	−4.1	0.03	−5.6	−10.4	−10.4	9.5	−7.0	−0.4	−27.6
1975	14.2	5.0	3.9	6.9	1.3	5.6	−5.4	0.5	−5.0	5.3	2.9	−1.0	38.3
1976	14.4	−0.3	2.8	−0.3	−2.2	2.8	−1.8	−1.1	1.7	−2.6	−1.8	6.1	17.9
1977	−5.0	−1.9	−1.8	0.8	−3.0	2.0	−2.9	−3.2	−1.7	−3.4	1.4	0.2	−17.3
1978	−7.4	−3.6	2.1	10.6	0.4	−2.6	5.3	1.7	−1.3	−8.5	0.8	0.7	−3.1
1979	4.2	−3.6	6.6	−0.8	−3.8	2.4	0.5	4.9	−1.0	−7.2	0.8	2.0	4.2
1980	4.4	−1.5	−9.0	4.0	4.1	2.0	7.8	−0.3	−0.02	−0.9	7.4	−3.0	14.9
1981	−1.7	2.9	3.0	−0.6	−0.6	−1.5	−2.5	−7.4	−3.6	0.3	4.3	−1.6	−9.2
1982	−0.4	−5.4	−0.2	3.1	−3.4	−0.9	−0.4	11.5	−0.6	10.7	4.8	0.7	19.6
1983	2.8	3.4	1.6	8.5	−2.1	1.8	−1.9	1.4	1.4	−0.6	4.1	−1.4	20.3
1984	−3.0	−5.4	0.9	0.5	−5.6	2.5	−1.5	9.8	−1.4	0.1	−1.5	1.9	−3.7
1985	6.2	−0.2	−1.3	−0.7	4.6	1.5	0.9	−1.0	−0.4	3.4	7.1	5.1	27.7
1986	1.6	8.8	6.4	−1.9	5.2	0.9	−6.2	6.9	−6.9	6.2	1.9	−1.0	22.6
1987	13.8	3.1	3.6	−0.8	0.2	5.5	6.3	3.5	−2.5	−23.2	−8.0	5.7	2.3
1988	1.0	5.8	−4.0	2.2	−0.1	5.4	−0.6	−4.6	4.0	1.7	−1.6	2.6	11.8
1989	8.0	−3.6	1.6	5.5	2.5	−1.6	9.0	2.9	−1.6	−1.8	2.3	1.7	27.0

continued

DOW JONES INDUSTRIALS MONTHLY PERCENT CHANGES SINCE 1950 (continued)

	Jan	Feb	Mar	Apr	May	Jun	Jul	Aug	Sep	Oct	Nov	Dec	Year
1990	−5.9	1.4	3.0	−1.9	8.3	0.1	0.9	−10.0	−6.2	−0.4	4.8	2.9	−4.3
1991	3.9	5.3	1.1	−0.9	4.8	−4.0	4.1	0.6	−0.9	1.7	−5.7	9.5	20.3
1992	1.7	1.4	−1.0	3.8	1.1	−2.3	2.3	−4.0	0.4	−1.4	2.4	−0.1	4.2
1993	0.3	1.8	1.9	−0.2	2.9	−0.3	0.7	3.2	−2.6	3.5	0.1	1.9	13.7
1994	6.0	−3.7	−5.1	1.3	2.1	−3.5	3.8	4.0	−1.8	1.7	−4.3	2.5	2.1
1995	0.2	4.3	3.7	3.9	3.3	2.0	3.3	−2.1	3.9	−0.7	6.7	0.8	33.5
1996	5.4	1.7	1.9	−0.3	1.3	0.2	−2.2	1.6	4.7	2.5	8.2	−1.1	26.0
1997	5.7	0.9	−4.3	6.5	4.6	4.7	7.2	−7.3	4.2	−6.3	5.1	1.1	22.6
1998	−0.02	8.1	3.0	3.0	−1.8	0.6	−0.8	−15.1	4.0	9.6	6.1	0.7	16.1
1999	1.9	−0.6	5.2	10.2	−2.1	3.9	−2.9	1.6	−4.5	3.8	1.4	5.7	25.2
2000	−4.8	−7.4	7.8	−1.7	−2.0	−0.7	0.7	6.6	−5.0	3.0	−5.1	3.6	−6.2
2001	0.9	−3.6	−5.9	8.7	1.6	−3.8	0.2	−5.4	−11.1	2.6	8.6	1.7	−7.1
2002	−1.0	1.9	2.9	−4.4	−0.2	−6.9	−5.5	−0.8	−12.4	10.6	5.9	−6.2	−16.8
2003	−3.5	−2.0	1.3	6.1	4.4	1.5	2.8	2.0	−1.5	5.7	−0.2	6.9	25.3
2004	0.3	0.9	−2.1	−1.3	−0.4	2.4	−2.8	0.3	−0.9	−0.5	4.0	3.4	3.1
2005	−2.7	2.6	−2.4	−3.0	2.7	−1.8	3.6	−1.5	0.8	−1.2	3.5	−0.8	−0.6
2006	1.4	1.2	1.1	2.3	−1.7	−0.2	0.3	1.7	2.6	3.4	1.2	2.0	16.3
2007	1.3	−2.8	0.7	5.7	4.3	−1.6	−1.5	1.1	4.0	0.2	−4.0	−0.8	6.4
2008	−4.6	−3.0	−0.03	4.5	−1.4	−10.2	0.2	1.5	−6.0	−14.1	−5.3	−0.6	−33.8
2009	−8.8	−11.7	7.7	7.3	4.1	−0.6	8.6	3.5	2.3	0.005	6.5	0.8	18.8
2010	−3.5	2.6	5.1	1.4	−7.9	−3.6	7.1	−4.3	7.7	3.1	−1.0	5.2	11.0
2011	2.7	2.8	0.8	4.0	−1.9	−1.2	−2.2	−4.4	−6.0	9.5	0.8	1.4	5.5
2012	3.4	2.5	2.0	0.01	−6.2	3.9	1.0	0.6	2.6	−2.5	−0.5	0.6	7.3
2013	5.8	1.4	3.7	1.8	1.9	−1.4	4.0	−4.4	2.2	2.8	3.5	3.0	26.5
2014	−5.3	4.0	0.8	0.7	0.8	0.7	−1.6	3.2	−0.3	2.0	2.5	−0.03	7.5
2015	−3.7	5.6	−2.0	0.4	1.0	−2.2	0.4	−6.6	−1.5	8.5	0.3	−1.7	−2.2
2016	−5.5	0.3	7.1	0.5	0.1	0.8	2.8	−0.2	−0.5	−0.9	5.4	3.3	13.4
2017	0.5	4.8	−0.7	1.3	0.3	1.6	2.5	0.3	2.1	4.3	3.8	1.8	25.1
2018	5.8	−4.3	−3.7	0.2	1.0	−0.6	4.7	2.2	1.9	−5.1	1.7	−8.7	−5.6
2019	7.2	3.7	0.1	2.6	−6.7	7.2	1.0	−1.7	1.9	0.5	3.7	1.7	22.3
2020	−1.0	−10.1	−13.7	11.1	4.3	1.7	2.4	7.6	−2.3	−4.6	11.8	3.3	7.2
2021	−2.0	3.2	6.6	2.7	1.9	−0.1	1.3	1.2	−4.3	5.8	−3.7	5.4	18.7
2022	−3.3	−3.5	2.3	−4.9	0.04	−6.7	6.7	−4.1	−8.8	14.0	5.7	−4.2	−8.8
2023	2.8	−4.2	1.9	2.5	−3.5	4.6	3.3	−2.4	−3.5	−1.4	8.8	4.8	13.7
2024	1.2	2.2	2.1	−5.0	2.3	1.1	4.4	1.8	1.8	−1.3	7.5	−5.3	12.9
2025	4.7	−1.6	−4.2	−3.2									
TOTALS	73.6	4.3	68.3	134.9	−1.8	−12.3	105.0	−7.3	−61.8	54.6	143.8	109.9	
AVG.	1.0	0.1	0.9	1.8	−0.02	−0.2	1.4	−0.1	−0.8	0.7	1.9	1.5	
# Up	48	44	49	51	41	36	50	42	30	44	52	52	
# Down	28	32	27	25	34	39	25	33	45	31	23	23	

DOW JONES INDUSTRIALS MONTHLY POINT CHANGES SINCE 1950

	Jan	Feb	Mar	Apr	May	Jun	Jul	Aug	Sep	Oct	Nov	Dec	Year
1950	1.66	1.65	2.61	8.28	9.09	−14.31	0.29	7.47	9.49	−1.35	2.59	7.81	235.41
1951	13.42	3.22	−4.11	11.19	−9.48	−7.01	15.22	12.39	0.91	−8.81	−1.08	7.96	269.23
1952	1.46	−10.61	9.38	−11.83	5.31	11.32	5.30	−4.52	−4.43	−1.38	14.43	8.24	291.90
1953	−2.13	−5.50	−4.40	−5.12	−2.47	−4.02	7.12	−14.16	2.82	11.77	5.56	−0.47	280.90
1954	11.49	2.15	8.97	15.82	8.16	6.04	14.39	−12.12	24.66	−8.32	34.63	17.62	404.39
1955	4.44	3.04	−2.17	15.95	−0.79	26.52	14.47	2.33	−1.56	−11.75	28.39	5.14	488.40
1956	−17.66	12.91	28.14	4.33	−38.07	14.73	25.03	−15.77	−26.79	4.60	−7.07	26.69	499.47
1957	−20.31	−14.54	10.19	19.55	10.57	−1.64	5.23	−24.17	−28.05	−15.26	8.83	−14.18	435.69
1958	14.33	−10.10	6.84	9.10	6.84	15.48	24.81	5.64	23.46	11.13	14.24	26.19	583.65
1959	10.31	9.54	−1.79	22.04	20.04	−0.19	31.28	−10.47	−32.73	14.92	12.58	20.18	679.36
1960	−56.74	7.50	−13.53	−14.89	23.80	15.12	−23.89	9.26	−45.85	0.22	16.86	18.67	615.89
1961	32.31	13.88	14.55	2.08	18.01	−12.76	21.41	14.57	−18.73	2.71	17.68	9.54	731.14
1962	−31.14	8.05	−1.10	−41.62	−51.97	−52.08	36.65	11.25	−30.20	10.79	59.53	2.80	652.10
1963	30.75	−19.91	19.58	35.18	9.26	−20.08	−11.45	33.89	3.47	22.44	−4.71	12.43	762.95
1964	22.39	14.80	13.15	−2.52	9.79	10.94	9.60	−2.62	36.89	−2.29	2.35	−1.30	874.13
1965	28.73	0.62	−14.43	33.26	−4.27	−50.01	13.71	11.36	37.48	30.24	−14.11	22.55	969.26
1966	14.25	−31.62	−27.12	8.91	−49.61	−13.97	−22.72	−58.97	−14.19	32.85	−15.48	−5.90	785.69
1967	64.20	−10.52	26.61	31.07	−44.49	7.70	43.98	−2.95	25.37	−46.92	−3.93	29.30	905.11
1968	−49.64	−14.97	0.17	71.55	−13.22	−1.20	−14.80	13.01	39.78	16.60	32.69	−41.33	943.75
1969	2.30	−40.84	30.27	14.70	−12.62	−64.37	−57.72	21.25	−23.63	42.90	−43.69	−11.94	800.36
1970	−56.30	33.53	7.98	−49.50	−35.63	−16.91	50.59	30.46	−3.90	−5.07	38.48	44.83	838.92
1971	29.58	10.33	25.54	37.38	−33.94	−16.67	−32.71	39.64	−10.88	−48.19	−7.66	58.86	890.20
1972	11.97	25.96	12.57	13.47	6.55	−31.69	−4.29	38.99	−10.46	2.25	62.69	1.81	1020.02
1973	−21.00	−43.95	−4.06	−29.58	−20.02	−9.70	34.69	−38.83	59.53	9.48	−134.33	28.61	850.86
1974	4.69	4.98	−13.85	−9.93	−34.58	0.24	−44.98	−78.85	−70.71	57.65	−46.86	−2.42	616.24
1975	87.45	35.36	29.10	53.19	10.95	46.70	−47.48	3.83	−41.46	42.16	24.63	−8.26	852.41
1976	122.87	−2.67	26.84	−2.60	−21.62	27.55	−18.14	−10.90	16.45	−25.26	−17.71	57.43	1004.65
1977	−50.28	−17.95	−17.29	7.77	−28.24	17.64	−26.23	−28.58	−14.38	−28.76	11.35	1.47	831.17
1978	−61.25	−27.80	15.24	79.96	3.29	−21.66	43.32	14.55	−11.00	−73.37	6.58	5.98	805.01
1979	34.21	−30.40	53.36	−7.28	−32.57	19.65	4.44	41.21	−9.05	−62.88	6.65	16.39	838.74
1980	37.11	−12.71	−77.39	31.31	33.79	17.07	67.40	−2.73	−0.17	−7.93	68.85	−29.35	963.99
1981	−16.72	27.31	29.29	−6.12	−6.00	−14.87	−24.54	−70.87	−31.49	2.57	36.43	−13.98	875.00
1982	−3.90	−46.71	−1.62	25.59	−28.82	−7.61	−3.33	92.71	−5.06	95.47	47.56	7.26	1046.54
1983	29.16	36.92	17.41	96.17	−26.22	21.98	−22.74	16.94	16.97	−7.93	50.82	−17.38	1258.64
1984	−38.06	−65.95	10.26	5.86	−65.90	27.55	−17.12	109.10	−17.67	0.67	−18.44	22.63	1211.57
1985	75.20	−2.76	−17.23	−8.72	57.35	20.05	11.99	−13.44	−5.38	45.68	97.82	74.54	1546.67
1986	24.32	138.07	109.55	−34.63	92.73	16.01	−117.41	123.03	−130.76	110.23	36.42	−18.28	1895.95
1987	262.09	65.95	80.70	−18.33	5.21	126.96	153.54	90.88	−66.67	−602.75	−159.98	105.28	1938.83
1988	19.39	113.40	−83.56	44.27	−1.21	110.59	−12.98	−97.08	81.26	35.74	−34.14	54.06	2168.57

continued

DOW JONES INDUSTRIALS MONTHLY POINT CHANGES SINCE 1950 (continued)

	Jan	Feb	Mar	Apr	May	Jun	Jul	Aug	Sep	Oct	Nov	Dec	Year
1989	173.75	−83.93	35.23	125.18	61.35	−40.09	220.60	76.61	−44.45	−47.74	61.19	46.93	2753.20
1990	−162.66	36.71	79.96	−50.45	219.90	4.03	24.51	−290.84	−161.88	−10.15	117.32	74.01	2633.66
1991	102.73	145.79	31.68	−25.99	139.63	−120.75	118.07	18.78	−26.83	52.33	−174.42	274.15	3168.83
1992	54.56	44.28	−32.20	123.65	37.76	−78.36	75.26	−136.43	14.31	−45.38	78.88	−4.05	3301.11
1993	8.92	60.78	64.30	−7.56	99.88	−11.35	23.39	111.78	−96.13	125.47	3.36	70.14	3754.09
1994	224.27	−146.34	−196.06	45.73	76.68	−133.41	139.54	148.92	−70.23	64.93	−168.89	95.21	3834.44
1995	9.42	167.19	146.64	163.58	143.87	90.96	152.37	−97.91	178.52	−33.60	319.01	42.63	5117.12
1996	278.18	90.32	101.52	−18.06	74.10	11.45	−125.72	87.30	265.96	147.21	492.32	−73.43	6448.27
1997	364.82	64.65	−294.26	425.51	322.05	341.75	549.82	−600.19	322.84	−503.18	381.05	85.12	7908.25
1998	−1.75	639.22	254.09	263.56	−163.42	52.07	−68.73	−1344.22	303.55	749.48	524.45	64.88	9181.43
1999	177.40	−52.25	479.58	1002.88	−229.30	411.06	−315.65	174.13	−492.33	392.91	147.95	619.31	11497.12
2000	−556.59	−812.22	793.61	−188.01	−211.58	−74.44	74.09	693.12	−564.18	320.22	−556.65	372.36	10786.85
2001	100.51	−392.08	−616.50	856.19	176.97	−409.54	20.41	−573.06	−1102.19	227.58	776.42	169.94	10021.50
2002	−101.50	186.13	297.81	−457.72	−20.97	−681.99	−506.67	−73.09	−1071.57	805.10	499.06	−554.46	8341.63
2003	−287.82	−162.73	101.05	487.96	370.17	135.18	248.36	182.02	−140.76	526.06	−18.66	671.46	10453.92
2004	34.15	95.85	−226.22	−132.13	−37.12	247.03	−295.77	34.21	−93.65	−52.80	400.55	354.99	10783.01
2005	−293.07	276.29	−262.47	−311.25	274.97	−192.51	365.94	−159.31	87.10	−128.63	365.80	−88.37	10717.50
2006	147.36	128.55	115.91	257.82	−198.83	−18.09	35.46	195.47	297.92	401.66	141.20	241.22	12463.15
2007	158.54	−353.06	85.72	708.56	564.73	−219.02	−196.63	145.75	537.89	34.38	−558.29	−106.90	13264.82
2008	−614.46	−383.97	−3.50	557.24	−181.81	−1288.31	28.01	165.53	−692.89	−1525.65	−495.97	−52.65	8776.39
2009	−775.53	−937.93	545.99	559.20	332.21	−53.33	724.61	324.67	216.00	0.45	632.11	83.21	10428.05
2010	−360.72	257.93	531.37	151.98	−871.98	−362.61	691.92	−451.22	773.33	330.44	−112.47	571.49	11577.51
2011	314.42	334.41	93.39	490.81	−240.75	−155.45	−271.10	−529.71	−700.15	1041.63	90.67	171.88	12217.56
2012	415.35	319.16	259.97	1.59	−820.18	486.64	128.59	82.16	346.29	−340.67	−70.88	78.56	13104.14
2013	756.44	193.91	524.05	261.26	275.77	−205.97	589.94	−689.23	319.36	416.08	540.66	490.25	16576.66
2014	−877.81	622.86	135.95	123.18	136.33	109.43	−263.30	535.15	−55.55	347.62	437.72	−5.17	17823.07
2015	−658.12	967.75	−356.58	64.40	170.16	−391.17	70.35	−1161.83	−244.03	1379.54	56.38	−294.89	17425.03
2016	−958.73	50.20	1168.59	88.55	13.56	142.79	502.25	−31.36	−92.73	−165.73	981.16	639.02	19762.60
2017	101.49	948.15	−149.02	277.29	68.14	340.98	541.49	56.98	456.99	972.15	895.11	446.87	24719.22
2018	1430.17	−1120.19	−926.09	60.04	252.69	−144.43	1143.78	549.63	493.49	−1342.55	422.70	−2211.00	23327.46
2019	1672.21	916.33	12.68	664.23	−1777.87	1784.92	264.31	−460.99	513.55	129.40	1005.18	487.03	28538.44
2020	−282.41	−2846.67	−3492.20	2428.56	1037.39	429.77	615.44	2001.73	−648.35	−1280.10	3137.04	967.84	30606.48
2021	−623.86	949.75	2049.18	893.30	654.60	−26.94	432.96	425.26	−1516.81	1975.64	−1335.84	1854.58	36338.30
2022	−1206.44	−1239.26	785.75	−1701.14	12.91	−2214.69	2069.70	−1334.70	−2784.92	4007.44	1856.82	−1442.52	33147.25
2023	938.79	−1429.34	617.45	824.01	−1189.89	1499.33	1151.93	−837.62	−1214.41	−454.63	2898.02	1738.65	37689.54
2024	460.76	846.09	810.98	−1991.45	870.40	432.54	1723.93	720.29	767.07	−566.69	3147.19	−2366.43	42544.22
2025	2000.44	−703.75	−1839.25	−1332.50									
TOTALS	2728.16	−2161.76	2032.85	6145.41	211.52	−103.43	10815.39	−1785.49	−6196.53	7595.07	17146.70	4041.34	
# Up	48	44	49	51	41	36	50	42	30	44	52	52	
# Down	28	32	27	25	34	39	25	33	45	31	23	23	

DOW JONES INDUSTRIALS MONTHLY CLOSING PRICES SINCE 1950

	Jan	Feb	Mar	Apr	May	Jun	Jul	Aug	Sep	Oct	Nov	Dec
1950	201.79	203.44	206.05	214.33	223.42	209.11	209.40	216.87	226.36	225.01	227.60	235.41
1951	248.83	252.05	247.94	259.13	249.65	242.64	257.86	270.25	271.16	262.35	261.27	269.23
1952	270.69	260.08	269.46	257.63	262.94	274.26	279.56	275.04	270.61	269.23	283.66	291.90
1953	289.77	284.27	279.87	274.75	272.28	268.26	275.38	261.22	264.04	275.81	281.37	280.90
1954	292.39	294.54	303.51	319.33	327.49	333.53	347.92	335.80	360.46	352.14	386.77	404.39
1955	408.83	411.87	409.70	425.65	424.86	451.38	465.85	468.18	466.62	454.87	483.26	488.40
1956	470.74	483.65	511.79	516.12	478.05	492.78	517.81	502.04	475.25	479.85	472.78	499.47
1957	479.16	464.62	474.81	494.36	504.93	503.29	508.52	484.35	456.30	441.04	449.87	435.69
1958	450.02	439.92	446.76	455.86	462.70	478.18	502.99	508.63	532.09	543.22	557.46	583.65
1959	593.96	603.50	601.71	623.75	643.79	643.60	674.88	664.41	631.68	646.60	659.18	679.36
1960	622.62	630.12	616.59	601.70	625.50	640.62	616.73	625.99	580.14	580.36	597.22	615.89
1961	648.20	662.08	676.63	678.71	696.72	683.96	705.37	719.94	701.21	703.92	721.60	731.14
1962	700.00	708.05	706.95	665.33	613.36	561.28	597.93	609.18	578.98	589.77	649.30	652.10
1963	682.85	662.94	682.52	717.70	726.96	706.88	695.43	729.32	732.79	755.23	750.52	762.95
1964	785.34	800.14	813.29	810.77	820.56	831.50	841.10	838.48	875.37	873.08	875.43	874.13
1965	902.86	903.48	889.05	922.31	918.04	868.03	881.74	893.10	930.58	960.82	946.71	969.26
1966	983.51	951.89	924.77	933.68	884.07	870.10	847.38	788.41	774.22	807.07	791.59	785.69
1967	849.89	839.37	865.98	897.05	852.56	860.26	904.24	901.29	926.66	879.74	875.81	905.11
1968	855.47	840.50	840.67	912.22	899.00	897.80	883.00	896.01	935.79	952.39	985.08	943.75
1969	946.05	905.21	935.48	950.18	937.56	873.19	815.47	836.72	813.09	855.99	812.30	800.36
1970	744.06	777.59	785.57	736.07	700.44	683.53	734.12	764.58	760.68	755.61	794.09	838.92
1971	868.50	878.83	904.37	941.75	907.81	891.14	858.43	898.07	887.19	839.00	831.34	890.20
1972	902.17	928.13	940.70	954.17	960.72	929.03	924.74	963.73	953.27	955.52	1018.21	1020.02
1973	999.02	955.07	951.01	921.43	901.41	891.71	926.40	887.57	947.10	956.58	822.25	850.86
1974	855.55	860.53	846.68	836.75	802.17	802.41	757.43	678.58	607.87	665.52	618.66	616.24
1975	703.69	739.05	768.15	821.34	832.29	878.99	831.51	835.34	793.88	836.04	860.67	852.41
1976	975.28	972.61	999.45	996.85	975.23	1002.78	984.64	973.74	990.19	964.93	947.22	1004.65
1977	954.37	936.42	919.13	926.90	898.66	916.30	890.07	861.49	847.11	818.35	829.70	831.17
1978	769.92	742.12	757.36	837.32	840.61	818.95	862.27	876.82	865.82	792.45	799.03	805.01
1979	839.22	808.82	862.18	854.90	822.33	841.98	846.42	887.63	878.58	815.70	822.35	838.74
1980	875.85	863.14	785.75	817.06	850.85	867.92	935.32	932.59	932.42	924.49	993.34	963.99
1981	947.27	974.58	1003.87	997.75	991.75	976.88	952.34	881.47	849.98	852.55	888.98	875.00
1982	871.10	824.39	822.77	848.36	819.54	811.93	808.60	901.31	896.25	991.72	1039.28	1046.54
1983	1075.70	1112.62	1130.03	1226.20	1199.98	1221.96	1199.22	1216.16	1233.13	1225.20	1276.02	1258.64
1984	1220.58	1154.63	1164.89	1170.75	1104.85	1132.40	1115.28	1224.38	1206.71	1207.38	1188.94	1211.57
1985	1286.77	1284.01	1266.78	1258.06	1315.41	1335.46	1347.45	1334.01	1328.63	1374.31	1472.13	1546.67
1986	1570.99	1709.06	1818.61	1783.98	1876.71	1892.72	1775.31	1898.34	1767.58	1877.81	1914.23	1895.95

continued

DOW JONES INDUSTRIALS MONTHLY CLOSING PRICES SINCE 1950 (continued)

	Jan	Feb	Mar	Apr	May	Jun	Jul	Aug	Sep	Oct	Nov	Dec
1987	2158.04	2223.99	2304.69	2286.36	2291.57	2418.53	2572.07	2662.95	2596.28	1993.53	1833.55	1938.83
1988	1958.22	2071.62	1988.06	2032.33	2031.12	2141.71	2128.73	2031.65	2112.91	2148.65	2114.51	2168.57
1989	2342.32	2258.39	2293.62	2418.80	2480.15	2440.06	2660.66	2737.27	2692.82	2645.08	2706.27	2753.20
1990	2590.54	2627.25	2707.21	2656.76	2876.66	2880.69	2905.20	2614.36	2452.48	2442.33	2559.65	2633.66
1991	2736.39	2882.18	2913.86	2887.87	3027.50	2906.75	3024.82	3043.60	3016.77	3069.10	2894.68	3168.83
1992	3223.39	3267.67	3235.47	3359.12	3396.88	3318.52	3393.78	3257.35	3271.66	3226.28	3305.16	3301.11
1993	3310.03	3370.81	3435.11	3427.55	3527.43	3516.08	3539.47	3651.25	3555.12	3680.59	3683.95	3754.09
1994	3978.36	3832.02	3635.96	3681.69	3758.37	3624.96	3764.50	3913.42	3843.19	3908.12	3739.23	3834.44
1995	3843.86	4011.05	4157.69	4321.27	4465.14	4556.10	4708.47	4610.56	4789.08	4755.48	5074.49	5117.12
1996	5395.30	5485.62	5587.14	5569.08	5643.18	5654.63	5528.91	5616.21	5882.17	6029.38	6521.70	6448.27
1997	6813.09	6877.74	6583.48	7008.99	7331.04	7672.79	8222.61	7622.42	7945.26	7442.08	7823.13	7908.25
1998	7906.50	8545.72	8799.81	9063.37	8899.95	8952.02	8883.29	7539.07	7842.62	8592.10	9116.55	9181.43
1999	9358.83	9306.58	9786.16	10789.04	10559.74	10970.80	10655.15	10829.28	10336.95	10729.86	10877.81	11497.12
2000	10940.53	10128.31	10921.92	10733.91	10522.33	10447.89	10521.98	11215.10	10650.92	10971.14	10414.49	10786.85
2001	10887.36	10495.28	9878.78	10734.97	10911.94	10502.40	10522.81	9949.75	8847.56	9075.14	9851.56	10021.50
2002	9920.00	10106.13	10403.94	9946.22	9925.25	9243.26	8736.59	8663.50	7591.93	8397.03	8896.09	8341.63
2003	8053.81	7891.08	7992.13	8480.09	8850.26	8985.44	9233.80	9415.82	9275.06	9801.12	9782.46	10453.92
2004	10488.07	10583.92	10357.70	10225.57	10188.45	10435.48	10139.71	10173.92	10080.27	10027.47	10428.02	10783.01
2005	10489.94	10766.23	10503.76	10192.51	10467.48	10274.97	10640.91	10481.60	10568.70	10440.07	10805.87	10717.50
2006	10864.86	10993.41	11109.32	11367.14	11168.31	11150.22	11185.68	11381.15	11679.07	12080.73	12221.93	12463.15
2007	12621.69	12268.63	12354.35	13062.91	13627.64	13408.62	13211.99	13357.74	13895.63	13930.01	13371.72	13264.82
2008	12650.36	12266.39	12262.89	12820.13	12638.32	11350.01	11378.02	11543.55	10850.66	9325.01	8829.04	8776.39
2009	8000.86	7062.93	7608.92	8168.12	8500.33	8447.00	9171.61	9496.28	9712.28	9712.73	10344.84	10428.05
2010	10067.33	10325.26	10856.63	11008.61	10136.63	9774.02	10465.94	10014.72	10788.05	11118.49	11006.02	11577.51
2011	11891.93	12226.34	12319.73	12810.54	12569.79	12414.34	12143.24	11613.53	10913.38	11955.01	12045.68	12217.56
2012	12632.91	12952.07	13212.04	13213.63	12393.45	12880.09	13008.68	13090.84	13437.13	13096.46	13025.58	13104.14
2013	13860.58	14054.49	14578.54	14839.80	15115.57	14909.60	15499.54	14810.31	15129.67	15545.75	16086.41	16576.66
2014	15698.85	16321.71	16457.66	16580.84	16717.17	16826.60	16563.30	17098.45	17042.90	17390.52	17828.24	17823.07
2015	17164.95	18132.70	17776.12	17840.52	18010.68	17619.51	17689.86	16528.03	16284.00	17663.54	17719.92	17425.03
2016	16466.30	16516.50	17685.09	17773.64	17787.20	17929.99	18432.24	18400.88	18308.15	18142.42	19123.58	19762.60
2017	19864.09	20812.24	20663.22	20940.51	21008.65	21349.63	21891.12	21948.10	22405.09	23377.24	24272.35	24719.22
2018	26149.39	25029.20	24103.11	24163.15	24415.84	24271.41	25415.19	25964.82	26458.31	25115.76	25538.46	23327.46
2019	24999.67	25916.00	25928.68	26592.91	24815.04	26599.96	26864.27	26403.28	26916.83	27046.23	28051.41	28538.44
2020	28256.03	25409.36	21917.16	24345.72	25383.11	25812.88	26428.32	28430.05	27781.70	26501.60	29638.64	30606.48
2021	29982.62	30932.37	32981.55	33874.85	34529.45	34502.51	34935.47	35360.73	33843.92	35819.56	34483.72	36338.30
2022	35131.86	33892.60	34678.35	32977.21	32990.12	30775.43	32845.13	31510.43	28725.51	32732.95	34589.77	33147.25
2023	34086.04	32656.70	33274.15	34098.16	32908.27	34407.60	35559.53	34721.91	33507.50	33052.87	35950.89	37689.54
2024	38150.30	38996.39	39807.37	37815.92	38686.32	39118.50	40842.79	41563.08	42330.15	41763.46	44910.65	42544.22
2025	44544.66	43840.91	42001.76	40669.36								

STANDARD & POOR'S 500 MONTHLY PERCENT CHANGES SINCE 1950

	Jan	Feb	Mar	Apr	May	Jun	Jul	Aug	Sep	Oct	Nov	Dec	Year
1950	1.7	1.0	0.4	4.5	3.9	-5.8	0.8	3.3	5.6	0.4	-0.1	4.6	21.8
1951	6.1	0.6	-1.8	4.8	-4.1	-2.6	6.9	3.9	-0.1	-1.4	-0.3	3.9	16.5
1952	1.6	-3.6	4.8	-4.3	2.3	4.6	1.8	-1.5	-2.0	-0.1	4.6	3.5	11.8
1953	-0.7	-1.8	-2.4	-2.6	-0.3	-1.6	2.5	-5.8	0.1	5.1	0.9	0.2	-6.6
1954	5.1	0.3	3.0	4.9	3.3	0.1	5.7	-3.4	8.3	-1.9	8.1	5.1	45.0
1955	1.8	0.4	-0.5	3.8	-0.1	8.2	6.1	-0.8	1.1	-3.0	7.5	-0.1	26.4
1956	-3.6	3.5	6.9	-0.2	-6.6	3.9	5.2	-3.8	-4.5	0.5	-1.1	3.5	2.6
1957	-4.2	-3.3	2.0	3.7	3.7	-0.1	1.1	-5.6	-6.2	-3.2	1.6	-4.1	-14.3
1958	4.3	-2.1	3.1	3.2	1.5	2.6	4.3	1.2	4.8	2.5	2.2	5.2	38.1
1959	0.4	-0.02	0.1	3.9	1.9	-0.4	3.5	-1.5	-4.6	1.1	1.3	2.8	8.5
1960	-7.1	0.9	-1.4	-1.8	2.7	2.0	-2.5	2.6	-6.0	-0.2	4.0	4.6	-3.0
1961	6.3	2.7	2.6	0.4	1.9	-2.9	3.3	2.0	-2.0	2.8	3.9	0.3	23.1
1962	-3.8	1.6	-0.6	-6.2	-8.6	-8.2	6.4	1.5	-4.8	0.4	10.2	1.3	-11.8
1963	4.9	-2.9	3.5	4.9	1.4	-2.0	-0.3	4.9	-1.1	3.2	-1.1	2.4	18.9
1964	2.7	1.0	1.5	0.6	1.1	1.6	1.8	-1.6	2.9	0.8	-0.5	0.4	13.0
1965	3.3	-0.1	-1.5	3.4	-0.8	-4.9	1.3	2.3	3.2	2.7	-0.9	0.9	9.1
1966	0.5	-1.8	-2.2	2.1	-5.4	-1.6	-1.3	-7.8	-0.7	4.8	0.3	-0.1	-13.1
1967	7.8	0.2	3.9	4.2	-5.2	1.8	4.5	-1.2	3.3	-2.9	0.1	2.6	20.1
1968	-4.4	-3.1	0.9	8.2	1.1	0.9	-1.8	1.1	3.9	0.7	4.8	-4.2	7.7
1969	-0.8	-4.7	3.4	2.1	-0.2	-5.6	-6.0	4.0	-2.5	4.4	-3.5	-1.9	-11.4
1970	-7.6	5.3	0.1	-9.0	-6.1	-5.0	7.3	4.4	3.3	-1.1	4.7	5.7	0.1
1971	4.0	0.9	3.7	3.6	-4.2	0.1	-4.1	3.6	-0.7	-4.2	-0.3	8.6	10.8
1972	1.8	2.5	0.6	0.4	1.7	-2.2	0.2	3.4	-0.5	0.9	4.6	1.2	15.6
1973	-1.7	-3.7	-0.1	-4.1	-1.9	-0.7	3.8	-3.7	4.0	-0.1	-11.4	1.7	-17.4
1974	-1.0	-0.4	-2.3	-3.9	-3.4	-1.5	-7.8	-9.0	-11.9	16.3	-5.3	-2.0	-29.7
1975	12.3	6.0	2.2	4.7	4.4	4.4	-6.8	-2.1	-3.5	6.2	2.5	-1.2	31.5
1976	11.8	-1.1	3.1	-1.1	-1.4	4.1	-0.8	-0.5	2.3	-2.2	-0.8	5.2	19.1
1977	-5.1	-2.2	-1.4	0.02	-2.4	4.5	-1.6	-2.1	-0.2	-4.3	2.7	0.3	-11.5
1978	-6.2	-2.5	2.5	8.5	0.4	-1.8	5.4	2.6	-0.7	-9.2	1.7	1.5	1.1
1979	4.0	-3.7	5.5	0.2	-2.6	3.9	0.9	5.3	N/C	-6.9	4.3	1.7	12.3
1980	5.8	-0.4	-10.2	4.1	4.7	2.7	6.5	0.6	2.5	1.6	10.2	-3.4	25.8
1981	-4.6	1.3	3.6	-2.3	-0.2	-1.0	-0.2	-6.2	-5.4	4.9	3.7	-3.0	-9.7
1982	-1.8	-6.1	-1.0	4.0	-3.9	-2.0	-2.3	11.6	0.8	11.0	3.6	1.5	14.8
1983	3.3	1.9	3.3	7.5	-1.2	3.5	-3.3	1.1	1.0	-1.5	1.7	-0.9	17.3
1984	-0.9	-3.9	1.3	0.5	-5.9	1.7	-1.6	10.6	-0.3	-0.01	-1.5	2.2	1.4
1985	7.4	0.9	-0.3	-0.5	5.4	1.2	-0.5	-1.2	-3.5	4.3	6.5	4.5	26.3
1986	0.2	7.1	5.3	-1.4	5.0	1.4	-5.9	7.1	-8.5	5.5	2.1	-2.8	14.6
1987	13.2	3.7	2.6	-1.1	0.6	4.8	4.8	3.5	-2.4	-21.8	-8.5	7.3	2.0
1988	4.0	4.2	-3.3	0.9	0.3	4.3	-0.5	-3.9	4.0	2.6	-1.9	1.5	12.4

continued

STANDARD & POOR'S 500 MONTHLY PERCENT CHANGES SINCE 1950 (continued)

	Jan	Feb	Mar	Apr	May	Jun	Jul	Aug	Sep	Oct	Nov	Dec	Year
1989	7.1	−2.9	2.1	5.0	3.5	−0.8	8.8	1.6	−0.7	−2.5	1.7	2.1	27.3
1990	−6.9	0.9	2.4	−2.7	9.2	−0.9	−0.5	−9.4	−5.1	−0.7	6.0	2.5	−6.6
1991	4.2	6.7	2.2	0.03	3.9	−4.8	4.5	2.0	−1.9	1.2	−4.4	11.2	26.3
1992	−2.0	1.0	−2.2	2.8	0.1	−1.7	3.9	−2.4	0.9	0.2	3.0	1.0	4.5
1993	0.7	1.0	1.9	−2.5	2.3	0.1	−0.5	3.4	−1.0	1.9	−1.3	1.0	7.1
1994	3.3	−3.0	−4.6	1.2	1.2	−2.7	3.1	3.8	−2.7	2.1	−4.0	1.2	−1.5
1995	2.4	3.6	2.7	2.8	3.6	2.1	3.2	−0.03	4.0	−0.5	4.1	1.7	34.1
1996	3.3	0.7	0.8	1.3	2.3	0.2	−4.6	1.9	5.4	2.6	7.3	−2.2	20.3
1997	6.1	0.6	−4.3	5.8	5.9	4.3	7.8	−5.7	5.3	−3.4	4.5	1.6	31.0
1998	1.0	7.0	5.0	0.9	−1.9	3.9	−1.2	−14.6	6.2	8.0	5.9	5.6	26.7
1999	4.1	−3.2	3.9	3.8	−2.5	5.4	−3.2	−0.6	−2.9	6.3	1.9	5.8	19.5
2000	−5.1	−2.0	9.7	−3.1	−2.2	2.4	−1.6	6.1	−5.3	−0.5	−8.0	0.4	−10.1
2001	3.5	−9.2	−6.4	7.7	0.5	−2.5	−1.1	−6.4	−8.2	1.8	7.5	0.8	−13.0
2002	−1.6	−2.1	3.7	−6.1	−0.9	−7.2	−7.9	0.5	−11.0	8.6	5.7	−6.0	−23.4
2003	−2.7	−1.7	1.0	8.0	5.1	1.1	1.6	1.8	−1.2	5.5	0.7	5.1	26.4
2004	1.7	1.2	−1.6	−1.7	1.2	1.8	−3.4	0.2	0.9	1.4	3.9	3.2	9.0
2005	−2.5	1.9	−1.9	−2.0	3.0	−0.01	3.6	−1.1	0.7	−1.8	3.5	−0.1	3.0
2006	2.5	0.05	1.1	1.2	−3.1	0.01	0.5	2.1	2.5	3.2	1.6	1.3	13.6
2007	1.4	−2.2	1.0	4.3	3.3	−1.8	−3.2	1.3	3.6	1.5	−4.4	−0.9	3.5
2008	−6.1	−3.5	−0.6	4.8	1.1	−8.6	−1.0	1.2	−9.1	−16.9	−7.5	0.8	−38.5
2009	−8.6	−11.0	8.5	9.4	5.3	0.02	7.4	3.4	3.6	−2.0	5.7	1.8	23.5
2010	−3.7	2.9	5.9	1.5	−8.2	−5.4	6.9	−4.7	8.8	3.7	−0.2	6.5	12.8
2011	2.3	3.2	−0.1	2.8	−1.4	−1.8	−2.1	−5.7	−7.2	10.8	−0.5	0.9	−0.003
2012	4.4	4.1	3.1	−0.7	−6.3	4.0	1.3	2.0	2.4	−2.0	0.3	0.7	13.4
2013	5.0	1.1	3.6	1.8	2.1	−1.5	4.9	−3.1	3.0	4.5	2.8	2.4	29.6
2014	−3.6	4.3	0.7	0.6	2.1	1.9	−1.5	3.8	−1.6	2.3	2.5	−0.4	11.4
2015	−3.1	5.5	−1.7	0.9	1.0	−2.1	2.0	−6.3	−2.6	8.3	0.1	−1.8	−0.7
2016	−5.1	−0.4	6.6	0.3	1.5	0.1	3.6	−0.1	−0.1	−1.9	3.4	1.8	9.5
2017	1.8	3.7	−0.04	0.9	1.2	0.5	1.9	0.1	1.9	2.2	2.8	1.0	19.4
2018	5.6	−3.9	−2.7	0.3	2.2	0.5	3.6	3.0	0.4	−6.9	1.8	−9.2	−6.2
2019	7.9	3.0	1.8	3.9	−6.6	6.9	1.3	−1.8	1.7	2.0	3.4	2.9	28.9
2020	−0.2	−8.4	−12.5	12.7	4.5	1.8	5.5	7.0	−3.9	−2.8	10.8	3.7	16.3
2021	−1.1	2.6	4.2	5.2	0.5	2.2	2.3	2.9	−4.8	6.9	−0.8	4.4	26.9
2022	−5.3	−3.1	3.6	−8.8	0.01	−8.4	9.1	−4.2	−9.3	8.0	5.4	−5.9	−19.4
2023	6.2	−2.6	3.5	1.5	0.2	6.5	3.1	−1.8	−4.9	−2.2	8.9	4.4	24.2
2024	1.6	5.2	3.1	−4.2	4.8	3.5	1.1	2.3	2.0	−1.0	5.7	−2.5	23.3
2025	2.7	−1.4	−5.8	−0.8									
TOTALS	82.0	−1.8	78.6	109.5	21.3	11.4	96.0	1.4	−51.2	66.6	140.4	107.3	
AVG.	1.1	−0.02	1.0	1.4	0.3	0.2	1.3	0.02	−0.7	0.9	1.9	1.4	
# Up	46	41	49	53	46	42	45	41	33	44	52	55	
# Down	30	35	27	23	29	33	30	34	41	31	23	20	

STANDARD & POOR'S 500 MONTHLY CLOSING PRICES SINCE 1950

	Jan	Feb	Mar	Apr	May	Jun	Jul	Aug	Sep	Oct	Nov	Dec
1950	17.05	17.22	17.29	18.07	18.78	17.69	17.84	18.42	19.45	19.53	19.51	20.41
1951	21.66	21.80	21.40	22.43	21.52	20.96	22.40	23.28	23.26	22.94	22.88	23.77
1952	24.14	23.26	24.37	23.32	23.86	24.96	25.40	25.03	24.54	24.52	25.66	26.57
1953	26.38	25.90	25.29	24.62	24.54	24.14	24.75	23.32	23.35	24.54	24.76	24.81
1954	26.08	26.15	26.94	28.26	29.19	29.21	30.88	29.83	32.31	31.68	34.24	35.98
1955	36.63	36.76	36.58	37.96	37.91	41.03	43.52	43.18	43.67	42.34	45.51	45.48
1956	43.82	45.34	48.48	48.38	45.20	46.97	49.39	47.51	45.35	45.58	45.08	46.67
1957	44.72	43.26	44.11	45.74	47.43	47.37	47.91	45.22	42.42	41.06	41.72	39.99
1958	41.70	40.84	42.10	43.44	44.09	45.24	47.19	47.75	50.06	51.33	52.48	55.21
1959	55.42	55.41	55.44	57.59	58.68	58.47	60.51	59.60	56.88	57.52	58.28	59.89
1960	55.61	56.12	55.34	54.37	55.83	56.92	55.51	56.96	53.52	53.39	55.54	58.11
1961	61.78	63.44	65.06	65.31	66.56	64.64	66.76	68.07	66.73	68.62	71.32	71.55
1962	68.84	69.96	69.55	65.24	59.63	54.75	58.23	59.12	56.27	56.52	62.26	63.10
1963	66.20	64.29	66.57	69.80	70.80	69.37	69.13	72.50	71.70	74.01	73.23	75.02
1964	77.04	77.80	78.98	79.46	80.37	81.69	83.18	81.83	84.18	84.86	84.42	84.75
1965	87.56	87.43	86.16	89.11	88.42	84.12	85.25	87.17	89.96	92.42	91.61	92.43
1966	92.88	91.22	89.23	91.06	86.13	84.74	83.60	77.10	76.56	80.20	80.45	80.33
1967	86.61	86.78	90.20	94.01	89.08	90.64	94.75	93.64	96.71	93.90	94.00	96.47
1968	92.24	89.36	90.20	97.59	98.68	99.58	97.74	98.86	102.67	103.41	108.37	103.86
1969	103.01	98.13	101.51	103.69	103.46	97.71	91.83	95.51	93.12	97.24	93.81	92.06
1970	85.02	89.50	89.63	81.52	76.55	72.72	78.05	81.52	84.21	83.25	87.20	92.15
1971	95.88	96.75	100.31	103.95	99.63	99.70	95.58	99.03	98.34	94.23	93.99	102.09
1972	103.94	106.57	107.20	107.67	109.53	107.14	107.39	111.09	110.55	111.58	116.67	118.05
1973	116.03	111.68	111.52	106.97	104.95	104.26	108.22	104.25	108.43	108.29	95.96	97.55
1974	96.57	96.22	93.98	90.31	87.28	86.00	79.31	72.15	63.54	73.90	69.97	68.56
1975	76.98	81.59	83.36	87.30	91.15	95.19	88.75	86.88	83.87	89.04	91.24	90.19
1976	100.86	99.71	102.77	101.64	100.18	104.28	103.44	102.91	105.24	102.90	102.10	107.46
1977	102.03	99.82	98.42	98.44	96.12	100.48	98.85	96.77	96.53	92.34	94.83	95.10
1978	89.25	87.04	89.21	96.83	97.24	95.53	100.68	103.29	102.54	93.15	94.70	96.11
1979	99.93	96.28	101.59	101.76	99.08	102.91	103.81	109.32	109.32	101.82	106.16	107.94
1980	114.16	113.66	102.09	106.29	111.24	114.24	121.67	122.38	125.46	127.47	140.52	135.76
1981	129.55	131.27	136.00	132.81	132.59	131.21	130.92	122.79	116.18	121.89	126.35	122.55
1982	120.40	113.11	111.96	116.44	111.88	109.61	107.09	119.51	120.42	133.71	138.54	140.64
1983	145.30	148.06	152.96	164.42	162.39	168.11	162.56	164.40	166.07	163.55	166.40	164.93
1984	163.41	157.06	159.18	160.05	150.55	153.18	150.66	166.68	166.10	166.09	163.58	167.24
1985	179.63	181.18	180.66	179.83	189.55	191.85	190.92	188.63	182.08	189.82	202.17	211.28
1986	211.78	226.92	238.90	235.52	247.35	250.84	236.12	252.93	231.32	243.98	249.22	242.17

continued

STANDARD & POOR'S 500 MONTHLY CLOSING PRICES SINCE 1950 (continued)

	Jan	Feb	Mar	Apr	May	Jun	Jul	Aug	Sep	Oct	Nov	Dec
1987	274.08	284.20	291.70	288.36	290.10	304.00	318.66	329.80	321.83	251.79	230.30	247.08
1988	257.07	267.82	258.89	261.33	262.16	273.50	272.02	261.52	271.91	278.97	273.70	277.72
1989	297.47	288.86	294.87	309.64	320.52	317.98	346.08	351.45	349.15	340.36	345.99	353.40
1990	329.08	331.89	339.94	330.80	361.23	358.02	356.15	322.56	306.05	304.00	322.22	330.22
1991	343.93	367.07	375.22	375.35	389.83	371.16	387.81	395.43	387.86	392.46	375.22	417.09
1992	408.79	412.70	403.69	414.95	415.35	408.14	424.21	414.03	417.80	418.68	431.35	435.71
1993	438.78	443.38	451.67	440.19	450.19	450.53	448.13	463.56	458.93	467.83	461.79	466.45
1994	481.61	467.14	445.77	450.91	456.50	444.27	458.26	475.49	462.69	472.35	453.69	459.27
1995	470.42	487.39	500.71	514.71	533.40	544.75	562.06	561.88	584.41	581.50	605.37	615.93
1996	636.02	640.43	645.50	654.17	669.12	670.63	639.95	651.99	687.31	705.27	757.02	740.74
1997	786.16	790.82	757.12	801.34	848.28	885.14	954.29	899.47	947.28	914.62	955.40	970.43
1998	980.28	1049.34	1101.75	1111.75	1090.82	1133.84	1120.67	957.28	1017.01	1098.67	1163.63	1229.23
1999	1279.64	1238.33	1286.37	1335.18	1301.84	1372.71	1328.72	1320.41	1282.71	1362.93	1388.91	1469.25
2000	1394.46	1366.42	1498.58	1452.43	1420.60	1454.60	1430.83	1517.68	1436.51	1429.40	1314.95	1320.28
2001	1366.01	1239.94	1160.33	1249.46	1255.82	1224.42	1211.23	1133.58	1040.94	1059.78	1139.45	1148.08
2002	1130.20	1106.73	1147.39	1076.92	1067.14	989.82	911.62	916.07	815.28	885.76	936.31	879.82
2003	855.70	841.15	849.18	916.92	963.59	974.50	990.31	1008.01	995.97	1050.71	1058.20	1111.92
2004	1131.13	1144.94	1126.21	1107.30	1120.68	1140.84	1101.72	1104.24	1114.58	1130.20	1173.82	1211.92
2005	1181.27	1203.60	1180.59	1156.85	1191.50	1191.33	1234.18	1220.33	1228.81	1207.01	1249.48	1248.29
2006	1280.08	1280.66	1294.83	1310.61	1270.09	1270.20	1276.66	1303.82	1335.85	1377.94	1400.63	1418.30
2007	1438.24	1406.82	1420.86	1482.37	1530.62	1503.35	1455.27	1473.99	1526.75	1549.38	1481.14	1468.36
2008	1378.55	1330.63	1322.70	1385.59	1400.38	1280.00	1267.38	1282.83	1166.36	968.75	896.24	903.25
2009	825.88	735.09	797.87	872.81	919.14	919.32	987.48	1020.62	1057.08	1036.19	1095.63	1115.10
2010	1073.87	1104.49	1169.43	1186.69	1089.41	1030.71	1101.60	1049.33	1141.20	1183.26	1180.55	1257.64
2011	1286.12	1327.22	1325.83	1363.61	1345.20	1320.64	1292.28	1218.89	1131.42	1253.30	1246.96	1257.60
2012	1312.41	1365.68	1408.47	1397.91	1310.33	1362.16	1379.32	1406.58	1440.67	1412.16	1416.18	1426.19
2013	1498.11	1514.68	1569.19	1597.57	1630.74	1606.28	1685.73	1632.97	1681.55	1756.54	1805.81	1848.36
2014	1782.59	1859.45	1872.34	1883.95	1923.57	1960.23	1930.67	2003.37	1972.29	2018.05	2067.56	2058.90
2015	1994.99	2104.50	2067.89	2085.51	2107.39	2063.11	2103.84	1972.18	1920.03	2079.36	2080.41	2043.94
2016	1940.24	1932.23	2059.74	2065.30	2096.96	2098.86	2173.60	2170.95	2168.27	2126.15	2198.81	2238.83
2017	2278.87	2363.64	2362.72	2384.20	2411.80	2423.41	2470.30	2471.65	2519.36	2575.26	2647.58	2673.61
2018	2823.81	2713.83	2640.87	2648.05	2705.27	2718.37	2816.29	2901.52	2913.98	2711.74	2760.16	2506.85
2019	2704.10	2784.49	2834.40	2945.83	2752.06	2941.76	2980.38	2926.46	2976.74	3037.56	3140.98	3230.78
2020	3225.52	2954.22	2584.59	2912.43	3044.31	3100.29	3271.12	3500.31	3363.00	3269.96	3621.63	3756.07
2021	3714.24	3811.15	3972.89	4181.17	4204.11	4297.50	4395.26	4522.68	4307.54	4605.38	4567.00	4766.18
2022	4515.55	4373.94	4530.41	4131.93	4132.15	3785.38	4130.29	3955.00	3585.62	3871.98	4080.11	3839.50
2023	4076.60	3970.15	4109.31	4169.48	4179.83	4450.38	4588.96	4507.66	4288.05	4193.80	4567.80	4769.83
2024	4845.65	5096.27	5254.35	5035.69	5277.51	5460.48	5522.30	5648.40	5762.48	5705.45	6032.38	5881.63
2025	6040.53	5954.50	5611.85	5569.06								

NASDAQ COMPOSITE MONTHLY PERCENT CHANGES SINCE 1971

	Jan	Feb	Mar	Apr	May	Jun	Jul	Aug	Sep	Oct	Nov	Dec	Year
1971	10.2	2.6	4.6	6.0	-3.6	-0.4	-2.3	3.0	0.6	-3.6	-1.1	9.8	27.4
1972	4.2	5.5	2.2	2.5	0.9	-1.8	-1.8	1.7	-0.3	0.5	2.1	0.6	17.2
1973	-4.0	-6.2	-2.4	-8.2	-4.8	-1.6	7.6	-3.5	6.0	-0.9	-15.1	-1.4	-31.1
1974	3.0	-0.6	-2.2	-5.9	-7.7	-5.3	-7.9	-10.9	-10.7	17.2	-3.5	-5.0	-35.1
1975	16.6	4.6	3.6	3.8	5.8	4.7	-4.4	-5.0	-5.9	3.6	2.4	-1.5	29.8
1976	12.1	3.7	0.4	-0.6	-2.3	2.6	1.1	-1.7	1.7	-1.0	0.9	7.4	26.1
1977	-2.4	-1.0	-0.5	1.4	0.1	4.3	0.9	-0.5	0.7	-3.3	5.8	1.8	7.3
1978	-4.0	0.6	4.7	8.5	4.4	0.05	5.0	6.9	-1.6	-16.4	3.2	2.9	12.3
1979	6.6	-2.6	7.5	1.6	-1.8	5.1	2.3	6.4	-0.3	-9.6	6.4	4.8	28.1
1980	7.0	-2.3	-17.1	6.9	7.5	4.9	8.9	5.7	3.4	2.7	8.0	-2.8	33.9
1981	-2.2	0.1	6.1	3.1	3.1	-3.5	-1.9	-7.5	-8.0	8.4	3.1	-2.7	-3.2
1982	-3.8	-4.8	-2.1	5.2	-3.3	-4.1	-2.3	6.2	5.6	13.3	9.3	0.04	18.7
1983	6.9	5.0	3.9	8.2	5.3	3.2	-4.6	-3.8	1.4	-7.4	4.1	-2.5	19.9
1984	-3.7	-5.9	-0.7	-1.3	-5.9	2.9	-4.2	10.9	-1.8	-1.2	-1.8	2.0	-11.2
1985	12.7	2.0	-1.7	0.5	3.6	1.9	1.7	-1.2	-5.8	4.4	7.3	3.5	31.4
1986	3.3	7.1	4.2	2.3	4.4	1.3	-8.4	3.1	-8.4	2.9	-0.3	-2.8	7.5
1987	12.2	8.4	1.2	-2.8	-0.3	2.0	2.4	4.6	-2.3	-27.2	-5.6	8.3	-5.4
1988	4.3	6.5	2.1	1.2	-2.3	6.6	-1.9	-2.8	3.0	-1.4	-2.9	2.7	15.4
1989	5.2	-0.4	1.8	5.1	4.4	-2.4	4.3	3.4	0.8	-3.7	0.1	-0.3	19.3
1990	-8.6	2.4	2.3	-3.6	9.3	0.7	-5.2	-13.0	-9.6	-4.3	8.9	4.1	-17.8
1991	10.8	9.4	6.5	0.5	4.4	-6.0	5.5	4.7	0.2	3.1	-3.5	11.9	56.8
1992	5.8	2.1	-4.7	-4.2	1.1	-3.7	3.1	-3.0	3.6	3.8	7.9	3.7	15.5
1993	2.9	-3.7	2.9	-4.2	5.9	0.5	0.1	5.4	2.7	2.2	-3.2	3.0	14.7
1994	3.0	-1.0	-6.2	-1.3	0.2	-4.0	2.3	6.0	-0.2	1.7	-3.5	0.2	-3.2
1995	0.4	5.1	3.0	3.3	2.4	8.0	7.3	1.9	2.3	-0.7	2.2	-0.7	39.9
1996	0.7	3.8	0.1	8.1	4.4	-4.7	-8.8	5.6	7.5	-0.4	5.8	-0.1	22.7
1997	6.9	-5.1	-6.7	3.2	11.1	3.0	10.5	-0.4	6.2	-5.5	0.4	-1.9	21.6
1998	3.1	9.3	3.7	1.8	-4.8	6.5	-1.2	-19.9	13.0	4.6	10.1	12.5	39.6
1999	14.3	-8.7	7.6	3.3	-2.8	8.7	-1.8	3.8	0.2	8.0	12.5	22.0	85.6

continued

Based on NASDAQ composite, prior to Feb. 5, 1971, based on National Quotation Bureau indices

NASDAQ COMPOSITE MONTHLY PERCENT CHANGES SINCE 1971 (continued)

	Jan	Feb	Mar	Apr	May	Jun	Jul	Aug	Sep	Oct	Nov	Dec	Year
2000	−3.2	19.2	−2.6	−15.6	−11.9	16.6	−5.0	11.7	−12.7	−8.3	−22.9	−4.9	−39.3
2001	12.2	−22.4	−14.5	15.0	−0.3	2.4	−6.2	−10.9	−17.0	12.8	14.2	1.0	−21.1
2002	−0.8	−10.5	6.6	−8.5	−4.3	−9.4	−9.2	−1.0	−10.9	13.5	11.2	−9.7	−31.5
2003	−1.1	1.3	0.3	9.2	9.0	1.7	6.9	4.3	−1.3	8.1	1.5	2.2	50.0
2004	3.1	−1.8	−1.8	−3.7	3.5	3.1	−7.8	−2.6	3.2	4.1	6.2	3.7	8.6
2005	−5.2	−0.5	−2.6	−3.9	7.6	−0.5	6.2	−1.5	−0.02	−1.5	5.3	−1.2	1.4
2006	4.6	−1.1	2.6	−0.7	−6.2	−0.3	−3.7	4.4	3.4	4.8	2.7	−0.7	9.5
2007	2.0	−1.9	0.2	4.3	3.1	−0.05	−2.2	2.0	4.0	5.8	−6.9	−0.3	9.8
2008	−9.9	−5.0	0.3	5.9	4.6	−9.1	1.4	1.8	−11.6	−17.7	−10.8	2.7	−40.5
2009	−6.4	−6.7	10.9	12.3	3.3	3.4	7.8	1.5	5.6	−3.6	4.9	5.8	43.9
2010	−5.4	4.2	7.1	2.6	−8.3	−6.5	6.9	−6.2	12.0	5.9	−0.4	6.2	16.9
2011	1.8	3.0	−0.04	3.3	−1.3	−2.2	−0.6	−6.4	−6.4	11.1	−2.4	−0.6	−1.8
2012	8.0	5.4	4.2	−1.5	−7.2	3.8	0.2	4.3	1.6	−4.5	1.1	0.3	15.9
2013	4.1	0.6	3.4	1.9	3.8	−1.5	6.6	−1.0	5.1	3.9	3.6	2.9	38.3
2014	−1.7	5.0	−2.5	−2.0	3.1	3.9	−0.9	4.8	−1.9	3.1	3.5	−1.2	13.4
2015	−2.1	7.1	−1.3	0.8	2.6	−1.6	2.8	−6.9	−3.3	9.4	1.1	−2.0	5.7
2016	−7.9	−1.2	6.8	−1.9	3.6	−2.1	6.6	1.0	1.9	−2.3	2.6	1.1	7.5
2017	4.3	3.8	1.5	2.3	2.5	−0.9	3.4	1.3	1.0	3.6	2.2	0.4	28.2
2018	7.4	−1.9	−2.9	0.04	5.3	0.9	2.2	5.7	−0.8	−9.2	0.3	−9.5	−3.9
2019	9.7	3.4	2.6	4.7	−7.9	7.4	2.1	−2.6	0.5	3.7	4.5	3.5	35.2
2020	2.0	−6.4	−10.1	15.4	6.8	6.0	6.8	9.6	−5.2	−2.3	11.8	5.7	43.6
2021	1.4	0.9	0.4	5.4	−1.5	5.5	1.2	4.0	−5.3	7.3	0.3	0.7	21.4
2022	−9.0	−3.4	3.4	−13.3	−2.1	−8.7	12.3	−4.6	−10.5	3.9	4.4	−8.7	−33.1
2023	10.7	−1.1	6.7	0.04	5.8	6.6	4.0	−2.2	−5.8	−2.8	10.7	5.5	43.4
2024	1.0	6.1	1.8	−4.4	6.9	6.0	−0.8	0.6	2.7	−0.5	6.2	0.5	28.6
2025	1.6	−4.0	−8.2	0.9									
TOTALS	144.7	28.0	36.4	73.0	59.2	53.9	47.3	17.2	−47.7	38.1	114.9	82.9	
AVG.	2.6	0.5	0.7	1.3	1.1	1.0	0.9	0.3	−0.9	0.7	2.1	1.5	
# Up	37	29	35	36	33	31	31	30	28	29	39	33	
# Down	18	26	20	19	21	23	23	24	26	25	15	21	

Based on NASDAQ composite, prior to Feb. 5, 1971, based on National Quotation Bureau indices

NASDAQ COMPOSITE MONTHLY CLOSING PRICES SINCE 1971

	Jan	Feb	Mar	Apr	May	Jun	Jul	Aug	Sep	Oct	Nov	Dec
1971	98.77	101.34	105.97	112.30	108.25	107.80	105.27	108.42	109.03	105.10	103.97	114.12
1972	118.87	125.38	128.14	131.33	132.53	130.08	127.75	129.95	129.61	130.24	132.96	133.73
1973	128.40	120.41	117.46	107.85	102.64	100.98	108.64	104.87	111.20	110.17	93.51	92.19
1974	94.93	94.35	92.27	86.86	80.20	75.96	69.99	62.37	55.67	65.23	62.95	59.82
1975	69.78	73.00	75.66	78.54	83.10	87.02	83.19	79.01	74.33	76.99	78.80	77.62
1976	87.05	90.26	90.62	90.08	88.04	90.32	91.29	89.70	91.26	90.35	91.12	97.88
1977	95.54	94.57	94.13	95.48	95.59	99.73	100.65	100.10	100.85	97.52	103.15	105.05
1978	100.84	101.47	106.20	115.18	120.24	120.30	126.32	135.01	132.89	111.12	114.69	117.98
1979	125.82	122.56	131.76	133.82	131.42	138.13	141.33	150.44	149.98	135.53	144.26	151.14
1980	161.75	158.03	131.00	139.99	150.45	157.78	171.81	181.52	187.76	192.78	208.15	202.34
1981	197.81	198.01	210.18	216.74	223.47	215.75	211.63	195.75	180.03	195.24	201.37	195.84
1982	188.39	179.43	175.65	184.70	178.54	171.30	167.35	177.71	187.65	212.63	232.31	232.41
1983	248.35	260.67	270.80	293.06	308.73	318.70	303.96	292.42	296.65	274.55	285.67	278.60
1984	268.43	252.57	250.78	247.44	232.82	239.65	229.70	254.64	249.94	247.03	242.53	247.35
1985	278.70	284.17	279.20	280.56	290.80	296.20	301.29	297.71	280.33	292.54	313.95	324.93
1986	335.77	359.53	374.72	383.24	400.16	405.51	371.37	382.86	350.67	360.77	359.57	349.33
1987	392.06	424.97	430.05	417.81	416.54	424.67	434.93	454.97	444.29	323.30	305.16	330.47
1988	344.66	366.95	374.64	379.23	370.34	394.66	387.33	376.55	387.71	382.46	371.45	381.38
1989	401.30	399.71	406.73	427.55	446.17	435.29	453.84	469.33	472.92	455.63	456.09	454.82
1990	415.81	425.83	435.54	420.07	458.97	462.29	438.24	381.21	344.51	329.84	359.06	373.84
1991	414.20	453.05	482.30	484.72	506.11	475.92	502.04	525.68	526.88	542.98	523.90	586.34
1992	620.21	633.47	603.77	578.68	585.31	563.60	580.83	563.12	583.27	605.17	652.73	676.95
1993	696.34	670.77	690.13	661.42	700.53	703.95	704.70	742.84	762.78	779.26	754.39	776.80
1994	800.47	792.50	743.46	733.84	735.19	705.96	722.16	765.62	764.29	777.49	750.32	751.96
1995	755.20	793.73	817.21	843.98	864.58	933.45	1001.21	1020.11	1043.54	1036.06	1059.20	1052.13
1996	1059.79	1100.05	1101.40	1190.52	1243.43	1185.02	1080.59	1141.50	1226.92	1221.51	1292.61	1291.03
1997	1379.85	1309.00	1221.70	1260.76	1400.32	1442.07	1593.81	1587.32	1685.69	1593.61	1600.55	1570.35

continued

Based on NASDAQ composite, prior to Feb. 5, 1971, based on National Quotation Bureau indices

NASDAQ COMPOSITE MONTHLY CLOSING PRICES SINCE 1971 (continued)

	Jan	Feb	Mar	Apr	May	Jun	Jul	Aug	Sep	Oct	Nov	Dec
1998	1619.36	1770.51	1835.68	1868.41	1778.87	1894.74	1872.39	1499.25	1693.84	1771.39	1949.54	2192.69
1999	2505.89	2288.03	2461.40	2542.85	2470.52	2686.12	2638.49	2739.35	2746.16	2966.43	3336.16	4069.31
2000	3940.35	4696.69	4572.83	3860.66	3400.91	3966.11	3766.99	4206.35	3672.82	3369.63	2597.93	2470.52
2001	2772.73	2151.83	1840.26	2116.24	2110.49	2160.54	2027.13	1805.43	1498.80	1690.20	1930.58	1950.40
2002	1934.03	1731.49	1845.35	1688.23	1615.73	1463.21	1328.26	1314.85	1172.06	1329.75	1478.78	1335.51
2003	1320.91	1337.52	1341.17	1464.31	1595.91	1622.80	1735.02	1810.45	1786.94	1932.21	1960.26	2003.37
2004	2066.15	2029.82	1994.22	1920.15	1986.74	2047.79	1887.36	1838.10	1896.84	1974.99	2096.81	2175.44
2005	2062.41	2051.72	1999.23	1921.65	2068.22	2056.96	2184.83	2152.09	2151.69	2120.30	2232.82	2205.32
2006	2305.82	2281.39	2339.79	2322.57	2178.88	2172.09	2091.47	2183.75	2258.43	2366.71	2431.77	2415.29
2007	2463.93	2416.15	2421.64	2525.09	2604.52	2603.23	2545.57	2596.36	2701.50	2859.12	2660.96	2652.28
2008	2389.86	2271.48	2279.10	2412.80	2522.66	2292.98	2325.55	2367.52	2091.88	1720.95	1535.57	1577.03
2009	1476.42	1377.84	1528.59	1717.30	1774.33	1835.04	1978.50	2009.06	2122.42	2045.11	2144.60	2269.15
2010	2147.35	2238.26	2397.96	2461.19	2257.04	2109.24	2254.70	2114.03	2368.62	2507.41	2498.23	2652.87
2011	2700.08	2782.27	2781.07	2873.54	2835.30	2773.52	2756.38	2579.46	2415.40	2684.41	2620.34	2605.15
2012	2813.84	2966.89	3091.57	3046.36	2827.34	2935.05	2939.52	3066.96	3116.23	2977.23	3010.24	3019.51
2013	3142.13	3160.19	3267.52	3328.79	3455.91	3403.25	3626.37	3589.87	3771.48	3919.71	4059.89	4176.59
2014	4103.88	4308.12	4198.99	4114.56	4242.62	4408.18	4369.77	4580.27	4493.39	4630.74	4791.63	4736.05
2015	4635.24	4963.53	4900.88	4941.42	5070.03	4986.87	5128.28	4776.51	4620.16	5053.75	5108.67	5007.41
2016	4613.95	4557.95	4869.85	4775.36	4948.05	4842.67	5162.13	5213.22	5312.00	5189.13	5323.68	5383.12
2017	5614.79	5825.44	5911.74	6047.61	6198.52	6140.42	6348.12	6428.66	6495.96	6727.67	6873.97	6903.39
2018	7411.48	7273.01	7063.44	7066.27	7442.12	7510.30	7671.79	8109.54	8046.35	7305.90	7330.54	6635.28
2019	7281.74	7532.53	7729.32	8095.39	7453.15	8006.24	8175.42	7962.88	7999.34	8292.36	8665.47	8972.60
2020	9150.94	8567.37	7700.10	8889.55	9489.87	10058.77	10745.27	11775.46	11167.51	10911.59	12198.74	12888.28
2021	13070.69	13192.35	13246.87	13962.68	13748.74	14503.95	14672.68	15259.24	14448.58	15498.39	15537.69	15644.97
2022	14239.88	13751.40	14220.52	12334.64	12081.39	11028.74	12390.69	11816.20	10575.62	10988.15	11468.00	10466.48
2023	11584.55	11455.54	12221.91	12226.58	12935.29	13787.92	14346.02	14034.97	13219.32	12851.24	14226.22	15011.35
2024	15164.01	16091.92	16379.46	15657.82	16735.02	17732.60	17599.40	17713.62	18189.17	18095.15	19218.17	19310.79
2025	19627.44	18847.28	17299.29	17446.34								

Based on NASDAQ composite, prior to Feb. 5, 1971, based on National Quotation Bureau indices

RUSSELL 1000 INDEX MONTHLY PERCENT CHANGES SINCE 1979

	Jan	Feb	Mar	Apr	May	Jun	Jul	Aug	Sep	Oct	Nov	Dec	Year
1979	4.2	-3.5	6.0	0.3	-2.2	4.3	1.1	5.6	0.02	-7.1	5.1	2.1	16.1
1980	5.9	-0.5	-11.5	4.6	5.0	3.2	6.4	1.1	2.6	1.8	10.1	-3.9	25.6
1981	-4.6	1.0	3.8	-1.9	0.2	-1.2	-0.1	-6.2	-6.4	5.4	4.0	-3.3	-9.7
1982	-2.7	-5.9	-1.3	3.9	-3.6	-2.6	-2.3	11.3	1.2	11.3	4.0	1.3	13.7
1983	3.2	2.1	3.2	7.1	-0.2	3.7	-3.2	0.5	1.3	-2.4	2.0	-1.2	17.0
1984	-1.9	-4.4	1.1	0.3	-5.9	2.1	-1.8	10.8	-0.2	-0.1	-1.4	2.2	-0.1
1985	7.8	1.1	-0.4	-0.3	5.4	1.6	-0.8	-1.0	-3.9	4.5	6.5	4.1	26.7
1986	0.9	7.2	5.1	-1.3	5.0	1.4	-5.9	6.8	-8.5	5.1	1.4	-3.0	13.6
1987	12.7	4.0	1.9	-1.8	0.4	4.5	4.2	3.8	-2.4	-21.9	-8.0	7.2	0.02
1988	4.3	4.4	-2.9	0.7	0.2	4.8	-0.9	-3.3	3.9	2.0	-2.0	1.7	13.1
1989	6.8	-2.5	2.0	4.9	3.8	-0.8	8.2	1.7	-0.5	-2.8	1.5	1.8	25.9
1990	-7.4	1.2	2.2	-2.8	8.9	-0.7	-1.1	-9.6	-5.3	-0.8	6.4	2.7	-7.5
1991	4.5	6.9	2.5	-0.1	3.8	-4.7	4.6	2.2	-1.5	1.4	-4.1	11.2	28.8
1992	-1.4	0.9	-2.4	2.3	0.3	-1.9	4.1	-2.5	1.0	0.7	3.5	1.4	5.9
1993	0.7	0.6	2.2	-2.8	2.4	0.4	-0.4	3.5	-0.5	1.2	-1.7	1.6	7.3
1994	2.9	-2.9	-4.5	1.1	1.0	-2.9	3.1	3.9	-2.6	1.7	-3.9	1.2	-2.4
1995	2.4	3.8	2.3	2.5	3.5	2.4	3.7	0.5	3.9	-0.6	4.2	1.4	34.4
1996	3.1	1.1	0.7	1.4	2.1	-0.1	-4.9	2.5	5.5	2.1	7.1	-1.8	19.7
1997	5.8	0.2	-4.6	5.3	6.2	4.0	8.0	-4.9	5.4	-3.4	4.2	1.9	30.5
1998	0.6	7.0	4.9	0.9	-2.3	3.6	-1.3	-15.1	6.5	7.8	6.1	6.2	25.1
1999	3.5	-3.3	3.7	4.2	-2.3	5.1	-3.2	-1.0	-2.8	6.5	2.5	6.0	19.5
2000	-4.2	-0.4	8.9	-3.3	-2.7	2.5	-1.8	7.4	-4.8	-1.2	-9.3	1.1	-8.8
2001	3.2	-9.5	-6.7	8.0	0.5	-2.4	-1.4	-6.2	-8.6	2.0	7.5	0.9	-13.6
2002	-1.4	-2.1	4.0	-5.8	-1.0	-7.5	-7.5	0.3	-10.9	8.1	5.7	-5.8	-22.9
2003	-2.5	-1.7	0.9	7.9	5.5	1.2	1.8	1.9	-1.2	5.7	1.0	4.6	27.5
2004	1.8	1.2	-1.5	-1.9	1.3	1.7	-3.6	0.3	1.1	1.5	4.1	3.5	9.5
2005	-2.6	2.0	-1.7	-2.0	3.4	0.3	3.8	-1.1	0.8	-1.9	3.5	0.01	4.4
2006	2.7	0.01	1.3	1.1	-3.2	0.003	0.1	2.2	2.3	3.3	1.9	1.1	13.3
2007	1.8	-1.9	0.9	4.1	3.4	-2.0	-3.2	1.2	3.7	1.6	-4.5	-0.8	3.9
2008	-6.1	-3.3	-0.8	5.0	1.6	-8.5	-1.3	1.2	-9.7	-17.6	-7.9	1.3	-39.0
2009	-8.3	-10.7	8.5	10.0	5.3	0.1	7.5	3.4	3.9	-2.3	5.6	2.3	25.5
2010	-3.7	3.1	6.0	1.8	-8.1	-5.7	6.8	-4.7	9.0	3.8	0.1	6.5	13.9
2011	2.3	3.3	0.1	2.9	-1.3	-1.9	-2.3	-6.0	-7.6	11.1	-0.5	0.7	-0.5
2012	4.8	4.1	3.0	-0.7	-6.4	3.7	1.1	2.2	2.4	-1.8	0.5	0.8	13.9
2013	5.3	1.1	3.7	1.7	2.0	-1.5	5.2	-3.0	3.3	4.3	2.6	2.5	30.4
2014	-3.3	4.5	0.5	0.4	2.1	2.1	-1.7	3.9	-1.9	2.3	2.4	-0.4	11.1
2015	-2.8	5.5	-1.4	0.6	1.1	-2.0	1.8	-6.2	-2.9	8.0	0.1	-2.0	-1.1
2016	-5.5	-0.3	6.8	0.4	1.5	0.1	3.7	-0.1	-0.1	-2.1	3.7	1.7	9.7
2017	1.9	3.6	-0.1	0.9	1.0	0.5	1.9	0.1	2.0	2.2	2.8	1.0	19.3
2018	5.4	-3.9	-2.4	0.2	2.3	0.5	3.3	3.2	0.2	-7.2	1.8	-9.3	-6.6
2019	8.2	3.2	1.6	3.9	-6.6	6.9	1.4	-2.0	1.6	2.0	3.6	2.7	28.9
2020	-0.01	-8.3	-13.4	13.1	5.1	2.1	5.7	7.2	-3.8	-2.5	11.6	4.1	18.9
2021	-0.9	2.8	3.7	5.3	0.3	2.4	2.0	2.8	-4.7	6.9	-1.5	3.9	24.8
2022	-5.7	-2.9	3.2	-9.0	-0.3	-8.5	9.2	-4.0	-9.4	7.9	5.2	-5.9	-20.4
2023	6.6	-2.5	3.0	1.1	0.3	6.6	3.3	-1.9	-4.8	-2.5	9.1	4.8	24.5
2024	1.3	5.2	3.1	-4.3	4.6	3.2	1.4	2.2	2.0	-0.8	6.3	-2.9	22.8
2025	3.1	-1.9	-5.9	-0.7									
TOTALS	52.7	8.7	39.3	69.2	43.4	20.1	54.7	14.9	-41.4	43.2	102.9	57.2	
AVG.	1.1	0.2	0.8	1.5	0.9	0.4	1.2	0.3	-0.9	0.9	2.2	1.2	
# Up	29	27	31	32	32	29	26	28	22	28	35	34	
# Down	18	20	16	15	14	17	20	18	24	18	11	12	

RUSSELL 1000 INDEX MONTHLY CLOSING PRICES SINCE 1979

	Jan	Feb	Mar	Apr	May	Jun	Jul	Aug	Sep	Oct	Nov	Dec
1979	53.76	51.88	54.97	55.15	53.92	56.25	56.86	60.04	60.05	55.78	58.65	59.87
1980	63.40	63.07	55.79	58.38	61.31	63.27	67.30	68.05	69.84	71.08	78.26	75.20
1981	71.75	72.49	75.21	73.77	73.90	73.01	72.92	68.42	64.06	67.54	70.23	67.93
1982	66.12	62.21	61.43	63.85	61.53	59.92	58.54	65.14	65.89	73.34	76.28	77.24
1983	79.75	81.45	84.06	90.04	89.89	93.18	90.18	90.65	91.85	89.69	91.50	90.38
1984	88.69	84.76	85.73	86.00	80.94	82.61	81.13	89.87	89.67	89.62	88.36	90.31
1985	97.31	98.38	98.03	97.72	103.02	104.65	103.78	102.76	98.75	103.16	109.91	114.39
1986	115.39	123.71	130.07	128.44	134.82	136.75	128.74	137.43	125.70	132.11	133.97	130.00
1987	146.48	152.29	155.20	152.39	152.94	159.84	166.57	172.95	168.83	131.89	121.28	130.02
1988	135.55	141.54	137.45	138.37	138.66	145.31	143.99	139.26	144.68	147.55	144.59	146.99
1989	156.93	152.98	155.99	163.63	169.85	168.49	182.27	185.33	184.40	179.17	181.85	185.11
1990	171.44	173.43	177.28	172.32	187.66	186.29	184.32	166.69	157.83	156.62	166.69	171.22
1991	179.00	191.34	196.15	195.94	203.32	193.78	202.67	207.18	204.02	206.96	198.46	220.61
1992	217.52	219.50	214.29	219.13	219.71	215.60	224.37	218.86	221.15	222.65	230.44	233.59
1993	235.25	236.67	241.80	235.13	240.80	241.78	240.78	249.20	247.95	250.97	246.70	250.71
1994	258.08	250.52	239.19	241.71	244.13	237.11	244.44	254.04	247.49	251.62	241.82	244.65
1995	250.52	260.08	266.11	272.81	282.48	289.29	299.98	301.40	313.28	311.37	324.36	328.89
1996	338.97	342.56	345.01	349.84	357.35	357.10	339.44	347.79	366.77	374.38	401.05	393.75
1997	416.77	417.46	398.19	419.15	445.06	462.95	499.89	475.33	500.78	483.86	504.25	513.79
1998	517.02	553.14	580.31	585.46	572.16	592.57	584.97	496.66	529.11	570.63	605.31	642.87
1999	665.64	643.67	667.49	695.25	679.10	713.61	690.51	683.27	663.83	707.19	724.66	767.97
2000	736.08	733.04	797.99	771.58	750.98	769.68	755.57	811.17	772.60	763.06	692.40	700.09
2001	722.55	654.25	610.36	658.90	662.39	646.64	637.43	597.67	546.46	557.29	599.32	604.94
2002	596.66	583.88	607.35	572.04	566.18	523.72	484.39	486.08	433.22	468.51	495.00	466.18
2003	454.30	446.37	450.35	486.09	512.92	518.94	528.53	538.40	532.15	562.51	568.32	594.56
2004	605.21	612.58	603.42	591.83	599.40	609.31	587.21	589.09	595.66	604.51	629.26	650.99
2005	633.99	646.93	635.78	623.32	644.28	645.92	670.26	663.13	668.53	656.09	679.35	679.42
2006	697.79	697.83	706.74	714.37	691.78	691.80	692.59	707.55	723.48	747.30	761.43	770.08
2007	784.11	768.92	775.97	807.82	835.14	818.17	792.11	801.22	830.59	844.20	806.44	799.82
2008	750.97	726.42	720.32	756.03	768.28	703.22	694.07	702.17	634.08	522.47	481.43	487.77
2009	447.32	399.61	433.67	476.84	501.95	502.27	539.88	558.21	579.97	566.50	598.41	612.01
2010	589.41	607.45	643.79	655.06	601.79	567.37	606.09	577.68	629.78	653.57	654.24	696.90
2011	712.97	736.24	737.07	758.45	748.75	734.48	717.77	674.79	623.45	692.41	688.77	693.36
2012	726.33	756.42	778.92	773.50	724.12	750.61	758.60	775.07	793.74	779.35	783.37	789.90
2013	831.74	840.97	872.11	886.89	904.44	890.67	937.16	909.28	939.50	979.68	1004.97	1030.36
2014	996.48	1041.36	1046.42	1050.20	1071.96	1094.59	1075.60	1117.71	1096.43	1121.98	1148.90	1144.37
2015	1111.85	1173.46	1156.35	1164.03	1176.67	1152.64	1173.55	1100.51	1068.46	1153.55	1154.66	1131.88
2016	1069.78	1066.58	1138.84	1143.76	1160.95	1161.57	1204.43	1203.05	1202.25	1177.22	1220.68	1241.66
2017	1265.35	1311.34	1310.06	1322.44	1336.18	1343.52	1368.57	1369.61	1396.90	1427.43	1467.42	1481.81
2018	1561.66	1501.23	1464.87	1468.28	1502.31	1509.96	1560.36	1610.70	1614.54	1498.65	1525.56	1384.26
2019	1498.36	1545.73	1570.23	1631.87	1524.42	1629.02	1652.40	1618.61	1644.18	1677.08	1736.85	1784.21
2020	1784.03	1635.21	1416.49	1601.82	1682.75	1717.47	1815.99	1946.15	1872.70	1825.67	2037.36	2120.87
2021	2101.36	2159.32	2238.17	2356.67	2364.53	2421.14	2469.17	2537.31	2418.16	2583.83	2545.78	2645.91
2022	2494.64	2422.79	2501.29	2276.45	2269.07	2075.96	2267.10	2176.45	1972.29	2128.36	2239.12	2105.90
2023	2244.91	2187.75	2253.36	2279.16	2285.65	2436.93	2518.42	2470.02	2351.35	2292.38	2501.69	2622.14
2024	2656.44	2795.56	2881.91	2757.14	2882.75	2974.64	3015.48	3082.73	3145.06	3120.81	3317.38	3221.05
2025	3320.99	3259.07	3066.32	3045.67								

RUSSELL 2000 INDEX MONTHLY PERCENT CHANGES SINCE 1979

	Jan	Feb	Mar	Apr	May	Jun	Jul	Aug	Sep	Oct	Nov	Dec	Year
1979	9.0	–3.2	9.7	2.3	–1.8	5.3	2.9	7.8	–0.7	–11.3	8.1	6.6	38.0
1980	8.2	–2.1	–18.5	6.0	8.0	4.0	11.0	6.5	2.9	3.9	7.0	–3.7	33.8
1981	–0.6	0.3	7.7	2.5	3.0	–2.5	–2.6	–8.0	–8.6	8.2	2.8	–2.0	–1.5
1982	–3.7	–5.3	–1.5	5.1	–3.2	–4.0	–1.7	7.5	3.6	14.1	8.8	1.1	20.7
1983	7.5	6.0	2.5	7.2	7.0	4.4	–3.0	–4.0	1.6	–7.0	5.0	–2.1	26.3
1984	–1.8	–5.9	0.4	–0.7	–5.4	2.6	–5.0	11.5	–1.0	–2.0	–2.9	1.4	–9.6
1985	13.1	2.4	–2.2	–1.4	3.4	1.0	2.7	–1.2	–6.2	3.6	6.8	4.2	28.0
1986	1.5	7.0	4.7	1.4	3.3	–0.2	–9.5	3.0	–6.3	3.9	–0.5	–3.1	4.0
1987	11.5	8.2	2.4	–3.0	–0.5	2.3	2.8	2.9	–2.0	–30.8	–5.5	7.8	–10.8
1988	4.0	8.7	4.4	2.0	–2.5	7.0	–0.9	–2.8	2.3	–1.2	–3.6	3.8	22.4
1989	4.4	0.5	2.2	4.3	4.2	–2.4	4.2	2.1	0.01	–6.0	0.4	0.1	14.2
1990	–8.9	2.9	3.7	–3.4	6.8	0.1	–4.5	–13.6	–9.2	–6.2	7.3	3.7	–21.5
1991	9.1	11.0	6.9	–0.2	4.5	–6.0	3.1	3.7	0.6	2.7	–4.7	7.7	43.7
1992	8.0	2.9	–3.5	–3.7	1.2	–5.0	3.2	–3.1	2.2	3.1	7.5	3.4	16.4
1993	3.2	–2.5	3.1	–2.8	4.3	0.5	1.3	4.1	2.7	2.5	–3.4	3.3	17.0
1994	3.1	–0.4	–5.4	0.6	–1.3	–3.6	1.6	5.4	–0.5	–0.4	–4.2	2.5	–3.2
1995	–1.4	3.9	1.6	2.1	1.5	5.0	5.7	1.9	1.7	–4.6	4.2	2.4	26.2
1996	–0.2	3.0	1.8	5.3	3.9	–4.2	–8.8	5.7	3.7	–1.7	4.0	2.4	14.8
1997	1.9	–2.5	–4.9	0.1	11.0	4.1	4.6	2.2	7.2	–4.5	–0.8	1.7	20.5
1998	–1.6	7.4	4.1	0.5	–5.4	0.2	–8.2	–19.5	7.6	4.0	5.2	6.1	–3.4
1999	1.2	–8.2	1.4	8.8	1.4	4.3	–2.8	–3.8	–0.1	0.3	5.9	11.2	19.6
2000	–1.7	16.4	–6.7	–6.1	–5.9	8.6	–3.2	7.4	–3.1	–4.5	–10.4	8.4	–4.2
2001	5.1	–6.7	–5.0	7.7	2.3	3.3	–5.4	–3.3	–13.6	5.8	7.6	6.0	1.0
2002	–1.1	–2.8	7.9	0.8	–4.5	–5.1	–15.2	–0.4	–7.3	3.1	8.8	–5.7	–21.6
2003	–2.9	–3.1	1.1	9.4	10.6	1.7	6.2	4.5	–2.0	8.3	3.5	1.9	45.4
2004	4.3	0.8	0.8	–5.2	1.5	4.1	–6.8	–0.6	4.6	1.9	8.6	2.8	17.0
2005	–4.2	1.6	–3.0	–5.8	6.4	3.7	6.3	–1.9	0.2	–3.2	4.7	–0.6	3.3
2006	8.9	–0.3	4.7	–0.1	–5.7	0.5	–3.3	2.9	0.7	5.7	2.5	0.2	17.0
2007	1.6	–0.9	0.9	1.7	4.0	–1.6	–6.9	2.2	1.6	2.8	–7.3	–0.2	–2.7
2008	–6.9	–3.8	0.3	4.1	4.5	–7.8	3.6	3.5	–8.1	–20.9	–12.0	5.6	–34.8
2009	–11.2	–12.3	8.7	15.3	2.9	1.3	9.5	2.8	5.6	–6.9	3.0	7.9	25.2
2010	–3.7	4.4	8.0	5.6	–7.7	–7.9	6.8	–7.5	12.3	4.0	3.4	7.8	25.3
2011	–0.3	5.4	2.4	2.6	–2.0	–2.5	–3.7	–8.8	–11.4	15.0	–0.5	0.5	–5.5
2012	7.0	2.3	2.4	–1.6	–6.7	4.8	–1.4	3.2	3.1	–2.2	0.4	3.3	14.6
2013	6.2	1.0	4.4	–0.4	3.9	–0.7	6.9	–3.3	6.2	2.5	3.9	1.8	37.0
2014	–2.8	4.6	–0.8	–3.9	0.7	5.2	–6.1	4.8	–6.2	6.5	–0.02	2.7	3.5
2015	–3.3	5.8	1.6	–2.6	2.2	0.6	–1.2	–6.4	–5.1	5.6	3.1	–5.2	–5.7
2016	–8.8	–0.1	7.8	1.5	2.1	–0.2	5.9	1.6	0.9	–4.8	11.0	2.6	19.5
2017	0.3	1.8	–0.1	1.0	–2.2	3.3	0.7	–1.4	6.1	0.8	2.8	–0.6	13.1
2018	2.6	–4.0	1.1	0.8	5.9	0.6	1.7	4.2	–2.5	–10.9	1.4	–12.0	–12.2
2019	11.2	5.1	–2.3	3.3	–7.9	6.9	0.5	–5.1	1.9	2.6	4.0	2.7	23.7
2020	–3.3	–8.5	–21.9	13.7	6.4	3.4	2.7	5.5	–3.5	2.0	18.3	8.5	18.4
2021	5.0	6.1	0.9	2.1	0.1	1.8	–3.6	2.1	–3.1	4.2	–4.3	2.1	13.7
2022	–9.7	1.0	1.1	–10.0	–0.003	–8.4	10.4	–2.2	–9.7	10.9	2.2	–6.6	–21.6
2023	9.7	–1.8	–5.0	–1.9	–1.1	7.9	6.1	–5.2	–6.0	–6.9	8.8	12.1	15.1
2024	–3.9	5.5	3.4	–7.1	4.9	–1.1	10.1	–1.6	0.6	–1.5	10.8	–8.4	10.0
2025	2.6	–5.4	–7.0	–2.4									
TOTALS	668.2	46.2	26.3	55.5	58.1	35.3	16.7	5.3	–36.3	–9.5	121.7	96.1	
AVG.	1.5	1.0	0.6	1.2	1.3	0.8	0.4	0.1	–0.8	–0.2	2.6	2.1	
# Up	26	27	32	28	29	29	25	25	24	26	32	34	
# Down	21	20	15	19	17	17	21	21	22	20	14	12	

RUSSELL 2000 INDEX MONTHLY CLOSING PRICES SINCE 1979

	Jan	Feb	Mar	Apr	May	Jun	Jul	Aug	Sep	Oct	Nov	Dec
1979	44.18	42.78	46.94	48.00	47.13	49.62	51.08	55.05	54.68	48.51	52.43	55.91
1980	60.50	59.22	48.27	51.18	55.26	57.47	63.81	67.97	69.94	72.64	77.70	74.80
1981	74.33	74.52	80.25	82.25	84.72	82.56	80.41	73.94	67.55	73.06	75.14	73.67
1982	70.96	67.21	66.21	69.59	67.39	64.67	63.59	68.38	70.84	80.86	87.96	88.90
1983	95.53	101.23	103.77	111.20	118.94	124.17	120.43	115.60	117.43	109.17	114.66	112.27
1984	110.21	103.72	104.10	103.34	97.75	100.30	95.25	106.21	105.17	103.07	100.11	101.49
1985	114.77	117.54	114.92	113.35	117.26	118.38	121.56	120.10	112.65	116.73	124.62	129.87
1986	131.78	141.00	147.63	149.66	154.61	154.23	139.65	143.83	134.73	139.95	139.26	135.00
1987	150.48	162.84	166.79	161.82	161.02	164.75	169.42	174.25	170.81	118.26	111.70	120.42
1988	125.24	136.10	142.15	145.01	141.37	151.30	149.89	145.74	149.08	147.25	142.01	147.37
1989	153.84	154.56	157.89	164.68	171.53	167.42	174.50	178.20	178.21	167.47	168.17	168.30
1990	153.27	157.72	163.63	158.09	168.91	169.04	161.51	139.52	126.70	118.83	127.50	132.16
1991	144.17	160.00	171.01	170.61	178.34	167.61	172.76	179.11	180.16	185.00	176.37	189.94
1992	205.16	211.15	203.69	196.25	198.52	188.64	194.74	188.79	192.92	198.90	213.81	221.01
1993	228.10	222.41	229.21	222.68	232.19	233.35	236.46	246.19	252.95	259.18	250.41	258.59
1994	266.52	265.53	251.06	252.55	249.28	240.29	244.06	257.32	256.12	255.02	244.25	250.36
1995	246.85	256.57	260.77	266.17	270.25	283.63	299.72	305.31	310.38	296.25	308.58	315.97
1996	315.38	324.93	330.77	348.28	361.85	346.61	316.00	333.88	346.39	340.57	354.11	362.61
1997	369.45	360.05	342.56	343.00	380.76	396.37	414.48	423.43	453.82	433.26	429.92	437.02
1998	430.05	461.83	480.68	482.89	456.62	457.39	419.75	337.95	363.59	378.16	397.75	421.96
1999	427.22	392.26	397.63	432.81	438.68	457.68	444.77	427.83	427.30	428.64	454.08	504.75
2000	496.23	577.71	539.09	506.25	476.18	517.23	500.64	537.89	521.37	497.68	445.94	483.53
2001	508.34	474.37	450.53	485.32	496.50	512.64	484.78	468.56	404.87	428.17	460.78	488.50
2002	483.10	469.36	506.46	510.67	487.47	462.64	392.42	390.96	362.27	373.50	406.35	383.09
2003	372.17	360.52	364.54	398.68	441.00	448.37	476.02	497.42	487.68	528.22	546.51	556.91
2004	580.76	585.56	590.31	559.80	568.28	591.52	551.29	547.93	572.94	583.79	633.77	651.57
2005	624.02	634.06	615.07	579.38	616.71	639.66	679.75	666.51	667.80	646.61	677.29	673.22
2006	733.20	730.64	765.14	764.54	721.01	724.67	700.56	720.53	725.59	766.84	786.12	787.66
2007	800.34	793.30	800.71	814.57	847.19	833.69	776.13	792.86	805.45	828.02	767.77	766.03
2008	713.30	686.18	687.97	716.18	748.28	689.66	714.52	739.50	679.58	537.52	473.14	499.45
2009	443.53	389.02	422.75	487.56	501.58	508.28	556.71	572.07	604.28	562.77	579.73	625.39
2010	602.04	628.56	678.64	716.60	661.61	609.49	650.89	602.06	676.14	703.35	727.01	783.65
2011	781.25	823.45	843.55	865.29	848.30	827.43	797.03	726.81	644.16	741.06	737.42	740.92
2012	792.82	810.94	830.30	816.88	761.82	798.49	786.94	812.09	837.45	818.73	821.92	849.35
2013	902.09	911.11	951.54	947.46	984.14	977.48	1045.26	1010.90	1073.79	1100.15	1142.89	1163.64
2014	1130.88	1183.03	1173.04	1126.86	1134.50	1192.96	1120.07	1174.35	1101.68	1173.51	1173.23	1204.70
2015	1165.39	1233.37	1252.77	1220.13	1246.53	1253.95	1238.68	1159.45	1100.69	1161.86	1198.11	1135.89
2016	1035.38	1033.90	1114.03	1130.84	1154.79	1151.92	1219.94	1239.91	1251.65	1191.39	1322.34	1357.13
2017	1361.82	1386.68	1385.92	1400.43	1370.21	1415.36	1425.14	1405.28	1490.86	1502.77	1544.14	1535.51
2018	1574.98	1512.45	1529.43	1541.88	1633.61	1643.07	1670.80	1740.75	1696.57	1511.41	1533.27	1348.56
2019	1499.42	1575.55	1539.74	1591.21	1465.49	1566.57	1574.61	1494.84	1523.37	1562.45	1624.50	1668.47
2020	1614.06	1476.43	1153.10	1310.66	1394.04	1441.37	1480.43	1561.88	1507.69	1538.48	1819.82	1974.86
2021	2073.64	2201.05	2220.52	2266.45	2268.97	2310.55	2226.25	2273.77	2204.37	2297.19	2198.91	2245.31
2022	2028.45	2048.09	2070.13	1864.10	1864.00	1707.99	1885.23	1844.12	1664.72	1846.86	1886.58	1761.25
2023	1931.95	1896.99	1802.48	1768.99	1749.65	1888.73	2003.18	1899.68	1785.10	1662.28	1809.02	2027.07
2024	1947.34	2054.84	2124.55	1973.91	2070.13	2047.69	2254.48	2217.63	2229.97	2196.65	2434.73	2230.16
2025	2287.69	2163.07	2011.91	1964.12								

10 BEST DAYS BY PERCENT AND POINT

	BY PERCENT CHANGE				BY POINT CHANGE		
DAY	CLOSE	PNT CHANGE	% CHANGE	DAY	CLOSE	PNT CHANGE	% CHANGE
DJIA 1901 to 1949							
3/15/33	62.10	8.26	15.3	10/30/29	258.47	28.40	12.3
10/6/31	99.34	12.86	14.9	11/14/29	217.28	18.59	9.4
10/30/29	258.47	28.40	12.3	10/5/29	341.36	16.19	5.0
9/21/32	75.16	7.67	11.4	10/31/29	273.51	15.04	5.8
8/3/32	58.22	5.06	9.5	10/6/31	99.34	12.86	14.9
2/11/32	78.60	6.80	9.5	11/15/29	228.73	11.45	5.3
11/14/29	217.28	18.59	9.4	6/19/30	228.97	10.13	4.6
12/18/31	80.69	6.90	9.4	9/5/39	148.12	10.03	7.3
2/13/32	85.82	7.22	9.2	11/22/28	290.34	9.81	3.5
5/6/32	59.01	4.91	9.1	10/1/30	214.14	9.24	4.5
DJIA 1950 to MAY 2, 2025							
3/24/2020	20704.91	2112.98	11.4	4/9/2025	40608.45	2962.86	7.9
10/13/2008	9387.61	936.42	11.1	3/24/2020	20704.91	2112.98	11.4
10/28/2008	9065.12	889.35	10.9	3/13/2020	23185.62	1985.00	9.4
10/21/1987	2027.85	186.84	10.2	4/6/2020	22679.99	1627.46	7.7
3/13/2020	23185.62	1985.00	9.4	11/6/2024	43729.93	1508.05	3.6
4/9/2025	40608.45	2962.86	7.9	3/26/2020	22552.17	1351.62	6.4
4/6/2020	22679.99	1627.46	7.7	3/2/2020	26703.32	1293.96	5.1
3/23/2009	7775.86	497.48	6.8	11/10/2022	33715.37	1201.43	3.7
11/13/2008	8835.25	552.59	6.7	3/4/2020	27090.86	1173.45	4.5
11/21/2008	8046.42	494.13	6.5	3/10/2020	25018.16	1167.14	4.9
S&P 500 1930 to MAY 2, 2025							
3/15/1933	6.81	0.97	16.6	4/9/2025	5456.90	474.13	9.5
10/6/1931	9.91	1.09	12.4	3/13/2020	2711.02	230.38	9.3
9/21/1932	8.52	0.90	11.8	3/24/2020	2447.33	209.93	9.4
10/13/2008	1003.35	104.13	11.6	11/10/2022	3956.37	207.80	5.5
10/28/2008	940.51	91.59	10.8	4/6/2020	2663.68	175.03	7.0
2/16/1935	10.00	0.94	10.4	3/26/2020	2630.07	154.51	6.2
8/17/1935	11.70	1.08	10.2	11/6/2024	5929.04	146.28	2.5
3/16/1935	9.05	0.82	10.0	3/17/2020	2529.19	143.06	6.0
9/12/1938	12.06	1.06	9.6	3/2/2020	3090.23	136.01	4.6
9/5/1939	12.64	1.11	9.6	3/10/2020	2882.23	135.67	4.9
NASDAQ 1971 to MAY 2, 2025							
1/3/2001	2616.69	324.83	14.2	4/9/2025	17124.97	1857.06	12.2
4/9/2025	17124.97	1857.06	12.2	11/10/2022	11114.15	760.98	7.4
10/13/2008	1844.25	194.74	11.8	3/13/2020	7874.88	673.08	9.4
12/5/2000	2889.80	274.05	10.5	3/24/2020	7417.86	557.19	8.1
10/28/2008	1649.47	143.57	9.5	11/6/2024	18983.47	544.30	3.0
3/13/2020	7874.88	673.08	9.4	4/6/2020	7913.24	540.16	7.3
4/5/2001	1785.00	146.20	8.9	3/16/2022	13436.55	487.93	3.8
4/18/2001	2079.44	156.22	8.1	11/30/2022	11468.00	484.22	4.4
3/24/2020	7417.86	557.19	8.1	7/27/2022	12032.42	469.85	4.1
5/30/2000	3459.48	254.37	7.9	1/31/2022	14239.88	469.31	3.4
RUSSELL 1000 1979 to MAY 2, 2025							
10/13/2008	542.98	56.75	11.7	4/9/2025	2980.19	260.20	9.6
10/28/2008	503.74	47.68	10.5	3/13/2020	1488.04	123.38	9.0
4/9/2025	2980.19	260.20	9.6	11/10/2022	2173.72	117.45	5.7
3/24/2020	1340.32	115.87	9.5	3/24/2020	1340.32	115.87	9.5
3/13/2020	1488.04	123.38	9.0	4/6/2020	1455.56	96.55	7.1
10/21/1987	135.85	11.15	8.9	11/6/2024	3240.37	83.93	2.7
4/6/2020	1455.56	96.55	7.1	3/26/2020	1442.70	83.87	6.2
3/23/2009	446.90	29.36	7.0	3/17/2020	1381.49	74.98	5.
11/13/2008	489.83	31.99	7.0	3/10/2020	1588.36	73.59	4.9
11/24/2008	456.14	28.26	6.6	3/2/2020	1708.13	72.92	4.5
RUSSELL 2000 1979 to MAY 2, 2025							
3/24/2020	1096.54	94.14	9.4	4/9/2025	1913.16	152.45	8.7
10/13/2008	570.89	48.41	9.3	11/6/2024	2392.92	132.08	5.8
4/9/2025	1913.16	152.45	8.7	11/10/2022	1867.93	107.53	6.1
11/13/2008	491.23	38.43	8.5	3/24/2020	1096.54	94.14	9.4
3/23/2009	433.72	33.61	8.4	11/14/2023	1798.32	92.82	5.4
4/6/2020	1138.78	86.73	8.2	3/13/2020	1210.13	87.20	7.8
3/13/2020	1210.13	87.20	7.8	4/6/2020	1138.78	86.73	8.2
10/21/1987	130.65	9.26	7.6	1/6/2021	2057.92	78.81	4.0
10/28/2008	482.55	34.15	7.6	5/18/2020	1333.69	76.70	6.1
11/24/2008	436.80	30.26	7.4	7/16/2024	2263.67	76.65	3.5

10 WORST DAYS BY PERCENT AND POINT

	BY PERCENT CHANGE				BY POINT CHANGE		
DAY	CLOSE	PNT CHANGE	% CHANGE	DAY	CLOSE	PNT CHANGE	% CHANGE
			DJIA 1901 to 1949				
10/28/1929	260.64	−38.33	−12.8	10/28/1929	260.64	−38.33	−12.8
10/29/1929	230.07	−30.57	−11.7	10/29/1929	230.07	−30.57	−11.7
11/6/1929	232.13	−25.55	−9.9	11/6/1929	232.13	−25.55	−9.9
8/12/1932	63.11	−5.79	−8.4	10/23/1929	305.85	−20.66	−6.3
3/14/1907	55.84	−5.05	−8.3	11/11/1929	220.39	−16.14	−6.8
7/21/1933	88.71	−7.55	−7.8	11/4/1929	257.68	−15.83	−5.8
10/18/1937	125.73	−10.57	−7.8	12/12/1929	243.14	−15.30	−5.9
2/1/1917	88.52	−6.91	−7.2	10/3/1929	329.95	−14.55	−4.2
10/5/1932	66.07	−5.09	−7.2	6/16/1930	230.05	−14.20	−5.8
9/24/1931	107.79	−8.20	−7.1	8/9/1929	337.99	−14.11	−4.0
			DJIA 1950 to MAY 2, 2025				
10/19/1987	1738.74	−508.00	−22.6	3/16/2020	20188.52	−2997.10	−12.9
3/16/2020	20188.52	−2997.10	−12.9	3/12/2020	21200.62	−2352.60	−10.0
3/12/2020	21200.62	−2352.60	−10.0	4/4/2025	38314.86	−2231.07	−5.5
10/26/1987	1793.93	−156.83	−8.0	3/9/2020	23851.02	−2013.76	−7.8
10/15/2008	8577.91	−733.08	−7.9	6/11/2020	25128.17	−1861.82	−6.9
3/9/2020	23851.02	−2013.76	−7.8	4/3/2025	40545.93	−1679.39	−4.0
12/1/2008	8149.09	−679.95	−7.7	3/11/2020	23553.22	−1464.94	−5.9
10/9/2008	8579.19	−678.91	−7.3	3/18/2020	19898.92	−1338.46	−6.3
10/27/1997	7161.15	−554.26	−7.2	9/13/2022	31104.97	−1276.37	−3.9
9/17/2001	8920.70	−684.81	−7.1	2/27/2020	25766.64	−1190.95	−4.4
			S&P 500 1930 to MAY 2, 2025				
10/19/1987	224.84	−57.86	−20.5	3/16/2020	2386.13	−324.89	−12.0
3/16/2020	2386.13	−324.89	−12.0	4/4/2025	5074.08	−322.44	−6.0
3/18/1935	8.14	−0.91	−10.1	4/3/2025	5396.52	−274.45	−4.8
4/16/1935	8.22	−0.91	−10.0	3/12/2020	2480.64	−260.74	−9.5
9/3/1946	15.00	−1.65	−9.9	3/9/2020	2746.56	−225.81	−7.6
3/12/2020	2480.64	−260.74	−9.5	4/10/2025	5268.05	−188.85	−3.5
10/18/1937	10.76	−1.10	−9.3	6/11/2020	3002.10	−188.04	−5.9
10/15/2008	907.84	−90.17	−9.0	12/18/2024	5872.16	−178.45	−3.0
12/1/2008	816.21	−80.03	−8.9	9/13/2022	3932.69	−177.72	−4.3
7/20/1933	10.57	−1.03	−8.9	5/18/2022	3923.68	−165.17	−4.0
			NASDAQ 1971 to MAY 2, 2025				
3/16/2020	6904.59	−970.29	−12.3	4/3/2025	16550.61	−1050.44	−6.0
10/19/1987	360.21	−46.12	−11.4	3/16/2020	6904.59	−970.29	−12.3
4/14/2000	3321.29	−355.49	−9.7	4/4/2025	15587.79	−962.82	−5.8
3/12/2020	7201.80	−750.25	−9.4	3/12/2020	7201.80	−750.25	−9.4
9/29/2008	1983.73	−199.61	−9.1	4/10/2025	16387.31	−737.66	−4.3
10/26/1987	298.90	−29.55	−9.0	3/10/2020	17468.32	−727.90	−4.0
10/20/1987	327.79	−32.42	−9.0	12/18/2024	19392.69	−716.37	−3.6
12/1/2008	1398.07	−137.50	−9.0	7/24/2024	17342.41	−654.94	−3.6
8/31/1998	1499.25	−140.43	−8.6	5/5/2022	12317.69	−647.17	−5.0
10/15/2008	1628.33	−150.68	−8.5	9/13/2022	11633.57	−632.84	−5.2
			RUSSELL 1000 1979 to MAY 2, 2025				
10/19/1987	121.04	−28.40	−19.0	3/16/2020	1306.51	−181.53	−12.2
3/16/2020	1306.51	−181.53	−12.2	4/4/2025	2772.12	−175.69	−6.0
3/12/2020	1364.66	−144.34	−9.6	4/3/2025	2947.81	−154.68	−5.0
10/15/2008	489.71	−49.11	−9.1	3/12/2020	1364.66	−144.34	−9.6
12/1/2008	437.75	−43.68	−9.1	3/9/2020	1514.77	−127.21	−7.8
9/29/2008	602.34	−57.35	−8.7	4/10/2025	2875.07	−105.12	−3.5
10/26/1987	119.45	−10.74	−8.3	6/11/2020	1660.70	−104.50	−5.9
3/9/2020	1514.77	−127.21	−7.8	12/18/2024	3217.90	−102.73	−3.1
10/9/2008	492.13	−40.05	−7.5	9/13/2022	2167.18	−97.21	−4.3
8/8/2011	617.28	−45.56	−6.9	5/18/2022	2154.00	−90.51	−4.0
			RUSSELL 2000 1979 to MAY 2, 2025				
3/16/2020	1037.42	−172.71	−14.3	3/16/2020	1037.42	−172.71	−14.3
10/19/1987	133.60	−19.14	−12.5	3/12/2020	1122.93	−141.37	−11.2
12/1/2008	417.07	−56.07	−11.9	3/9/2020	1313.44	−135.78	−9.4
3/12/2020	1122.93	−141.37	−11.2	4/4/2025	1910.55	−134.81	−6.6
3/18/2020	991.16	−115.35	−10.4	3/18/2020	991.16	−115.35	−10.4
10/15/2008	502.11	−52.54	−9.5	6/11/2020	1356.22	−111.17	−7.6
3/9/2020	1313.44	−135.78	−9.4	12/18/2024	2231.51	−102.57	−4.4
10/26/1987	110.33	−11.26	−9.3	3/11/2020	1264.30	−86.60	−6.4
10/20/1987	121.39	−12.21	−9.1	6/13/2022	1714.60	−85.68	−4.8
8/8/2011	650.96	−63.67	−8.9	11/26/2021	2245.94	−85.52	−3.7

10 BEST WEEKS BY PERCENT AND POINT

	BY PERCENT CHANGE				BY POINT CHANGE		
WEEK ENDS	CLOSE	PNT CHANGE	% CHANGE	WEEK ENDS	CLOSE	PNT CHANGE	% CHANGE
			DJIA 1901 to 1949				
8/6/1932	66.56	12.30	22.7	12/7/1929	263.46	24.51	10.3
6/25/1938	131.94	18.71	16.5	6/25/1938	131.94	18.71	16.5
2/13/1932	85.82	11.37	15.3	6/27/1931	156.93	17.97	12.9
4/22/1933	72.24	9.36	14.9	11/22/1929	245.74	17.01	7.4
10/10/1931	105.61	12.84	13.8	8/17/1929	360.70	15.86	4.6
7/30/1932	54.26	6.42	13.4	12/22/1928	285.94	15.22	5.6
6/27/1931	156.93	17.97	12.9	8/24/1929	375.44	14.74	4.1
9/24/1932	74.83	8.39	12.6	2/21/1929	310.06	14.21	4.8
8/27/1932	75.61	8.43	12.6	5/10/1930	272.01	13.70	5.3
3/18/1933	60.56	6.72	12.5	11/15/1930	186.68	13.54	7.8
			DJIA 1950 to MAY 2, 2025				
3/27/2020	21636.78	2462.80	12.8	4/9/2020	23719.37	2666.84	12.7
4/9/2020	23719.37	2666.84	12.7	3/27/2020	21636.78	2462.80	12.8
10/11/1974	658.17	73.61	12.6	5/27/2022	33212.96	1951.06	6.2
10/31/2008	9325.01	946.06	11.3	11/8/2024	43988.99	1936.80	4.6
8/20/1982	869.29	81.24	10.3	4/11/2025	40212.71	1897.85	5.0
11/28/2008	8829.04	782.62	9.7	11/6/2020	28323.40	1821.80	6.9
3/13/2009	7223.98	597.04	9.0	3/18/2022	34754.93	1810.74	5.5
10/8/1982	986.85	79.11	8.7	10/28/2022	32861.80	1779.24	5.7
3/21/2003	8521.97	662.26	8.4	6/5/2020	27110.98	1727.87	6.8
8/3/1984	1202.08	87.46	7.9	11/3/2023	34061.32	1643.73	5.1
			S&P 500 1930 to MAY 2, 2025				
8/6/1932	7.22	1.12	18.4	4/9/2020	2789.82	301.17	12.1
6/25/1938	11.39	1.72	17.8	4/11/2025	5363.36	289.28	5.7
7/30/1932	6.10	0.89	17.1	11/8/2024	5995.54	266.74	4.7
4/22/1933	7.75	1.09	16.4	3/18/2022	4463.12	258.81	6.2
10/11/1974	71.14	8.80	14.1	5/27/2022	4158.24	256.88	6.6
2/13/1932	8.80	1.08	14.0	4/25/2025	5525.21	242.51	4.6
9/24/1932	8.52	1.02	13.6	11/3/2023	4358.34	240.97	5.9
10/10/1931	10.64	1.27	13.6	11/6/2020	3509.44	239.48	7.3
8/27/1932	8.57	1.01	13.4	6/24/2022	3911.74	236.90	6.5
3/18/1933	6.61	0.77	13.2	3/27/2020	2541.47	236.55	10.3
			NASDAQ 1971 to MAY 2, 2025				
6/2/2000	3813.38	608.27	19.0	4/11/2025	16724.46	1136.67	7.3
4/12/2001	1961.43	241.07	14.0	4/25/2025	17382.94	1096.49	6.7
11/28/2008	1535.57	151.22	10.9	3/18/2022	13893.84	1050.03	8.2
10/31/2008	1720.95	168.92	10.9	11/8/2024	19286.78	1046.86	5.7
3/13/2009	1431.50	137.65	10.6	9/13/2024	17683.98	993.15	6.0
4/9/2020	8153.58	780.50	10.6	11/6/2020	11895.23	983.64	9.0
4/20/2001	2163.41	201.98	10.3	8/16/2024	17631.72	886.42	5.3
12/8/2000	2917.43	272.14	10.3	11/11/2022	11323.33	848.08	8.1
4/20/2000	3643.88	322.59	9.7	11/3/2023	13478.28	835.27	6.6
10/11/1974	60.42	5.26	9.5	6/24/2022	11607.62	809.27	7.5
			RUSSELL 1000 1979 to MAY 2, 2025				
4/9/2020	1530.05	171.04	12.6	4/9/2020	1530.05	171.04	12.6
11/28/2008	481.43	53.55	12.5	4/11/2025	2926.05	153.93	5.6
10/31/2008	522.47	50.94	10.8	11/8/2024	3285.81	152.93	4.9
3/13/2009	411.10	39.88	10.7	3/18/2022	2466.14	146.57	6.3
3/27/2020	1394.65	133.96	10.6	5/27/2022	2285.42	140.71	6.6
8/20/1982	61.51	4.83	8.5	11/6/2020	1962.60	136.93	7.5
6/2/2000	785.02	57.93	8.0	3/27/2020	1394.65	133.96	10.6
9/28/2001	546.46	38.48	7.6	11/3/2023	2384.64	133.93	6.0
10/16/1998	546.09	38.45	7.6	4/25/2025	3021.54	133.76	4.6
8/3/1984	87.43	6.13	7.5	6/24/2022	2149.71	132.36	6.6
			RUSSELL 2000 1979 to MAY 2, 2025				
4/9/2020	1246.73	194.68	18.5	4/9/2020	1246.73	194.68	18.5
11/28/2008	473.14	66.60	16.4	11/8/2024	2399.64	189.51	8.6
10/31/2008	537.52	66.40	14.1	3/12/2021	2352.79	160.58	7.3
6/2/2000	513.03	55.66	12.2	2/5/2021	2233.33	159.69	7.7
3/13/2009	393.09	42.04	12.0	11/5/2021	2437.08	139.89	6.1
3/27/2020	1131.99	118.10	11.7	11/3/2023	1760.70	123.76	7.6
12/2/2011	735.02	68.86	10.3	7/12/2024	2148.27	121.54	6.0
11/11/2016	1282.38	118.94	10.2	11/11/2016	1282.38	118.94	10.2
10/14/2011	712.46	56.25	8.6	3/27/2020	1131.99	118.10	11.7
11/8/2024	2399.64	189.51	8.6	1/8/2021	2091.66	116.80	5.9

10 WORST WEEKS BY PERCENT AND POINT

	BY PERCENT CHANGE				BY POINT CHANGE		
WEEK ENDS	CLOSE	PNT CHANGE	% CHANGE	WEEK ENDS	CLOSE	PNT CHANGE	% CHANGE
DJIA 1901 to 1949							
7/22/1933	88.42	–17.68	–16.7	11/8/1929	236.53	–36.98	–13.5
5/18/1940	122.43	–22.42	–15.5	12/8/1928	257.33	–33.47	–11.5
10/8/1932	61.17	–10.92	–15.2	6/21/1930	215.30	–28.95	–11.9
10/3/1931	92.77	–14.59	–13.6	10/19/1929	323.87	–28.82	–8.2
11/8/1929	236.53	–36.98	–13.5	5/3/1930	258.31	–27.15	–9.5
9/17/1932	66.44	–10.10	–13.2	10/31/1929	273.51	–25.46	–8.5
10/21/1933	83.64	–11.95	–12.5	10/26/1929	298.97	–24.90	–7.7
12/12/1931	78.93	–11.21	–12.4	5/18/1940	122.43	–22.42	–15.5
5/8/1915	62.77	–8.74	–12.2	2/8/1929	301.53	–18.23	–5.7
6/21/1930	215.30	–28.95	–11.9	10/11/1930	193.05	–18.05	–8.6
DJIA 1950 to MAY 2, 2025							
10/10/2008	8451.19	–1874.19	–18.2	3/20/2020	19173.98	–4011.64	–17.3
3/20/2020	19173.98	–4011.64	–17.3	2/28/2020	25409.36	–3583.05	–12.4
9/21/2001	8235.81	–1369.70	–14.3	4/4/2025	38314.86	–3269.04	–7.9
10/23/1987	1950.76	–295.98	–13.2	3/13/2020	23185.62	–2679.16	–10.4
2/28/2020	25409.36	–3583.05	–12.4	10/10/2008	8451.19	–1874.19	–18.2
3/13/2020	23185.62	–2679.16	–10.4	10/30/2020	26501.60	–1833.97	–6.5
10/16/1987	2246.74	–235.47	–9.5	12/21/2018	22445.37	–1655.14	–6.9
4/4/2025	38314.86	–3269.04	–7.9	1/21/2022	34265.37	–1646.44	–4.6
10/13/1989	2569.26	–216.26	–7.8	6/10/2022	31392.79	–1506.91	–4.6
3/16/2001	9823.41	–821.21	–7.7	6/12/2022	25605.54	–1505.44	–5.6
S&P 500 1930 to MAY 2, 2025							
7/22/1933	9.71	–2.20	–18.5	4/4/2025	5074.08	–506.86	–9.1
10/10/2008	899.22	–200.01	–18.2	3/20/2020	2304.92	–406.10	–15.0
5/18/1940	9.75	–2.05	–17.4	2/28/2020	2954.22	–383.53	–11.5
10/8/1932	6.77	–1.38	–16.9	1/21/2022	4397.94	–264.91	–5.7
3/20/2020	2304.92	–406.10	–15.0	3/13/2020	2711.02	–261.35	–8.8
9/17/1932	7.50	–1.28	–14.6	9/6/2024	5408.42	–239.98	–4.3
10/21/1933	8.57	–1.31	–13.3	6/17/2022	3674.84	–226.02	–5.8
10/3/1931	9.37	–1.36	–12.7	6/10/2022	3900.86	–207.68	–5.1
10/23/1987	248.22	–34.48	–12.2	10/10/2008	899.22	–200.01	–18.2
12/12/1931	8.20	–1.13	–12.1	10/30/2020	3269.96	–195.43	–5.6
NASDAQ 1971 to MAY 2, 2025							
4/14/2000	3321.29	–1125.16	–25.3	4/4/2025	15587.79	–1735.20	–10.0
10/23/1987	328.45	–77.88	–19.2	4/14/2000	3321.29	–1125.16	–25.3
9/21/2001	1423.19	–272.19	–16.1	1/21/2022	13768.92	–1124.83	–7.6
10/10/2008	1649.51	–297.88	–15.3	9/6/2024	16690.83	–1022.79	–5.8
3/20/2020	6879.52	–995.36	–12.6	2/28/2020	8567.37	–1009.22	–10.5
11/10/2000	3028.99	–422.59	–12.2	3/20/2020	6879.52	–995.36	–12.6
10/3/2008	1947.39	–235.95	–10.8	4/19/2024	15282.01	–893.08	–5.5
7/28/2000	3663.00	–431.45	–10.5	1/7/2022	14935.90	–709.07	–4.5
2/28/2020	8567.37	–1009.22	–10.5	3/13/2020	7874.88	–700.74	–8.2
4/4/2025	15587.79	–1735.20	–10.0	2/26/2021	13192.35	–682.11	–4.9
RUSSELL 1000 1979 to MAY 2, 2025							
10/10/2008	486.23	–108.31	–18.2	4/4/2025	2772.12	–279.44	–9.2
3/20/2020	1260.69	–227.35	–15.3	3/20/2020	1260.69	–227.35	–15.3
10/23/1987	130.19	–19.25	–12.9	2/28/2020	1635.21	–214.22	–11.6
9/21/2001	507.98	–67.59	–11.7	3/13/2020	1488.04	–153.94	–9.4
2/28/2020	1635.21	–214.22	–11.6	1/21/2022	2427.56	–149.96	–5.8
4/14/2000	715.20	–90.39	–11.2	9/6/2024	2950.08	–132.65	–4.3
10/3/2008	594.54	–65.15	–9.9	6/17/2022	2017.35	–126.66	–5.9
3/13/2020	1488.04	–153.94	–9.4	6/10/2022	2144.01	–114.51	–5.1
4/4/2025	2772.12	–279.44	–9.2	10/30/2020	1825.67	–110.60	–5.7
10/16/1987	149.44	–14.42	–8.8	3/10/2023	2120.53	–109.44	–4.9
RUSSELL 2000 1979 to MAY 2, 2025							
10/23/1987	121.59	–31.15	–20.4	3/13/2020	1210.13	–239.09	–16.5
3/13/2020	1210.13	–239.09	–16.5	2/28/2020	1476.43	–202.18	–12.0
4/14/2000	453.72	–89.27	–16.4	3/20/2020	1013.89	–196.24	–16.2
3/20/2020	1013.89	–196.24	–16.2	4/4/2025	1827.03	–196.24	–9.7
10/10/2008	522.48	–96.92	–15.7	1/21/2022	1987.92	–174.54	–8.1
9/21/2001	378.89	–61.84	–14.0	3/10/2023	1772.70	–155.56	–8.1
10/3/2008	619.40	–85.39	–12.1	8/2/2024	2109.31	–150.76	–6.7
2/28/2020	1476.43	–202.18	–12.0	6/17/2022	1665.69	–134.59	–7.5
11/21/2008	406.54	–49.98	–11.0	9/6/2024	2091.41	–126.22	–5.7
10/24/2008	471.12	–55.31	–10.5	6/12/2020	1387.68	–119.47	–7.9

10 BEST MONTHS BY PERCENT AND POINT

	BY PERCENT CHANGE				BY POINT CHANGE		
MONTH	CLOSE	PNT CHANGE	% CHANGE	MONTH	CLOSE	PNT CHANGE	% CHANGE
DJIA 1901 to 1949							
Apr-1933	77.66	22.26	40.2	Nov-1928	293.38	41.22	16.3
Aug-1932	73.16	18.90	34.8	Jun-1929	333.79	36.38	12.2
Jul-1932	54.26	11.42	26.7	Aug-1929	380.33	32.63	9.4
Jun-1938	133.88	26.14	24.3	Jun-1938	133.88	26.14	24.3
Apr-1915	71.78	10.95	18.0	Aug-1928	240.41	24.41	11.3
Jun-1931	150.18	21.72	16.9	Apr-1933	77.66	22.26	40.2
Nov-1928	293.38	41.22	16.3	Feb-1931	189.66	22.11	13.2
Nov-1904	52.76	6.59	14.3	Jun-1931	150.18	21.72	16.9
May-1919	105.50	12.62	13.6	Aug-1932	73.16	18.90	34.8
Sep-1939	152.54	18.13	13.5	Jan-1930	267.14	18.66	7.5
DJIA 1950 to APRIL 2025							
Jan-1976	975.28	122.87	14.4	Oct-2022	32732.95	4007.44	14.0
Jan-1975	703.69	87.45	14.2	Nov-2024	44910.65	3147.19	7.5
Oct-2022	32732.95	4007.44	14.0	Nov-2020	29638.64	3137.04	11.8
Jan-1987	2158.04	262.09	13.8	Nov-2023	35950.89	2898.02	8.8
Nov-2020	29638.64	3137.04	11.8	Apr-2020	24345.72	2428.56	11.1
Aug-1982	901.31	92.71	11.5	Jul-2022	32845.13	2069.70	6.7
Apr-2020	24345.72	2428.56	11.1	Mar-2021	32981.55	2049.18	6.6
Oct-1982	991.72	95.47	10.7	Aug-2020	28430.05	2001.73	7.6
Oct-2002	8397.03	805.10	10.6	Jan-2025	44544.66	2000.44	4.7
Apr-1978	837.32	79.96	10.6	Oct-2021	35819.56	1975.64	5.8
S&P 500 1930 to APRIL 2025							
Apr-1933	8.32	2.47	42.2	Nov-2023	4567.80	374.00	8.9
Jul-1932	6.10	1.67	37.7	Nov-2020	3621.63	351.67	10.8
Aug-1932	8.39	2.29	37.5	Jul-2022	4130.29	344.91	9.1
Jun-1938	11.56	2.29	24.7	Apr-2020	2912.43	327.84	12.7
Sep-1939	13.02	1.84	16.5	Nov-2023	6032.38	326.93	5.7
Oct-1974	73.90	10.36	16.3	Oct-2021	4605.38	297.84	6.9
May-1933	9.64	1.32	15.9	Oct-2022	3871.98	286.36	8.0
Apr-1938	9.70	1.20	14.1	Jun-2023	4450.38	270.55	6.5
Jun-1931	14.83	1.81	13.9	Feb-2024	5096.27	250.62	5.2
Jan-1987	274.08	31.91	13.2	May-2024	5277.51	241.82	4.8
NASDAQ 1971 to APRIL 2025							
Dec-1999	4069.31	733.15	22.0	Nov-2023	14226.22	1374.98	10.7
Feb-2000	4696.69	756.34	19.2	Jul-2022	12390.69	1361.95	12.4
Oct-1974	65.23	9.56	17.2	Nov-2020	12198.74	1287.15	11.8
Jan-1975	69.78	9.96	16.7	Apr-2020	8889.55	1189.45	15.5
Jun-2000	3966.11	565.20	16.6	Nov-2024	19218.17	1123.02	6.2
Apr-2020	8889.55	1189.45	15.5	Jan-2023	11584.55	1118.07	10.7
Apr-2001	2116.24	275.98	15.0	May-2024	16735.02	1077.20	6.9
Jan-1999	2505.89	313.20	14.3	Oct-2021	15498.39	1049.81	7.3
Nov-2001	1930.58	240.38	14.2	Aug-2020	11775.46	1030.19	9.6
Oct-2002	1329.75	157.69	13.5	Jun-2024	17732.60	997.58	6.0
RUSSELL 1000 1979 to APRIL 2025							
Apr-2020	1601.82	185.33	13.1	Nov-2020	2037.36	211.69	11.6
Jan-1987	146.48	16.48	12.7	Nov-2023	2501.69	209.31	9.1
Nov-2020	2037.36	211.69	11.6	Nov-2024	3317.38	196.57	6.3
Oct-1982	73.34	7.45	11.3	Jul-2022	2267.10	191.14	9.2
Aug-1982	65.14	6.60	11.3	Apr-2020	1601.82	185.33	13.1
Dec-1991	220.61	22.15	11.2	Oct-2021	2583.83	165.67	6.9
Oct-2011	692.41	68.96	11.1	Oct-2022	2128.36	156.07	7.9
Aug-1984	89.87	8.74	10.8	Jun-2023	2436.93	151.28	6.6
Nov-1980	78.26	7.18	10.1	Feb-2024	2795.56	139.12	5.2
Apr-2009	476.84	43.17	10.0	Jan-2023	2244.91	139.01	6.6
RUSSELL 2000 1979 to APRIL 2025							
Nov-2020	1819.82	281.34	18.3	Nov-2020	1819.82	281.34	18.3
Feb-2000	577.71	81.48	16.4	Nov-2024	2434.73	238.08	10.8
Apr-2009	487.56	64.81	15.3	Dec-2023	2027.07	218.05	12.1
Oct-2011	741.06	96.90	15.0	Jul-2024	2254.48	206.79	10.1
Oct-1982	80.86	10.02	14.1	Oct-2022	1846.86	182.14	10.9
Apr-2020	1310.66	157.56	13.7	Jul-2022	1885.23	177.24	10.4
Jan-1985	114.77	13.28	13.1	Jan-2023	1931.95	170.70	9.7
Sep-2010	676.14	74.08	12.3	Apr-2020	1310.66	157.56	13.7
Dec-2023	2027.07	218.05	12.1	Dec-2020	1974.86	155.04	8.5
Aug-1984	106.21	10.96	11.5	Jan-2019	1499.42	150.86	11.2

10 WORST MONTHS BY PERCENT AND POINT

	BY PERCENT CHANGE				BY POINT CHANGE		
MONTH	CLOSE	PNT CHANGE	% CHANGE	MONTH	CLOSE	PNT CHANGE	% CHANGE
DJIA 1901 to 1949							
Sep-1931	96.61	−42.80	−30.7	Oct-1929	273.51	−69.94	−20.4
Mar-1938	98.95	−30.69	−23.7	Jun-1930	226.34	−48.73	−17.7
Apr-1932	56.11	−17.17	−23.4	Sep-1931	96.61	−42.80	−30.7
May-1940	116.22	−32.21	−21.7	Sep-1929	343.45	−36.88	−9.7
Oct-1929	273.51	−69.94	−20.4	Sep-1930	204.90	−35.52	−14.8
May-1932	44.74	−11.37	−20.3	Nov-1929	238.95	−34.56	−12.6
Jun-1930	226.34	−48.73	−17.7	May-1940	116.22	−32.21	−21.7
Dec-1931	77.90	−15.97	−17.0	Mar-1938	98.95	−30.69	−23.7
Feb-1933	51.39	−9.51	−15.6	Sep-1937	154.57	−22.84	−12.9
May-1931	128.46	−22.73	−15.0	May-1931	128.46	−22.73	−15.0
DJIA 1950 to APRIL 2025							
Oct-1987	1993.53	−602.75	−23.2	Mar-2020	21917.16	−3492.20	−13.7
Aug-1998	7539.07	−1344.22	−15.1	Feb-2020	25409.36	−2846.67	−10.1
Oct-2008	9325.01	−1525.65	−14.1	Sep-2022	28725.51	−2784.92	−8.8
Nov-1973	822.25	−134.33	−14.0	Dec-2024	42544.22	−2366.43	−5.3
Mar-2020	21917.16	−3492.20	−13.7	Jun-2022	30775.43	−2214.69	−6.7
Sep-2002	7591.93	−1071.57	−12.4	Dec-2018	23327.46	−2211.00	−8.7
Feb-2009	7062.93	−937.93	−11.7	Apr-2024	37815.92	−1991.45	−5.0
Sep-2001	8847.56	−1102.19	−11.1	Mar-2025	42001.76	−1839.15	−4.2
Sep-1974	607.87	−70.71	−10.4	May-2019	24815.04	−1777.87	−6.7
Aug-1974	678.58	−78.85	−10.4	Apr-2022	32977.21	−1701.14	−4.9
S&P 500 1930 to APRIL 2025							
Sep-1931	9.71	−4.15	−29.9	Apr-2022	4131.93	−398.48	−8.8
Mar-1938	8.50	−2.84	−25.0	Mar-2020	2584.59	−369.63	−12.5
May-1940	9.27	−2.92	−24.0	Sep-2022	3585.62	−369.38	−9.3
May-1932	4.47	−1.36	−23.3	Jun-2022	3785.38	−346.77	−8.4
Oct-1987	251.79	−70.04	−21.8	Mar-2025	5611.85	−342.65	−5.8
Apr-1932	5.83	−1.48	−20.2	Feb-2020	2954.22	−271.30	−8.4
Feb-1933	5.66	−1.28	−18.4	Dec-2018	2506.85	−253.31	−9.2
Oct-2008	968.75	−197.61	−16.9	Jan-2022	4515.55	−250.63	−5.3
Jun-1930	20.46	−4.03	−16.5	Dec-2022	3839.50	−240.61	−5.9
Aug-1998	957.28	−163.39	−14.6	Sep-2023	4288.05	−219.61	−4.9
NASDAQ 1971 to APRIL 2025							
Oct-1987	323.30	−120.99	−27.2	Apr-2022	12334.64	−1885.88	−13.3
Nov-2000	2597.93	−771.70	−22.9	Mar-2025	17299.29	−1547.99	−8.2
Feb-2001	2151.83	−620.90	−22.4	Jan-2022	14239.88	−1405.09	−9.0
Aug-1998	1499.25	−373.14	−19.9	Sep-2022	10575.62	−1240.58	−10.5
Oct-2008	1720.95	−370.93	−17.7	Jun-2022	11028.74	−1052.65	−8.7
Mar-1980	131.00	−27.03	−17.1	Dec-2022	10466.48	−1001.52	−8.7
Sep-2001	1498.80	−306.63	−17.0	Mar-2020	7700.10	−867.27	−10.1
Oct-1978	111.12	−21.77	−16.4	Sep-2023	13219.32	−815.65	−5.8
Apr-2000	3860.66	−712.17	−15.6	Sep-2021	14448.58	−810.66	−5.3
Nov-1973	93.51	−16.66	−15.1	Feb-2025	18847.28	−780.16	−4.0
RUSSELL 1000 1979 to APRIL 2025							
Oct-1987	131.89	−36.94	−21.9	Apr-2022	2276.45	−224.84	−9.0
Oct-2008	522.47	−111.61	−17.6	Mar-2020	1416.49	−218.72	−13.4
Aug-1998	496.66	−88.31	−15.1	Sep-2022	1972.29	−204.16	−9.4
Mar-2020	1416.49	−218.72	−13.4	Jun-2022	2075.96	−193.11	−8.5
Mar-1980	55.79	−7.28	−11.5	Mar-2025	3066.42	−192.65	−5.9
Sep-2002	433.22	−52.86	−10.9	Jan-2022	2494.64	−151.27	−5.7
Feb-2009	399.61	−47.71	−10.7	Feb-2020	1635.21	−148.82	−8.3
Sep-2008	634.08	−68.09	−9.7	Dec-2018	1384.26	−141.30	−9.3
Aug-1990	166.69	−17.63	−9.6	Dec-2022	2105.90	−133.22	−5.9
Feb-2001	654.25	−68.30	−9.5	Apr-2024	2757.14	−124.77	−4.3
RUSSELL 2000 1979 to APRIL 2025							
Oct-1987	118.26	−52.55	−30.8	Mar-2020	1153.10	−323.33	−21.9
Mar-2020	1153.10	−323.33	−21.9	Jan-2022	2028.45	−216.86	−9.7
Oct-2008	537.52	−142.06	−20.9	Apr-2022	1864.10	−206.03	−10.0
Aug-1998	337.95	−81.80	−19.5	Dec-2024	2230.16	−204.57	−8.4
Mar-1980	48.27	−10.95	−18.5	Oct-2018	1511.41	−185.16	−10.9
Jul-2002	392.42	−70.22	−15.2	Dec-2018	1348.56	−184.71	−12.0
Aug-1990	139.52	−21.99	−13.6	Sep-2022	1664.72	−179.40	−9.7
Sep-2001	404.87	−63.69	−13.6	Jun-2022	1707.99	−156.05	−8.4
Feb-2009	389.02	−54.51	−12.3	Mar-2025	2011.91	−151.16	−7.0
Dec-2018	1348.56	−184.71	−12.0	Apr-2024	1973.91	−150.64	−7.1

10 BEST QUARTERS BY PERCENT AND POINT

	BY PERCENT CHANGE			BY POINT CHANGE			
QUARTER	CLOSE	PNT CHANGE	% CHANGE	QUARTER	CLOSE	PNT CHANGE	% CHANGE
DJIA 1901 to 1949							
Jun-1933	98.14	42.74	77.1	Dec-1928	300.00	60.57	25.3
Sep-1932	71.56	28.72	67.0	Jun-1933	98.14	42.74	77.1
Jun-1938	133.88	34.93	35.3	Mar-1930	286.10	37.62	15.1
Sep-1915	90.58	20.52	29.3	Jun-1938	133.88	34.93	35.3
Dec-1928	300.00	60.57	25.3	Sep-1927	197.59	31.36	18.9
Dec-1904	50.99	8.80	20.9	Sep-1928	239.43	28.88	13.7
Jun-1919	106.98	18.13	20.4	Sep-1932	71.56	28.72	67.0
Sep-1927	197.59	31.36	18.9	Jun-1929	333.79	24.94	8.1
Dec-1905	70.47	10.47	17.4	Sep-1939	152.54	21.91	16.8
Jun-1935	118.21	17.40	17.3	Sep-1915	90.58	20.52	29.3
DJIA 1950 to MARCH 2025							
Mar-1975	768.15	151.91	24.7	Dec-2022	33147.25	4421.74	15.4
Mar-1987	2304.69	408.74	21.6	Dec-2023	37689.54	4182.04	12.5
Jun-2020	25812.88	3895.72	17.8	Jun-2020	25812.88	3895.72	17.8
Mar-1986	1818.61	271.94	17.6	Sep-2024	42330.15	3211.29	8.2
Mar-1976	999.45	147.04	17.3	Dec-2020	30606.48	2824.78	10.2
Dec-1998	9181.43	1338.81	17.1	Mar-2019	25928.68	2601.22	11.2
Dec-1982	1046.54	150.29	16.8	Dec-2021	36338.30	2494.38	7.4
Jun-1997	7672.79	1089.31	16.6	Mar-2021	32981.55	2375.07	7.8
Dec-1985	1546.67	218.04	16.4	Dec-2017	24719.22	2314.13	10.3
Dec-2022	33147.25	4421.74	15.4	Sep-2018	26458.31	2186.90	9.0
S&P 500 1930 to MARCH 2025							
Jun-1933	10.91	5.06	86.5	Jun-2020	3100.29	515.70	20.0
Sep-1932	8.08	3.65	82.4	Mar-2024	5254.35	484.52	10.2
Jun-1938	11.56	3.06	36.0	Dec-2023	4769.83	481.78	11.2
Mar-1975	83.36	14.80	21.6	Dec-2021	4766.18	458.64	10.7
Dec-1998	1229.23	212.22	20.9	Dec-2020	3756.07	393.07	11.7
Jun-1935	10.23	1.76	20.8	Jun-2023	4450.38	341.07	8.3
Mar-1987	291.70	49.53	20.5	Mar-2019	2834.40	327.55	13.1
Jun-2020	3100.29	515.70	20.0	Jun-2021	4297.50	324.61	8.2
Sep-1939	13.02	2.16	19.9	Sep-2024	5762.48	302.00	5.5
Mar-1943	11.58	1.81	18.5	Mar-2023	4109.31	269.81	7.0
NASDAQ 1971 to MARCH 2025							
Dec-1999	4069.31	1323.15	48.2	Jun-2020	10058.77	2358.67	30.6
Jun-2020	10058.77	2358.67	30.6	Dec-2023	15011.35	1792.03	13.6
Dec-2001	1950.40	451.60	30.1	Mar-2023	12221.91	1755.43	16.8
Dec-1998	2192.69	498.85	29.5	Dec-2020	12888.28	1720.77	15.4
Mar-1991	482.30	108.46	29.0	Jun-2023	13787.92	1566.01	12.8
Mar-1975	75.66	15.84	26.5	Mar-2024	16379.46	1368.11	9.1
Dec-1982	232.41	44.76	23.9	Jun-2024	17732.60	1353.14	8.3
Mar-1987	430.05	80.72	23.1	Dec-1999	4069.31	1323.15	48.2
Jun-2003	1622.80	281.63	21.0	Jun-2021	14503.95	1257.08	9.5
Jun-1980	157.78	26.78	20.4	Dec-2021	15644.97	1196.39	8.3
RUSSELL 1000 1979 to MARCH 2025							
Dec-1998	642.87	113.76	21.5	Jun-2020	1717.47	300.98	21.3
Jun-2020	1717.47	300.98	21.3	Dec-2023	2622.14	270.79	11.5
Mar-1987	155.20	25.20	19.4	Mar-2024	2881.91	259.77	9.9
Dec-1982	77.24	11.35	17.2	Dec-2020	2120.87	248.17	13.3
Jun-1997	462.95	64.76	16.3	Dec-2021	2645.91	227.75	9.4
Dec-1985	114.39	15.64	15.8	Mar-2019	1570.23	185.97	13.4
Jun-2009	502.27	68.60	15.8	Jun-2023	2436.93	183.57	8.2
Dec-1999	767.97	104.14	15.7	Jun-2021	2421.14	182.97	8.2
Sep-2009	579.97	77.70	15.5	Sep-2024	3145.06	170.42	5.7
Jun-2003	518.94	68.59	15.2	Sep-2020	1872.70	155.23	9.0
RUSSELL 2000 1979 to MARCH 2025							
Dec-2020	1974.86	467.17	31.0	Dec-2020	1974.86	467.17	31.0
Mar-1991	171.01	38.85	29.4	Jun-2020	1441.37	288.27	25.0
Dec-1982	88.90	18.06	25.5	Mar-2021	2220.52	245.66	12.4
Jun-2020	1441.37	288.27	25.0	Dec-2023	2027.07	241.97	13.6
Mar-1987	166.79	31.79	23.6	Mar-2019	1539.74	191.18	14.2
Jun-2003	448.37	83.83	23.0	Sep-2024	2229.97	182.28	8.9
Sep-1980	69.94	12.47	21.7	Dec-2019	1668.47	145.10	9.5
Dec-2001	488.50	83.63	20.7	Jun-2018	1643.07	113.64	7.4
Jun-2009	508.28	85.53	20.2	Dec-2010	783.65	107.51	15.9
Jun-1983	124.17	20.40	19.7	Dec-2016	1357.13	105.48	8.4

10 WORST QUARTERS BY PERCENT AND POINT

	BY PERCENT CHANGE				BY POINT CHANGE		
QUARTER	CLOSE	PNT CHANGE	% CHANGE	QUARTER	CLOSE	PNT CHANGE	% CHANGE
			DJIA 1901 to 1949				
Jun-1932	42.84	–30.44	–41.5	Dec-1929	248.48	–94.97	–27.7
Sep-1931	96.61	–53.57	–35.7	Jun-1930	226.34	–59.76	–20.9
Dec-1929	248.48	–94.97	–27.7	Sep-1931	96.61	–53.57	–35.7
Sep-1903	33.55	–9.73	–22.5	Dec-1930	164.58	–40.32	–19.7
Dec-1937	120.85	–33.72	–21.8	Dec-1937	120.85	–33.72	–21.8
Jun-1930	226.34	–59.76	–20.9	Sep-1946	172.42	–33.20	–16.1
Dec-1930	164.58	–40.32	–19.7	Jun-1932	42.84	–30.44	–41.5
Dec-1931	77.90	–18.71	–19.4	Jun-1940	121.87	–26.08	–17.6
Mar-1938	98.95	–21.90	–18.1	Mar-1939	131.84	–22.92	–14.8
Jun-1940	121.87	–26.08	–17.6	Dec-1931	150.18	–22.18	–12.9
			DJIA 1950 to MARCH 2025				
Dec-1987	1938.83	–657.45	–25.3	Mar-2020	21917.16	–6621.28	–23.2
Sep-1974	607.87	–194.54	–24.2	Jun-2022	30775.43	–3902.92	–11.3
Mar-2020	21917.16	–6621.28	–23.2	Dec-2018	23327.46	–3130.85	–11.8
Jun-1962	561.28	–145.67	–20.6	Dec-2008	8776.39	–2074.27	–19.1
Dec-2008	8776.39	–2074.27	–19.1	Sep-2022	28725.51	–2049.92	–6.7
Sep-2002	7591.93	–1651.33	–17.9	Mar-2022	34678.35	–1659.95	–4.6
Sep-2001	8847.56	–1654.84	–15.8	Sep-2001	8847.56	–1654.84	–15.8
Sep-1990	2452.48	–428.21	–14.9	Sep-2002	7591.93	–1651.33	–17.9
Mar-2009	7608.92	–1167.47	–13.3	Sep-2011	10913.38	–1500.96	–12.1
Sep-1981	849.98	–126.90	–13.0	Sep-2015	16284.00	–1335.51	–7.6
			S&P 500 1930 to MARCH 2025				
Jun-1932	4.43	–2.88	–39.4	Jun-2022	3785.38	–745.03	–16.4
Sep-1931	9.71	–5.12	–34.5	Mar-2020	2584.59	–646.19	–20.0
Sep-1974	63.54	–22.46	–26.1	Dec-2018	2506.85	–407.13	–14.0
Dec-1937	10.55	–3.21	–23.3	Mar-2025	5611.85	–269.78	–4.6
Dec-1987	247.08	–74.75	–23.2	Dec-2008	903.25	–263.11	–22.6
Dec-2008	903.25	–263.11	–22.6	Mar-2022	4530.41	–235.77	–4.9
Jun-1962	54.75	–14.80	–21.3	Sep-2022	3585.62	–199.76	–5.3
Mar-2020	2584.59	–646.19	–20.0	Sep-2011	1131.42	–189.22	–14.3
Mar-1938	8.50	–2.05	–19.4	Sep-2001	1040.94	–183.48	–15.0
Jun-1970	72.72	–16.91	–18.9	Sep-2002	815.28	–174.54	–17.6
			NASDAQ 1971 to MARCH 2025				
Dec-2000	2470.52	–1202.30	–32.7	Jun-2022	11028.74	–3191.78	–22.4
Sep-2001	1498.80	–661.74	–30.6	Mar-2025	17299.29	–2011.50	–10.4
Sep-1974	55.67	–20.29	–26.7	Mar-2022	14220.52	–1424.45	–9.1
Dec-1987	330.47	–113.82	–25.6	Dec-2018	6635.28	–1411.07	–17.5
Mar-2001	1840.26	–630.26	–25.5	Mar-2020	7700.10	–1272.50	–14.2
Sep-1990	344.51	–117.78	–25.5	Dec-2000	2470.52	–1202.30	–32.7
Dec-2008	1577.03	–514.85	–24.6	Sep-2001	1498.80	–661.74	–30.6
Jun-2022	11028.74	–3191.78	–22.4	Mar-2001	1840.26	–630.26	–25.5
Jun-2002	1463.21	–382.14	–20.7	Jun-2000	3966.11	–606.72	–13.3
Sep-2002	1172.06	–291.15	–19.9	Sep-2023	13219.32	–568.60	–4.1
			RUSSELL 1000 1979 to MARCH 2025				
Dec-2008	487.77	–146.31	–23.1	Jun-2022	2075.96	–425.33	–17.0
Dec-1987	130.02	–38.81	–23.0	Mar-2020	1416.49	–367.72	–20.6
Mar-2020	1416.49	–367.72	–20.6	Dec-2018	1384.26	–230.28	–14.3
Sep-2002	433.22	–90.50	–17.3	Mar-2025	3066.42	–154.63	–4.8
Jun-2022	2075.96	–425.33	–17.0	Dec-2008	487.77	–146.31	–23.1
Sep-2001	546.46	–100.18	–15.5	Mar-2022	2501.29	–144.62	–5.5
Sep-1990	157.83	–28.46	–15.3	Sep-2011	623.45	–111.03	–15.1
Sep-2011	623.45	–111.03	–15.1	Sep-2022	1972.29	–103.67	–5.0
Dec-2018	1384.26	–230.28	–14.3	Sep-2001	546.46	–100.18	–15.5
Jun-2002	523.72	–83.63	–13.8	Sep-2002	433.22	–90.50	–17.3
			RUSSELL 2000 1979 to MARCH 2025				
Mar-2020	1153.10	–515.37	–30.9	Mar-2020	1153.10	–515.37	–30.9
Dec-1987	120.42	–50.39	–29.5	Jun-2022	1707.99	–362.14	–17.5
Dec-2008	499.45	–180.13	–26.5	Dec-2018	1348.56	–348.01	–20.5
Sep-1990	126.70	–42.34	–25.0	Mar-2025	2011.91	–218.25	–9.8
Sep-2011	644.16	–183.27	–22.1	Sep-2011	644.16	–183.27	–22.1
Sep-2002	362.27	–100.37	–21.7	Dec-2008	499.45	–180.13	–26.5
Sep-2001	404.87	–107.77	–21.0	Mar-2022	2070.13	–175.18	–7.8
Dec-2018	1348.56	–348.01	–20.5	Sep-2015	1100.69	–153.26	–12.2
Sep-1998	363.59	–93.80	–20.5	Sep-2001	404.87	–107.77	–21.0
Sep-1981	67.55	–15.01	–18.2	Sep-2021	2204.37	–106.18	–4.6

10 **BEST** YEARS BY PERCENT AND POINT

	BY PERCENT CHANGE				BY POINT CHANGE		
YEAR	CLOSE	PNT CHANGE	% CHANGE	YEAR	CLOSE	PNT CHANGE	% CHANGE
			DJIA 1901 to 1949				
1915	99.15	44.57	81.7	1928	300.00	97.60	48.2
1933	99.90	39.97	66.7	1927	202.40	45.20	28.8
1928	300.00	97.60	48.2	1915	99.15	44.57	81.7
1908	63.11	20.07	46.6	1945	192.91	40.59	26.6
1904	50.99	15.01	41.7	1935	144.13	40.09	38.5
1935	144.13	40.09	38.5	1933	99.90	39.97	66.7
1905	70.47	19.48	38.2	1925	156.66	36.15	30.0
1919	107.23	25.03	30.5	1936	179.90	35.77	24.8
1925	156.66	36.15	30.0	1938	154.76	33.91	28.1
1927	202.40	45.20	28.8	1919	107.23	25.03	30.5
			DJIA 1950 to 2024				
1954	404.39	123.49	44.0	2021	36338.30	5731.82	18.7
1975	852.41	236.17	38.3	2019	28538.44	5210.98	22.3
1958	583.65	147.96	34.0	2017	24719.22	4956.62	25.1
1995	5117.12	1282.68	33.5	2024	42544.22	4854.68	12.9
1985	1546.67	335.10	27.7	2023	37689.54	4542.29	13.7
1989	2753.20	584.63	27.0	2013	16576.66	3472.52	26.5
2013	16576.66	3472.52	26.5	2016	19762.60	2337.57	13.4
1996	6448.27	1331.15	26.0	1999	11497.12	2315.69	25.2
2003	10453.92	2112.29	25.3	2003	10453.92	2112.29	25.3
1999	11497.12	2315.69	25.2	2020	30606.48	2068.04	7.3
			S&P 500 1930 to 2024				
1933	10.10	3.21	46.6	2024	5881.63	1111.80	23.3
1954	35.98	1.17	45.0	2021	4766.18	1010.11	26.9
1935	13.43	3.93	41.4	2023	4769.83	930.33	24.2
1958	55.21	15.22	38.1	2019	3230.78	723.93	28.9
1995	615.93	156.66	34.1	2020	3756.07	525.29	16.3
1975	90.19	21.63	31.5	2017	2673.61	434.78	19.4
1997	970.43	229.69	31.0	2013	1848.36	422.17	29.6
1945	17.36	4.08	30.7	1998	1229.23	258.80	26.7
2013	1848.36	422.17	29.6	1999	1469.25	240.02	19.5
2019	3230.78	723.93	28.9	2003	1111.92	232.10	26.4
			NASDAQ 1971 to 2024				
1999	4069.31	1876.62	85.6	2023	15011.35	4544.87	43.4
1991	586.34	212.50	56.8	2024	19310.79	4299.44	28.6
2003	2003.37	667.86	50.0	2020	12888.28	3915.68	43.6
2009	2269.15	692.12	43.9	2021	15644.97	2756.69	21.4
2020	12888.28	3915.68	43.6	2019	8972.60	2337.32	35.2
2023	15011.35	4544.87	43.4	1999	4069.31	1876.62	85.6
1995	1052.13	300.17	39.9	2017	6903.39	1520.27	28.2
1998	2192.69	622.34	39.6	2013	4176.59	1157.08	38.3
2013	4176.59	1157.08	38.3	2009	2269.15	692.12	43.9
2019	8972.60	2337.32	35.2	2003	2003.37	667.86	50.0
			RUSSELL 1000 1979 to 2024				
1995	328.89	84.24	34.4	2024	3221.05	598.91	22.8
1997	513.79	120.04	30.5	2021	2645.91	525.04	24.8
2013	1030.36	240.46	30.4	2023	2622.14	516.24	24.5
2019	1784.21	399.95	28.9	2019	1784.21	399.95	28.9
1991	220.61	49.39	28.9	2020	2120.87	336.66	18.9
2003	594.56	128.38	27.5	2013	1030.36	240.46	30.4
1985	114.39	24.08	26.7	2017	1481.81	240.15	19.3
1989	185.11	38.12	25.9	1998	642.87	129.08	25.1
1980	75.20	15.33	25.6	2003	594.56	128.38	27.5
2009	612.01	124.24	25.5	1999	767.97	125.10	19.5
			RUSSELL 2000 1979 to 2024				
2003	556.91	173.82	45.4	2019	1668.47	319.91	23.7
1991	189.94	57.78	43.7	2013	1163.64	314.29	37.0
1979	55.91	15.39	38.0	2020	1974.86	306.39	18.4
2013	1163.64	314.29	37.0	2021	2245.31	270.45	13.7
1980	74.80	18.89	33.8	2023	2027.07	265.82	15.1
1985	129.87	28.38	28.0	2016	1357.13	221.24	19.5
1983	112.27	23.37	26.3	2024	2230.16	203.09	10.0
1995	315.97	65.61	26.2	2017	1535.51	178.38	13.1
2010	783.65	158.26	25.3	2003	556.91	173.82	45.4
2009	625.39	125.94	25.2	2010	783.65	158.26	25.3

10 WORST YEARS BY PERCENT AND POINT

	BY PERCENT CHANGE				BY POINT CHANGE		
YEAR	CLOSE	PNT CHANGE	% CHANGE	YEAR	CLOSE	PNT CHANGE	% CHANGE
			DJIA 1901 to 1949				
1931	77.90	−86.68	−52.7	1931	77.90	−86.68	−52.7
1907	43.04	−26.08	−37.7	1930	164.58	−83.90	−33.8
1930	164.58	−83.90	−33.8	1937	120.85	−59.05	−32.8
1920	71.95	−35.28	−32.9	1929	248.48	−51.52	−17.2
1937	120.85	−59.05	−32.8	1920	71.95	−35.28	−32.9
1903	35.98	−11.12	−23.6	1907	43.04	−26.08	−37.7
1932	59.93	−17.97	−23.1	1917	74.38	−20.62	−21.7
1917	74.38	−20.62	−21.7	1941	110.96	−20.17	−15.4
1910	59.60	−12.96	−17.9	1940	131.13	−19.11	−12.7
1929	248.48	−51.52	−17.2	1932	59.93	−17.97	−23.1
			DJIA 1950 to 2024				
2008	8776.39	−4488.43	−33.8	2008	8776.39	−4488.43	−33.8
1974	616.24	−234.62	−27.6	2022	33147.25	−3191.05	−8.8
1966	785.69	−183.57	−18.9	2002	8341.63	−1679.87	−16.8
1977	831.17	−173.48	−17.3	2018	23327.46	−1391.76	−5.6
2002	8341.63	−1679.87	−16.8	2001	10021.50	−765.35	−7.1
1973	850.86	−169.16	−16.6	2000	10786.85	−710.27	−6.2
1969	800.36	−143.39	−15.2	2015	17425.03	−398.04	−2.2
1957	435.69	−63.78	−12.8	1974	616.24	−234.62	−27.6
1962	652.10	−79.04	−10.8	1966	785.69	−183.57	−18.9
1960	615.89	−63.47	−9.3	1977	831.17	−173.48	−17.3
			S&P 500 1930 to 2024				
1931	8.12	−7.22	−47.1	2022	3839.50	−926.68	−19.4
1937	10.55	−6.63	−38.6	2008	903.25	−565.11	−38.5
2008	903.25	−565.11	−38.5	2002	879.82	−268.26	−23.4
1974	68.56	−28.99	−29.7	2001	1148.08	−172.20	−13.0
1930	15.34	−6.11	−28.5	2018	2506.85	−166.76	−6.2
2002	879.82	−268.26	−23.4	2000	1320.28	−148.97	−10.1
2022	3839.50	−926.68	−19.4	1974	68.56	−28.99	−29.7
1941	8.69	−1.89	−17.9	1990	330.22	−23.18	−6.6
1973	97.55	−20.50	−17.4	1973	97.55	−20.50	−17.4
1940	10.58	−1.91	−15.3	2015	2043.94	−14.96	−0.7
			NASDAQ 1971 to 2024				
2008	1577.03	−1075.25	−40.5	2022	10466.48	−5178.49	−33.1
2000	2470.52	−1598.79	−39.3	2000	2470.52	−1598.79	−39.3
1974	59.82	−32.37	−35.1	2008	1577.03	−1075.25	−40.5
2022	10466.48	−5178.49	−33.1	2002	1335.51	−614.89	−31.5
2002	1335.51	−614.89	−31.5	2001	1950.40	−520.12	−21.1
1973	92.19	−41.54	−31.1	2018	6635.28	−268.11	−3.9
2001	1950.40	−520.12	−21.1	1990	373.84	−80.98	−17.8
1990	373.84	−80.98	−17.8	2011	2605.15	−47.72	−1.8
1984	247.35	−31.25	−11.2	1973	92.19	−41.54	−31.1
1987	330.47	−18.86	−5.4	1974	59.82	−32.37	−35.1
			RUSSELL 1000 1979 to 2024				
2008	487.77	−312.05	−39.0	2022	2105.90	−540.01	−20.4
2002	466.18	−138.76	−22.9	2008	487.77	−312.05	−39.0
2022	2105.90	−540.01	−20.4	2002	466.18	−138.76	−22.9
2001	604.94	−95.15	−13.6	2018	1384.26	−97.55	−6.6
1981	67.93	−7.27	−9.7	2001	604.94	−95.15	−13.6
2000	700.09	−67.88	−8.8	2000	700.09	−67.88	−8.8
1990	171.22	−13.89	−7.5	1990	171.22	−13.89	−7.5
2018	1384.26	−97.55	−6.6	2015	1131.88	−12.49	−1.1
1994	244.65	−6.06	−2.4	1981	67.93	−7.27	−9.7
2015	1131.88	−12.49	−1.1	1994	244.65	−6.06	−2.4
			RUSSELL 2000 1979 to 2024				
2008	499.45	−266.58	−34.8	2022	1761.25	−484.06	−21.6
2002	383.09	−105.41	−21.6	2008	499.45	−266.58	−34.8
2022	1761.25	−484.06	−21.6	2018	1348.56	−186.95	−12.2
1990	132.16	−36.14	−21.5	2002	383.09	−105.41	−21.6
2018	1348.56	−186.95	−12.2	2015	1135.89	−68.81	−5.7
1987	120.42	−14.58	−10.8	2011	740.92	−42.73	−5.5
1984	101.49	−10.78	−9.6	1990	132.16	−36.14	−21.5
2015	1135.89	−68.81	−5.7	2007	766.03	−21.63	−2.7
2011	740.92	−42.73	−5.5	2000	483.53	−21.22	−4.2
2000	483.53	−21.22	−4.2	1998	421.96	−15.06	−3.4

STRATEGY PLANNING AND RECORD SECTION

CONTENTS

- 185   Portfolio at Start of 2026
- 186   Additional Purchases
- 188   Short-Term Transactions
- 190   Long-Term Transactions
- 192   Interest/Dividends Received During 2026/Brokerage Account Data 2026
- 193   Weekly Portfolio Price Record 2026
- 195   Weekly Indicator Data 2026
- 197   Monthly Indicator Data 2026
- 198   Portfolio at End of 2026
- 199   If You Don't Profit from Your Investment Mistakes, Someone Else Will; Performance Record of Recommendations
- 200   Individual Retirement Accounts: Most Awesome Investment Incentive Ever Devised
- 201   G.M. Loeb's "Battle Plan" for Investment Survival
- 202   G.M. Loeb's Investment Survival Checklist

These forms are available at our website, www.stocktradersalmanac.com under "Forms" located at the bottom of the homepage.

PORTFOLIO AT START OF 2026

DATE ACQUIRED	NO. OF SHARES	SECURITY	PRICE	TOTAL COST	PAPER PROFITS	PAPER LOSSES

ADDITIONAL PURCHASES

DATE ACQUIRED	NO. OF SHARES	SECURITY	PRICE	TOTAL COST	REASON FOR PURCHASE PRIME OBJECTIVE, ETC.

ADDITIONAL PURCHASES

DATE ACQUIRED	NO. OF SHARES	SECURITY	PRICE	TOTAL COST	REASON FOR PURCHASE PRIME OBJECTIVE, ETC.

SHORT-TERM TRANSACTIONS

Pages 188–191 can accompany next year's income tax return (Schedule D). Enter transactions as completed to avoid last-minute pressures.

NO. OF SHARES	SECURITY	DATE ACQUIRED	DATE SOLD	SALE PRICE	COST	LOSS	GAIN	TOTALS: Carry over to next page

SHORT-TERM TRANSACTIONS (continued)

NO. OF SHARES	SECURITY	DATE ACQUIRED	DATE SOLD	SALE PRICE	COST	LOSS	GAIN
TOTALS:							

LONG-TERM TRANSACTIONS

Pages 188–191 can accompany next year's income tax return (Schedule D). Enter transactions as completed to avoid last-minute pressures.

NO. OF SHARES	SECURITY	DATE ACQUIRED	DATE SOLD	SALE PRICE	COST	LOSS	GAIN

TOTALS: Carry over to next page

LONG-TERM TRANSACTIONS *(continued)*

NO. OF SHARES	SECURITY	DATE ACQUIRED	DATE SOLD	SALE PRICE	COST	LOSS	GAIN
TOTALS:							

INTEREST/DIVIDENDS RECEIVED DURING 2026

SHARES	STOCK/BOND	FIRST QUARTER	SECOND QUARTER	THIRD QUARTER	FOURTH QUARTER
		$	$	$	$

BROKERAGE ACCOUNT DATA 2026

	MARGIN INTEREST	TRANSFER TAXES	CAPITAL ADDED	CAPITAL WITHDRAWN
JAN				
FEB				
MAR				
APR				
MAY				
JUN				
JUL				
AUG				
SEP				
OCT				
NOV				
DEC				

WEEKLY PORTFOLIO PRICE RECORD 2026 (FIRST HALF)

Place purchase price above stock name and weekly closes below.

STOCKS										
Week Ending	1	2	3	4	5	6	7	8	9	10

JANUARY
Week Ending	1	2	3	4	5	6	7	8	9	10
2										
9										
16										
23										
30										

FEBRUARY
Week Ending	1	2	3	4	5	6	7	8	9	10
6										
13										
20										
27										

MARCH
Week Ending	1	2	3	4	5	6	7	8	9	10
6										
13										
20										
27										

APRIL
Week Ending	1	2	3	4	5	6	7	8	9	10
3										
10										
17										
24										

MAY
Week Ending	1	2	3	4	5	6	7	8	9	10
1										
8										
15										
22										
29										

JUNE
Week Ending	1	2	3	4	5	6	7	8	9	10
5										
12										
19										
26										

WEEKLY PORTFOLIO PRICE RECORD 2026 (SECOND HALF)

Place purchase price above stock name and weekly closes below.

STOCKS Week Ending	1	2	3	4	5	6	7	8	9	10
JULY 3										
10										
17										
24										
31										
AUGUST 7										
14										
21										
28										
SEPTEMBER 4										
11										
18										
25										
OCTOBER 2										
9										
16										
23										
30										
NOVEMBER 6										
13										
20										
27										
DECEMBER 4										
11										
18										
25										

WEEKLY INDICATOR DATA 2026 (FIRST HALF)

Week Ending	Dow Jones Industrial Average	Net Change for Week	Net Change on Friday	Net Change Next Monday	S&P or NASDAQ	NYSE Advances	NYSE Declines	New Highs	New Lows	CBOE Put/Call Ratio	90-Day Treas. Rate	Moody's AAA Rate
JANUARY												
2												
9												
16												
23												
30												
FEBRUARY												
6												
13												
20												
27												
MARCH												
6												
13												
20												
27												
APRIL												
3												
10												
17												
24												
MAY												
1												
8												
15												
22												
29												
JUNE												
5												
12												
19												
26												

WEEKLY INDICATOR DATA 2026 (SECOND HALF)

	Week Ending	Dow Jones Industrial Average	Net Change for Week	Net Change on Friday	Net Change Next Monday	S&P or NASDAQ	NYSE Advances	NYSE Declines	New Highs	New Lows	CBOE Put/Call Ratio	90-Day Treas. Rate	Moody's AAA Rate
JULY	3												
	10												
	17												
	24												
	31												
AUGUST	7												
	14												
	21												
	28												
SEPTEMBER	4												
	11												
	18												
	25												
OCTOBER	2												
	9												
	16												
	23												
	30												
NOVEMBER	6												
	13												
	20												
	27												
DECEMBER	4												
	11												
	18												
	25												

MONTHLY INDICATOR DATA 2026

	DJIA% Last 3 + 1st 2 Days	DJIA% 9th to 11th Trading Days	DJIA% Change Rest of Month	DJIA% Change Whole Month	% Change Your Stocks	Gross Domestic Product	Prime Rate	Trade Deficit $ Billion	CPI % Change	% Unem- ployment Rate
JAN										
FEB										
MAR										
APR										
MAY										
JUN										
JUL										
AUG										
SEP										
OCT										
NOV										
DEC										

INSTRUCTIONS:

Weekly Indicator Data (pages 195–196). Keeping data on several indicators may give you a better feel of the market. In addition to the closing Dow and its net change for the week, post the net change for Friday's Dow and also the following Monday's. A series of "down Fridays" followed by "down Mondays" often precedes a downswing (see page 78). Tracking either the S&P or NASDAQ composite, and advances and declines, will help prevent the Dow from misleading you. New highs and lows and put/call ratios (www.cboe.com) are also useful indicators. Many of these weekly figures appear in weekend papers or *Barron's* (https://www.barrons.com/market-data/market-lab). Data for the 90-day Treasury Rate and 30-year Treasury Rate are quite important for tracking short- and long-term interest rates. These figures are available from:

https://fred.stlouisfed.org/

Monthly Indicator Data. The purpose of the first three columns is to enable you to track the market's bullish bias near the end, beginning and middle of the month, which has been shifting lately (see pages 72, 147, and 148). Market direction, performance of your stocks, gross domestic product, prime rate, trade deficit, Consumer Price Index, and unemployment rate are worthwhile indicators to follow. Or, readers may wish to gauge other data.

PORTFOLIO AT END OF 2026

DATE ACQUIRED	NO. OF SHARES	SECURITY	PRICE	TOTAL COST	PAPER PROFITS	PAPER LOSSES

IF YOU DON'T PROFIT FROM YOUR INVESTMENT MISTAKES, SOMEONE ELSE WILL

No matter how much we may deny it, almost every successful person on Wall Street pays a great deal of attention to trading suggestions—especially when they come from "the right sources."

One of the hardest things to learn is to distinguish between good tips and bad ones. Usually, the best tips have a logical reason behind them, which accompanies the tip. Poor tips usually have no reason to support them.

The important thing to remember is that the market discounts. It does not review, it does not reflect. The Street's real interest in "tips," inside information, buying and selling suggestions, and everything else of this kind emanates from a desire to find out just what the market has on hand to discount. The process of finding out involves separating the wheat from the chaff—and there is plenty of chaff.

HOW TO MAKE USE OF STOCK "TIPS"

- The source should be **reliable**. (By listing all "tips" and suggestions on a Performance Record of Recommendations, such as the form below, and then periodically evaluating the outcomes, you will soon know the "batting average" of your sources.)
- The story should make sense. Would the merger violate antitrust laws? Are there too many computers on the market already? How many years will it take to become profitable?
- The stock should not have had a recent sharp run-up. Otherwise, the story may already be discounted, and confirmation or denial in the press would most likely be accompanied by a sell-off in the stock.

PERFORMANCE RECORD OF RECOMMENDATIONS

STOCK RECOMMENDED	BY WHOM	DATE	PRICE	REASON FOR RECOMMENDATION	SUBSEQUENT ACTION OF STOCK

INDIVIDUAL RETIREMENT ACCOUNTS: MOST AWESOME INVESTMENT INCENTIVE EVER DEVISED

MAX IRA INVESTMENTS OF $7,000* A YEAR COMPOUNDED AT VARIOUS INTEREST RATES OF RETURN FOR DIFFERENT PERIODS

Annual Rate	5 Yrs	10 Yrs	15 Yrs	20 Yrs	25 Yrs	30 Yrs	35 Yrs	40 Yrs	45 Yrs	50 Yrs
1%	$36,064	$73,968	$113,805	$155,674	$199,679	$245,929	$294,538	$345,627	$399,321	$455,755
2%	37,157	78,181	123,475	173,483	228,696	289,656	356,961	431,270	513,314	603,897
3%	38,279	82,655	134,098	193,735	262,871	343,019	435,932	543,643	668,510	813,265
4%	39,431	87,404	145,772	216,784	303,182	408,298	536,188	691,786	881,094	1,111,416
5%	40,613	92,448	158,602	243,035	350,794	488,326	663,854	887,878	1,173,796	1,538,708
6%	41,827	97,801	172,708	272,949	407,095	586,612	826,846	1,148,334	1,578,557	2,154,292
7%	43,073	103,485	188,216	307,056	473,735	707,511	1,035,394	1,495,267	2,140,262	3,044,902
8%	44,352	109,518	205,270	345,960	552,681	856,421	1,302,715	1,958,467	2,921,982	4,337,702
9%	45,663	115,922	224,024	390,352	646,268	1,040,027	1,645,873	2,578,043	4,012,302	6,219,088
10%	47,009	122,718	244,648	441,017	757,272	1,266,604	2,086,888	3,407,963	5,535,567	8,962,096
11%	48,390	129,930	267,330	498,856	888,991	1,546,392	2,654,151	4,520,789	7,666,182	12,966,352
12%	49,806	137,582	292,273	564,891	1,045,338	1,892,048	3,384,242	6,013,997	10,648,523	18,816,143
13%	51,259	145,700	319,702	640,289	1,230,951	2,319,206	4,324,245	8,018,401	14,824,642	27,364,701
14%	52,749	154,312	349,862	726,379	1,451,329	2,847,159	5,534,710	10,709,360	20,672,707	39,856,280
15%	54,276	163,445	383,022	824,671	1,712,984	3,499,698	7,093,420	14,321,677	28,860,284	58,102,616
16%	55,842	173,130	419,475	936,884	2,023,618	4,306,131	9,100,189	19,169,349	40,318,024	84,737,468
17%	57,448	183,400	459,542	1,064,970	2,392,339	5,302,526	11,682,961	25,671,734	56,341,390	123,583,019
18%	59,094	194,286	503,573	1,211,147	2,829,905	6,533,230	15,005,542	34,388,140	78,730,827	180,176,154
19%	60,781	205,825	551,951	1,377,932	3,349,014	8,052,712	19,277,400	46,063,475	109,984,524	262,522,752
20%	62,509	218,053	605,095	1,568,179	3,964,641	9,927,805	24,766,066	61,688,406	153,563,003	382,176,402

* At Press Time - 2026 Contribution Limit will be indexed to inflation

G. M. LOEB'S "BATTLE PLAN" FOR INVESTMENT SURVIVAL

LIFE IS CHANGE: Nothing can ever be the same a minute from now as it was a minute ago. Everything you own is changing in price and value. You can find that last price of an active security on the stock ticker, but you cannot find the next price anywhere. The value of your money is changing. Even the value of your home is changing, though no one walks in front of it with a sandwich board consistently posting the changes.

RECOGNIZE CHANGE: Your basic objective should be to profit from change. The art of investing is being able to recognize change and to adjust investment goals accordingly.

WRITE THINGS DOWN: You will score more investment success and avoid more investment failures if you write things down. Very few investors have the drive and inclination to do this.

KEEP A CHECKLIST: If you aim to improve your investment results, get into the habit of keeping a checklist on every issue you consider buying. Before making a commitment, it will pay you to write down the answers to at least some of the basic questions—How much am I investing in this company? How much do I think I can make? How much do I have to risk? How long do I expect to take to reach my goal?

HAVE A SINGLE RULING REASON: Above all, writing things down is the best way to find "the ruling reason." When all is said and done, there is invariably a single reason that stands out above all others, why a particular security transaction can be expected to show a profit. All too often, many relatively unimportant statistics are allowed to obscure this single important point.

Any one of a dozen factors may be the point of a particular purchase or sale. It could be a technical reason—an increase in earnings or dividend not yet discounted in the market price—a change of management—a promising new product—an expected improvement in the market's valuation of earnings—or many others. But, in any given case, one of these factors will almost certainly be more important than all the rest put together.

CLOSING OUT A COMMITMENT: If you have a loss, the solution is automatic, provided you decide what to do at the time you buy. Otherwise, the question divides itself into two parts. Are we in a bull or bear market? Few of us really know until it is too late. For the sake of the record, if you think it is a bear market, just put that consideration first and sell as much as your conviction suggests and your nature allows.

If you think it is a bull market, or at least a market where some stocks move up, some mark time and only a few decline, do not sell unless:

- ✓ You see a bear market ahead.
- ✓ You see trouble for a particular company in which you own shares.
- ✓ Time and circumstances have turned up a new and seemingly far better buy than the issue you like least in your list.
- ✓ Your shares stop going up and start going down.

A subsidiary question is, which stock to sell first? Two further observations may help:

- ✓ Do not sell solely because you think a stock is "overvalued."
- ✓ If you want to sell some of your stocks and not all, in most cases it is better to go against your emotional inclinations and sell first the issues with losses, small profits or none at all, the weakest, the most disappointing, and so on.

Mr. Loeb is the author of *The Battle for Investment Survival*, John Wiley & Sons.

G. M. LOEB'S INVESTMENT SURVIVAL CHECKLIST

OBJECTIVES AND RISKS

Security		Price	Shares	Date
"Ruling reason" for commitment			Amount of commitment $	
			% of my investment capital _____%	
Price objective	Est. time to achieve it	I will risk _____ points	Which would be $	

TECHNICAL POSITION

Price action of stock:
- ❏ Hitting new highs
- ❏ Pausing in an uptrend
- ❏ Acting stronger than market
- ❏ In a trading range
- ❏ Moving up from low ground
- ❏ _____

Dow Jones Industrial Average

Trend of market

SELECTED YARDSTICKS

	Price Range		Earnings Per Share Actual or Projected	Price/Earnings Ratio Actual or Projected
	High	Low		
Current year				
Previous year				
Merger possibilities				Years for earnings to double in past
Comment on future				Years for market price to double in past

PERIODIC RECHECKS

Date	Stock Price	DJIA	Comment	Action taken, if any

COMPLETED TRANSACTIONS

Date closed	Period of time held	Profit or loss
Reason for profit or loss		

NOTES

NOTES